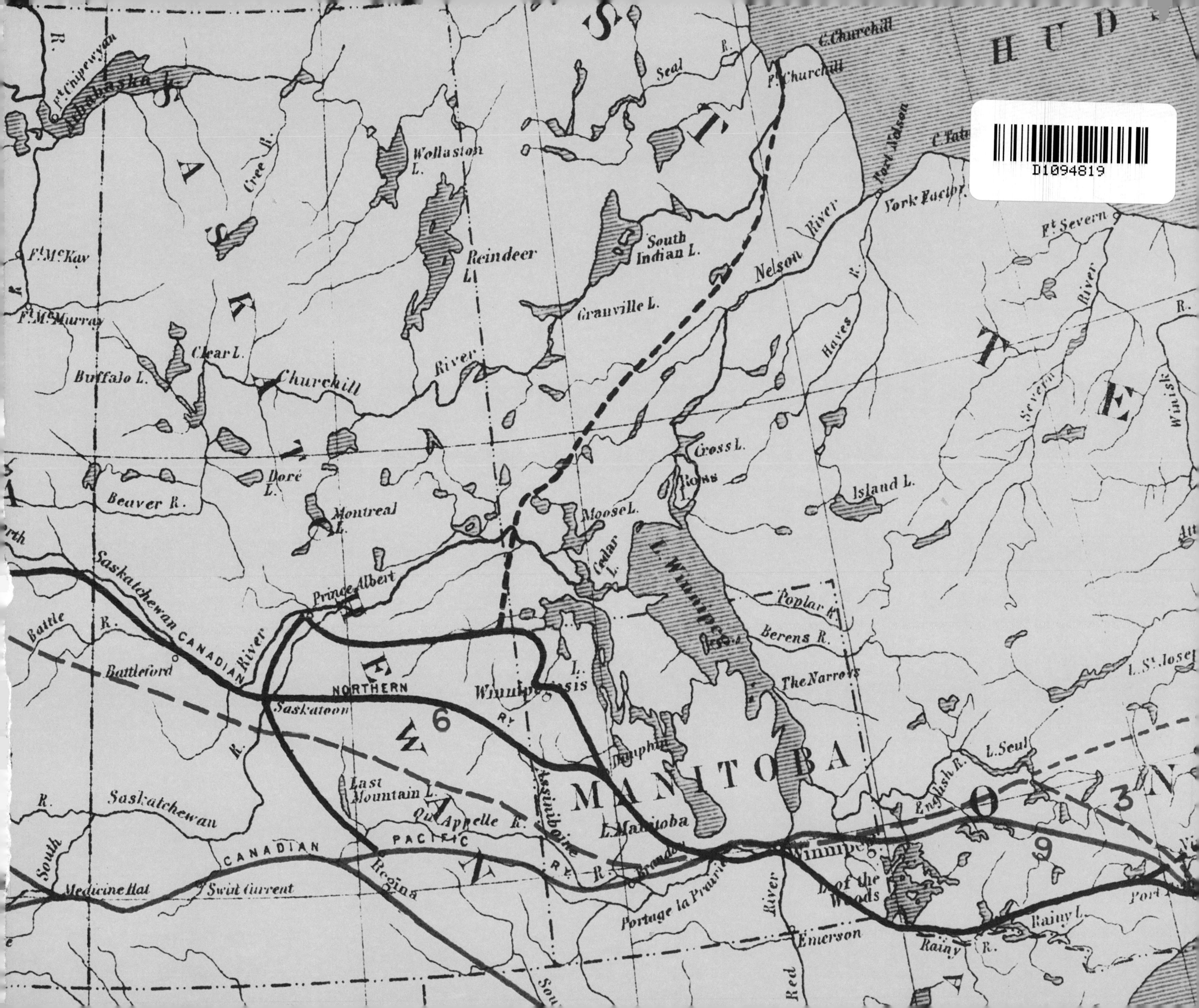
HUD
C. Churchill
Ft. Churchill
Seal
Port Nelson
C. Tatn
York Factory
Ft. Severn
Ft. Chipewyan
Athabaska L.
Wollaston L.
Cree R.
Reindeer L.
South Indian L.
Nelson River
Ft. McKay
Ft. McMurray
Granville L.
Clear L.
Buffalo L.
Churchill
River
Hayes R.
Severn River
Winisk
Cross L.
Ross
Island L.
Doré L.
Beaver R.
Montreal L.
Moose L.
Cedar L.
L. Winnipeg
Poplar R.
Berens R.
The Narrows
L. St. Joseph
Prince Albert
Saskatchewan
Battle R.
Battleford
CANADIAN
NORTHERN
RY.
River
Saskatoon
L. Winnipegosis
Dauphin
MANITOBA
L. Seul
English R.
Last Mountain L.
Qu'Appelle R.
Assiniboine
L. Manitoba
Saskatchewan
R.
South
CANADIAN
PACIFIC
RY.
Regina
Brandon
Winnipeg
L. of the Woods
Medicine Hat
Swift Current
Portage la Prairie
Red River
Emerson
Rainy L.
Rainy R.
Port
S
A
S
K
A
T
T
E
N
O
6
9
3
E
W
A
T

The Golden Age of

CANADIAN RAILWAYS

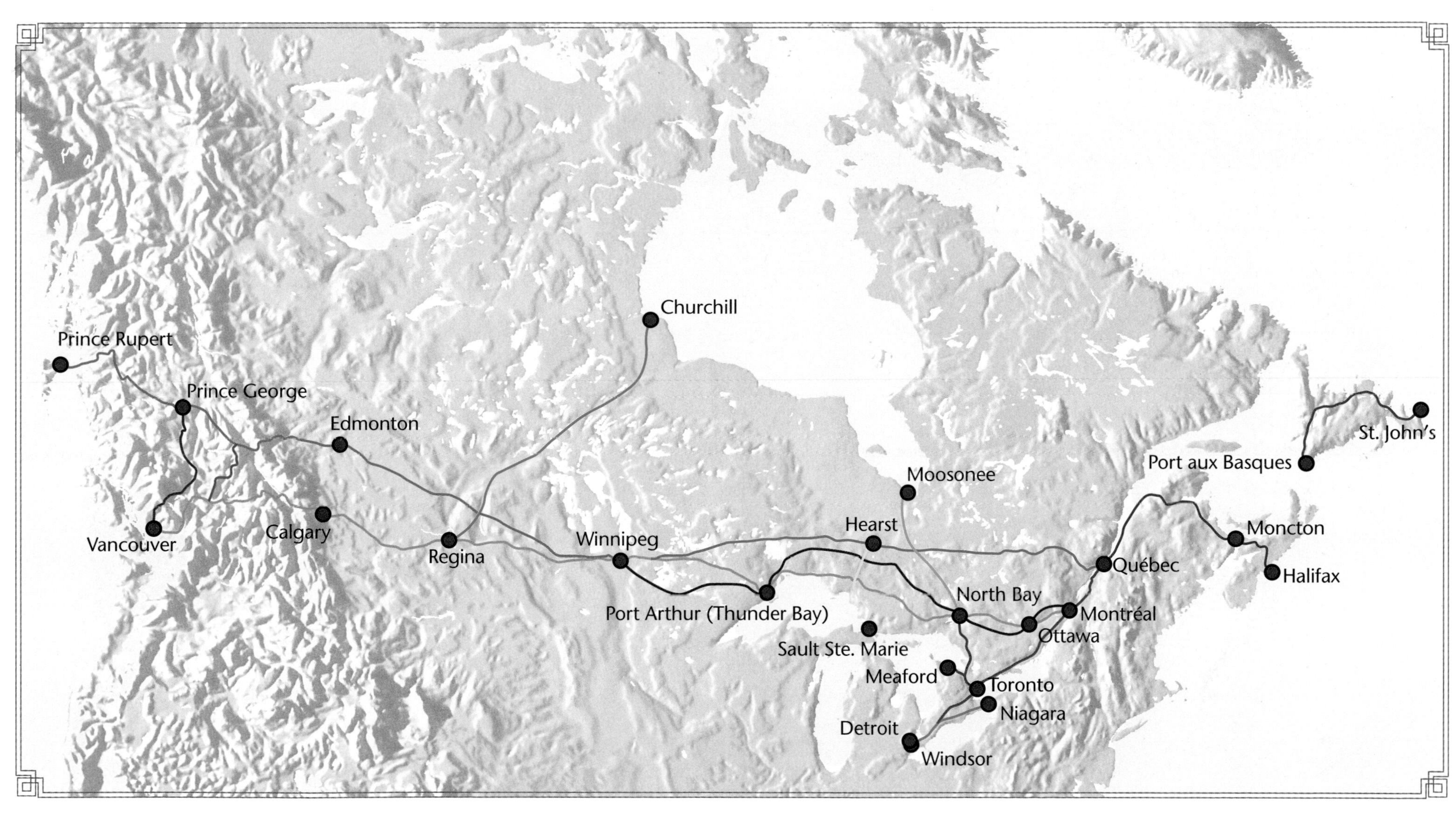

The Golden Age of

CANADIAN RAILWAYS

Introduction by Charlotte Gray

Bruce Clement Cooper
CONSULTANT EDITOR

A Canadian Pacific train powers through the Selkirks in this dramatic image produced by A.C. Leighton for a 1929 CPR brochure.

This edition first published in 2010 by Worth Press
Reprinted 2011, 2013

Production and international sales co-ordination by Worth Press
A Bookcraft Ltd/Worth Press co-production

The endpaper maps are reproduced from *Atlas of Canada*,
published by the Canadian Department of the Interior in 1906

ISBN 978 1 903025 19 2

Project manager John Button
Design manager Lucy Guenot

Set in Stone Sans and Serif (text), Argos, Grant Antique and Orbit Antique (display), and designed by Bookcraft Ltd, Stroud, Gloucestershire, United Kingdom

Printed in Malaysia for Imago

A classic Canadian Pacific poster from the early 1940s by Scottish-born artist James Crockart. Crockart emigrated to Canada in 1911 and opened his own studio in Montréal in 1925.

5924
5924
LITHOGRAPHED IN CANA

CONTENTS

"In the Rockies—The Three Sisters," painted by Frederick Talbot, from *Peeps at Great Railways: Canadian Pacific Railway*, 1922 (left).

Canadian National No. 6100, a 4–8–4 Northern Class locomotive, built in 1927 at the end of the "golden age," from *Canadian National Railway Magazine*, October 1927 (top right).

THE CONTRIBUTORS

Meredith MacArdle, Editorial Director for the project, is an editor and author who has written *The Timechart History of Canada* amongst other books. She has researched extensively into the development of railroads in both Canada and the United States.

Bruce Clement Cooper, Consultant Editor for the book, is an author, historian, avid railroad collector, and the great-great-grandson of Lewis M. Clement, chief assistant engineer on the US Central Pacific line from 1862 to 1881. His family's website on the Central Pacific is considered to be the most complete resource on North American railroad history on the web.

Christopher Andreae is a heritage planner with Golder Associates, and is currently completing a heritage impact assessment of Toronto Union Station. Over the past thirty years he has written many books, the best-known being *Lines of Country: An Atlas of Railway and Waterway History in Canada.* Chris Andreae's contributions to this volume are:

The Nova Scotia Railway
The Newfoundland Railway
The National Transcontinental Railway—Introduction
The National Transcontinental Railway—Features
The Hudson Bay Railway

Elisabeth Bailey grew up in the train town of Galesburg, Illinois, at that time the only city in the United States to be serviced by Amtrak and Santa Fe at separate stations. A writer and editor living in the UNESCO world heritage village of Lunenburg, Nova Scotia, she rides the rails at every opportunity. For this volume, Elisabeth Bailey has contributed:

The Grand Trunk Railway—Introduction
The Grand Trunk Railway—Features
The Canadian Pacific Railway—Introduction
The Canadian Pacific Railway—Features
The Grand Trunk Pacific—Introduction
The Great Western Railway— Niagara Bridge Feature

Ron Brown is a freelance travel writer and a tour director for a leading Ontario tour operator. He has authored more than twenty titles featuring the lesser-known aspects of the heritage of Ontario and Canada. He lives in Toronto and is past chair of the Writers' Union of Canada. In this volume, Ron Brown has written:

The Northern Railway
The Great Western Railway
The Ontario Northland Railway

Ken Cruikshank is a historian at McMaster University who is interested in the interaction of business, state, and society in Canada and the United States. Railway historians turn to his *Close Ties* when they have questions about the history of early railway freight rate regulation in Canada. For this volume, Ken Cruikshank has contributed:

The Intercolonial Railway
The Prince Edward Island Railway

Image from *The Railway that Glue Built,* Frederick A. Stokes Co., New York, 1908.

R.B. (Rae) Fleming believes that history begins at home. Memories of growing up in a general store in Argyle, Ontario, led to two books, a prize-winning biography of Sir William Mackenzie, born in nearby Kirkfield, and a history of Canadian general stores. Rae Fleming has written:

The Canadian Northern—Introduction

The Canadian Northern—Features

Charlotte Gray is one of Canada's best-known non-fiction writers, and the author of eight award-winning books on Canadian history including *Sisters in the Wilderness.* Chair of Canada's History Society, she hosted a CBC documentary on Sir John A. Macdonald, Canada's first prime minister, which included a trip by train through the Rockies, taking in the location of the original Canadian Pacific "last spike." For this volume, Charlotte Gray has contributed:

Main Introduction

Big Bear and the Railway

Sandford Fleming, Canadian Time Lord

Canadian Railway Disasters

The White Pass and Yukon Railway

Patrick Hind came to British Columbia from England in 1947 and has had a lifelong interest in railways, both Canadian and British. Having retired from municipal government service and later working with various heritage organizations, he became an archivist at the West Coast Railway Association in Squamish. An expert on the Pacific Great Eastern, he has written two books on that railway. Patrick Hind's contributions to this volume are:

The Pacific Great Eastern—Introduction

The Pacific Great Eastern—Features

The Kettle Valley Railway

The Esquimalt and Nanaimo Railway

Nick Kingsley is Industry Editor of *Railway Gazette International*, the market-leading international trade journal for the rail industry. Nick studied at the Institute of Railway Studies at the National Railway Museum in York as part of his degree at the University of York. For this volume, Nick Kingsley has written:

Museums and Places to Visit

Duncan McDowall is a professor of history at Carleton University in Canada's capital, Ottawa. He has written widely on the emergence of Canada's modern economy, and is a winner of the National Business Book Award. In this volume, Duncan McDowall has written:

The Algoma Central Railway

Brian Solomon is a lecturer and writer on both contemporary and historical railroad subjects. His many books include *North American Railroad Bridges, Working on the Railroad, Railroad Photography*, and *Railway Masterpieces.* He is also known for his distinctive railroad photography. For this volume, Brian Solomon has contributed:

Classic Canadian Locomotives

Railway Equipment and Rolling Stock

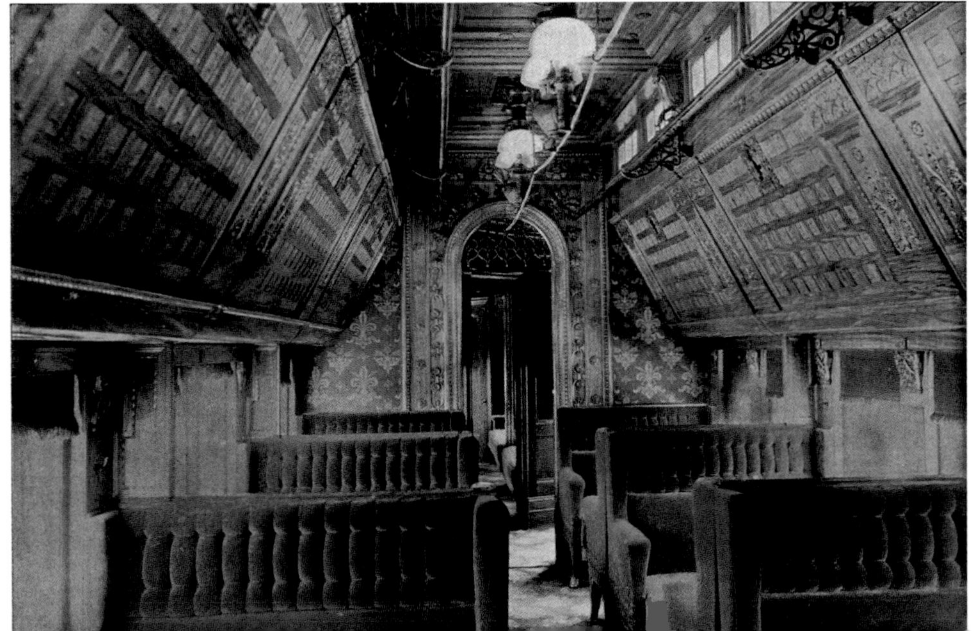

Interior of a Canadian Pacific sleeping car, from *Autour du Monde*, 1899.

INTRODUCTION

Charlotte Gray

Without railways, there might be no Canada.

In the late 1860s, the immense, under-populated territories in the northern half of North America were being sucked inexorably into the sway of the thriving republic to the south. It seemed that only a transcontinental spine of steel could stop the new Confederation of Canada from becoming the economic backyard of the United States, and so it was that politics triggered the explosive development of Canadian railways. Hero worship is not a Canadian trait, but the success of Canada's late-nineteenth-century railwaymen, whose extraordinary engineering feats helped create a country, has earned them a reputation as nation-builders.

"The Valley of the Illecillewaet below Mount Sir Donald," painted by Frederick Talbot, from *Peeps at Great Railways: Canadian Pacific Railway*, 1922.

However, if politics were responsible for the "golden age" of Canadian railways, economics had laid its foundation half a century earlier. The commercial promise of railways was recognized long before the idea of a Canadian Confederation was born.

Transport was the key to prosperity in British North America in the early nineteenth century. There were six autonomous little British colonies: Newfoundland, New Brunswick, Nova Scotia, and Prince Edward Island on the Atlantic coast, and further west (but still closer to the Atlantic than the Pacific), Lower Canada (Québec) and Upper Canada (today's Ontario). In 1841, Upper and Lower Canada were reluctantly united, eventually becoming the Province of Canada. Apart from a handful of colonial cities, most people lived in scattered and isolated settlements, dominated by churches, gristmills, and breweries, and surrounded by wilderness. The English writer Susanna Moodie, who arrived in Upper Canada in 1832, wrote despairingly of the isolation:

Oh! Land of waters, how my spirit tires
In the dark prison of thy boundless woods …

The economies of these British colonies depended on hauling raw materials over vast distances to the coastline for shipment to Britain. The Hudson's Bay Company shipped bundles of furs by canoe, and later by York boat, across lakes and down rivers. Lumber companies floated rafts of maple, birch, pine, and oak logs down mighty waterways like the St. Lawrence and Ottawa Rivers. But with the liquid highways frozen for up to five months each year, and an almost non-existent road system, commerce on the docks of Montréal and Québec City in Lower Canada, of Nova Scotia's Halifax and Saint John, New Brunswick, ground to a halt each November.

Freeze-up—*la prise des glaces,* as French Canadians call it—enraged colonial businessmen like Thomas Keefer, a prominent engineer and entrepreneur who championed the development of railways. Winter, he wrote in 1850, laid "an embargo which no human power can remove … on our ports." But railways, "the iron civilizer," would have an impact in Canada "which can only be compared to that which the discovery of printing had exercised upon the mind." Trains would conquer the deep silence of winter because they could operate year round, day and night, regardless of the ice that paralyzed boat traffic or the mud and snowdrifts that sabotaged stagecoach travel. Railroad construction soaked up a huge amount of capital, but early railway promoters had little difficulty in finding eager investors, in both Montréal, British North America's largest city, and in London, the heart of the British Empire to which these shabby colonies clung.

The first Canadian set of tracks was a ramshackle affair with wooden rails joined by iron splice plates, but crowds came out to watch its locomotive's inaugural run. This was the Champlain and Saint Lawrence Railroad (C&SL), which opened on July 21, 1836, covering fourteen miles from La Prairie, south of Montréal, to St.-Jean-sur-Richelieu. Backed by John Molson, the Montréal brewer, its little locomotive, *Dorchester,* had been built in Newcastle, England, by Robert Stephenson who, with his father George, had built the famed *Rocket* seven years earlier. *Dorchester* ran at an average speed of 14 miles (22.5 km) per

THE CHAMPLAIN AND ST. LAWRENCE RAILROAD COMPANY.

IN connection with the Steamer PRINCESS VICTORIA, will be prepared to convey Passengers between MONTREAL and ST. JOHNS, on MONDAY, the 25th instatn, as follows:—

Steamer. FROM MONTREAL.	*Locomotive.* FROM LAPRAIRIE.
8 o'clock, A. M.	9 o'clock, A. M.
2 do P. M.	5 do P. M.
4 do P. M.	

Locomotive. FROM ST. JOHNS.	*Steamer* FROM LAPRAIRIE.
8 o'clock, A. M.	6 o'clock, A. M.
2 do P. M.	9 do A. M.
	3 do P. M.

July 23, 1836.

103

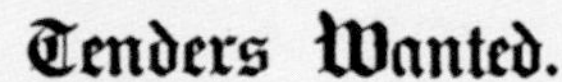

Tenders Wanted.

TO RAILWAY CONTRACTORS.

Nova Scotia Railway.

EXTENSION FROM TRURO TO PICTOU.

THIS Extension, over forty miles in length, will be placed under contract, as soon as the Surveys now in progress are sufficiently advanced. The line to be constructed will be divided into eight sections, of about five miles in length, and due notice will be given when each section shall be ready for contract.

TENDERS

For the construction of works on the first Section from Truro Station, will be received at this office, till

Monday, the 25th day of July next,

At TWELVE o'clock, noon.

Specifications, forms of Tenders and any other information required by intending contractors, may be had on application at the Engineer's office, in Halifax, Truro and Pictou, on and after the fifteenth day of July next. The work to be finished at the time, and on the terms stated in he Specification.

JAS. McDONALD,
Commissioner.

Railway Office,
Halifax, June 25, 1864.

4441 1mo

hour, and was nicknamed "Kitten" because its short wheelbase resulted in a skittish ride. By 1851, the C&SL was a year-round, iron-railed line that crossed the American border and connected with the Vermont Central. In 1853, another railway company, the St. Lawrence and Atlantic, completed a two-hundred-mile track from Montréal south through Sherbrooke to the ice-free Atlantic port of Portland, Maine.

Soon Canadians were train-crazy, and every small community lobbied to be connected to a rail track. Short lines snaked across the map of eastern Canada. With little local capital available, the governments of both New Brunswick and Nova Scotia found they had to finance and undertake railway construction themselves. In the 1850s, two lines were built to connect Atlantic ports with surrounding areas. The Nova Scotia Railway (NSR) linked Halifax to its hinterland, particularly the ferry route from Pictou in the north to Prince Edward Island, and to the agriculturally rich Annapolis Valley to the west. In New Brunswick, the splendidly named European and North American Railway (the E&NA, which was originally envisioned to extend to Europe via New England) linked the Bay of Fundy port of Saint John to Shediac.

Rail lines also spread through the region north of the Great Lakes. The Great Western Railway, which covered the eighty miles between Niagara Falls and Windsor, was completed in

Champlain and St. Lawrence Railroad Company (top right); the wood-burning *Dorchester* on its way to St. Johns on the Richelieu River, 1832, a painting by J.D. Kelly (top left). Nova Scotia Railway Engine No. 6, *The Pictou* (above).

Mail steamer passing under Victoria Bridge, Montréal, from *Picturesque Canada*, 1882.

1854 thanks to a loan from the Province of Canada. The most ambitious and expensive project during this period, however, was the Grand Trunk Railway (GTR) between Montréal and Toronto and Sarnia (a hub for Chicago-bound traffic), which its promoters declared would allow Montréal to dominate trade and traffic between the Great Lakes region and the Atlantic seaboard. The GTR spawned some impressive engineering feats, including the Victoria Bridge at Montréal that was officially opened in 1860. Two miles long, it was the first bridge to span the St. Lawrence River, and at the time it was the longest bridge in the world. One of its designers was the same Robert Stephenson whose company had built the *Dorchester*. However, by the time the first engine steamed along the line from Montréal to Sarnia, the GTR owed £800,000 to British banks and teetered on the edge of bankruptcy. A new managing director of the company, Sir Edward Watkin, declared that the GTR was "an organized mess" and set about cleaning it up with iron-fisted gusto. In 1862 the Canadian legislature rescued the railway's finances with the Grand Trunk Arrangements Act, which injected new capital.

In 1850, only sixty miles of track were in operation in Canada: by 1864, more than three thousand miles of track had been laid. Government leaders began to talk about a rail system that linked the various British colonies together. Joseph Howe, editor of the newspaper *Nova Scotian* and a future premier of the province, predicted in 1851 that "in five years we shall make the journey hence to Québec and Montréal, and home through Portland and St. John, by rail; and I believe that many in this room will live to hear the whistle of the steam engine in the passes of the Rocky Mountains, and to make the journey from Halifax to the Pacific in five or six days."

At the time, this looked like an impossible ambition. So far, the development of railways in British North America had been haphazard, dependent on unreliable promoters, ill-informed investors and reluctant governments. Most of the major lines ran south to US ports, or linked into the US rail system. Moreover, Canadian railway projects had proved a grand way to lose money. Sources of British capital dried up as investors realized that Canadian labour was expensive, terrain brutal, construction costs astronomical, and there were several months when nothing could be done. Corruption, usually bribes to politicians for charters, loans, and land grants, was rampant. A British engineer, Sir Edmund Hornby, remarked, "Upon my word, I do not think that there is much to be said for Canadians over Turks when contracts, places, free tickets on railways or even cash is in question."

The major obstacle was not the technology required, but the fact that there were not enough people in British North America to sustain a profitable level of traffic. But railways

were transforming the landscape even as immigrants surged across the Atlantic. Steel rails tied together scattered settlements, opened up new markets, and created demand for fuel, iron, steel, and rolling stock. The first Canadian-built locomotive was produced in 1853 by James Good of Toronto, to run on the Ontario, Simcoe and Huron Union Railroad.

Belleville, an established town on Lake Ontario, illustrates the impact of early railways. In 1856 the town became the site of one of the GTR's signature stone stations, characterized by a mansard roof and round-arched windows, and thanks to the GTR, Belleville then acquired not only a water tank and coal dock but also additional businesses such as hotels, feed mills, and perhaps even a brothel. Susanna Moodie, the British immigrant who had found Canada's boundless woods so oppressive when she first arrived, lived nearby. Now the author of one of Canada's earliest bestsellers, *Roughing It in the Bush*, she watched the first GTR trains steam through town and saw that they would conquer the tyrannies of geography and climate. "I never saw a locomotive engine at work before," she wrote to a friend in England. "The sight filled me with awe."

Nevertheless, until the 1860s, Canadian railway activity was restricted to the Atlantic coast, the basin of the St. Lawrence River, and the northern shores of the Great Lakes. Beyond these areas stretched thousands of square miles of muskeg bog and rocks on the Canadian Shield, grasslands across the Prairies, and towering mountain ranges in the Rockies. Distributed across this vast land were about 34,000 Native Canadians and fur traders, plus two small colonial settlements—the Red River settlement, which clustered around the old Hudson's Bay Company post at the junction of the Red and Assiniboine Rivers at what is now Winnipeg, Manitoba, and the new British Columbia colony, perched far away on the Pacific coast. The costs of constructing a railroad across this uncharted landmass would be crushing. It would take more than commerce to drive steel rails all the way from Atlantic to Pacific and help create a brand new transcontinental nation.

The political imperative for railway construction came with the establishment in 1867 of the Dominion of Canada—the union of New Brunswick and Nova Scotia with the large and powerful Province of Canada. Several different factors

The *Toronto*, the first locomotive built in Canada (left).

Great Western Railway 0–4–2T standard gauge switcher No. 208, London, Ontario, 1863 (top right).

A Great Western Railway freight train pulled by a wood-burning steam locomotive, *c.*1870 (bottom right).

Prime Minister John A. Macdonald (right).
The steam shovel, the railway builders' most serviceable tool (left).

contributed to this bold initiative, not the least of which was a desire for self-government within Canada, and British fatigue with paying its colonies' bills. Canadian politicians haggled for several years over the terms of the deal. Serious discussion had begun in 1864, yet it was three more years before the British North America Act passed into law in the British Parliament. Two issues were clear throughout the prolonged negotiations. The first was that Canadians were coming together to defend themselves against American aggression, particularly after a series of cross-border raids by American Fenians dedicated to Irish independence. And the second was that railways were crucial to the deal, promoting both vigorous industrial growth and a sense of nationhood.

Canadians had watched with trepidation the expansion of the American railroad system. Despite the disruption of the American Civil War, American settlers had been pouring west and the American appetite for expansion was voracious. In February 1869 the *Daily Alta California* newspaper of San Francisco had declared, "When the fever is on, our people do not seem to know when and where to stop, but keep on swallowing so long as there is anything in reach." Construction crews of the Union Pacific and Central Pacific railroad companies moved inexorably toward each other, and when they met at Promontory Summit in Utah on May 10, 1869, the rails of the first North American transcontinental railroad were joined.

"Meeting of engines; laying the last rail, Promontory." Detail of a stereograph by Charles R. Savage, taken at Promontory Summit, Utah, May 10, 1869.

Canada's first prime minister, Sir John A. Macdonald, was always determined that his fledgling nation should remain closer to Britain than to the United States; he cherished his Scottish roots. Too frequently caricatured today as an exuberant man with wild hair and a large thirst, in reality Macdonald was a brilliant strategist who knew (in the words of biographer Richard Gwyn) "how to herd political cats." He could see that the promise of a railway would persuade the small Atlantic provinces to unite with the Province of Canada, by then split into Québec and Ontario but still dominant in land, population, and resources. The 1867 British North America Act formally recorded an agreement that construction should begin at once on an Intercolonial Railway (ICR), because it was "essential to the Consolidation of the Union of British North America, and to the Assent thereto of Nova Scotia and New Brunswick." The new Canadian federal government in Ottawa demonstrated its good faith (and determination to make the deal stick) by immediately assuming the operations and debts of the old eastern lines, the NSR and E&NA, which would be absorbed into the ICR. The route was controversial:

DO NOT MISS THE FREE SHOW
A
GRAND EXHIBITION
OF THE
AGRICULTURAL WEALTH
OF THE
GOLDEN
NORTH-WEST
GIVEN FREE
TO THE
PEOPLE OF CANADA
BY THE
Canadian Pacific
RAILWAY.
Smith's Falls, Nov. 29
Brockville, - - Dec. 1
Carleton Jct. Dec. 2
ALL ARE CORDIALLY INVITED
COME AND SEE AND YOU WILL BE CONVINCED
THAT THE
CANADIAN NORTH-WEST
IS THE
GRANARY OF THE WORLD

"Interior of an emigrant car," from *Peeps at Great Railways: Canadian Pacific Railway*, 1922 (right). Advertisement for a CPR-sponsored exhibition of 1884 (far right).

contractors found themselves under pressure to lay track as far as possible from the American border, and as close as possible to the homes of politically well-connected landlords. For this reason it took another decade before construction was completed. But by 1876, Halifax was linked to Québec City.

Meanwhile, tiny Prince Edward Island reconsidered its determination to stay out of the Confederation. In 1871, the government there had decided to build its own 136-mile railroad, financed with British capital. The Prince Edward Island Railway took a meandering path across the island's gentle countryside (construction contractors were paid by the mile), and local demand led to the erection of one railway station for every two and a half miles of track. Within twelve months the railway threatened to bankrupt the province, and in 1873 the debt forced the island to join the Confederation so that Canada could bail it out. (Newfoundland would not become part of Canada until 1949.)

So railways gradually knit together British North America's oldest colonies, despite their ruggedly individual characters. But Canada was still only a fragment of British North America as a whole, and Sir John A. Macdonald had bigger dreams. He knew that if the Dominion of the North were to become a muscular, independent country, it needed to spread across the millions of arable acres west of the Great Lakes and include the two additional British colonies—the Red River settlement and British Columbia. And that required some East–West glue.

At Confederation, Macdonald had pledged that a railroad would be built from sea to sea, but only when the new Dominion's finances would permit. However, American settlers had already pushed as far west as they could, and were drifting north into the Canadian Prairies, while at the same time American prospectors were flooding into British Columbia where gold had been found in river beds. The US population of 38.5 million dwarfed that of Canada, which hovered around 3.5 million. Canada needed more people, but immigrants would arrive only if they were offered lands ripe for agricultural settlement and a railroad to carry them west. Canada certainly had the land—nearly one-third of today's

Canadian artist Robert Harris's 1884 painting "The Fathers of Confederation" from an 1885 photograph of an earlier painting (right). The original painting was destroyed in the 1916 Parliament Buildings fire.

By contrast, when the first American transcontinental railroad was completed in 1869 in Utah, there had been crowds, fanfares, and a gold spike. Despite the modest gesture, however, the CPR achieved its political purpose. Immigrants from eastern Europe flooded into the West. New cities and small towns, from Winnipeg to Vancouver, were soon strung along the tracks like beads on a necklace. The Canadian Prairies became the breadbasket of the British Empire, as Marquis wheat, a Canadian-developed hybrid, flourished in the northern climate. The CPR fostered the growth of more than eight hundred communities in the three prairie provinces, each with a grain elevator from which grain could be loaded onto CPR hopper cars and taken to market.

Between 1867, the year of Confederation, and 1911 the population of Canada doubled to more than seven million. Now both commerce and politics drove railway construction. However, the CPR soon proved inadequate to service the growing transcontinental nation. Branch lines began to crisscross the West, and a second transcontinental road, the Canadian Northern Railway (CNoR), was established in 1899 along the route originally proposed by Sandford Fleming and thus challenged the CPR's monopoly. Next, with Ottawa's enthusiastic (and not particularly wise) encouragement, the GTR joined the race with a third set of tracks to the Pacific. But the railway bubble in Canada burst with the onset of hostilities in Europe in 1914. European immigration temporarily petered out, and so did access to the British capital that had helped underwrite much of the expansion.

John Macdonald crossing Rogers Pass on his first transcontinental trip to the Pacific Coast, a painting by C.W. Jefferys, from *Steel of Empire*, 1935 (left). First train through the slide, Frank, Alberta, 1903 postcard (top).

CPR advertisement, mid-1890s (right). St. Thomas, Ontario, from Kettle Creek Bridge, 1882 (left).

Until the advent of commercial aviation, railways continued to be the most efficient way to reach isolated resource-rich regions in a country that, in area, is the second largest in the world (after Russia). So Canadians kept laying track, particularly into the inaccessible North, but the age of railway heroes was over. When bean-counters calculate how much the golden age of railways in Canada cost the public purse in cash, subsidies, tax breaks, bond guarantees, and land grants, they purse their lips. The CNoR alone received public assistance of one-quarter of a billion dollars.

Yet few historians question the railways' contribution to nation-building—a contribution that was psychological as well as political and economic. The plaintive hoot of a steam locomotive's whistle became a sound that drew Canadians together, coast to coast. Rail travel also opened the eyes of Canadians to the magnificence of their young country. Pauline Johnson, a poet of mixed English–Mohawk background, crossed Canada on the CPR at least fifteen times, becoming the first national celebrity with her stirring recitals in every small town where the train stopped. On her first transcontinental trip in 1894, she wrote to a friend, "This 'great, lone land' of ours is so absorbing, so lovely … The magnitude of this country impresses me as it never has before."

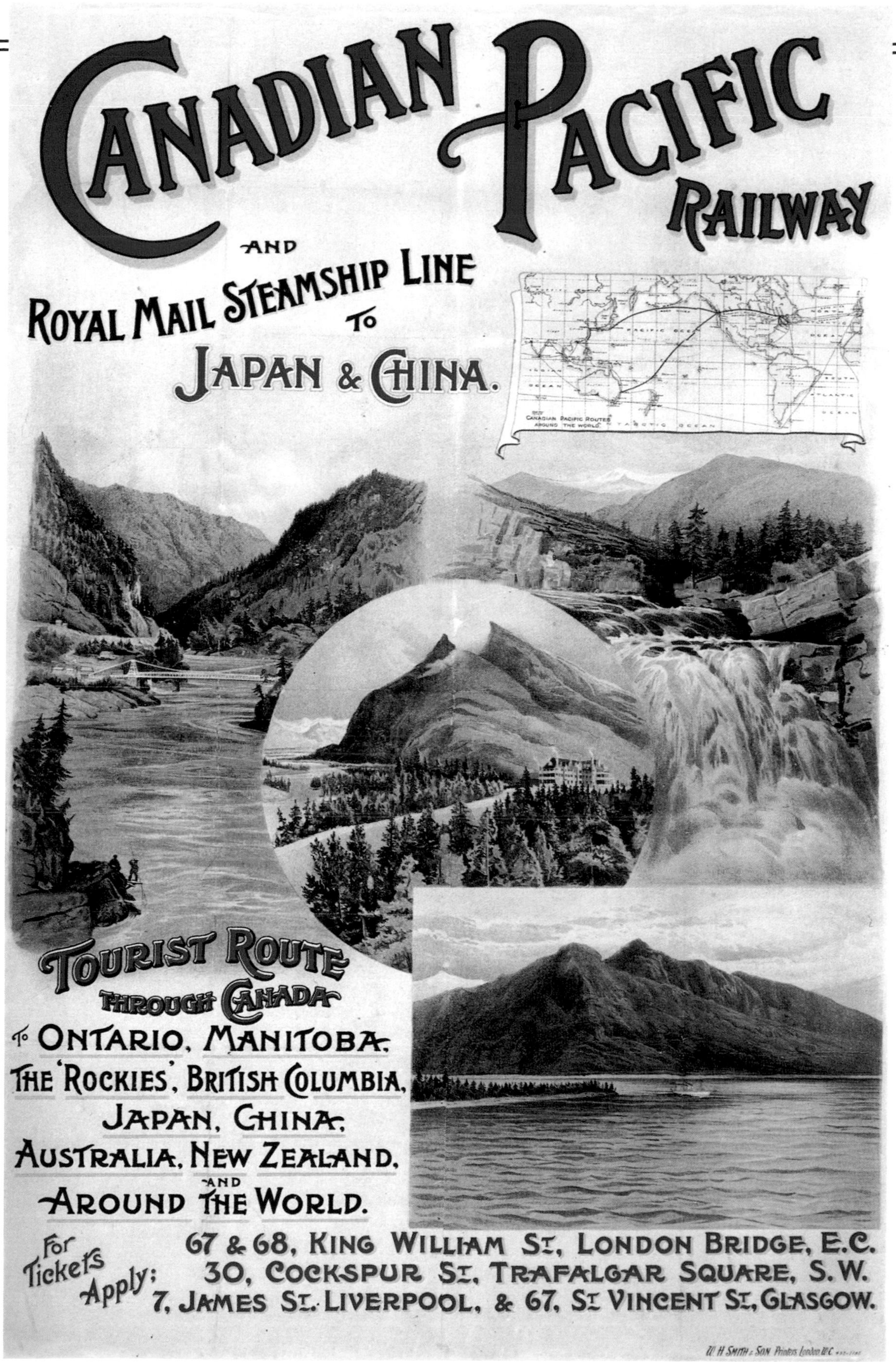

Canadian Pacific Railway

and

Royal Mail Steamship Line to Japan & China.

Canadian Pacific Routes Around the World

Tourist Route through Canada

to Ontario, Manitoba. The 'Rockies', British Columbia. Japan, China. Australia, New Zealand. and Around the World.

For Tickets Apply: 67 & 68, King William St, London Bridge, E.C.
30, Cockspur St, Trafalgar Square, S.W.
7, James St. Liverpool, & 67, St Vincent St, Glasgow.

W. H. Smith & Son Printers London W.C.

BIG BEAR AND THE RAILWAY

Before Canadian Pacific rails could bisect the Prairies, the Canadian government needed to make terms with the First Nations, including the Cree, Blackfoot, and Assiniboines, who had hunted across the grasslands for hundreds of years. For the nomadic warriors of the Canadian Prairies, the arrival of the railways spelt the wholesale obliteration of their way of life.

Several leaders struggled to protect their followers, including Crowfoot (Isapo-Muxica) and Poundmaker (Potikwahanapiwoyin.) The most famous, and perhaps most tragic, was Big Bear (Mistahimaskwa, 1825–88), a stocky, stubborn Cree chief who was both an independent-minded thinker and a brilliant orator. Big Bear embodied the aboriginal belief that the land, water, air, and buffalo were gifts from the Great Spirit for everybody: no one had the right to claim ownership of these natural resources or prevent others from using them. In 1876, he was the first important chief on the Canadian Prairies to refuse to sign a land settlement treaty, Treaty No. 6, which dealt with the rights to 120,000 square miles of land (about 310,800 square kilometres) and would have confined his band to a small reserve. He argued that the incentives to sign were inadequate, and he stopped railway surveyors charting land in present-day Southern Alberta.

But over-hunting had destroyed the huge herds of buffalo on which Big Bear's followers depended. By 1882, the Cree were reduced to eating dogs and gophers, and Big Bear reluctantly signed Treaty No. 6 at the Saskatchewan North-West Mounted Police camp, Fort Walsh. He remained defiant, however, and sent messages to the other chiefs to bring their people (over two thousand in all) to a ceremony called "a Thirst Dance." In the face of European invasion, he argued that they should make a joint demand for one huge reserve on the North Saskatchewan River for all Plains Indians, hoping that unity might secure a negotiated settlement with the government in Ottawa before the railway arrived.

It was not to be: the federal government was far too busy pushing steel tracks towards the Pacific to listen to First Nations' demands. In April 1885, in a little Saskatchewan settlement called Frog Lake, Big Bear lost control of the younger warriors. The Catholic Church was destroyed and nine non-native men, including two Oblate priests, were killed. The insurrection spread, despite Big Bear's attempts to rein in the warriors and warn the Mounties. He knew that violence was entirely counter-productive: the Cree could not win against Ottawa's superior force. He gave himself up to a startled Mountie at Fort Carlton on July 2, 1885, and was charged with treason.

Sentenced to three years in Stony Mountain penitentiary, he made an impassioned speech in court on behalf of his people. According to the only contemporary testimony (there was no court record of the trial), he spread his arms wide and cried, "Many of my band are hiding in the woods, paralyzed with terror … I plead again to you, the chiefs of the white men's laws, for pity and help to the outcasts of my band!" He was ignored.

Big Bear was dead within three years, although he was released from prison early because of ill health. By then the grasslands were tilled and fenced, and First Nations had been herded into reserves and told to become self-sufficient farmers. They were soon impoverished, demoralized shadows of their once proud selves. Their children were rounded up and sent off to residential schools while snorting locomotives brought trainloads of settlers onto their old hunting grounds.

SANDFORD FLEMING, CANADIAN TIME LORD

The fingerprints of Sir Sandford Fleming (1827–1915) can be found all over the history of Canadian railways.

Fleming arrived in Upper Canada (present-day Ontario) in 1845 as an eighteen-year-old surveyor, and within seven years he had designed Canada's first postage stamp (the "Threepenny Beaver") and become assistant engineer of the Toronto, Simcoe and Lake Huron Union Railroad, one of the first little lines snaking north from Toronto. (It was later absorbed into the Northern Railway, for which Fleming served as chief engineer.) The young Scot quickly grasped the potential of railways to conquer wilderness, and in 1862 he submitted to the government the first carefully-drawn plan for a Pacific railroad. He even travelled to London the following year, to try to impress the imperial government with the project.

Fleming got nowhere in Britain, but back in Canada his enthusiasm persuaded Sir John A. Macdonald to appoint him chief surveyor of the Intercolonial Railway in 1867. Fighting off political interference, Fleming was an engineering genius who built his roads for permanence rather than quick profit. He insisted on stone and iron instead of wood for bridge construction, introduced snowsheds for the deep cuts through eastern Québec's Matapédia Valley in order to shelter the line from heavy snow falls, and switched the ICR from broad to standard gauge, to ensure its compatibility with US lines.

In 1871, Fleming took on the additional position of chief engineer of the Canadian Pacific Railway. A hearty outdoorsman who loved exploration, he organized detailed surveys of the immense transcontinental route and took part in many of them himself, including an expedition to the Rockies in 1883 to find a pass through the Selkirk Mountains. In the famous "Last Spike" photo, he holds centre stage with his top hat and bushy beard.

Today, Sandford Fleming is celebrated as one of the key figures in the universal measurement of time. Until 1883, the practice of keeping local time across North America made railway scheduling a nightmare. The Canadian surveyor helped lead the fight for Railway Standard Time, with four different time zones across North America. In 1918, this system would be extended into twenty-four zones around the globe, with the Greenwich Meridian as the start point.

Standard Time was one of many examples of Fleming's belief that technology, contained by rules, would modernize the world. His family and close friends were fond of this vigorous champion of his own ideas for one particular idiosyncratic rule—he could never remember the birthdays of his numerous grandchildren and godchildren, so the rule was that he sent them all presents on his birthday.

Sandford Fleming as a young man (above), and standing just behind Lord Strathcona at Craigellachie, November 7, 1885 (left).

CANADIAN RAILWAY DISASTERS

The mid-nineteenth-century railway boom in Canada was not risk-free for travellers. The Great Western Railway, in a rush to get passenger traffic moving before the line was properly completed, had a terrible reputation in the 1850s for accidents. Collisions between regular trains and ballast and construction trains were common, and scheduled services often ran on lines with incomplete or untested signalling. Within its first year of operation the Great Western had notched up more than fifteen serious accidents, including a collision at St. Baptiste between a mail train and a gravel train which had been left unguarded on the main line. Fifty-two people were killed and many more were injured as the wooden train burned.

Worse was to come. On March 12, 1857 a Great Western Railway train from Toronto was crossing a timber suspension bridge over the Desjardins Canal, heading for Hamilton in Southern Ontario. A broken axle threw the train from the track, hurled it through the bridge deck, and sent it crashing down a sixty-foot chasm. The engine and tender broke through two feet of ice, sinking into the freezing water and pulling the

passenger cars with it. Fifty-nine of the hundred passengers were killed, and another eighteen suffered serious injury. An investigation showed that cheaper pine had been used for the bridge in place of the more expensive but sturdier oak. Even so, it would have been strong enough to hold a train under normal conditions, but the jury found that it had "no margin of safety for derailment."

The Desjardins derailment did not hold the record as Canada's worst train accident for long, however, as seven years later, on June 29, 1864, the driver of a Grand Trunk Railroad train failed to see a red stop light that signalled an open swing bridge across the Richelieu River at St.-Hilaire in Québec. At 1.20 a.m. the locomotive and eleven carriages fell through the open gap, one on top of the other, crushing a passing barge. The train was carrying between 354 and 475 passengers, many of them German and Polish immigrants, from Québec City to Montréal. An estimated ninety-nine people were killed, and at least another hundred were rushed through the dark night to Montréal hospitals with severe injuries. The St.-Hilaire calamity remains Canada's worst railway disaster.

Safety standards gradually rose, but the dangers presented by hastily constructed viaducts, careless drivers, winter blizzards, and animals on the tracks continued. Early train travellers took their lives in their own hands when they purchased their tickets.

A typical GWR accident between London and Kamoka in 1874 (far left).
The Desjardins Canal disaster in 1857 (left).
"The wrecking crane at work," a painting by E.P. Kinsella (top right).
The Beloeil Bridge railway accident at Richelieu River, June 1864 (middle left).
A wreck near New Annan, Nova Scotia, 1903 (middle right).
A partially-collapsed bridge on the Transcontinental Railway near Hearst, 1911 (bottom).

THE BOOK THAT GATHERS NO DUST

Nothing better reflects the reach of the nation's once-extensive railway network than a single bulky periodical, *The Official Guide of the Railways and Steam Navigation Lines of the United States, Porto Rico, Canada, Mexico and Cuba.* At one time it was the world's biggest monthly publication—more than sixteen hundred pages of train schedules and related information. The first issue appeared in June 1868 in New York City, and the last *Official Guide* was published as late as 1995. It has been described as "the book that gathers no dust," because for years it enjoyed heavy use in every railroad station across North America.

Month after month for more than a century, the publication's pages faithfully chronicled the expansion, consolidation, and contraction of the North American railway network. For any given minute the *Official Guide* showed where every scheduled passenger train in the continent was supposed to be.

For several of the routes in this volume, we have reproduced facsimile pages from the July 1906 edition, with detailed information about main line and connecting services, and the facilities offered en route.

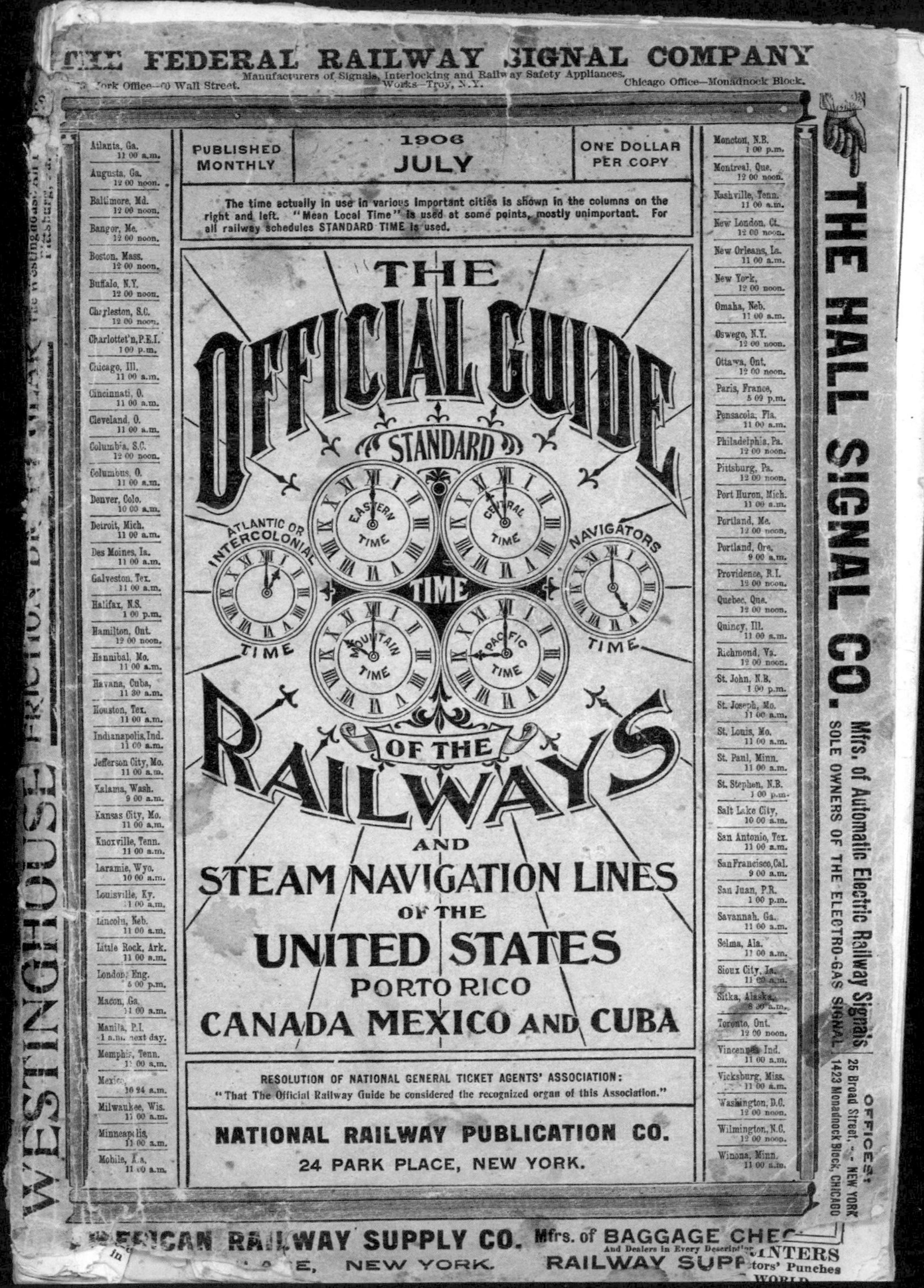

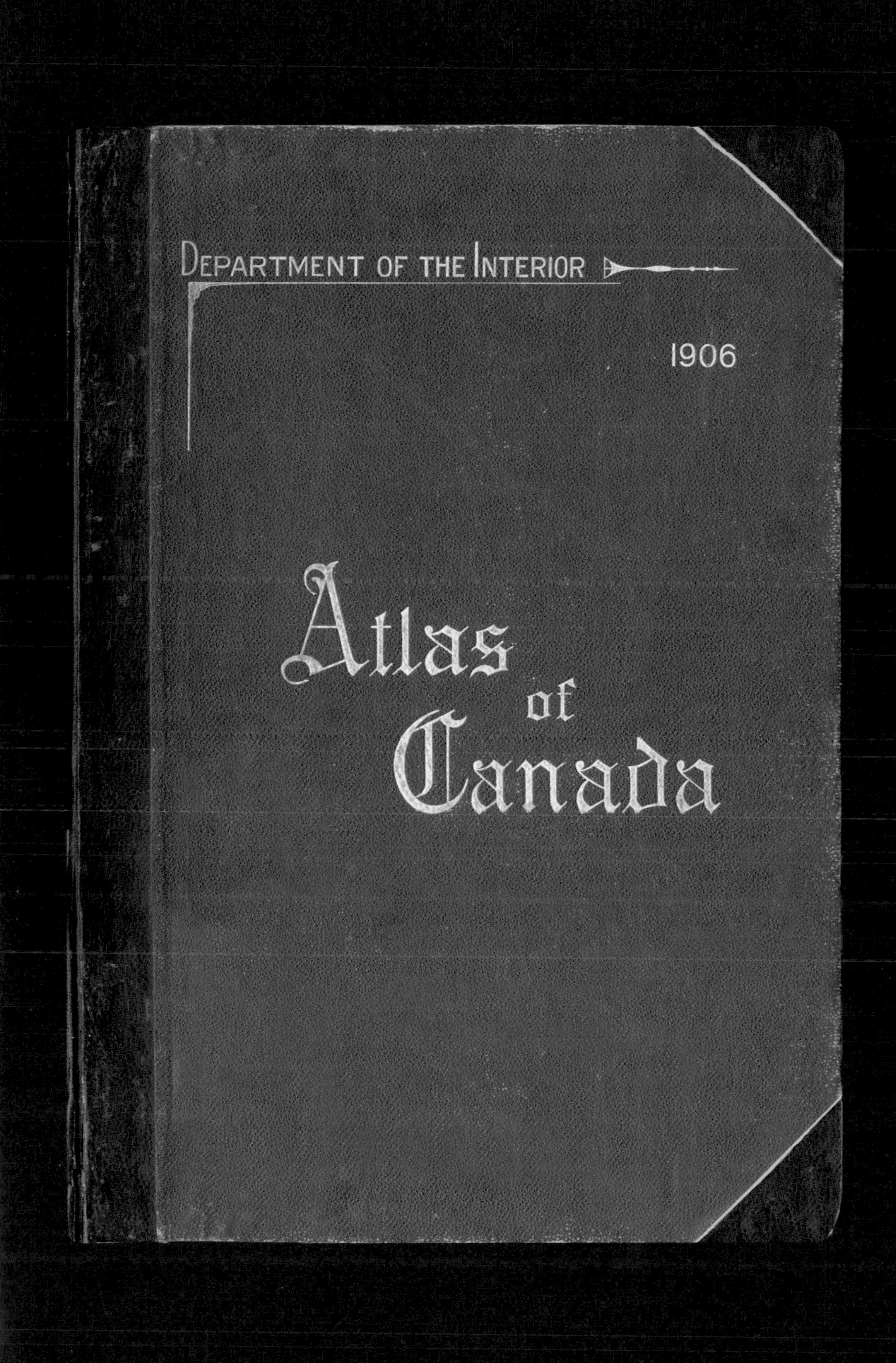

THE 1906 ATLAS OF CANADA

The maps in *The Golden Age of Canadian Railways* are taken from the first edition of the official *Atlas of Canada*, which was published as a bound volume by the Canadian Department of the Interior in 1906. This pioneering atlas, designed to be an overview of a proud and unified nation shortly after Saskatchewan and Alberta had joined the Confederation in September 1905, consists of sixty-five plates, thirty-seven of which are maps along with twenty-eight graphs and tables.

Five of the atlas plates show Canada's railway system at the point when most of the railways in the Maritimes and Ontario and the Canadian Pacific main line were well established, but the Grand Trunk Pacific line had only just been established and was under construction.

We have used the four regional atlas plates as the base for the maps of routes which were already established in 1906. For the Grand Trunk Pacific route from Winnipeg to Prince Rupert we have superimposed the route as completed on the relevant sections of the *Atlas of Canada* Plates 20 and 21, which show the projected route. For routes constructed after 1906, including the Canadian Northern, the National Transcontinental, the Hudson Bay Railway, and the Ontario Northland, we have used *Atlas of Canada* relief maps Plates 2 and 3 as the base.

The endpaper maps are based on *Atlas of Canada's* Plate 21, Transcontinental Railways, which was clearly drafted after the main railway maps in the atlas, and shows the projected routes of the Canadian Northern and Hudson Bay lines in addition to the Grand Trunk Pacific.

For the Newfoundland Railway, as Newfoundland did not join the Confederation until 1949, we have used as a base the Newfoundland map from Keith Johnston's *Royal Atlas of Modern Geography*, published in Edinburgh in 1905.

DAVENPORT

THE NORTHERN RAILWAY

TORONTO TO MEAFORD AND NORTH BAY—THE NORTHERN DREAM

The first railways in Canada were built simply as an alternative to canals: heavily travelled waterways were connected by a series of overland portages, and it was these cumbersome links that the early railway advocates sought to replace–though there were many who felt that the prohibitive cost of railway construction would prevent their introduction, and who instead advocated the improvement of existing waterways using canals. Many of the earliest Canadian railways slipped into the niche which had up until that point been dominated by stagecoaches–transporting passengers between waterways.

The engines of these early locomotives burned wood voraciously, which necessitated wooding-up stations at regular points along the lines to replenish fuel. Trains could easily be immobilized by heavy snow in winter, and both the crew and all able-bodied male passengers were called on to dig the train out in the event of a snowdrift. Both heat and lighting were erratic at best, so travelling by rail in the early days required a good deal of endurance.

Possibly the greatest success of this period was the Champlain and St. Lawrence Railway, opened in 1836, which ran between Montréal and Lachine, with many Montréalers making one or more excursions just for the thrill of travelling by train, a journey which was very affordable at only seven shillings and sixpence. By 1852, the line had grown from $14\frac{1}{2}$ to 43 miles in length. In the meantime, inspired by the Champlain and St. Lawrence's success, other railways were being built elsewhere, perhaps most notably the Montréal and New York Railroad. The two became fierce rivals, each attempting to undercut each other's prices, a struggle which brought them both to the brink of bankruptcy, and eventually led to a merger, the new company being known as the Montréal and Champlain Railroad, which lasted for six years before being absorbed into the Grand Trunk Railway of Canada.

Meanwhile, in the 1830s, businessmen in Toronto had conceived of another grand vision: a northern railway to transport grain and lumber to their city for onwards export. For many years, the intransigence of city politicians ensured that this dream remained just that, a dream. Nevertheless, in 1853, Ontario's first steam locomotive puffed away from a simple station on Lake Ontario and into the hinterland.

At that time named The Ontario, Simcoe and Huron Union Railway, this "portage" line forged north through Allandale (Barrie) and on to the shores of Georgian Bay at Collingwood and eventually to Meaford, giving western grain shippers a new route from the upper Great Lakes to the port of Toronto.

Davenport station, Toronto, built in 1853 as Canada's first passenger station for the Ontario, Simcoe and Huron Railway (later the Northern Railway), *The Canadian Illustrated News*, 1863 (far left).

Barrie, *Picturesque Canada*, 1882 (above).

A metal token used on the Montréal and Lachine line instead of paper tickets (left).

From Allandale a branch line veered northeasterly into the timber lands of Muskoka to a new lakeside terminal at Gravenhurst, where wealthy Toronto vacationers boarded lake steamers to reach their summer homes and lakeside resorts.

In 1858 the line became the Northern Railway Company of Canada, a company that was also anxious to connect with the transcontinental line, the Canadian Pacific Railway, and, as the Northern and Pacific Junction Railway, did indeed link with the CPR near North Bay.

From 1888, under Grand Trunk ownership, the lines to Meaford and North Bay continued to prosper, carrying vacationers to the lakes and hauling grain from the bustling ports of Collingwood and Meaford. But with the arrival of the auto age, the tourists and the grain haulers abandoned the railways and the legacy of the Northern Railway faded, although it did not entirely vanish.

Although vacant, the grand wooden station at Allandale, with its pillared dining room once staffed by uniformed servers, still stands. Ships no longer call at Collingwood and the line services only a single industry–grain transport. Yet the massive grain elevators also survive to celebrate the line's heritage, and in Gravenhurst, while the branch line to the lake is now trackless, a replica station is the ticket office for a refurbished HMS *Seguin*, the same coal-fired steamboat that once carried travellers from the trains to their lakeshore retreats.

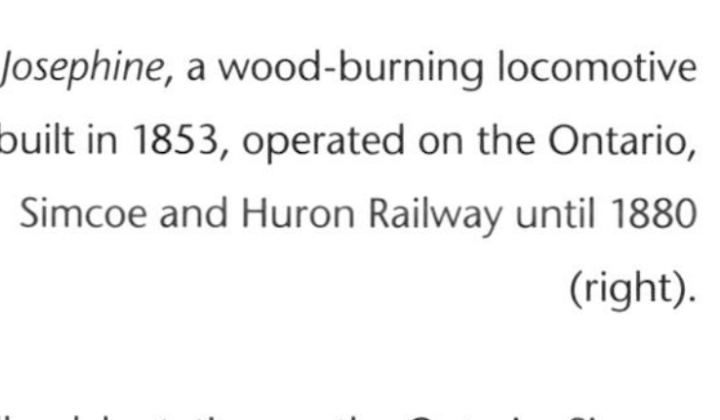

Josephine, a wood-burning locomotive built in 1853, operated on the Ontario, Simcoe and Huron Railway until 1880 (right).

Allendale station on the Ontario, Simcoe and Huron Railway (below).

On the Northern Railway, *Picturesque Canada*, 1882 (bottom right).

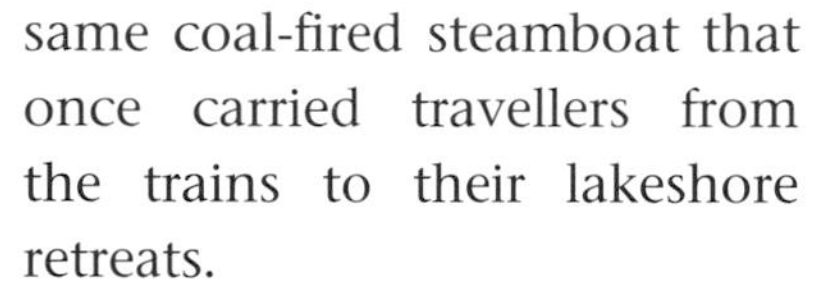

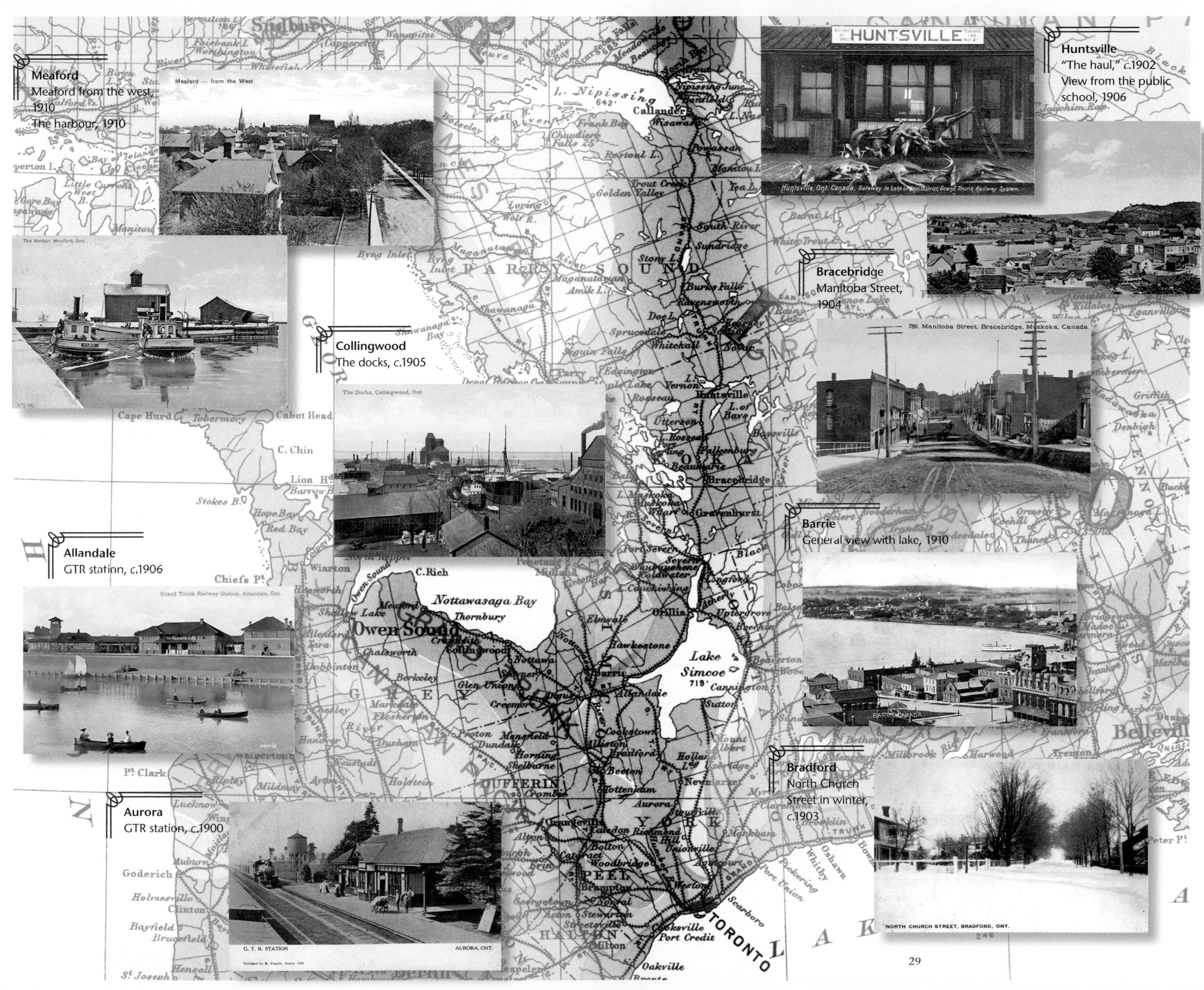

Meaford
Meaford from the west, 1910
The harbour, 1910

Collingwood
The docks, c.1905

Allandale
GTR station, c.1906

Aurora
GTR station, c.1900

Huntsville
"The haul," c.1902
View from the public school, 1906

Bracebridge
Manitoba Street, 1904

Barrie
General view with lake, 1910

Bradford
North Church Street in winter, c.1903

W. T. Smedley

THE GREAT WESTERN RAILWAY

NIAGARA TO WINDSOR, AND A PAIR OF ONTARIO FIRSTS

From its beginning in 1853, the Great Western Railway represented a pair of "firsts" in Ontario's railway history. It became Ontario's first main line operation, beating the Grand Trunk by two years, and it also was the victim of Ontario's first—and one of its worst—railway disasters.

In the 1830s Ontario dignitaries Allan Napier McNab (1798–1862) and Thomas Talbot (1771–1853) met in McNab's magnificent home Dundurn Castle atop Hamilton's Burlington Heights to discuss the need for a rail line across southwestern Ontario. But another dozen years would pass before government support made the Great Western Railway a reality, a new main line which would stretch from Niagara Falls to Windsor and Sarnia.

The first trains began running in 1853 between Niagara Falls and Hamilton, the line's headquarters. By 1856 the road reached Toronto and a decade later it connected to Sarnia and the booming oil fields of Petrolia. To avoid double-tracking its route, the GW cleverly built a loop line several miles to the south known as the Canada Air Line.

Sadly, however, after only four years of operation, the GW experienced another "first," as the victim of one of Canada's worst railway tragedies. In March 1857, a Hamilton-bound passenger train derailed and plunged through a high trestle into the Desjardins Canal, ironically located only yards away from McNab's grand castle. Fifty-nine people perished in the ice-choked waters far below.

GWR station, Hamilton, from *Picturesque Canada*, 1882 (opposite).

Great Western Railway freight train, c.1870 (below left).

Col. Thomas Talbot (centre).

GWR station, Toronto, in an 1867 photograph and an 1870 Notman and Fraser engraving (below right).

View from the Dundas Mountain near Hamilton, with the GWR main line running below, from *Picturesque Canada*, 1882.

But the GW survived this setback, and as it grew it also built some of Ontario's finest early stations, conceived by its architect and engineer Joseph Hobson (1834–1917). However, when the Grand Trunk and GW merged in 1882, the Great Western imprint vanished.

Crossing Ontario's finest farmlands and accessing American markets in both Michigan and New York, the GW's former routes continued to prosper. With the coming of the auto age, however, its branch lines were abandoned as was the once vital Air Line. But the main lines between Niagara Falls, Toronto, Sarnia, and Windsor remain among Canada's busiest, still carrying both freight and passengers today. The GW's legacy also lives on in Hobson's grand stations in Niagara Falls, Woodstock, Chatham, and Sarnia, while McNab's Dundurn Castle, now a museum, still looks out over the GW's former Hamilton yards.

GWR's Hamilton yards and station with locomotive shops, grain elevators and, in the distance, sailing schooners, 1870 (above).

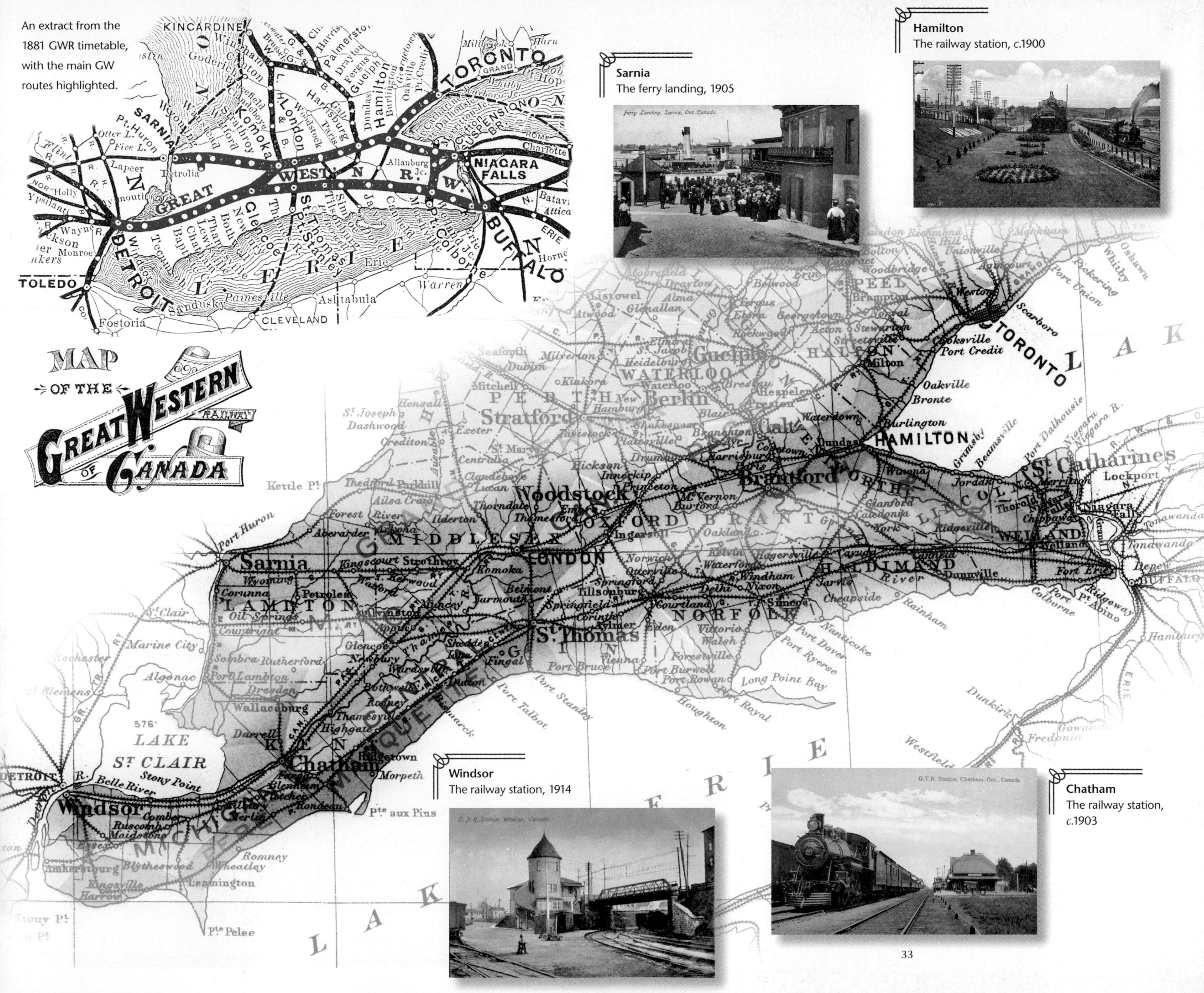

An extract from the 1881 GWR timetable, with the main GW routes highlighted.

Sarnia
The ferry landing, 1905

Hamilton
The railway station, c.1900

Windsor
The railway station, 1914

Chatham
The railway station, *c*.1903

THE NIAGARA BRIDGE

Suspended near the Falls

In 1846 the state of New York, the government of Canada, and Queen Victoria of England all approved charters to form the Niagara Falls International Bridge Company in the United States and the Niagara Falls Suspension Bridge Company in Canada. These companies aimed to build the largest suspension bridge in North America. Prior to the construction of the suspension bridge, passage across the river was by steamer ship only.

As the result of a collaboration of two companies from different countries, the bridge was known by several different names. In the United States it was called the International Suspension Bridge. In Canada it was more commonly known as the Niagara Railway Suspension Bridge or the Niagara Suspension Bridge. The finished structure was a suspension bridge spanning 823 feet (251 m) with two decks; trains travelled on the upper deck, while pedestrians and carriage traffic used the lower one. The span was constructed of wood, limestone, cast iron, and wrought iron—although this was eventually and gradually replaced with steel—and was sited 2½ miles (4 km) downstream from Niagara Falls; at its apex it measured 251 feet (76 m). The location of the bridge was based on both convenience and aesthetics—while there could have been less challenging places to put the bridge, the location was relatively narrow and presented a full, unobstructed view of the falls.

The prime motivating force behind the suspension bridge was the drive of Canadian legislator and entrepreneur William Hamilton Merritt (1793–1862) to increase trade with the United States. At the time, many bridge-builders (not to mention the general public) were sceptical that a suspension bridge over the Niagara could safely transport trains. A few who disagreed with that opinion built the bridge—and history.

The first civil engineer to work on the design of the bridge was Charles Ellet Jr. (1810–62). He had been educated at the École Nationale des Ponts et Chaussées in France, making him the only native-born US citizen at the time with a European education in engineering. Inspired by the Freibourg Suspension Bridge of Switzerland, he built his first suspension bridge, known as the "Wire Bridge," over the Schuylkill River in Philadelphia, Pennsylvania in 1842. With the help of a line laid by a kite across the 787-foot (240-m) chasm, Ellet built a temporary bridge in 1848. (The kite concept was inspired by both Leonardo da Vinci and Benjamin Franklin.) He offered five dollars to any boy who flew a kite across the gorge and secured his string to the other side: 15-year-old Homan Walsh was the first to succeed in doing so.

After a disagreement with the bridge companies, however, Ellet left the project. A three-year hiatus later, the companies hired engineer John Augustus Roebling to finish the job. A Prussian engineer who had designed a series of his own wire cables, Roebling created a pulley winding system which

The Niagara Falls Suspension Bridge, a lithograph by Clay, Cosack and Co., 1876 (right).

strengthened the suspension bridge and which was used for other suspension bridges for several decades. He used Ellet's temporary bridge as scaffolding to build a double-decked bridge. In 1854 the lower deck opened to pedestrian and carriage traffic, and on March 18, 1855 the completed bridge officially opened as the first passenger train crossed the upper deck at a grand five miles an hour.

Three distinct railway lines used the bridge—the Great Western Railway, New York Central Railroad, and New York and Erie Railroad. Unfortunately for the bridge builders, all three lines used different gauges on their tracks. To accommodate them all, the bridge used a triple gauge system which overlapped two tracks beside each other and utilized one rail from each to form a third track.

The construction of the bridge drew traffic and commerce to the region on both sides of the border. Not only did tourists visit the bridge itself to marvel at its sophisticated engineering, they also enjoyed the tightrope artists performing tricks against the magnificent background of the falls. These visitors brought their dollars to spend on both sides of the border. The bridge was also an integral part of the Underground Railroad, bringing liberated slaves to freedom in Canada.

As popular as the bridge was, crossing it was not necessarily a comfortable experience. According to American humorist Mark Twain, "You drive over to Suspension Bridge and divide your misery between the chances of smashing down two hundred feet into the river below, and the chances of having a railway-train overhead smashing down onto you. Either possibility is discomforting taken by itself, but, mixed together, they amount in the aggregate to positive unhappiness."

In 1886, the bridge's decaying wooden components were replaced with steel and iron counterparts. As the century came to a close, however, new heavier trains exceeded the maximum support capacity of the bridge. Larger and more powerful locomotives were required to pull cars that handled an increasing number of passengers and goods; compared to the 23-short-ton (21 ton) locomotives crossing the bridge in the 1850s, 170-short-ton (150 ton) locomotives were the common engines forty years later. Eventually the Niagara Bridge closed on August 27, 1897 and was replaced by the Steel Arch Bridge, later renamed the Whirlpool Rapids Bridge.

An 1856 Currier & Ives hand-coloured print of the Niagara Railway Suspension Bridge (above).

The double-track double-decker steel arch bridge built by GTR in 1897 to replace the Niagara Suspension Bridge (below).

GRAND TRUNK BRIDGE

THE GRAND TRUNK RAILWAY

QUEBEC AND PORTLAND TO DETROIT AND CHICAGO

There had been many years of comprehensive railway planning in the provinces of Canada during the early part of the nineteenth century, but it wasn't until the 1850s that construction began in earnest. There were two obvious approaches to take in planning the network: it could either link North America together in a contiguous system, or it could define the British colonies separately from the United States, thus reinforcing the Canadian railroads' independence from the United States and strengthening their ties to Britain. With proponents of both systems involved in the processes of planning railways, a regional system with strong ties to the United States was realized in the Grand Trunk Railway (GTR), which would extend the entire length of the St. Lawrence valley from the western boundary of Canada to the eastern ports of Montréal and Portland, Maine.

Previous to the construction of the GTR, several small railways had sprung up in the East. In Nova Scotia and New Brunswick the two governments built short provincial railways. The Champlain and St. Lawrence (C&SL) was also one of the first railways in British North America. Financed by Montréal brewer and entrepreneur John Molson, this line connected the St. Lawrence River valley with Lake Champlain, shortening travel time from Montréal to New York. Construction began early in 1835 when a locomotive was ordered from Newcastle upon Tyne in England, freight cars were built in Montréal, and passenger cars were purchased from the United States. The C&SL opened on July 21, 1836, and was extended to Rouses Point, New York in 1851. In 1857, the C&SL merged with the Montréal and New York Railroad to form the Montréal and Champlain Railroad. This was leased in 1864 by the Grand Trunk Railway, which went on to purchase it eight years later, subsequently converting the track from broad gauge to standard gauge as part of a system-wide conversion.

Three commercial companies, the Northern, the Great Western, and the GTR were founded largely with British capital and received extensive government support. The GTR was physically headquartered in Montréal, but the corporate office for the line was in London. Though the Northern and the Great Western were relatively small

CONTRACT.

Grand Trunk Railway of Canada.

EXCAVATORS and BUILDERS desirous of contracting for execution of the Grading and Brickwork on the Grand Trunk Railway, in the Townships of York and Scarboro, can see the plans, sections and specifications, on and after the 15th instant, at Messrs. Jackson, Peto, Brassey & Betts' office King Street, Toronto, between the hours of 9 and 5 o'clock.

Tenders to be delivered at their office, on the 25th inst., marked Tenders for Works in the Township of ———

Messrs. Jackson, Pete, Brassey & Betts do not bind themselves to accept the lowest tender, or any tender.

Plant or Stock, such as earth, waggons, barrows, planks and rails, will be provided on certain terms and conditions.

Toronto, March 14th, 1854. 1223-10t

WANTED,

TWO Hundred Men to work on the G. T. Railroad and Bridges in Belleville, Canada West. Work to be commenced about the 20th of July next.

C. R. MILKS & Co.

Belleville, June 24, 1854. 44

Hand-coloured lithograph of the Grand Trunk bridge and canal lock at Ste. Anne's, Montréal, 1882 (opposite).

GTR "Men Wanted" and contract notice, 1854 (left).

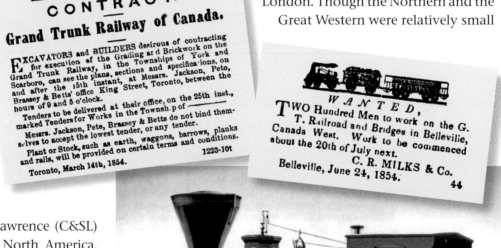

A 4-4-0 woodburner built in 1850 for the Atlantic and St. Lawrence Railroad, which was bought by the Grand Trunk in 1853 (below).

Cape Diamond from St. Romuald, Québec, from *Picturesque Canada*, 1882.

GTR timetable, August 1887 (above).

in comparison with the Grand Trunk, all three railways were planned to attract a part of the general East–West traffic of the continent. The model of the Grand Trunk Railway is based on a tree trunk—a strong main line with many branches.

Incorporated as the Grand Trunk Railway Company of Canada on November 10, 1852, the GTR was charged with building a railway line between Toronto and Montréal, and soon afterward the charter extended east to Portland, Maine and west to Sarnia, Ontario. In 1853, the Grand Trunk Railway bought the St. Lawrence and Atlantic Railroad, which covered the route from Montréal to the Québec/Vermont border, as well as its American partner company, the Atlantic and St. Lawrence Railroad, which owned track from the border to the harbour in Portland, Maine. In 1855 the company also built a line to Lévis from Montréal. That same year, the GTR purchased the Toronto and Guelph Railroad, extending the line to Sarnia to serve as a hub for traffic to and from Chicago to the south. Like other Canadian railway lines, the GTR built and ran its own hotels at the beginning of the twentieth century. These included the Chateau Laurier, Jasper Park Lodge, Hotel Macdonald, Fort Garry Hotel, and Highland Inn.

Violent tension with America complicated construction of the railway, as raids by the Fenian Brotherhood, an American Irish terrorist organization, plagued Canadians of the mid-nineteenth century. The Fenians attempted to pressure Britain to withdraw from Ireland by raiding army forts, custom posts and similar targets, and the threat from the Fenian Brotherhood was a constant background anxiety throughout the building of the railroad, necessitating the posting of British warships at the railhead in Vancouver when the Canadian Pacific Railway opened in 1886. Ironically, the tension actually encouraged Canadians to support Confederation in 1867, but Canadian–American tensions over the Fenian Brotherhood (and what was perceived as *laissez-faire* treatment of terrorists by the US government) continued until World War II.

Security concerns about the Fenian Brotherhood contributed to public demand for a year-round transportation system, so that British troops could be dispatched quickly to anywhere in Canada should there be additional attacks. Many of the British colonists and other Canadian citizens felt that the combined measures of finishing the railway and incorporating the colonies in federation so they could share the cost of the railway were steps for self-preservation.

We are the Fenian Brotherhood, skilled in the arts of war,
And we're going to fight for Ireland, the land we adore,
Many battles we have won, along with the boys in blue,
And we'll go and capture Canada, for we've nothing else to do.

Fenian soldiers' song

The Battle of Ridgeway, June 2, 1866, showing the charge of General O'Neill's Fenians on British troops and Canadian militia (right).

The worst accident in the history of Canadian rail took place on the Grand Trunk Railway on June 28, 1864. On that day, a passenger train running from Lévis to Montréal missed the signal indicating an open drawbridge over the Richelieu River and consequently fell into the river, landing on top of a barge and killing 99 European immigrants onboard the train.

By 1867, the Grand Trunk Railway was the largest railroad system in the world, with over 1,277 miles (2,055 km) of track. By then, the railroad was already world-renowned for its feats of construction, including the Victoria Bridge over the St. Lawrence River at Montréal in 1860 and the tunnel beneath the St. Clair River between Sarnia, Ontario, and Port Huron, Michigan in 1890. Best of all, however, was the bridging of the Niagara River between Fort Erie, Ontario, and Buffalo, New York.

Originally, the GTR used a broad gauge (also known as Provincial or Portland Gauge) of 5′ 6″ (1.676 m). In order to run trains from American tracks to GTR tracks the company experimented with variable gauge axles but with poor success. By 1873, they had changed to a standard gauge of 4′ $8\frac{1}{2}$″ (1.435 m).

Throughout the 1860s and 1870s the GTR expanded through western Québec and southern Ontario, purchasing many smaller railway companies and laying new trackage. The largest of these acquisitions was the Great Western Railway in 1882, which ran 852 miles (1,371 km) from Toronto to Niagara Falls.

After Confederation, the federal government offered the Grand Trunk Railway the opportunity to build the proposed rail line to British Columbia, but the GTR declined the offer. As a result, the Canadian Pacific Railway was born. This was the decisive moment that launched the ascendancy of the CPR as the most influential railway in Canada's history, and it was the same moment at which the GTR gave up that position. By this time, the three main subsidiaries of the Grand Trunk Railway were the Central Vermont Railway, which operated in Québec, Massachusetts, Vermont, and Connecticut; the Grand Trunk Pacific Railway, which operated in British Columbia, Saskatchewan, Alberta, and Manitoba; and the Grand Trunk Western Railroad, which operated in Illinois, Indiana, and Michigan. A fourth subsidiary was planned but never completed–the Southern New England Railway, chartered in 1910, which was meant to connect the Central Vermont line with the deep-water port of Providence, Rhode Island. Intermittent construction was abandoned in the early 1930s with the advent of the Great Depression.

Early in the twentieth century the GTR desired to participate in the vibrant economy of moving immigrants to the West and raw materials to the East. At the urging of the federal government the company tried to negotiate a cooperative venture with the Canadian Northern Railway (CNoR) but they failed to reach agreement. CNoR subsequently chose to construct an independent transcontinental line. The GTR then negotiated an

Building the GTR tunnel under the St. Claire River between Sarnia and Port Huron in 1890.

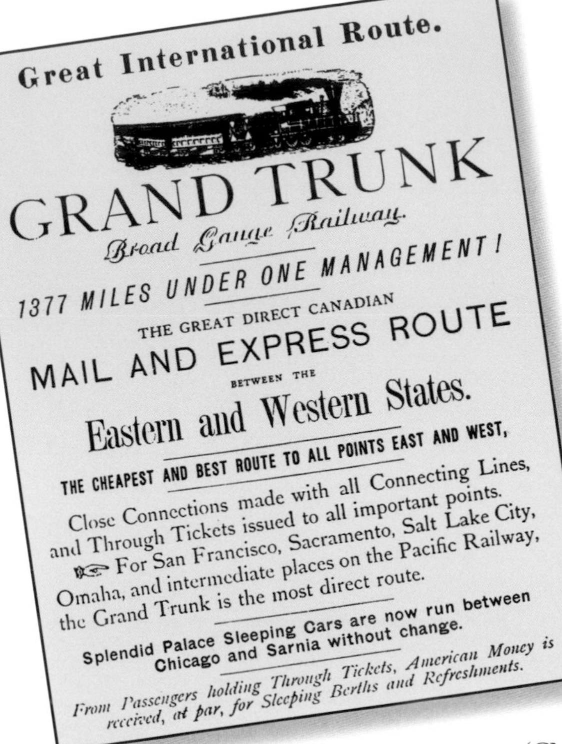

agreement with the federal government to operate the Grand Trunk Pacific Railway from Winnipeg to Prince Rupert, which would work in conjunction with the National Transcontinental Railway (NTR) between Winnipeg and Moncton, New Brunswick. To supplement this system, the GTR purchased the Canada Atlantic Railway (CAR) in 1905: CAR trains covered the territory from Ottawa south into Vermont and west to Georgian Bay.

The GTPR/NTR began construction in 1905, opening for rail traffic in 1914. In 1919 the GTR defaulted on the federal loan, was repossessed by the government, and was then placed under the auspices of the Canadian National Railways (CNR) in July of 1920. The GTPR routes were highly speculative and expensive to build. After the death of GTR president Charles Melville Hays—he had, most unfortunately, chosen to sail on the *Titanic*—the management of the GTR deteriorated, resulting in the abandonment of the Southern New England Railway. In 1923, the GTR was completely absorbed into the CNR as they merged into a Crown corporation.

An 1869 poster for the GTR express broad gauge service (above).

A 1906 postcard of Muskoka Wharf station, and a Wills cigarette card of 1910 featuring Canada's famous train ferries (below).

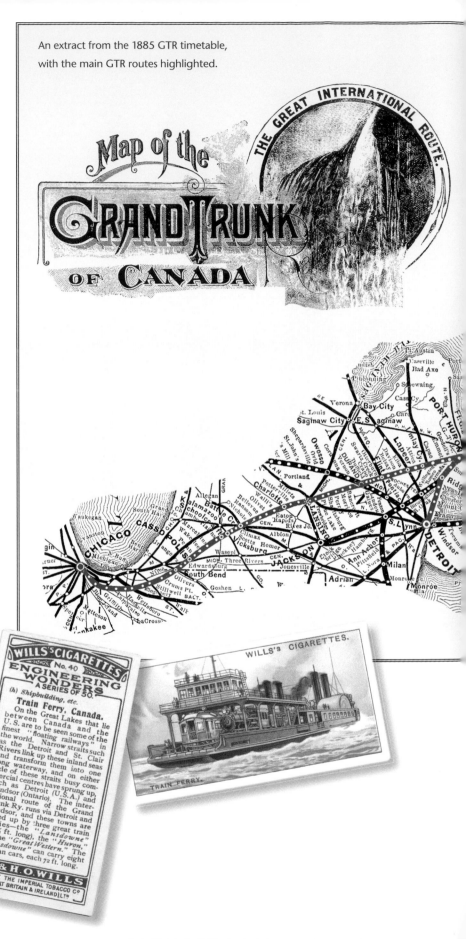

An extract from the 1885 GTR timetable, with the main GTR routes highlighted.

QUEBEC
POINT LEVI
MONTREAL
OTTAWA
SHERBROOKE
ARTHABASKA
RICHMOND
SOREL
ST. JOHNS
KINGSTON
BROCKVILLE
PRESCOTT
CORNWALL
OGDENSBURG
THOUSAND ISLANDS
TORONTO
LAKE ONTARIO
HAMILTON
BRANTFORD
GUELPH
STRATFORD
LONDON
ST. THOMAS
PALMERSTON
WIARTON
KINCARDINE
GODERICH
NIAGARA FALLS
BUFFALO
ROCHESTER
LAKE ERIE
PORTLAND
LEWISTON
MONTPELIER
Gravenhurst
Haliburton
Peterborough
Watertown
Oswego
Rome
Utica
Sarnia
Chatham
Petrolia
Wingham
Clinton
Listowel
Berlin
Galt
Woodstock
St. Catharines
Welland
Tillsonburg
Simcoe
Port Dover
Orillia
Lindsay
Belleville
Trenton
Cobourg
Whitby
Three Rivers
Doucet's Landing
Coaticook
Island Pond
Auburn
Salamanca
Corry
G.T.R. Double Track through the Garden of Canada
Grand Trunk Central Station, Ottawa, Canada
ONLY DOUBLE-TRACK RAILWAY BETWEEN MONTREAL, TORONTO AND OTHER PRINCIPAL CITIES IN CANADA.
JULY 1, 1905.
GRAND TRUNK RAILWAY SYSTEM
COMPLETE
TIME TABLES
CHAS. M. HAYS.
W. E. DAVIS.
G. T. BELL.
MONTREAL
MONTREAL
MONTREAL
GEORGE VAUX.
H. G. ELLIOTT.
MONTREAL

GRAND TRUNK TIMETABLES, 1906

CONDENSED THROUGH TIME-TABLES.

MONTREAL AND BOSTON, VIA CENTRAL VERMONT LINE.

Exp.	Exp.	(*Eastern time.*)	Exp.	Exp.	Exp.
P M	A M	LEAVE] [ARRIVE	P M	P M	A M
*8 40	*9 01	**Montreal**...(*Gr. Tk.*)	8 10	10 10	7 25
9 30	9 45	**St. Johns**..(*Cent. Vt.*)	7 20	8 20	6 35
10 43	10 57	**St. Albans**.. "	6 05	8 05	5 20
3 30	2 35	**White River Jn** (*B.& M.*)	1 24	4 00	12 20
5 47	4 44	**Concord**.... "	11 05	1 35	9 47
6 50	5 46	**Nashua**..... "	10 03	12 34	8 37
7 17	6 11	**Lowell**....... "	9 39	12 09	8 10
8 05	6 55	**Boston**...... "	†9 00	*11 30	*7 30
A M	P M	ARRIVE] [LEAVE	A M	A M	P M

Express from Montreal 9 01 a.m. Pullman Parlor Car Montreal to Boston, and Pullman Parlor Car Montreal to Springfield, via Grand Trunk and Central Vermont Line.

Express from Montreal 8 40 p.m. Pullman Sleeping Car Chicago through Montreal to Boston daily, via Grand Trunk and Central Vermont Line. Pullman Sleeping Car Montreal to Springfield daily.

Express from Boston 9 00 a.m. Pullman Parlor Car Boston to Montreal.

Express from Boston 11 30 a.m. Pullman Sleeping Car Boston to Montreal and Chicago.

Express from Boston 7 30 p.m. Pullman Sleeping Car Boston to Montreal. Pullman Sleeping Car Springfield to Montreal daily.

MONTREAL, MOOER'S JUNCTION AND MASSENA SPRINGS.

For Sleeping and Parlor Car Arrangements, see page 98.

56	54	52	Mls.	*June* 24, 1906.	51	55	171	175
P M	P M	A M		(*Eastern time.*)	A M	P M		
†4 50	†4 20	†7 00	0	lve..‖**Montreal** ♁ arr.	8 50	4 30		
4 55	4 25	7 05	1.50	......St. Henri.... ♁	8 44	4 24		
4 59	4 29	7 10	3.00	...Point St. Charles. ♁	8 36	4 16		
5 05	4 35	7 16	6.32	......St. Lambert... ♁	8 30	4 10		
5 15	4 48	7 26	12.00	...Brosseau's Junc. ♁	8 19	4 00		
P M	4 53	7 32	14.30	......Laprairie.... ♁	8 11	3 50		
	5 02	7 42	19.88	.....St. Constant... ♁	8 01	3 38		
	5 11	7 53	23.38	ar. **St. Isidore Jn** ♁ lv.	7 53	3 30		
	5 15	8 10	23.38	lv. **St. Isidore Jn**..ar.	7 45	3 30		
	5 23	8 20	27.00	...Cote Ste. Therese...	7 37	3 20		
	5 30	8 35	29.78	.......St. Remi..... ♁	7 30	3 05		
	5 39	8 50	33.47	......St. Michel......	7 21	2 25		
	5 48	9 05	37.20	......Sherrington......	7 12	2 15		
	5 56	9 30	40.18	......Barrington......	7 04	2 02	A M	P M
	6 05	10 10	44.67	....Hemmingford.. ♁	†6 55	†1 50	9 45	6 40
	6 20	10 25	50.10	arr. **Mooer's Jn** ♁ lve.	A M	P M	†9 30	†6 25
	5 11	7 53	23.38	lv.. **St. Isidore Jn**.ar.	7 53	3 30	A M	P M
	5 18	8 05	27.39	......St. Isidore......	7 39	3 18		
	5 24	8 10	30.41	....Ste. Philomene....	7 33	3 10		
	5 31	8 16	33.66	**Ste. Martine Junc** ♁	7 25	3 03		
	5 43	8 27	38.86	.......Howick...... ♁	7 12	2 50		
	5 45	8 29	39.80	.. Howick Junction ..	7 07	2 46		
	5 56	8 37	43.66	.........Bryson's.......	7 01	2 38		
	6 03	8 47	47.32	......Ormstown.... ♁	6 54	2 30		
	6 12	8 58	52.16	.....Dewittville.....	6 45	2 18		
	6 23	9 07	56.74	.....Huntingdon.... ♁	6 36	2 10		
	6 34	9 18	62.38	........Carr's........	6 25	1 56		
	6 39	9 23	64.44	........White's........	6 21	1 50		
	6 49	9 32	69.29	......Ste. Agnes......	6 13	1 41		
	7 00	9 45	74.20	... Fort Covington . ♁	†6 05	1 32		
	P M	9 57	79.70	........Bombay..... ♁	A M	1 19		
		10 13	87.20	........Helena..... ♁		1 05		
		10 30	95.70	**Massena Springs** ♁		†12 50		
		A M		ARRIVE] [LEAVE		Noon		

Beauharnois Branch.—Train leaves **Ste. Martine Junction** *g* 10 10 a.m., arrives Beauharnois (6 miles) 10 25 a.m. Leaves Beauharnois *g* 10 30 a.m., arrives **Ste. Martine Junction** 10 45 a.m.

Baggage from Canada to the United States may, for convenience, be examined, passed Customs and checked to destination at Montreal, Toronto, Stratford or London, and likewise baggage for Canada may be passed Customs and checked to destination at the Dearborn Street Station, Chicago. Baggage to and from United States points passing through Canada is bonded while in transit and not examined by the Customs officials. The frontier Customs examination stations are Island Pond, Fort Covington, Suspension Bridge, Niagara Falls, Detroit and Port Huron.

* Daily; † daily, except Sunday; *c* Sunday arrives 10 05 a.m.; *g* Monday, Wednesday and Friday only; *h* on Sunday leaves 11 30 p.m.

PORT DOVER AND HAMILTON.

43	41	Mls.	*December* 3, 1905.	40	42
P M	A M		LEAVE] [ARRIVE	A M	P M
†5 40	†7 55	0	.....**Port Dover**... ♁	10 40	8 05
5 55	8 20	9.00	.......**Jarvis**..... ♁	10 20	7 45
6 00	8 28	11.50	........Garnett.......	10 15	7 05
6 10	8 45	14.50	......Hagersville.... ♁	10 10	7 00
6 14	8 48	16.25	.......Ballsville......	10 05	6 55
6 30	9 15	24.00	ar. } **Caledonia** ♁ { lv.	9 52	6 40
7 25	9 15	24.00	lv. } **Caledonia** ♁ { ar.	9 52	6 40
7 35	9 23	29.00	.......Glanford.......	9 42	6 20
7 45	9 33	34.50	........Rymal........	9 33	6 10
8 00	9 45		.....*King Street*... ♁	9 10	5 55
8 10	9 55		.....*Stuart Street*... ♁	†9 00	†5 50
P M	A M	40.25	arr..‖**Hamilton**..lve.	A M	P M

JARVIS AND PORT ROWAN.

63	61	Mls.	*December* 3, 1905.	62	64
P M	A M	31.25	lve..‖**Hamilton**..arr.	A M	P M
†5 50	†9 00		....*Stuart Street*....	9 55	8 10
5 55	9 10		.... *King Street*.....	9 45	8 00
†7 45	†10 30	0	lve....**Jarvis**....arr.	8 15	5 18
7 55	10 45	6.02	........Renton........	8 02	5 07
8 05	11 00	10.58	.**Simcoe** (Loop Line) ♁	7 55	4 57
8 15	11 10	11.67	Loop Line Junction ♁	7 35	3 25
8 20	11 35	13.42	**Simcoe** (G. B. & L. E.) ♁	7 30	3 15
8 30	11 50	18.56	........Vittoria...... ♁	6 53	2 20
8 40	12 01	21.79	........Walsh........	6 47	2 05
8 45	12 10	24.44	......Forestville......	6 40	1 50
8 52	12 17	26.95	.....St. Williams... ♁	6 34	1 40
9 05	12 30	30.42	....**Port Rowan**.. ♁	†6 25	†1 30
P M	Noon		ARRIVE] [LEAVE	A M	P M

TORONTO, NEW YORK AND PHILADELPHIA, VIA NIAGARA FALLS AND LEHIGH VALLEY RAILROAD.

Exp.	Exp.	Exp.	Exp.	(*Eastern time.*)	Exp.	Exp.	Exp.	Exp.
A M	P M	P M	P M	LEAVE] [ARRIVE	A M	A M	A M	A M
†7 35	*6 10	*5 00	*11 20	.......**Toronto**.......	10 05	11 15	*c*8 25	*c*8 25
8 40	7 05	5 55	2 25	.......**Hamilton**..arr.	8 55	10 20	1 05	1 05
9 55	8 50	6 55	3 25	**Niagara Falls** (*G. T. R.*)	7 55	9 20	12 01	12 01
11 00	10 40	7 40	.....	**Buffalo**..(*L. V. R.R.*)	6 25	8 00	10 30	10 30
1 10	12 55	10 10	†6 35	**Geneva**..... "	3 39	5 15	8 00	7 28
2 13	.....	11 20	7 45	**Ithaca**...... "	.....	.....	.....	6 18
5 30	4 58	2 50	11 15	**Wilkes-Barre** "	11 42	1 20	4 34	2 52
7 00	6 34	4 39	1 01	**Mauch Chunk** "	9 43	11 30	3 04	1 21
7 47	7 25	5 29	1 56	**Bethlehem** "	8 28	10 31	*2 12	12 19
9 15	9 15	7 15	3 45	Philadelphia (P. & R. Ry.)	6 30	*8 40	*12 30	*10 02
10 08	10 00	8 03	4 33	**New York** (*L. V. R.R.*)	*5 40	*7 55	*11 55	*9 55
P M	A M	A M	P M	arr. *West 23d Street* lve.	P M	P M	A M	A M

MONTREAL AND NEW YORK, VIA DELAWARE & HUDSON CO.

Exp	Exp	Exp	Express.	(*Eastern time.*)	Exp	Exp	Express.	Exp
P M	P M	A M	....	LEAVE] [ARRIVE	P M	P M	....	P M
*11 30	*8 10	†10 15	†7 21 A M	**Montreal**.......(*G. T.*)	9 46	8 20	7 15 A M	2 15
11 45	8 25	10 30	7 37 A M	**St. Lambert**.... "	9 24	8 05	6 58 A M	2 33
12 17	8 55	11 00	8 14 A M	**St. Johns**....... "	8 52	7 35	6 27 A M	2 01
1 05	9 40	11 40	9 10 A M	Rouses Point...(*D. & H.*)	8 05	7 00	5 45 A M	1 15
1 45	10 20	11 20	9 55 A M	**Plattsburgh**.. "	7 20	6 25	5 00 A M	12 30
1 50	10 25	12 27	10 03 A M	Hotel Champlain "	6 45	6 12	4 42 A M	12 10
7 00	1 55	3 45	2 35 P M	**Saratoga**..... "	1 40	2 50	12 55 Night	8 15
8 10	2 45	4 55	– –	**Troy**.......... "	12 25	1 45	11 40 P M	7 00
8 20	3 15	.....	4 00 P M	**Albany**........ "	12 25	.....	11 00 P M	*7 00
1 30	7 18	9 00	8 00 P M	**New York**..... "	†8 45	†9 45	*7 00 P M	†12 10
P M	A M	P M	....	ARRIVE] [LEAVE	A M	A M	....	Night

Express from Montreal 10 15 a.m., except Sunday. Parlor Car Montreal to New York. Dining Car Plattsburg to Whitehall.

Express from Montreal 7 21 a.m., except Sunday. Parlor Car Montreal to Albany.

Express from Montreal 8 10 p.m. daily. Sleeping Cars Montreal to New York.

Express from New York 7 00 p.m. daily. Sleeping Car New York to Montreal. Sleeping Car New York to Plattsburg.

Express from New York 9 45 a.m. Parlor Car New York to Montreal. Dining Car Whitehall to Rouses Point.

Express from New York 12 10 night. Parlor Car Plattsburg to Montreal.

Express from New York 8 45 a.m. Parlor Car Montreal to Albany.

Express from Montreal 11 30 p.m. daily. Pullman Sleeping Car Montreal to Albany.

QUEBEC AND BOSTON, VIA PORTLAND.

Express.	Express.	(*Eastern time.*)	Express.	Express.
†6 35 A M	†7 00 P M	lve.....**Quebec**.....arr.	*8 05 A M	†11 00 P M
†7 05 A M	†7 30 P M	lve...**Point Levi**...arr	7 35 A M	†10 30 P M
*10 40 A M	*10 55 P M	.......**Richmond**.......	4 25 A M	4 00 P M
11 32 A M	11 40 P M	......**Sherbrooke**.......	3 45 A M	3 10 P M
1 24 P M	1 48 A M	...**North Stratford**...	1 16 A M	12 55 Noon
1 48 P M	2 12 A M	.......**Groveton**.......	12 52 Night	12 30 Noon
2 50 P M	3 21 A M	........**Gorham**........	11 48 P M	11 30 A M
4 42 P M	5 35 A M	..**Danville Junction**..	9 32 P M	9 15 A M
5 45 P M	6 40 A M	arr....**Portland**....lve.	*8 30 P M	*8 15 A M
6 21 P M	†7 25 A M	ar. Old Orchard (B. & M.). lv.	†7 27 P M	....
9 10 P M	†10 15 A M	arr.. **Boston** (B. & M.). lve.	†4 15 P M	....

HAMILTON AND SOUTHAMPTON.

45	19	43	17	Miles.	*June* 17, 1906.	44	18	20	22
P M	P M	A M	A M	......	LEAVE] [ARRIVE	A M	P M	P M	P M
†7 06	†3 55	†9 00	†8 00	......	........**Hamilton**...... ♁	8 20	1 35	5 20	9 00
†8 30	†4 05	†10 20	†9 05	......	lve....**Brantford** ♁ . arr.	8 05	12 10	4 25	7 25
†9 00	†4 40	†11 00	9 30	0	lve..‖**Harrisburg** ♁.arr.	7 30	11 45	4 00	7 05
9 13	4 50	11 30	9 40	6.08	.........Branchton...... ♁	7 15	11 30	3 45	6 52
9 25	5 05	12 05	9 55	11.73	arr.........**Galt** ♁......lve.	7 05	11 15	3 35	6 40
9 25	5 05	12 05	9 55	11.73	lve.........**Galt**.......arr.	7 05	11 15	3 35	6 40
9 40	5 13	12 30	10 02	15.79	..........Preston........ ♁	6 40	11 05	3 22	6 30
9 56	5 22	12 55	10 08	19.16	.... Hespeler...... ♁	6 30	10 57	3 15	6 23
– –	– –	– –	10 17	24.06	.........Gourock.........	– –	– –	3 05	– –
10 15	5 35	1 15	10 25	26.76	arr...**Guelph Junc** ♁ lve.	6 10	10 42	3 00	6 10
10 25	5 48	1 25	10 35	27.92	arr...**Guelph City** ♁ .lve.	†6 00	10 15	2 50	5 45
P M	6 05	1 25	10 50	27.92	lve...**Guelph City**...arr.	A M	10 05	2 50	5 40
	6 10	1 55	– –	26.76	lve...**Guelph Junc**..arr.		– –	2 44	– –
.....	6 17	2 37	11 03	30.86	..........Marden.........	.....	9 47	2 37	5 25
.....	6 34	3 00	11 24	40.29	...........Elora......... ♁	.....	9 33	2 25	5 14
.....	6 42	3 30	11 35	42.91	..........Fergus......... ♁	.....	9 26	2 19	5 08
.....	6 54	3 45	11 45	49.00	...........Alma.......... ♁	.....	9 13	2 07	4 56
.....	7 05	4 00	11 56	54.56	........Goldstone....... ♁	.....	9 00	1 55	4 44
.....	7 13	4 36	12 04	58.15	.........Drayton......... ♁	.....	8 52	1 46	4 36
41	7 22	4 55	12 13	62.30	........Moorefield...... ♁	42	8 44	1 35	4 28
A M	7 35	5 25	12 30	69.34	arr..‖**Palmerston** ♁ lve.	A M	8 30	†1 20	4 15
†6 00	8 00	P M	1 00	69.34	lve...**Palmerston**...arr.	11 30	7 55	P M	4 00
6 50	8 10	.....	1 10	74.99	arr....**Harriston** ♁ ..lve.	11 10	7 40	.....	3 50
6 50	8 10	.....	1 10	74.99	lve....**Harriston**....arr.	11 10	7 40	.....	3 50
7 10	8 16	.....	1 17	79.08	.........Fulton's.........	10 38	7 32	.....	3 35
7 26	8 22	.....	1 24	81.67	.........Clifford........ ♁	10 30	7 26	.....	3 28
8 30	8 36	.....	1 40	90.47	.... Mildmay........ ♁	9 50	7 11	.....	3 12
9 30	8 50	.....	1 54	96.29	........Walkerton....... ♁	9 30	6 59	.....	3 00
9 45	9 00	.....	2 02	101.17	.........Dunkeld.........	8 40	6 46	.....	2 47
10 00	9 06	.....	2 07	103.70	.... Cargill........ ♁	8 30	6 40	.....	2 42
10 10	9 10	.....	2 10	105.03	.........Pinkerton.........	8 20	6 36	.....	2 38
11 00	9 25	.....	2 27	111.36	..........Paisley........ ♁	8 00	6 24	.....	2 27
11 15	9 37	.....	2 42	118.67	.........Turner's.........	7 30	6 10	.....	2 12
11 45	9 50	.....	2 56	124.26	........Port Elgin...... ♁	7 20	6 00	.....	2 00
12 05	10 00	.....	3 10	128.28	.....**Southampton**... ♁	†7 00	†5 50	.....	†1 50
Noon	P M	.....	P M	......	ARRIVE] [LEAVE	A M	A M	.....	P M

GRAND TRUNK RAILWAY SYSTEM.

CHICAGO, PORT HURON, TORONTO, MONTREAL AND PORTLAND.

64	8	2	6	10	26	12	4	Miles.	*December* 3, 1905.	7	3	9	25	5	9	3	13	65	67
	A M		P M	A M	P M		P M		(*Central time.*)	P M	P M	P M	A M	A M					
	*11 05		*10 30	†8 32	*4 02		*3 02	0	lve......‖**Chicago** ♁.....arr.	2 00	9 10	7 00	9 30	7 42					
	11 10		10 35	8 37	4 07		3 07	1.25	.......Archer Avenue...... ♁	1 55	9 06	6 55	9 25	7 37					
	11 19		10 44	8 46	4 16		3 16	4.20	.........47th Street........ ♁	1 46	8 56	6 46	9 13	7 28					
	– –		– –	9 30	5 02		– –	19.34	.........Blue Island........ ♁	– –	– –	6 00	8 21	– –					
	– –		– –	10 05	5 37		– –	36.09	.... **Griffith**.......... ♁	– –	– –	5 23	7 44	– –					
	12 48		12 21	10 47	6 32		4 48	55.50	........‖**Valparaiso**........ ♁	12 15	7 23	4 48	*6 45	5 43					
	– –		– –	11 01	P M		– –	63.57	..........**Haskells**......... ♁	– –	– –	4 25	A M	– –					
	– –		– –	11 12			– –	69.83	.........Union Mills......... ♁	– –	– –	4 14		– –					
	– –		– –	11 15			– –	70.75	.........**Wellsboro**......... ♁	– –	– –	4 11		– –					
	– –		– –	11 23			– –	74.73	..........Kingsbury......... ♁	– –	– –	4 02		– –					
	1 24		12 58	11 33			5 26	79.86	..........**Stillwell**......... ♁	11 40	6 45	3 54		5 03					
	– –		– –	11 41		A M	– –	84.18	.........Mill Creek......... ♁	– –	– –	3 42		– –			P M		
	2 00		1 32	12 25		†7 00	6 02	100.14	.........**South Bend**......... ♁	11 03	6 09	3 07		4 25			7 30		
	– –		– –	12 31		7 08	– –	103.72	.........Mishawaka......... ♁	– –	– –	3 00		– –			7 22		
	– –		– –	12 43		7 19	6 20	110.56	..........**Granger**......... ♁	10 48	– –	2 48		– –			7 10		
	– –		*c* –	12 50		7 25	– –	113.65	........Edwardsburg......... ♁	– –	– –	2 41		– –			7 03		
	2 32		2 12	1 07		7 41	6 42	122.34	.........**Cassopolis**......... ♁	10 29	5 35	2 28		3 49			6 48		
	– –		– –	1 24		8 01	– –	131.13	..........Wakelee......... ♁	– –	– –	2 07		– –			6 30		
	– –		*c* –	1 34		8 12	7 06	135.67	.........Marcellus......... ♁	10 08	– –	1 59		– –			6 21		
	– –		*c* –	1 54		8 32	– –	146.45	........**Schoolcraft**......... ♁	9 51	– –	1 38		– –			6 01		
	3 14		3 00	2 06		8 44	7 33	151.91	.........**Vicksburg**......... ♁	9 42	4 51	1 28		2 57			5 50		
	– –		– –	2 15		8 52	– –	156.87	..........Pavilion......... ♁	– –	– –	1 16		– –			5 39		
	– –		– –	2 31		9 08	– –	164.64	..........Clima......... ♁	– –	– –	1 01	‖	– –			5 25		
	– –	A M	– –	2 38		9 18	– –	168.81	..........Renton.........	– –	– –	12 52	P M	– –			5 17		
	3 55	†7 00	3 45	2 55		9 40	8 15	175.11	......‖**Battle Creek**..... ♁	9 08	4 17	12 40	9 00	2 17			5 05		
	– –	7 05	– –	3 00		9 45	– –	176.21	..........Nichols.........	– –	– –	12 20	8 55	– –			4 55		
	– –	7 15	– –	3 10		9 55	– –	181.77	..........Penfield......... ♁	– –	– –	12 10	8 43	– –			4 42		
	– –	7 28	– –	3 22		10 08	– –	188.47	..........Bellevue......... ♁	– –	– –	12 00	8 32	– –			4 30		
	c –	7 38	– –	3 31		10 18	– –	193.60	..........Olivet......... ♁	8 35	– –	11 50	8 22	– –			4 20		
	4 34	7 53	4 30	3 45		10 33	8 55	201.57	.........**Charlotte**......... ♁	8 22	3 34	11 36	8 07	1 27			4 05		
	– –	8 05	– –	3 57		10 45	– –	207.98	.........Potterville......... ♁	– –	– –	11 25	7 54	– –			3 54		
	4 57	8 30	4 58	4 21		11 10	9 23	220.19	..........**Lansing**......... ♁	7 57	3 08	11 03	7 30	12 56			3 33		
	– –	8 37	– –	4 28		11 17	– –	222.73	.........**Trowbridge**......... ♁	– –	– –	10 53	7 22	– –			3 26		
	– –	8 48	– –	4 39		11 28	– –	228.33	........Haslett Park......... ♁	– –	– –	10 42	7 13	– –			3 16		
	– –	9 00	– –	4 51		11 40	– –	234.98	.........Shaftsburg......... ♁	– –	– –	10 30	7 01	– –			3 06		
	– –	9 11	– –	5 01		11 51	– –	239.29	...........Perry......... ♁	– –	– –	10 20	6 52	– –			2 57		
	– –	9 18	– –	5 07		11 58	– –	241.47	..........Morrice......... ♁	– –	– –	10 14	6 46	– –			2 52		
	– –	9 28	– –	5 19		12 10	– –	247.75	..........Bancroft......... ♁	– –	– –	10 02	6 34	– –			2 42		
	5 40	9 40	5 55	5 30		12 20	10 10	252.55	arr.......‖**Durand** ♁.....lve.	7 15	*2 25	9 50	6 20	12 05			2 35		
	7 45	12 20	*8 20	7 45		†2 40		319.65	arr..‖**Detroit** (D. & M. Div.)..lve.		†11 30	†7 00	†3 30	*10 00			†11 30		
	P M	9 50	5 55	6 20		12 45	10 10	252.55	lve.......‖**Durand**........arr.	7 15	2 25	9 40	5 50	11 50			2 15		
		9 56	– –	6 27		12 51	– –	256.49	..........Duffield......... ♁	– –	– –	9 30	5 39	– –			2 05		
		10 04	– –	6 35		12 58	– –	260.74	........Swartz Creek......... ♁	– –	– –	9 22	5 31	– –			1 58		
		10 09	– –	6 40		1 03	– –	263.32	..........Otterburn......... ♁	– –	– –	9 16	5 26	– –			1 52		
		10 25	6 28	6 55		1 15	10 40	269.49	...........**Flint**......... ♁	6 47	1 57	9 04	5 12	11 15			1 37		
		10 32	– –	7 08		1 22	– –	274.48	...........Belsay......... ♁	– –	– –	8 49	4 58	– –			1 22		
		10 48	– –	7 24		1 38	– –	282.51	...........Elba......... ♁	– –	– –	8 33	4 43	– –			1 02		
		11 02	7 01	7 39		1 52	11 12	289.41	..........**Lapeer**......... ♁	6 17	1 28	8 20	4 31	10 35			12 48		
		11 15	– –	7 52		2 05	– –	296.53	...........Attica......... ♁	– –	– –	8 06	4 18	– –			12 32		
		11 25	7 20	8 02		2 15	– –	301.23	........**Imlay City**......... ♁	– –	– –	7 57	4 10	10 14			12 20		
		11 38	7 33	8 16		2 28	– –	308.60	...........Capac......... ♁	– –	– –	7 44	3 57	10 00			12 05		
		11 52	7 47	8 32		2 42	– –	317.19	..........Emmett......... ♁	– –	– –	7 29	3 43	8 44			11 49		
	P M	12 20	8 15	9 00		3 10	12 20	335.00	arr....‖**Port Huron** ♁ ...lve.	*5 15	*12 25	†7 00	†3 10	*9 15		P M	†11 15		
	*7 55	*10 45	*10 45	P M		P M	*10 30	0	lv.‖**Detroit** (*Via Pt. Huron*) ar.		Noon	A M	†6 00	†8 35		*2 00	A M		
	9 35	12 20	12 20				12 05	57.02	arr.....‖**Port Huron**....lve.				†4 05	†6 50		*12 25			
	P M								lv. **Detroit** (*Via Windsor*) ar.				P M						
		*12 25	*12 25				*12 42		lv. ‖**Port Huron** (Via Stratford) ar.				*1 50	†6 25		†11 35			
	9 45	*12 50	*8 25			†3 15	*12 36		lv...**Port Huron** (Via London)..ar.	*5 05			P M	*9 00		A M			
	P M	Noon	A M			P M	Night		(*Central time.*)	A M				P M					
	72	2				6	4		*June* 17, 1906.	7			3	5		11			
	P M	P M				A M	A M		(*Eastern time.*)	P M			P M	P M		A M			
	†4 40	*1 45				†6 00	*2 02	338.08	lv..**Sarnia** (*Tunnel Sta.*) ♁ .ar	10 10			2 35	7 10		10 45			
	4 55	1 55				6 10	– –	344.34	..........Blackwell......... ♁	9 55			2 23	6 53		10 35			
	5 05	2 00				6 15	– –	348.03	...........Perch...........	– –			2 16	6 45		10 28			
	5 18	2 10				6 22	– –	352.67	.........Camlachie......... ♁	9 40			2 10	6 40		10 17			
	5 44	2 26				6 39	2 39	361.73	..........Forrest......... ♁	9 25			2 00	6 23		9 59			
	6 10	2 41				6 56	– –	370.74	.........Thedford......... ♁	9 10			1 45	6 10		9 43			
	6 35	2 56				7 10	3 05	379.41	..........Parkhill......... ♁	8 58			1 20	5 55		9 27			
	7 00	3 10	66			7 25	3 20	386.82	........Ailsa Craig......... ♁	8 47			1 05	5 42		9 15			
	– –	– –	&			– –	– –	391.83	.......Lucan Crossing ⊡.....	– –			– –	5 30		9 05			
	7 25	3 25	10	8	62	7 40	– –	393.88	...........Lucan......... ♁	8 35		1	12 51	5 20		8 55	63		
P M	7 40	3 35	P M	A M	A M	7 50	– –	399.84	arr.........Granton ♁......lve.	8 25		A M	12 41	5 05	P M	8 45	A M	P M	P M
†2 50			†5 00	†6 20	†10 45			431.85	lve.......‖**London**.......arr.			10 55		6 35	10 55		10 40	1 25	6 35
3 45	8 10	3 55	5 45	7 08	†11 35	8 10	4 02	409.23	....**St. Mary's Junction**.. ♁	8 10		– –	12 28	4 50	10 10	8 30	9 55	12 35	5 45
3 53	8 20	4 05	5 53	7 15	11 42	8 20	– –	414.21	..........St. Paul's......... ♁	8 00		– –	12 19	4 40	– –	8 20	9 47	12 28	5 32
4 05	8 35	4 20	6 05	7 25	11 55	8 30	4 20	419.29	arr. } ....‖**Stratford** ♁ ... { lve.	7 50		10 05	12 10	4 30	9 55	†8 05	†9 40	†12 20	†5 25
P M	P M	4 30	6 50	7 30	A M	8 45	4 30	419.29	lve. } ....‖**Stratford** ♁ ... { arr.	7 35		10 00	11 59	4 20	9 50	A M	A M	Noon	P M
		4 42	7 00	– –		8 57	– –	425.89	........Shakespeare......... ♁	7 22		– –	11 47	4 08	– –				
		4 52	7 10	7 50		9 10	– –	432.96	.......New Hamburg......... ♁	7 10		9 41	11 37	3 56	9 28				
		4 58	7 15	7 54		9 16	– –	435.40	...........Baden......... ♁	6 55		– –	11 33	3 51	– –				
		5 05	7 22	– –		9 32	– –	438.81	........Petersburg......... ♁	6 48		– –	11 27	3 43	– –				
		5 20	7 45	8 10		9 50	5 20	445.29	...........**Berlin**......... ♁	6 30		9 19	11 15	3 30	9 08				
		5 28	7 51	– –		9 59	– –	449.56	..........Breslau......... ♁	6 20		– –	11 02	3 15	– –				
		5 43	– –	– –		10 15	– –	458.08	.....**Guelph Junction**..... ♁	6 07		– –	10 48	2 58	– –				
		5 55	8 10	8 30		10 40	5 50	459.24	..........**Guelph**......... ♁	5 55		8 55	10 40	2 50	8 45				
		6 10	8 32	– –		10 54	– –	466.60	.........Rockwood......... ♁	5 40		– –	10 24	2 35	– –				
		6 24	8 45	8 53		11 05	6 18	472.28	........Acton West......... ♁	5 30		8 31	10 14	2 25	8 23				
		6 40	8 57	9 05		11 20	6 33	478.54	........**Georgetown**......... ♁	5 10		8 15	9 55	2 08	8 08				
		6 49	9 01	9 10		11 26	– –	480.94	..........Norval......... ♁	5 00		– –	9 40	2 00	– –				
		7 00	9 13	9 24		11 37	6 50	486.53	.........Brampton......... ♁	4 50		8 00	9 24	1 49	7 45				
		7 10	9 23	– –		11 46	7 00	492.51	..........Malton......... ♁	4 36		– –	9 08	1 36	– –				
		7 20	9 33	9 41		11 58	7 12	499.22	..........Weston......... ♁	4 22		– –	8 55	1 22	7 20				
		7 30	9 41	– –		12 06	– –	502.53	......Toronto Junction..... ♁	4 15		– –	8 48	1 15	– –				
		7 40	9 50	9 52		12 13	7 30	505.35	....North Parkdale Junction. ♁	4 08		7 30	8 40	1 08	7 07				
		7 50	10 03	10 00		12 20	7 40	507.63	........‖**Toronto**......... ♁	†4 00		†7 20	*8 30	†1 00	†7 00				
		P M	P M	A M		Noon	A M		ARRIVE] [LEAVE	P M		A M	A M	P M	P M				

* Daily; † daily, except Sunday; ‡ Sunday only; *b* stops Saturday to leave passengers; *c* stops to leave passengers from Chicago. ‖ Meals.

⊡ No tickets sold at, or baggage checked at, to, from or via Lucan Crossing; stops are made there only for passengers for or from Main Line trains.

NOTE.—The Through Connection of Train No. 4 from Port Huron to Toronto is via Stratford, and of Train No. 6 is via London.

☞ For Sleeping and Parlor Car Arrangements, see page 98.

GRAND TRUNK RAILWAY SYSTEM.

CHICAGO, PORT HURON, TORONTO, MONTREAL AND PORTLAND.

KINGSTON AND KINGSTON JUNCTION.

28	22	44	52	32	24	38	42	36	.....	Mls	*June 17, 1906.*
A M	A M	A M	A M	Noon	P M	P M	P M	Night			[LEAVE
*1 48	*2 26	†8 16	*9 15	*12 16	*1 00	†3 19	†7 03	*12 45		0	Kingston ♁
2 00	2 38	8 28	9 27	12 28	1 12	3 31	7 15	12 57		2.25	Kingston Junction‖ ♁
A M	A M	A M	A M	Noon	P M	P M	P M	Night			[ARRIVE

25	39	23	57	41	21	35	27	43	.....	Mls	*(Eastern time.)*
A M	A M	A M	A M	A M	Noon	P M	P M	P M			[LEAVE
*1 03	*2 10	*2 53	†8 35	†9 35	*12 37	*1 17	†3 39	†7 26		0	Kingston Junction
1 15	2 22	3 05	8 47	9 47	12 49	1 29	3 51	7 38		2.25	Kingston
A M	A M	A M	A M	A M	Noon	P M	P M	P M			[ARRIVE

6	26	22	30	.....	8	2	4	Miles.	*June 17, 1906.*	15	7	11	.....	1	11	.....	5	.....
A M			P M		P M	Noon	Night		LEAVE] [ARRIVE	P M	A M	A M		A M			P M	
*8 25			†3 15		*9 45	*12 50	*12 35	335.00	Port Huron (*Central time*)	9 00	5 05	*11 50		*11 50			9 00	
*9 45			†4 35		*11 00	*2 10	*1 55	338.08	Sarnia (*Eastern time*)	9 45	5 50	12 35		12 35			9 45	
*11 30			†6 55		*12 20	*4 25	*3 25	397.04	lve. London arr.	7 47	4 00	11 00		11 00			6 25	
*1 35			†9 00		*2 20	*6 55	*5 25	472.95	arr. Hamilton arr.	5 20	12 30	7 40		8 30			3 25	
*3 00	P M	A M	†10 00		A M	8 15	n8 25	511.66	arr. Toronto lve.	*4 30	*11 20	†6 20		*7 35			*2 00	
A M	†6 05	*11 10	A M			*2 45		0	lve. Detroit (*Via Windsor*) arr.	9 50	†9 30	1 20		1 20			9 50	
*11 30	*12 20	4 25				*6 55		111.20	lve. London arr.	7 47	4 00	11 00		11 00			6 25	
*1 35	*2 20	*6 55				*9 00		187.11	lve. Hamilton arr.	5 20	12 30	7 40		8 30			3 25	
*3 00	†8 25	*8 15				*10 00		225.82	arr. Toronto lve.	*4 30	*11 20	†6 20		*7 35			*2 00	

28	26	24	76	14	8	12	14	6	2	4	Miles	*(Eastern time.)*	1	7	5	13	3	.....	13	P M	.....		
					P M	P M	P M	A M	P M	A M		LEAVE] [ARRIVE	P M	P M	A M	A M	A M	P M					
			Additional Train—Leaves Cornwall e7 30 a.m., arrives Montreal 9 15 a.m.		*9 00	†1 50	†5 10	†7 45	*10 15	*9 00	507.63	‖Toronto ♁	4 20	9 20	*6 10	9 45	7 15	3 20					
					– –	– –	– –	– –	– –	– –	509.31	Don	International Limited.	– –	– –	– –	– –	– –					
					j9 09	2 01	5 22	7 56	– –	– –	510.01	Riverdale		9 07	j6 00	9 30	– –	3 08					
					– –	2 05	5 26	– –	– –	– –	511.63	Golf Grounds		9 04	5 57	9 25	– –	3 03					
					– –	2 10	5 30	8 05	– –	– –	513.06	York ♁		9 02	5 55	9 23	– –	2 58					
					9 23	2 18	5 37	8 10	– –	– –	516.61	Scarboro Junction ♁		8 56	5 45	9 15	– –	2 50					
					– –	2 32	5 50	8 22	– –	– –	525.53	Port Union ♁		8 37	5 29	8 56	– –	2 32					
					a9 37	2 37	5 53	8 25	– –	– –	527.13	Rosebank		8 32	5 26	8 51	– –	2 28					
					– –	2 43	5 58	8 29	– –	– –	528.26	Dunbarton		8 25	– –	8 46	– –	2 23					
					– –	2 47	6 04	8 33	– –	– –	530.93	Pickering ♁		8 20	– –	8 41	– –	2 18					
					9 55	3 01	6 19	8 45	– –	s9 49	537.19	**Whitby Junction** ♁		8 05	5 06	8 28	– –	2 05					
					10 05	3 12	6 29	8 52	– –	9 55	541.06	**Oshawa Junction** ♁		7 55	4 59	8 19	– –	1 56					
					*10 15	†3 20	†6 40	†9 10		*10 10	542.63	arr. **Oshawa** lve.		†7 35	*4 40	†7 55		†1 30					
					*9 40	†2 45	†6 00	†8 40		*9 35	542.63	lve. (*Via Oshawa Ry.*) arr.		†8 05	*5 10	†8 30		2 15					
					– –	3 25	6 40	9 00	– –	– –	547.05	lve. **Darlington** ♁ arr.	– –	7 42	– –	8 06	– –	1 43					
					10 24	3 36	6 49	9 06	– –	10 10	550.34	Bowmanville ♁	– –	7 33	4 40	7 57	– –	1 36					
					– –	3 47	6 58	9 15	– –	– –	554.72	Newcastle ♁	– –	7 23	– –	7 46	– –	1 25					
					– –	4 05	7 16	9 30	– –	– –	562.68	Newtonville ♁	– –	7 07	– –	7 30	– –	1 10					
					11 02	4 25	7 31	9 44	12 01	10 40	570.32	arr. **Port Hope** ♁ lve.	2 45	6 51	4 02	7 15	5 15	12 55					
						†[illegible]			†[illegible]		[illegible]	arr. **Peterboro** lve.						‖11 45					
					11 17	4 40	7 45	9 57	12 16	10 52	577.13	arr. ‖**Cobourg** ♁ lve.	2 35	6 37	3 47	7 00	5 05	12 40					
					11 17	4 40	7 45	9 57	12 16	10 52	577.13	lve. arr.	2 35	‖6 17	3 47	7 00	5 05	‖12 20					
					– –	4 53	7 58	10 10	– –	– –	584.93	Grafton ♁	– –	6 04	3 32	6 43	– –	12 06					
					11 42	5 04	8 11	10 22	– –	– –	591.58	Colborne ♁	– –	5 53	3 21	6 34	– –	11 53					
					11 57	5 15	8 26	10 35	– –	– –	599.18	Brighton ♁	– –	5 40	3 09	6 23	– –	11 39					
					12 19	5 30	8 48	10 50	– –	11 41	608.53	Trenton ♁	– –	5 25	2 51	6 09	– –	11 24					
				A M	12 40	5 50	8 10	11 10	1 25	12 01	620.42	arr. **Belleville** ♁ lve.	1 40	5 03	2 30	†5 50	4 02	11 03	P M				
				†7 00	12 45	5 56	P M	11 13	1 30	12 06	620.42	lve. arr.	1 37	4 58	2 25	A M	3 57	11 00	8 50				
				7 14	– –	6 10		11 25	– –	– –	627.52	Shannonville ♁	– –	4 45	– –		– –	10 46	8 35				
				7 26	– –	6 20		11 37	– –	– –	634.04	Marysville ♁	– –	4 35	– –		– –	10 35	8 25				
				†8 15	†2 35	†7 10		†1 30	†2 35	†1 30	641.31	arr. **Deseronto** lve.	†11 35	†3 45	†12 50		b2 50	†9 50	†7 40				
				†7 20	†12 50	†6 10		†11 40	†12 50	†11 40		lve. (*Via B. of Q. Ry.*) arr.	†1 30	†4 50	†2 35		b3 55	†10 55	8 35				
				7 43	1 24	6 40		11 52	*2 06	12 38	642.12	lve. **Napanee** ♁ lve.	1 08	4 23	1 45		b –	10 20	8 11				
				7 52	– –	6 50		12 02	– –	– –	647.28	lve. **Fredericksburg** arr.	– –	4 11	– –		– –	10 10	7 57				
				8 03	– –	7 00		12 12	– –	– –	652.98	Ernestown ♁	– –	4 02	– –		– –	10 00	7 48				
				8 17	– –	7 12		12 25	– –	– –	660.52	Collins' Bay ♁	– –	3 51	– –		– –	9 45	7 35				
				8 35	2 10	7 25		12 37	2 51	1 17	668.34	arr. ‖**Kingston Junc** ♁ lve.	12 34	3 39	1 03		2 45	9 30	7 23				
				†8 47	*2 22	†7 38		†12 49	*3 05	*1 29	670.59	arr. **Kingston** ♁ lve.	*12 16	†3 19	*12 45		*2 26	†9 15	†7 03				
				†8 16	*1 48	†7 03		†12 16	*2 26	*1 00	670.59	lve. arr.	*12 49	†3 51	*1 15		*3 05	†9 47	†7 38				
				8 35	2 10	7 45		12 37	2 51	1 17	668.34	lve. **Kingston Junction** arr.	12 34	3 39	1 03		2 45	9 30	7 23				
				8 43	– –	7 52		12 50	– –	– –	672.23	Rideau	– –	3 27	– –		– –	9 20	7 10				
				9 09	2 43	8 14		1 20	g –	1 48	687.09	ar. **Thousand Islands Jn** ♁ lv.	12 08	3 08	12 32		b –	8 53	6 47				
				†9 35	*3 15	†8 40		†2 15	g4 00	*2 15	689.63	arr. **Gananoque** lve.	11 35	†2 35	*11 45		b1 50	†8 20	†6 05				
				†8 20	*2 10	†7 40		†12 55	g1 50	*12 55		lve. (*Via T. I. Ry.*) arr.	12 35	3 35	*1 00		b4 00	9 35	†7 20				
				9 23	– –	8 27		1 35	– –	– –	694.52	lve. **Lansdowne** ♁ arr.	– –	2 55	12 19		– –	8 38	6 35				
				9 37	3 08	8 39		1 50	– –	– –	702.74	Mallorytown ♁	– –	2 41	12 07		– –	8 23	6 22				
				9 52	– –	8 52		2 07	– –	– –	711.20	Lyn ♁	– –	2 27	h –		– –	8 08	6 08				
				10 00	3 30	9 00		2 15	4 10	2 30	715.40	arr. **Brockville** lve.	11 33	†2 20	11 48		1 36	†8 00	†6 00				
				A M		P M	12		*9 41	†6 00	788.40	arr. **Ottawa** lve.		†11 30	*6 45	11	*6 45	A M	P M				
			P M				A M		A M	P M	788.40	lve. (*Via C. P. Ry.*) arr.		A M	P M	P M	P M						
			§4 00		3 35		†6 40	2 50	4 15	2 35	715.40	lve. **Brockville** ♁ arr.	11 30	*2 05	11 43	8 15	1 31						
			4 08		– –		6 48	3 02	– –	– –	720.46	Maitland ♁	– –	1 52	– –	8 03	– –						
			4 20		3 53		6 59	3 15	4 34	2 54	727.12	**Prescott** ♁	11 14	1 40	11 21	7 53	b –						
			4 34		i –		7 13	3 32	– –	– –	736.24	Cardinal ♁	– –	1 22	11 03	7 37	– –						
			4 43		4 14		7 21	3 43	– –	– –	741.53	Iroquois ♁	– –	1 11	10 52	7 27	– –						
			4 55		4 24		7 33	3 58	– –	3 27	748.36	Morrisburg ♁	– –	12 59	10 39	7 15	– –						
			5 08		– –		7 46	4 14	– –	– –	756.87	Aultsville ♁	– –	12 44	– –	7 01	– –						
			5 12		– –		7 50	4 20	– –	– –	759.18	Farran's Point	– –	12 39	– –	6 57	– –						
			5 20		– –		7 58	4 29	– –	– –	763.57	Wales ♁	– –	12 30	10 13	6 49	– –						
			5 29		– –		8 07	4 40	– –	– –	768.41	Mille Roches ♁	– –	12 20	10 06	6 41	– –			13			
			5 36		– –		8 13	4 47	– –	– –	771.76	**Cornwall Junction** ♁	– –	12 13	– –	6 33	– –			P M			
			5 41		5 06		8 19	4 59	5 45	4 09	773.26	‖**Cornwall** ♁	10 20	12 10	9 57	6 30	12 10			3 40			
			5 55		– –		8 32	5 13	– –	– –	781.20	Summerstown ♁	– –	11 38	– –	6 11	– –			3 25			
			6 05		5 25		8 42	5 23	– –	l –	786.90	Lancaster ♁	– –	11 28	9 34	6 01	– –			3 15			
			6 16		– –		8 51	5 33	– –	– –	792.24	Bainsville ♁	– –	11 18	– –	5 50	– –			3 05			
			6 25		s –		9 00	5 43	– –	– –	797.48	River Beaudette ♁	– –	11 08	8 15	5 40	– –			2 55			
28	26	24	6 32		– –	22	9 07	– –	– –	– –	801.00	arr. **St. Zotique** lve.	– –	– –	– –	5 34	– –	21	23	2 49	25	.....	27
P M †7 15	P M †5 00	P M *3 30		16		A M	12 40			†7 10	880.87	arr. **Ottawa** lve.		*8 35	†5 00	†3 30		A M	Noon		P M	15	P M
				A M		*8 35	– –				880.87	lve. **Ottawa** arr.		A M	P M	P M		11 00	12 40		7 10	P M	10 30
†9 25	†7 10	*5 30	6 37	†8 15	5 51	*10 45	9 15	5 53	6 30	*4 55	802.97	lve. **Coteau Junction** ♁ arr.	– –	10 58	9 05	5 30	c –	8 45	10 30	2 45	5 00	6 30	8 20
– –	– –	– –	6 42	8 21	– –	– –	9 23	6 00	– –	– –	806.06	Riviere Rouge	– –	10 52	– –	5 20	– –	– –	– –	2 38	– –	6 22	– –
– –	– –	– –	6 49	8 28	– –	– –	9 31	6 08	– –	– –	809.57	St. Dominique ♁	– –	10 46	– –	5 13	– –	– –	– –	2 31	– –	6 16	– –
– –	– –	– –	6 53	8 32	– –	– –	9 38	6 12	– –	– –	811.63	Cedars	– –	10 42	– –	5 08	– –	– –	– –	2 26	– –	6 11	– –
9 40	– –	– –	7 10	8 45	6 10	11 00	9 50	6 20	6 50	5 15	816.38	Vaudreuil ♁	– –	10 35	8 46	5 02	– –	– –	10 12	2 20	4 43	6 05	8 03
– –	– –	– –	8 07	9 26	6 52	– –	10 41	7 08	7 28	– –	839.13	St. Henri ♁	– –	9 50	8 05	4 26	10 35	8 05	9 45	1 41	– –	5 20	– –
10 15	8 00	6 30	8 10	9 33	*7 01	11 35	10 50	†7 15	*7 40	*8 00	840.63	‖**Montreal** ♁	*9 00	*9 45	*8 00	†4 21	*10 30	†8 00	*9 40	k1 36	†4 10	†5 15	*7 30
P M	P M	P M	P M	A M	A M	A M	A M	P M	A M	P M		ARRIVE] [LEAVE	A M	A M	P M	P M	P M	A M	A M	P M	P M	P M	P M
								P M	A M	P M		(*Via C. V. and B. & M. R.Rs.*)	A M		P M		P M						
								*8 40	*9 01	*8 40	0	lve. **Montreal** arr.	7 25		8 10		10 15						
								8 05	6 55	8 05	334.00	**Boston**	*7 30		†9 00		*11 30						
								A M	P M	A M		ARRIVE] [LEAVE	P M		A M		A M						

NOTE—Nos. 6, 7, 9, 10 and 76 will stop on signal at Moulinette between Wales and Mille Roches.

* Daily; † daily, except Sunday; § Sunday only; a stops to leave passengers from Toronto; b stops to let off passengers from Montreal or beyond; c stops for passengers from Ottawa Division points for Toronto and beyond; e Monday only; g stops for passengers from west of Toronto; h stops to leave from Toronto or beyond; j stops to take or leave passengers for or from Montreal and East; k Saturday only; l stops to leave passengers from points on Ottawa Division; n on Sunday arrives at 10 05 a.m.; s stops on Sunday. ♁ Telegraph stations.

For Sleeping and Parlor Car Arrangements, see page 98.

GRAND TRUNK RAILWAY SYSTEM.

CHICAGO, PORT HURON, TORONTO, MONTREAL AND PORTLAND.

150	200	12	8	146	34	6	152	4	2	Miles.	*June 17, 1906.*	3	1	5	151	199	7	145	33	153
P M	P M	P M	P M	P M	Noon	P M	A M	P M	A M		(*Eastern time.*)	P M	A M	P M	A M	A M	A M	A M	P M	P M
¶11 45	‡7 31	k1 45	x5 16	†3 50	‡12 01	†4 16	†7 25	*8 15	*8 01	840.63	lve. **Montreal** ♁ arr.	6 50	7 20	1 00	6 45	7 00	8 35	9 40	6 01	10 00
– –	– –	1 50	5 21	3 55	– –	4 21	– –	– –	8 05	842.13	St. Henri ♁	6 43	7 14	12 54	– –	– –	8 29	9 34	– –	9 55
– –	– –	1 56	5 25	– –	– –	4 25	– –	– –	8 11	843.63	Point St. Charles ♁	6 34	7 09	12 48	– –	– –	8 21	– –	– –	9 48
12 05	7 43	2 03	5 31	4 05	12 19	4 32	7 38	8 30	8 17	846.95	**St. Lambert** ♁	6 27	7 03	12 40	6 25	6 39	8 15	9 22	5 42	9 40
12 15	7 50	2 10	5 38	4 15	12 30	4 39	7 46	8 38	8 22	850.67	St. Hubert ♁	6 18	6 55	12 30	6 14	– –	8 08	9 12	5 34	– –
12 25	– –	2 20	5 45	4 23	– –	4 50	7 56	e –	8 30	855.54	St. Bruno ♁	6 10	s –	12 18	6 01	– –	7 56	9 02	– –	9 22
12 30	– –	2 25	5 50	4 28	– –	4 55	a –	s –	8 37	857.79	St. Bazile	6 07	s –	12 11	a –	– –	7 50	8 56	– –	a –
12 40	– –	2 32	6 00	4 38	c12 48	5 02	8 12	9 00	8 45	861.75	Belœil ♁	6 00	6 33	12 05	5 47	– –	7 42	8 50	c –	– –
– –	– –	2 33	6 01	– –	– –	5 03	– –	– –	– –	862.13	Otterburn Park	– –	– –	12 03	– –	– –	7 40	– –	– –	– –
12 42	– –	2 35	6 03	4 40	c12 51	5 08	8 14	9 03	8 48	862.86	St. Hilaire ♁	5 57	6 31	12 02	5 45	– –	7 39	8 48	c –	9 03
– –	– –	2 38	6 05	4 42	– –	– –	– –	– –	– –	863.63	St. Hilaire East	– –	– –	– –	– –	– –	7 38	8 42	– –	– –
12 54	– –	2 50	6 17	4 58	– –	5 18	8 30	9 14	8 59	868.79	Ste. Madeleine ♁	5 47	6 20	11 50	5 32	– –	7 31	8 30	– –	8 50
1 10	8 35	3 10	6 35	5 12	1 15	5 32	8 45	9 30	9 14	876.30	St. Hyacinthe ♁	5 32	6 05	11 35	5 17	5 50	†7 20	8 15	4 45	8 35
1 15	8 40	P M	P M	5 20	1 20	5 37	8 50	– –	9 19	878.64	**Ste. Rosalie** ♁	5 20	5 59	11 26	‡5 10	¶5 45	A M	†8 10	*4 40	†8 25
A M	P M			P M	P M	5 46	A M	– –	– –	883.24	Britannia Mills ♁	– –	– –	11 18	A M	A M		A M	P M	P M
						5 50		9 48	9 31	885.54	St. Liboire ♁	5 04	5 42	11 13						
						5 56		9 53	9 35	888.63	Upton ♁	4 57	5 35	11 08						
						6 09		10 06	9 46	895.03	Actonvale ♁	4 45	5 22	10 56						
						6 25		10 20	10 02	902.63	Danby	4 33	5 05	10 43						
						6 35		10 30	10 12	906.79	South Durham ♁	4 27	4 58	10 36						
						6 41		– –	10 19	909.78	Lisgar ♁	4 22	s –	10 30						
						6 48		– –	– –	912.38	Gore	– –	– –	10 25						
						7 00		10 50	10 35	917.09	arr. ‖**Richmond** ♁ lve.	*4 10	*4 35	†10 15						
						10 30	10	*7 35	†1 45	1013.59	arr. **Point Levi** lve.	†1 10	†7 30	7 05			9			
						11 00	Noon	*8 05	†2 15	1013.59	arr. **Quebec** lve.	†12 40	†7 00	†6 35			P M			
						†12 40	†12 40	†7 00	†6 35		lve. **Quebec** arr.	†11 00	*8 05	2 15			11 00			
						1 10	1 10	†7 30	7 05		lve. **Point Levi** arr.	10 30	7 35	1 45			10 30			
						†7 15	†4 05	*10 55	*10 40	917.09	lve. ‖**Richmond** arr.	4 00	4 25	10 05			7 15			
						7 22	4 13	– –	– –	921.46	Rockland	– –	– –	9 53			7 02			
						7 33	4 23	11 13	10 55	927.34	Windsor ♁	3 35	4 08	9 40			6 53			
						7 40	4 30	– –	– –	930.88	Titus	– –	– –	9 31			6 47			
						7 50	4 37	[illegible]	[illegible]	[illegible]	Bromptonville ♁	3 22	3 55	[illegible]			6 40			
						8 05	4 50	11 40	11 22	941.73	**Sherbrooke** ♁	3 10	3 45	9 15			6 30			
						8 11	4 57	11 48	11 30	944.75	**Lennoxville** ♁	3 00	3 35	9 05			6 20			
						8 26	5 10	12 01	11 45	951.75	Waterville ♁	2 48	3 20	8 52			6 06			
						8 31	5 16	– –	11 52	955.04	Compton ♁	2 43	3 15	8 45			6 00			
						8 36	5 22	– –	– –	957.82	Hillhurst	– –	– –	8 40			5 54			
						8 50	5 35	12 24	12 08	963.18	Coaticooke ♁	2 27	2 58	8 30			†5 45			
						9 00	P M	– –	12 18	968.24	Dixville	2 16	– –	8 20			P M			
						9 10		12 43	12 27	972.74	Norton Mills ♁	2 08	2 37	8 13						
				74	6	9 30		– –	– –	982.01	Summit	– –	– –	7 57	73	5				
				A M	A M	9 45		1 10	12 50	988.46	arr. ‖**Island Pond** ♁ lve.	1 40	2 10	†7 45	P M	P M				
				†6 45	†6 30	P M		1 20	12 55	988.46	lve. **Island Pond**‖ arr.	1 30	1 50	A M	2 30	7 50				
				7 00	6 37			– –	– –	992.70	East Brighton	– –	– –		2 15	7 38				
				7 20	6 43			– –	– –	995.88	Wenlock ♁	– –	– –		2 05	7 33				
				8 17	6 55			1 48	1 24	1003.40	**North Stratford** ♁	12 55	1 16		1 40	7 18				
				8 30	7 02			– –	– –	1007.10	Beatties	– –	– –		12 20	– –				
				8 45	7 07			– –	1 37	1011.55	Stratford Hollow ♁	12 38	– –		11 53	7 00				
				9 30	7 15			2 12	1 48	1015.79	**Groveton** ♁	12 30	12 52		11 15	6 50				
				9 50	7 26			– –	– –	1021.56	Stark	12 18	– –		10 45	6 39				
				10 30	7 31			2 30	2 05	1023.63	Percy ♁	12 14	12 36		10 30	6 34				
				10 40	7 37			– –	– –	1026.41	Crystal	– –	– –		9 55	6 25				
			8	11 00	7 42			– –	2 13	1028.63	West Milan ♁	12 04	– –		9 40	6 20	7			
			P M	11 56	7 53			– –	– –	1034.35	Copperville ♁	– –	– –		9 25	6 08	Noon			
			§4 00	12 45	8 05			3 06	2 35	1040.05	**Berlin, N.H.** ♁	11 47	12 06		9 10	5 57	12 15			
			4 16	1 15	8 20			3 21	2 50	1046.48	‖**Gorham** ♁	11 30	11 48		†8 20	5 40	12 01			
			4 28	P M	8 30			– –	3 00	1052.14	Shelburne ♁	11 16	11 33		A M	5 04	11 45			
			4 41		8 40			3 45	3 10	1057.87	Gilead ♁	11 07	11 22			4 51	11 35			
			4 55		8 50			3 57	3 20	1063.93	West Bethel ♁	10 57	11 10			4 35	11 22			
			5 05		9 00			4 05	3 28	1067.87	**Bethel** ♁	10 50	11 03			4 25	11 12			
			5 14		9 10			– –	3 37	1072.62	Locke's Mills ♁	10 41	10 53			4 15	11 03			
			5 25		9 18			4 22	3 43	1076.16	Bryant's Pond ♁	10 34	10 45			4 05	10 55			
			5 40		9 30			4 33	3 52	1082.30	West Paris ♁	10 22	10 30			3 52	10 40			
			6 00		9 44			4 51	4 04	1090.68	**South Paris** ♁	10 07	10 15			3 26	10 22			
			6 15		9 55			5 05	4 15	1097.12	Oxford ♁	9 55	10 02			3 13	10 07			
			6 28		10 03			– –	– –	1101.42	P. & R. F. Crossing	– –	– –			3 02	9 58			
			6 30		10 05			5 17	4 24	1101.69	**Mechanic Falls** ♁	9 42	9 53			3 00	9 57			
			6 37		10 14			5 26	– –	1106.00	Empire Road	9 32	9 42			2 50	9 46			
			6 45		10 25	12	10	5 30	4 38	1108.19	arr. **Lewiston Junc** ♁ lve.	9 25	9 38	9	11	2 45	9 41			
			7 05		10 45	P M	A M	5 50	4 55	1113.69	arr. **Lewiston** ♁ lve.	*9 05	*9 20	A M	P M	†2 25	§9 05			
			§6 25		†10 05	†5 20	†7 00	*5 10	*4 20	1113.69	lve. arr.	9 45	9 55	8 15	6 35	3 05	10 00			
			6 45		10 25	5 35	7 15	5 30	4 38	1108.19	lve. **Lewiston Junction** arr.	9 25	9 38	8 00	6 20	2 45	9 41			
			6 53		10 32	5 40	7 20	5 35	4 42	1110.41	**Danville Junction** ♁	9 15	9 32	7 52	6 12	2 38	9 34			
			7 04		10 40	5 48	7 28	– –	– –	1115.26	New Gloucester ♁	– –	– –	7 42	6 05	2 27	9 24			
			7 14		10 48	5 56	7 35	– –	– –	1119.47	Pownal ♁	– –	– –	7 35	5 56	2 17	9 15			
			7 23		10 55	6 03	7 42	– –	– –	1122.62	North Yarmouth ♁	– –	– –	7 30	5 46	2 08	9 07			
			7 30		11 03	6 09	7 48	6 08	5 09	1125.78	**Yarmouth Junction** ♁	8 42	9 01	7 25	5 40	2 00	9 00			
			7 35		11 05	6 11	7 50	6 10	5 13	1126.64	Yarmouth ♁	8 39	8 59	7 23	5 38	1 57	8 58			
			7 42		11 10	6 16	7 55	– –	– –	1129.04	Cumberland ♁	– –	– –	7 18	5 33	1 51	8 52			
			7 48		11 17	6 20	8 00	– –	– –	1132.42	Falmouth ♁	– –	– –	7 13	5 26	1 44	8 44			
			7 52		11 24	6 26	8 07	– –	– –	1136.20	Deering	– –	– –	7 08	5 19	1 36	8 38			
			7 55		11 25	6 30	8 10	6 35	5 35	1136.69	**Portland and Rochester Junc** ♁	8 20	8 40	7 05	5 18	1 35	8 35			
			8 00		11 30	6 35	8 15	6 40	5 45	1137.88	‖**Portland** (*G. T. Station*) ♁	*8 15	*8 30	†7 00	†5 15	†1 30	§8 30			
			P M		A M	P M	A M	A M	P M		ARRIVE] [LEAVE	A M	P M	A M	P M	P M	A M			
					A M		A M	A M	P M		(*Via B. & M. R.R.*)	A M	P M		P M	P M				
					†11 41		†8 30	*6 40	†5 45	1136.69	lve. **Port. and Roch Jn.** arr.	8 18	8 30		5 15	1 26				
					11 51		8 40	6 50	5 55	1139.12	arr. **Portland** (*Union Sta.*) lve.	†8 10	*8 20		†5 05	†1 16				
					†12 30		†8 50	*7 00	†6 05	0	lve. **Portland** (*Union Sta.*) arr.	8 06	7 50		5 00	12 15				
					12 48		9 09	7 33	6 21	11.00	arr. **Old Orchard**	†7 44	7 27		4 42	11 52				
					4 00		12 20	x10 15	9 10	115.00	arr. **Boston** lve.	A M	†4 15		†2 00	†8 45				
					P M		Noon	A M	P M		(*Western Division.*)		P M		P M	A M				
					†12 45		†9 00	†9 00	†6 00	0	lve. **Portland** (*Union Sta.*) arr.		4 40		4 40	12 40				
					3 55		12 25	12 25	9 05	115.00	arr. **Boston** lve.		†1 00		†1 00	†10 00				
					P M		Noon	Noon	P M		(*Eastern Division.*)		P M		P M	A M				

LEWISTON AND LEWISTON JUNCTION.

34	10	44	38	46	32	12	42	48	.....	Ms.	*June 17, 1906.* (*Eastern time.*)
A M	A M	A M	A M	P M	P M	P M	P M	P M			
*5 10	†7 00	*9 05	†10 05	†2 25	*4 20	†5 20	*9 20	§6 25		0	lve. Lewiston ♁ arr.
5 12	7 02	9 07	10 07	2 28	4 25	5 22	9 22	6 27		.36	Auburn
5 19	7 09	9 14	10 14	2 35	4 30	5 29	9 29	6 34		3.72	Littlefield
5 25	7 15	9 20	10 20	2 40	4 35	5 35	9 35	6 40		5.50	Lewiston Junc. ♁ [LEAVE
A M	A M	A M	A M	P M	P M	P M	P M	P M			ARRIVE]

45	9	33	47	35	43	11	31	37	49	Stations
A M	A M	A M	A M	P M	P M	P M	P M	A M	P M	
5 50	8 15	9 45	10 45	3 05	4 55	6 35	9 55	10 00	7 05	Lewiston ♁ arr.
5 45	8 10	9 40	10 40	3 00	4 50	6 30	9 50	9 55	7 00	Auburn
5 38	8 03	9 33	10 33	2 53	4 43	6 23	9 43	9 48	6 53	Littlefield
*5 35	†8 00	†9 30	†10 30	†2 50	*4 40	†6 20	*9 40	§9 45	§6 50	Lewiston Junc. ♁ [LEAVE
A M	A M	A M	A M	P M	P M	P M	P M	A M	P M	

NORWAY AND SOUTH PARIS.

58	62	52	66	64	56	54	Mls	*June 17, 1906.* (*Eastern time.*)	65	67	53	55	63	51	59	69
P M	P M	P M	P M	A M	A M	A M		[LEAVE	A M	A M	A M	P M	P M	P M	A M	P M
§5 50	*10 05	*3 55	†3 15	*9 55	†9 35	*4 40	0	lve. **Norway** arr.	5 00	9 50	10 15	3 35	4 10	10 25	10 30	8 10
5 55	10 10	4 00	3 20	10 00	9 40	4 45	1.50	**South Paris**	*4 55	†9 45	*10 10	†3 30	*4 05	*10 20	§10 25	§8 05
P M	P M	P M	P M	A M	A M	A M		ARRIVE]	A M	A M	A M	P M	P M	P M	A M	P M

§ Stops Sunday only. ‖ Meals. ♁ Telegraph stations.

MONTREAL AND OTTAWA.

27	25	23	21	STATIONS.	22	24	26	28
P M	P M	A M	A M	LEAVE] [ARRIVE	A M	P M	P M	P M
*7 30	*4 10	*9 40	†8 00	**Montreal** (*G. T.*)	11 35	6 30	8 00	10 15
8 20	x5 00	10 30	8 50	**Coteau Junc.** "	10 45	5 30	7 10	9 25
10 30	7 10	12 40	11 00	**Ottawa** "	*8 35	*3 30	†5 00	†7 15
9 45	†6 12	11 20	9 45	**Valleyfield** "	*10 10	*5 15	†6 10	†8 15
P M	P M	A M	A M	ARRIVE] [LEAVE	A M	P M	P M	P M

Trains Nos. 21, 22, 23, 24, 25, 26 and 28 are solid vestibule trains with Parlor Cars between Montreal and Ottawa.

* Daily; † daily, except Sunday; ‡ daily, except Saturday; ¶ daily, except Monday; § Sunday only; a stops to take for or leave from Drummondsville and east; c stops to leave from or to take for Montreal or leave from or take for St. Hyacinthe and points east; e stops Saturday and Sunday; x daily, except Saturday and Sunday.

For Sleeping and Parlor Car Arrangements, see page 98.

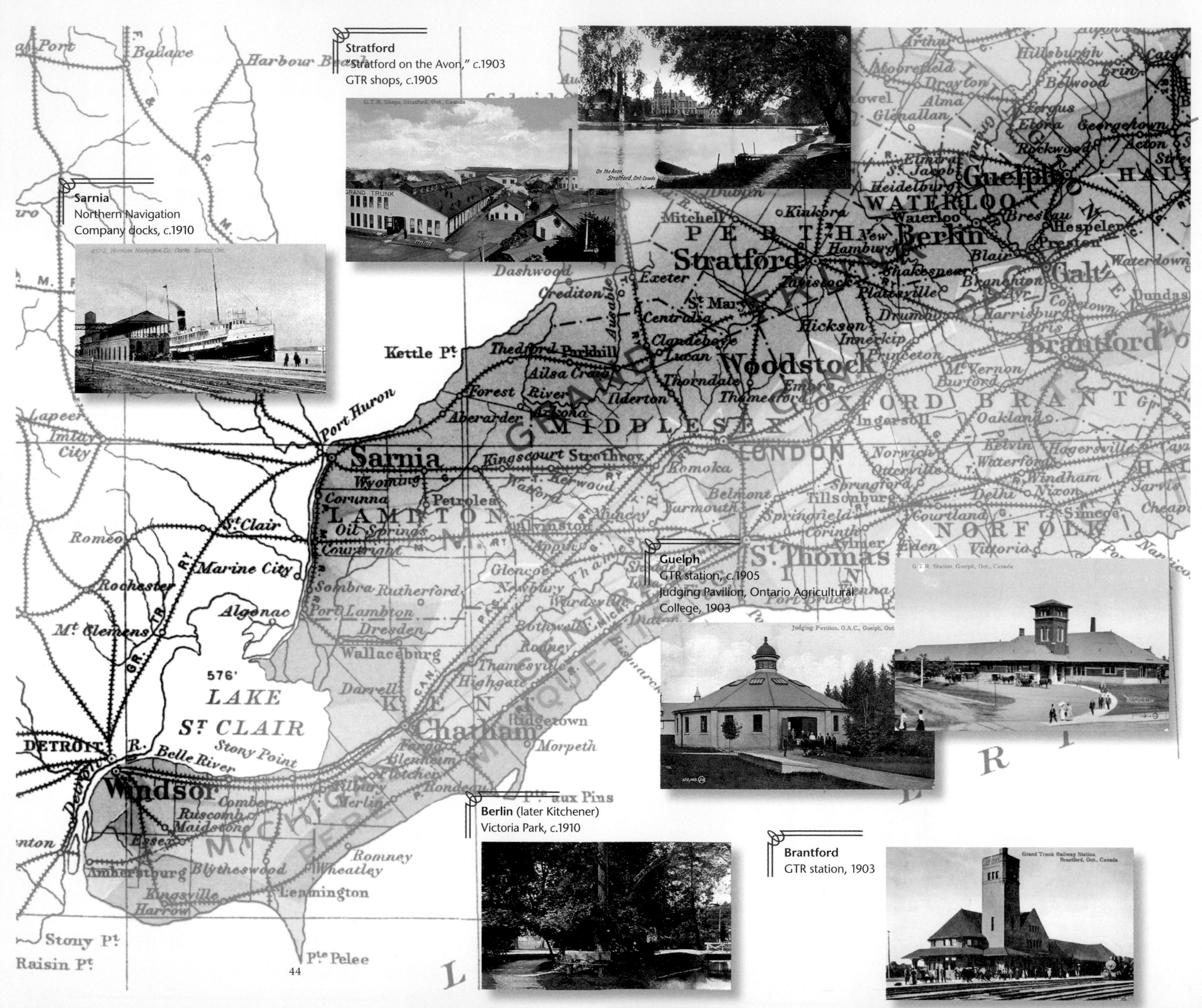

Stratford
"Stratford on the Avon," c.1903
GTR shops, c.1905

Sarnia
Northern Navigation Company docks, c.1910

Guelph
GTR station, c.1905
Judging Pavilion, Ontario Agricultural College, 1903

Berlin (later Kitchener)
Victoria Park, c.1910

Brantford
GTR station, 1903

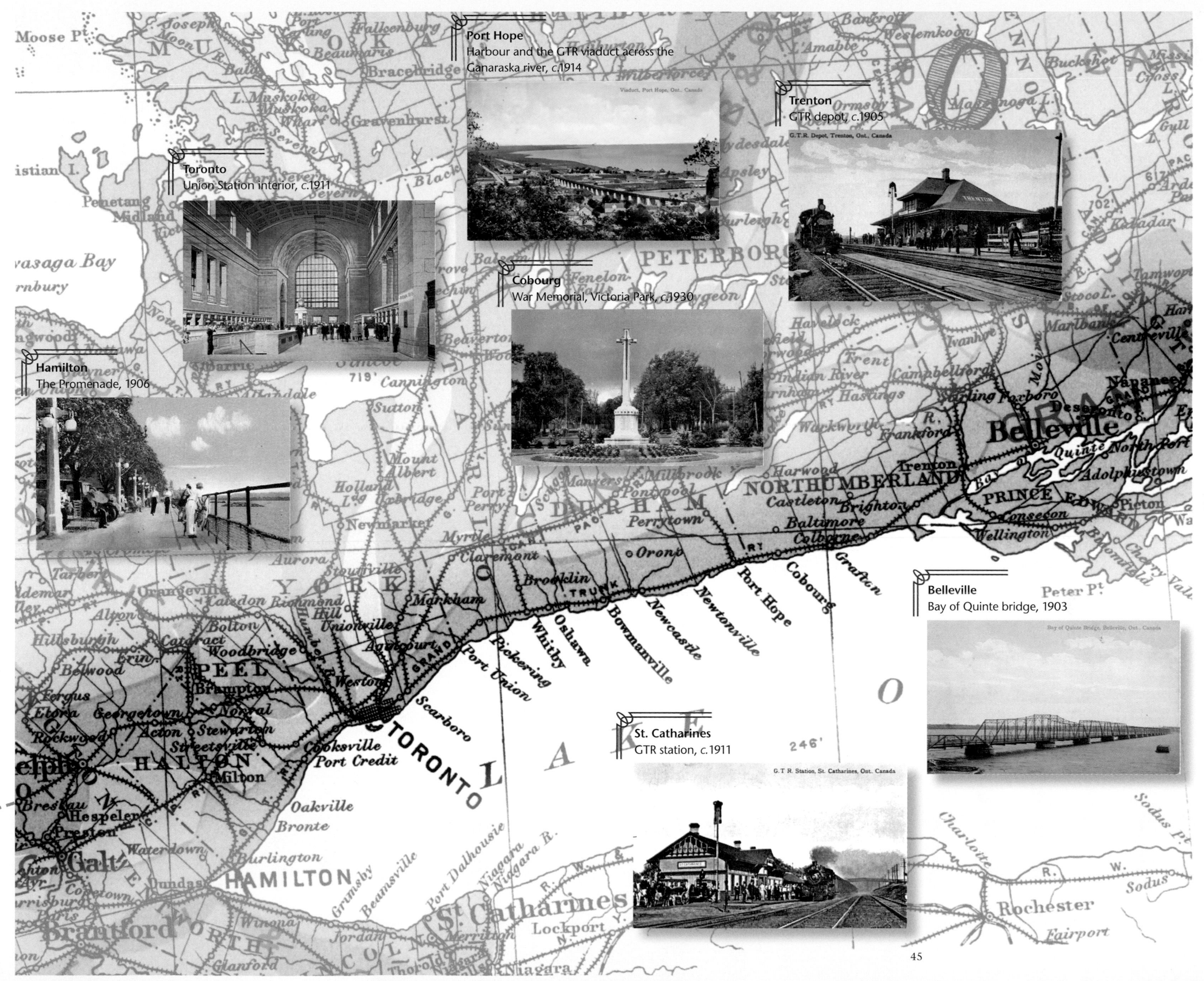

Port Hope
Harbour and the GTR viaduct across the Ganaraska river, *c.*1914

Trenton
GTR depot, *c.*1905

Toronto
Union Station interior, *c.*1911

Cobourg
War Memorial, Victoria Park, *c.*1930

Hamilton
The Promenade, 1906

Belleville
Bay of Quinte bridge, 1903

St. Catharines
GTR station, *c.*1911

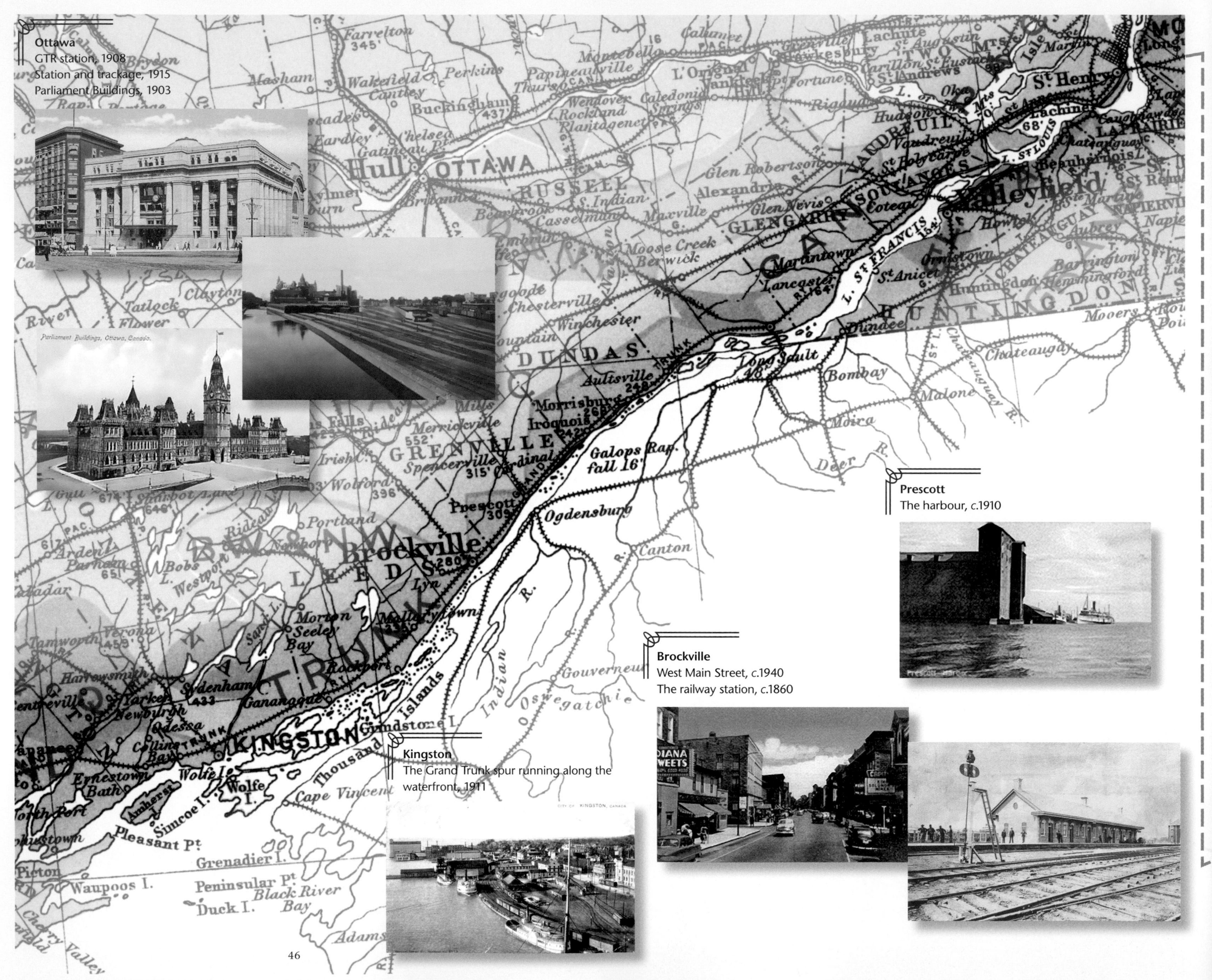

Ottawa
GTR station, 1908
Station and trackage, 1915
Parliament Buildings, 1903

Prescott
The harbour, *c.*1910

Brockville
West Main Street, *c.*1940
The railway station, *c.*1860

Kingston
The Grand Trunk spur running along the waterfront, 1911

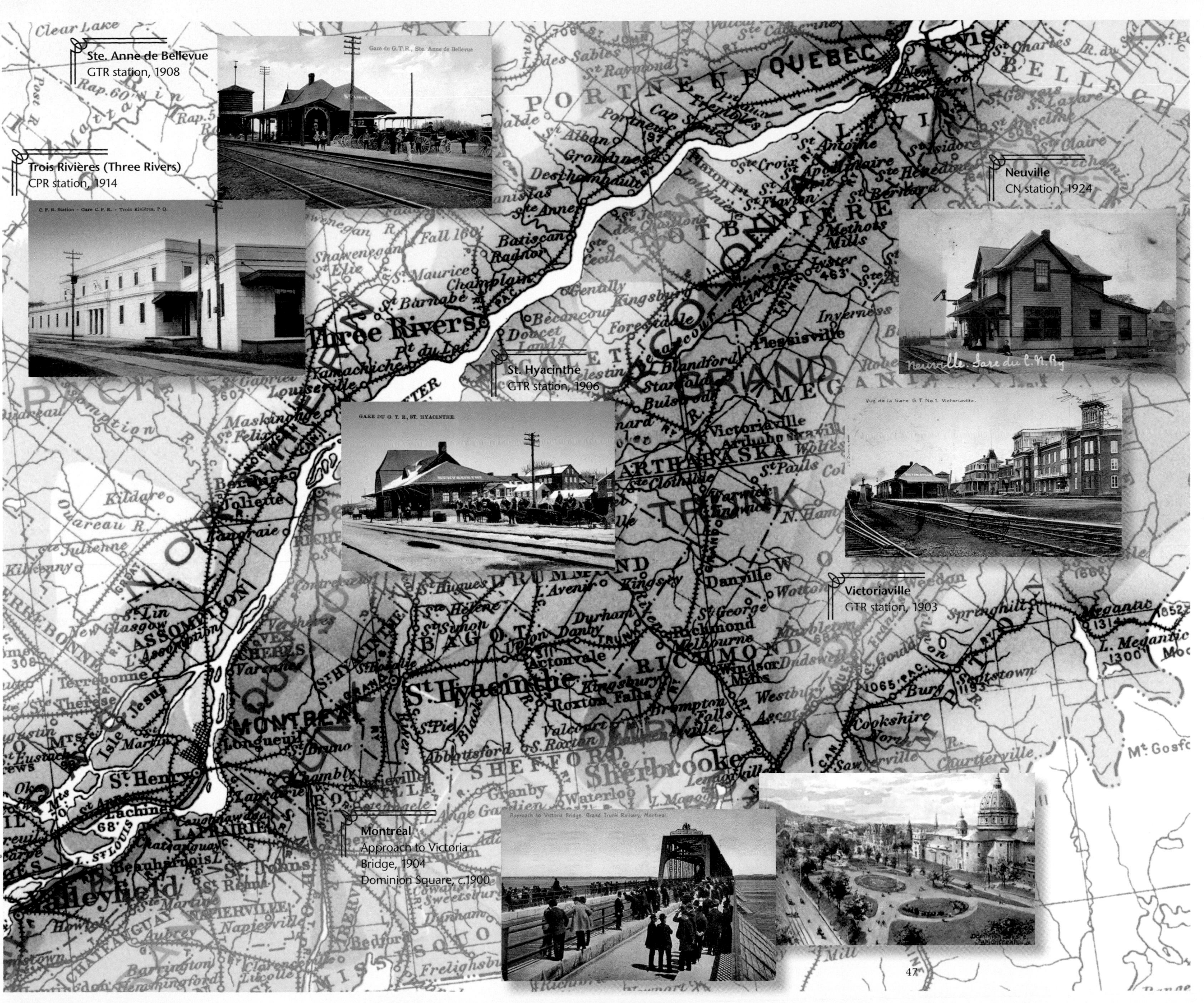

Ste. Anne de Bellevue
GTR station, 1908

Trois Rivières (Three Rivers)
CPR station, 1914

Neuville
CN station, 1924

St. Hyacinthe
GTR station, 1906

Victoriaville
GTR station, 1903

Montréal
Approach to Victoria Bridge, 1904
Dominion Square, c.1900

J.V.

THE INTERCOLONIAL RAILWAY

HALIFAX TO RIVIERE-DU-LOUP, QUEBEC CITY AND MONTREAL

The British North America Act 1867 contained "a novelty not to be found in the constitution of any country"–Section 145 obliged the new national government to construct a railway. In the 1840s and 1850s, railway promoters in England and the independent colonies of Nova Scotia, New Brunswick, and Upper and Lower Canada originally envisioned a line connecting Halifax to the St. Lawrence River as a prelude to the union of the colonies. Its early name–the Intercolonial Railway–stuck, even though the project was not started until after, and as a condition of, that union.

The government of the new Dominion of Canada–spurred on and assisted by a generous British loan guarantee–completed construction of the railway within a decade. On July 3, 1876 the first passenger train left Halifax on a 700-mile (1,126 km), 27-hour journey to Québec City. It travelled across Nova Scotia through Truro and Amherst, via the north shore of New Brunswick, through the Matapédia Valley to the south shore of the St. Lawrence, from where it travelled upriver on its own lines to Rivière-du-Loup and then on the lines of the Grand Trunk Railway the remainder of the way. It was not the shortest route that was available between Halifax and Québec City, but it was considered safe by the British government, who wanted to be able to transport troops from the naval port of Halifax to Québec and Ontario in the event of war with the United States. Just as important for the Dominion government was the fact that the chosen route did not offend important political and economic interests: it would serve the existing lumbering and fishing towns of New Brunswick rather than opening up new territory, while also, of all the potential routes, it gave the least competitive advantage to Halifax's rival, Saint John, as an Atlantic seaport.

The famed Canadian engineer, Sir Sandford Fleming (1827–1915), oversaw construction of the new railway, and

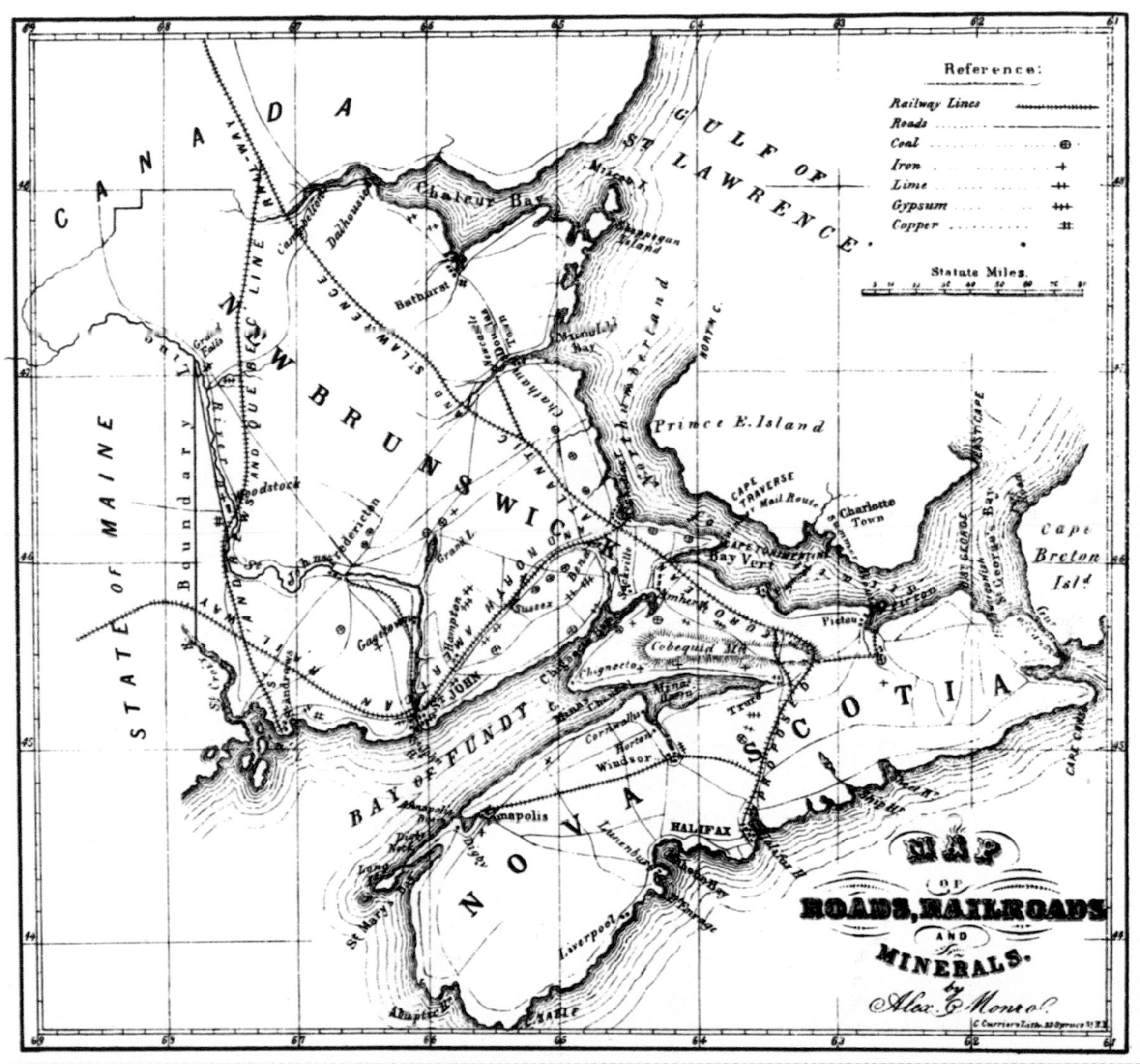

A map of proposed roads and railroads for Nova Scotia, New Brunswick, and Maine, 1850 (above).

The ICR station in Truro, 1906 (opposite).

Intercolonial Railway of Canada.

THE DIRECT ROUTE TO THE Famous * Seaside * Resorts OF THE Lower St. Lawrence AND THE Maritime Provinces.

PASSENGER TIME TABLE.

Summer of 1890.

RAILWAY OFFICE, MONCTON, JULY 1ST, 1890.

RAILWAY INTERCOLONIAL OF CANADA

INTERCOLONIAL

RAILWAY OF CANADA.

Pocket Time Table

SUMMER OF 1890

GEO. TAYLOR, GENERAL FREIGHT AGENT

A. BUSBY, GENERAL PASS'R AGENT.

D. POTTINGER, CHIEF SUPERINTENDENT

The first locomotive to be built in the Intercontinental Railway's Moncton shops, New Brunswick, in 1876 (top).

Howe Truss, one of the few wooden bridges on the ICR, built in 1876 (above).

An Intercolonial Railway passenger timetable for summer 1890 (right).

most commentators agree that he convinced the government to focus on long-term investment rather than short-term cost savings. He insisted that most of the road's bridges should be iron or iron-framed rather than wooden, and that the track should be standard gauge, with its rails made of steel rather than iron. With so much of the railway's grade routed through heavy snowfall areas, Fleming also paid considerable attention to constructing a roadbed that would be able to cope with extremes of snow, frosts, and floods. But, no matter how well-built the road was originally, a tenfold increase in freight and passenger traffic between its opening and World War I meant that the Intercolonial was required to invest substantial sums in ever more powerful locomotives, larger and specialized freight cars, safety devices such as automatic couplers and air brakes, additional ballasting on roadbeds, heavier steel rails and stronger bridges, and larger and more sophisticated yards and ocean terminals. In the 1880s, the average train on the railway carried about 80 tons of freight; in the years leading up to the war, locomotives were hauling trainloads of 275 tons.

The government railway gradually expanded up the St. Lawrence and through the coal, iron, and steel districts of eastern Nova Scotia. In 1879 it took direct control of the then seriously neglected Grand Trunk line that it had been using between Rivière-du-Loup and Point Lévis, across the river from Québec City. The Intercolonial acquired another road running from New Glasgow to the Strait of Canso in 1884, and in 1890 and 1891 lines running through the Bras d'Or Lake region of Cape Breton Island to Sydney and North Sydney were also added to the system. Wilfrid Laurier's Liberal government then had to weather a storm of protest in 1898 as it extended the railway's connections further up the St. Lawrence to Canada's economic centre, Montréal.

The passenger and freight service of "The People's Railway" both contributed to and benefited from the economic growth of eastern Canada. Its main business reflected the economy it served, which involved moving freight within the region,

particularly coal, lumber, and iron products. As a government-owned and -operated railway, the Intercolonial was not expected to pay a return on capital, but most political leaders hoped that its operating costs would be covered by income. The railway struggled to do this, and was not always able to meet its expenses. Critics blamed these operating losses on government ownership, although the railway's difficulties appear to have had more to do with attracting sufficient traffic than with excessive spending. Following World War I, the Intercolonial lost its independent, regional identity, as it was gradually incorporated into the new, transcontinental Canadian National Railways system.

HALIFAX TO MONTREAL LUXURY PASSENGER SERVICE

Unlike American railways, but like other Canadian railways, freight operations during the golden age of rail travel grew faster and became more profitable than the passenger service. Between 1899 and 1914, freight tonnage tripled and earnings from this grew by more than three and a half times, whereas the number of travellers on the Intercolonial increased two and a half times and revenues from the passenger business tripled. The Intercolonial paid particular attention to the through express service between Montréal and Halifax, as well as from Boston to the region. The railway's managers also invested in tourist travel, in part hoping that by entertaining wealthy business leaders they might attract economic investment to the region.

As early as 1885, the railway's managers decided to end its contract with the prestigious Pullman Company that had been operating its specialized sleeping and parlour cars on their trains (and thereby taking large profits from the railway company for those services) and decided to take charge of this side of the business itself. By 1896 the railway operated fifteen of its own first-class and seven second-class sleeping cars, as

Intercontinental Railway station, Halifax, 1903 (top).

Intercolonial Bridge, Grand Narrows, Cape Breton, Nova Scotia (centre).

Interior of an Intercolonial Railway sleeping car, 1901 (left).

A 1900 postcard of Petit Métis (Métis-sur-Mer), Québec (right).

well as five parlour cars, and within twenty years the fleet had grown to forty-eight first-class and fifty-nine second-class sleeping cars, eight parlours, and sixteen dining cars. The first-class sleeping and passenger cars, as well as the dining cars, offered the "procured luxury" that wealthy American travellers would have expected. They featured polished mahogany inlaid with lighter woods, ceilings of green and gold in the empire style, plate glass mirrors, Pintsch gas lighting, Wilton rugs, solid silver settings at the dining tables, and plenty of space for the traveller to move around.

TOURING EASTERN CANADA

The Intercolonial worked with other railways and steamship companies to develop a number of summer "tours," and by the early twentieth century it offered thirty-two tours for the traveller leaving from Montréal. Some were simple: one tour consisted of just a train ride over the Intercolonial to Saint John, and a return trip by way of the Canadian Pacific Railway Short Line. Others were more elaborate. For $24, a traveller could take a journey from Montréal to the beautiful Matapédia Valley on the Intercolonial, transfer to a smaller railway that traversed the south shore of the Gaspe Peninsula to New Carlisle, take a steamer around to Gaspe in order to see Percé Rock, and then return by steamer back down Baie-des-Chaleurs to Dalhousie, from where the Intercolonial took trippers back to Montréal. For $47, one could travel from Montréal either to Halifax or Saint John, hop on a steamer to Boston, travel by American railways to Niagara Falls, and by the Grand Trunk back to Montréal. (The price for these "tours" did not include accommodation or meals.)

FASHIONABLE RESORTS

By the late nineteenth century, the Intercolonial catered to wealthy families from Québec City, Montréal, and the United States who sought to escape the summer heat of their growing cities. Special tickets allowed families to move their belongings for extended stays at luxury hotels, villas, and cottages, while Montréal businessmen could take specially scheduled trains that left in the evening and arrived in the morning, either to join their families by the seaside, or to return to the city. The favoured resorts were located in the lower St. Lawrence and included Murray Bay (Malbaie), a north shore location that required a rail and steamer connection, and Cacouna and Little Métis (Métis-sur-Mer), both of which were further from the cities but had a direct connection. Each resort featured "health giving and bracing air" in an era before air conditioning, as well as opportunities to see and be seen by other members of high society, whether at the beach, the races, the tennis court, the golf course, or in the dining hall.

SPORTING PARADISE

Just east of these fashionable, family resorts the railway journeyed through what at the time was largely a tourist world designed to cater to elite men. The Matapédia Valley of Québec, as well as Campbellton and Dalhousie in New Brunswick, represented a gateway to a land of sport fishing and game hunting. The Intercolonial tourist promoters promised men easy access to moose, caribou, and abundant

The Dufferin Hotel in Saint John, New Brunswick (above).

trout in undesecrated forests and pristine rivers, although only those with the money and connections could expect to enjoy salmon fishing on the rivers of eastern Québec and northern New Brunswick. There was a good reason that the symbol of the Intercolonial Railway was the head of a moose!

THREE PROVINCIAL CAPITALS

The Intercolonial provided direct rail connections between Halifax, Saint John, and Québec City, three capitals that offered visitors distinct experiences. Halifax represented the British garrison city, where visitors could visit older fortifications on Citadel Hill and newer ones on McNab's and George's islands, or admire naval and other ships along the docks of the harbour. Saint John, much of which was largely rebuilt after a major fire in 1877, looked like a more modern, business port. The most frequently noted tourist site was a natural phenomenon, the "reversing falls" on the Saint John River, created by the tides of the Bay of Fundy. In contrast to Saint John, Québec City allowed visitors to step into the past. The citadel, the fortifications, and the old town overlooking the St. Lawrence attracted travellers in the late nineteenth century as much as they do now.

Two highly-illustrated Québec and Lake St. John route brochures (above).

The Intercolonial *Tours to Summer Haunts* brochure, 1910 (left).

INTERCOLONIAL RAILWAY

MONTREAL, QUEBEC, HALIFAX AND ST. JOHN.

150	146	152	34	200	Mls	*June* 24, 1906.	33	199	153	151	145
†23 45	†15 50	†7 25	‡12 00	‡19 30	0	lve..+ **Montreal**....arr.	18 00	¶7 00	22 00	†6 45	9 40
24 05	16 05	7 38	12 19	19 43	7	St. Lambert	17 42	6 39	21 40	6 25	9 22
24 15	16 15	7 46	12 30	19 50	10	St. Hubert	17 34	– –	– –	6 14	9 12
24 54	16 58	8 30	– –	– –	28	+ Ste. Madeleine	– –	– –	20 50	5 32	8 30
1 10	17 12	8 45	13 15	20 35	36	+ **St. Hyacinthe**	16 45	5 50	20 35	5 15	8 15
1 15	17 20	8 50	13 20	20 40	38	**St. Rosalie**	16 40	5 45	20 25	5 10	8 10
2 30	18 36	9 39	14 05	21 20	65	+ **Drummondville**	15 55	5 04	19 33	4 08	7 14
3 23	19 30	10 13	– –	– –	84	**St. Leonard Junction**	– –	– –	18 58	3 23	†6 35
6 27		12 25	16 40	– –	154	**Chaudiere**	13 09	– –	16 40	24 34	
6 29	.....	12 27	– –	– –	155	Chaudiere Junction	– –	– –	16 38	– –	.....
6 47	.....	12 48	– –	– –	162	Pointe Levis	– –	– –	16 18	24 09	.....
¶6 50	.....	12 52	17 05	24 05	163	arr. **Levis** lve.	*12 45	2 30	16 15	24 05	.....
.....	.....	.....	17 50	.....	.....	arr. + **Quebec** { Via } lve.	*11 50	.....	.....	.....	.....
.....	48	.....	17 00	.....	.....	lve. **Quebec** {Ferry} arr.	.....	.....	.....	.....	45
†7 45	†17 00	13 05	17 20	24 10	163	lve. + **Levis** arr.	12 35	2 25	16 05	23 35	9 50
7 56	17 11	13 16	– –	– –	168	+ Harlaka Junction	– –	– –	15 54	– –	9 39
8 15	17 30	13 35	17 50	– –	177	+ St. Charles Junction	12 05	– –	15 35	23 05	9 20
8 37	17 53	13 56	– –	– –	187	+ St. Valier	– –	– –	15 15	22 40	8 59
8 48	18 05	14 06	– –	– –	192	+ St. Francois	– –	– –	15 05	22 29	8 48
8 54	18 12	14 12	– –	– –	195	+ St. Pierre	– –	– –	14 59	22 21	8 40
9 04	18 43	14 22	18 32	1 11	200	+ Montmagny	11 25	1 11	14 49	22 09	8 28
9 18	18 58	14 35	– –	– –	207	+ Cap St. Ignace	– –	– –	14 35	21 53	8 13
9 32	19 15	14 48	18 55	– –	213	+ L'Islet	11 02	– –	14 21	21 38	7 58
9 49	19 35	15 03	*c r*	– –	222	+ St. Jean Port Joli	*c r*	– –	14 03	21 18	7 39
10 05	19 54	15 15	– –	– –	229	+ Ste. Louise	– –	– –	13 47	21 00	7 22
10 21	20 12	15 30	19 38	– –	237	+ Ste. Anne	10 21	– –	13 31	20 43	7 04
10 34	20 29	15 43	19 48	2 18	243	+ **Riviere Ouelle**	10 07	– –	13 18	20 29	6 50
10 43	20 38	15 53	– –	– –	247	+ St. Phillippe de Neri	– –	– –	13 10	20 19	6 42
10 57	20 52	16 05	20 06	– –	252	+ St. Paschal	9 50	– –	12 58	20 06	6 29
11 11	21 07	16 18	– –	– –	258	+ Ste. Helene	– –	– –	12 47	19 53	6 16
11 30	21 28	16 37	– –	– –	266	+ St. Alexandre	*a*9 32	– –	12 31	19 36	5 58
12 20	22 00	17 15	21 05	3 20	278	+ **Riviere du Loup**	9 10	23 15	12 05	19 10	†5 30
12 32		17 26	*r*21 15	– –	283	+ Cacouna	*r*8 45	– –	11 44	18 40	
12 37	.....	17 32	– –	– –	285	+ Ste. Arsene	– –	– –	11 39	18 33	*a* Stops to leave from Chatham Junction and east.
12 55	.....	17 48	21 37	– –	294	+ Isle Verte	8 25	– –	11 22	18 09	
13 18	.....	18 08	21 58	– –	305	+ Trois Pistoles	8 05	– –	11 00	17 43	
13 37	.....	18 28	– –	– –	313	+ St. Simon	– –	– –	10 42	17 25	
13 58	.....	18 47	22 34	– –	323	+ St. Fabien	7 32	– –	10 21	17 07	
14 18	.....	19 07	22 50	– –	333	+ Bic	7 10	– –	9 58	16 46	
14 41	.....	19 28	23 08	5 01	343	+ **Rimouski**	6 50	21 26	9 37	16 28	
15 25	.....	20 05	23 45	5 35	361	+ Ste. Flavie	6 20	21 00	9 00	15 50	
15 47	.....	20 25	24 08	5 55	370	+ Little Metis	*5 55	– –	8 34	‡15 30	
16 48	.....		*m* –	– –	397	+ Cedar Hall	m5 04	– –	7 39	99	
18 47	.....	.....	– –	– –	448	St. Alexis	*r*3 25	– –	5 53	20 20	
19 01	.....	.....	2 47	8 13	453	+ **Matapedia**	3 15	18 17	5 43	20 07	
19 35	.....	.....	†3 10	†8 35	...	ar. (*Eastern Time*) lv.	¶2 50	†17 55	†5 15	†19 35	
.....	.....	36	.....	.....	466	+ **Campbellton**	.....	.....		35	.....
72	158	†6 50	†4 20	†9 40	...	lv. (*Atlantic Time*) ar.	¶3 40	18 50	53	17 15	157
†19 40	†11 55	7 10	4 36	9 54	475	**Dalhousie Junction**	3 25	18 36	7 05	16 53	11 45
20 00	12 15	7 35	5 05	10 20	482	arr. + **Dalhousie** lve.	¶2 55	†18 10	†6 45	†16 25	†11 25
	.....	7 44	*o*5 00	– –	491	New Mills	*o*3 00	– –		16 14	.....
.....	.....	8 06	*o*5 16	– –	501	+ Jacquet River	*o*2 44	– –	.....	15 50	*c* Stops to take for or leave from Riviere du Loup and east.
Mix.	.....	8 43	*o*5 43	– –	518	Petite Roche	*o*2 16	– –	Mix.	15 08	
60	.....	9 09	6 03	11 14	529	+ Bathurst	1 57	17 13	59	14 40	
†16 10	.....	10 45	7 20	12 25	573	+ **Newcastle**	24 45	16 05	10 30	13 10	
16 25	.....	10 52	– –	– –	577	**Derby Junction**	– –	– –	10 15	12 57	
16 37	.....	.....	.....	.....	581	**Millerton**	.....	.....	10 03	.....	
17 10	.....	.....	.....	.....	591	arr. **Indiantown** lve.	.....	.....	†9 30	.....	
.....	.....	10 57	7 31	12 34	579	+ **Chatham Junction**	24 25	15 50	.....	12 50	
.....	.....	11 30	8 15	13 25	591	arr. + **Chatham** lve.	23 45	15 10	*r* Stops to take for or leave from Levis and west; *w* to leave from New Glasgow and west.	11 55	
.....	.....	.....	12 05	.....	687	arr. + **Fredericton** lve.	†17 00	15 00		5 00	
.....	.....	.....	.....	5 00	....	lve. **Fredericton** arr.	.....	.....		.....	
.....	.....	10 20	6 50	11 55	....	lve. **Chatham** arr.	1 00	16 30		13 25	
.....	.....	10 57	7 31	12 34	579	**Chatham Junction**	24 25	15 50		12 50	
.....	.....	12 30	8 32	13 28	615	+ **Harcourt**	23 23	14 57		11 30	
Train leaves Dalhousie Junction for Dalhousie ‡3 35, †17 00.	Leaves Dalhousie for Dalhousie Junction ‡4 05, †9 30.	13 50	9 35	14 25	651	arr. **Moncton** lve.	22 20	14 00		9 50	.....
		14 35	9 50	14 35	651	lve. + **Moncton** arr.	22 00	13 45		9 25	**Mixed Train**—Leaves Riviere du Loup †21 10, arrives Levis ¶5 30.
		17 15	12 50	17 15	740	arr. + **St. John** lve.	†19 00	†11 00		†6 00	
		14 45	9 45	14 35	651	lve. **Moncton** arr.	22 10	13 50		9 35	
		15 00	10 00	14 48	659	**Painsec Junction**	21 55	– –		9 18	
		15 23	10 27	– –	670	+ Memramcook	21 31	– –		8 50	
		15 38	10 43	15 23	678	+ Dorchester	21 17	12 58		8 33	
		16 00	11 07	15 42	689	+ Sackville	20 55	12 37		8 07	
		16 21	11 29	16 00	699	+ Amherst	20 34	12 17		7 44	
		16 37	11 45	– –	709	+ **Maccan**	20 18	– –		7 26	
		17 00	12 10	16 35	716	**Spring Hill Junction**	20 00	11 45		7 05	
		17 23	12 34	16 59	729	+ **Oxford Junction**	19 28	11 16		†6 35	
		17 45	12 58	– –	742	Westchester	19 02	– –		.....	
		18 15	13 29	– –	758	+ Londonderry	18 28	– –		.....	
		18 55	14 15	18 30	775	+ **Truro**	17 55	9 45		.....	
		19 32	14 49	– –	797	Shubenacadie	17 10	– –		.....	
		20 16	15 32	19 51	823	+ **Windsor Junction**	16 28	8 25		.....	
		20 45	16 00	20 15	837	arr. + **Halifax** lve.	†16 00	†8 00	.....	.....	

THROUGH CAR SERVICE.—**No. 150**—Sleeper Montreal and Levis. **No. 151**—Sleeping Car Little Metis, Riviere Ouelle and Levis to Montreal. **Nos. 33 and 34**—Dining and Sleeping and Colonist Sleeping Cars between Montreal and Halifax. Sleeper Moncton and St. John. **Nos. 152 and 153**—Buffet Sleeping Car between Montreal and Little Metis. Sleeping Car Montreal and Riviere Ouelle on **Nos. 151 199 and 200**—Sleeper Montreal and Halifax to St. John; to Montreal on **199**. Montreal to Riviere Ouelle and Little Metis on **200**.

† Daily, except Sunday; ‡ daily, except Saturday; ¶ daily, except Monday.

Hon. H. R. EMMERSON,
Minister of Railways and Canals, Ottawa, Ont.
M. J. BUTLER, C. E.,
Deputy Minister of Railways and Canals, Ottawa, Ont.
L. K. JONES, Secretary Railways and Canals, "
D. POTTINGER, General Manager, Moncton, N.B.
E. TIFFIN, General Traffic Manager, "
THOMAS WILLIAMS, Chief Acct. and Treasurer, "
J. J. WALLACE, General Freight Agent, "
JNO. M. LYONS, Gen. Pas. and Ticket Agent, "
W. B. MACKENZIE, Chief Engineer, "
G. R. JOUGHINS, Supt. of Motive Power, "
W. F. TAYLOR, General Storekeeper, "
T. C. BURPEE, Eng. Maintenance of Way and Works, "
T. E. HENDERSON, Superintendent Car Service, "
G. M. JARVIS, Supt. Halifax and St. John Dist., Truro, N.S.
EVAN PRICE, Supt. Moncton & Ste. Flavie Dist., Campbellton, N.B.
Y. C. CAMPBELL, Supt. S. O. & T. Dist., New Glasgow, N.S.
W. A. DUBE, Supt. Montreal and Ste. Flavie Dist., Levis, P.Q.
W. H. OLIVE, Asst. Gen. Freight Agent, Montreal, P.Q.
J. R. BRUCE, Traffic Auditor, Moncton, N.B.
H. H. SCHAEFER, Division Freight Agent, St. John, N.B.
D. A. STORY, Division Freight Agent, Halifax, N.S.
OWEN CAMERON, Freight Claim Agent, Moncton, N.B.
H. A. PRICE, Asst. Gen. Passenger Agent, Montreal, P.Q.
J. B. LAMBKIN, Asst. Gen. Passenger Agent, Halifax, N.S.
L. B. ARCHIBALD, Supt. Parlor, Sleep. & Dining Cars, Halifax, N.S.
J. CAMPBELL, Car Accountant, Moncton, N.B.
GEO. C. ALLEN, General Baggage Agent, "
N. WEATHERSTON, Agent, 51 King Street, East,
King Edward Hotel Block, Toronto, Ont.

UNITED STATES AGENCIES.

BOSTON, 306 Washington Street, R. W. CHIPMAN.
CHICAGO, 249 Clark Street, cor Jackson Boulevard, J. H. BURGIS.
CHICAGO, 34 Wabash Ave., J. A. BOAK, Freight Agent.

HALIFAX, PICTOU, MULGRAVE AND SYDNEY.

13	85	19	Mls	*June* 4, 1905.	20	86	18	
†17 00	†12 30	†6 45	....	lve. **Halifax** (Atl. time) arr.	20 10	23 00	11 40	**Additional Trains**—Lv. Hopewell †6 15, †7 15, †18 30, ar. New Glasgow 6 38, 7 50, 19 45. Lv. New Glasgow †6 48, †18 00, ar. Hopewell 7 10, 18 25.
†19 45	†14 25	†9 15	0	lve. + **Truro** arr.	17 30	21 05	9 10	
19 55	– –	9 25	5	Valley	17 19	– –	9 00	
20 03	– –	9 35	9	Union	17 10	– –	8 51	
20 12	– –	9 43	13	+ Riversdale	17 02	– –	8 42	
20 27	15 03	10 01	21	+ West River	16 44	20 27	8 25	
20 34	– –	10 08	26	Gordon Summit	16 38	– –	8 18	
20 44	– –	10 18	29	Glengarry	16 28	– –	8 08	
20 57	15 29	10 32	35	+ Hopewell	16 13	19 58	7 54	
21 10	15 40	10 45	41	arr. **Stellarton** lve.	16 00	19 45	7 40	
21 55	16 45	11 45	55	arr. **Pictou** lve.	14 50	18 40	†6 45	
†18 40	†14 50	†10 00	55	lve. **Pictou** arr.	16 45	21 55	8 30	
21 15	15 50	10 55	41	lve. + **Stellarton** arr.	15 50	19 35	7 35	
21 20	15 55	11 15	43	+ **New Glasgow**	15 40	19 30	†7 30	
	– –	11 30	49	Woodburn	15 20	– –		
.....	*w* –	11 40	53	West Merigomish	15 09	– –	.....	
.....	*w* –	11 48	57	+ Merigomish	15 01	19 00	.....	
.....	*w* –	12 00	62	Piedmont	14 47	– –	.....	
.....	*w* –	12 09	65	+ Avondale	14 38	18 40	*g* Monday only. + Coupon stations.	
.....	– –	12 14	67	Barney's River	14 33	– –		
.....	*w* –	12 33	75	James River	14 13	18 18		
.....	– –	12 43	79	Brierly's Brook	14 02	– –		
.....	17 32	12 56	85	+ Antigonish	13 44	17 57		
.....	– –	13 10	89	South River	13 35	– –		
.....	– –	13 21	95	+ Pomquet	13 21	– –		
.....	– –	13 27	97	+ Heatherton	13 16	– –		
.....	– –	13 32	99	Bayfield Road	13 11	– –		
.....	– –	13 36	101	Afton	13 07	– –		
.....	18 17	13 47	105	+ Tracadie	12 57	17 14	.....	
.....	– –	13 58	109	Linwood	12 45	– –	.....	
Mix.	18 34	14 09	113	+ Harbour au Bouche	12 35	16 56	.....	
105	18 55	14 35	123	arr. + **Mulgrave** lve.	†12 10	16 35	104	102
†6 00	19 35	15 15	124	lve. + **Point Tupper** arr.	11 15	16 00	15 05	23 30
6 05	– –	15 20	125	Hawkesbury	11 10	– –	15 00	23 25
6 30	– –	15 42	131	+ MacIntyre's Lake	10 52	– –	14 35	23 02
6 57	– –	15 56	138	+ West Bay Road	10 36	– –	14 08	22 35
7 28	– –	16 12	141	+ River Denys	10 17	– –	13 38	22 07
7 59	20 32	16 29	149	+ Orangedale	10 00	14 58	13 07	21 36
8 45	– –	16 52	160	McKinnon's Harbor	9 37	– –	12 24	20 53
9 04	– –	17 03	165	+ Iona	9 26	14 28	12 04	20 21
9 20	21 04	17 09	166	+ **Grand Narrows**	9 20	14 26	11 58	20 15
9 54	– –	17 27	175	+ Shenacadie	9 03	– –	11 10	19 45
10 28	– –	17 44	184	Boisdale	8 47	– –	10 28	19 17
11 07	– –	18 06	195	George's River	8 26	– –	9 53	18 38
11 20	22 05	18 15	199	arr. **North Sydney Jn** lve.	†8 18	13 25	9 40	18 25
11 35	22 15	18 30	204	arr. } + **North Sydney** { lve.	7 58	13 10	9 25	18 00
12 20	21 50	18 00	204	lve. } { arr.	7 48	13 40	9 05	18 30
12 35	22 05	18 20	199	lve. **North Sydney Jn** arr.	8 13	13 25	8 50	18 10
13 30	22 30	18 50	214	arr. + **Sydney** lve.	†7 45	†13 00	†8 10	†17 25

PICTOU LANDING BRANCH.

.....	†16 50	†7 40	†6 30	0	lv. + **Stellarton** ar.	6 55	.....	18 10	.....
.....	16 55	8 05	6 38	2	+ **New Glasgow**	6 48	9 20	18 00	.....
.....	16 59	8 08	6 42	3	Trenton	†6 45	9 15	17 57	.....
.....	17 20	8 25	.....	10	ar. **Pictou L'd'g** lv.	.....	†8 55	†17 35	.....

o Stops only to receive or leave for or from Moncton and east, or Levis and west; *m* stops to take or let off for or from Campbellton and east, and to take or let off for or from Rimouski or west.

INTERCOLONIAL RAILWAY

STANDARD—*Atlantic time.*

HALIFAX AND ST. JOHN.

9	13	33	199	85	25	19	Ms.	*June* 24, 1906.	10	18	34	20	26	200
‡20 40	†17 00	†16 00	†8 00	†12 30	†8 10	†6 45	0	lv. + **Halifax**..ar.	¶19 05	11 40	16 00	20 10	20 45	20 15
– –	17 03	– –	– –	– –	– –	6 48	1	... Richmond ...	– –	11 37	– –	20 07	– –	– –
20 49	17 09	– –	– –	– –	– –	6 54	4	.. Rockingham ..	8 56	11 28	– –	20 00	20 37	– –
21 00	17 20	16 20	– –	12 50	8 25	7 03	9	+ .. Bedford	8 46	11 16	15 40	19 50	20 25	– –
– –	17 29	– –	– –	– –	– –	7 12	12	...Lake View...	– –	11 09	– –	19 42	– –	– –
21 11	17 33	16 28	8 25	12 59	8 35	7 15	14	+ **Windsor Junc**..	8 35	11 05	15 32	19 38	20 16	19 51
– –	17 50	– –	– –	– –	– –	7 30	22	...Wellington...	– –	10 50	– –	19 20	– –	– –
– –	17 54	– –	– –	– –	– –	7 33	23	.. Grand Lake ..	– –	10 46	– –	19 16	– –	– –
– –	17 57	– –	– –	– –	– –	7 36	24	.... Oakfield	– –	10 44	– –	19 14	– –	– –
21 38	18 05	– –	– –	– –	– –	7 44	28	+ ...Enfield.....	7 57	10 37	– –	19 05	– –	– –
21 42	18 11	– –	– –	13 25	– –	7 52	30	+ ..Elmsdale....	7 52	10 31	– –	18 59	– –	– –
21 54	18 25	– –	– –	– –	– –	8 05	37	.... Milford	7 41	10 18	– –	18 45	– –	– –
22 02	18 35	17 10	– –	13 41	9 18	8 14	40	+ **Shubenacadie**..	7 35	10 10	14 49	18 35	19 32	– –
22 10	18 45	17 17	– –	13 48	9 26	8 22	45	+ . Stewiacke ...	7 27	10 01	14 42	18 26	19 24	– –
– –	18 55	– –	– –	– –	– –	8 32	49	..... Alton	– –	9 52	– –	18 15	– –	– –
22 30	19 09	– –	– –	14 03	– –	8 43	54	+ . Brookfield ...	– –	9 42	14 27	18 03	– –	– –
– –	19 19	– –	– –	– –	– –	8 50	57	.....Hilden.....	– –	9 33	– –	17 54	– –	– –
22 55	19 30	17 55	9 45	14 15	10 05	9 20	62	+ ... **Truro**	6 55	†9 20	14 15	17 45	18 55	18 30
– –	– –	– –	– –	– –	– –	9 36	70	.... Belmont	6 20		– –	16 02	– –	– –
23 28	.....	18 28	– –	.....	10 38	9 53	79	+ **Londonderry**	6 02		13 29	15 37	18 15	– –
23 53	**83**	18 52	– –		– –	10 20	91	+ . Wentworth ..	5 38		– –	15 10	17 53	– –
24 02	**and**	19 02	– –		11 11	10 28	96	+ . Westchester ..	5 30		12 58	14 59	17 45	– –
24 19	**133**	– –	– –		– –	10 46	104	... Thomson ...	5 13		– –	14 39	17 30	– –
24 28	†6 35	19 28	11 16		11 35	10 54	108	+ **Oxford Junc.**	5 04		12 34	14 28	17 23	16 59
– –	6 47	– –	– –		– –	11 07	115	.. Salt Springs ..	– –		– –	14 15	– –	– –
1 00	7 05	20 00	11 45		12 05	11 25	121	+ **Spring Hill Jn**	4 40		12 10	14 00	17 00	16 35
– –	7 17	– –	– –		– –	11 37	127	..... Athol	4 24		– –	13 35	16 43	– –
1 21	7 26	20 18	– –		12 24	11 45	130	+ . **Maccan** ...	4 17		11 45	13 25	16 37	– –
[illegible]	7 34	[illegible]	– –		– –	11 55	134	.... Nappan	4 10		– –	13 16	16 29	– –
1 37	7 44	20 34	12 17		12 40	12 05	138	+ . **Amherst** ...	4 02		11 29	†13 05	16 21	16 00
– –	7 58	– –	– –		12 55		144	..... Aulac	– –		11 15		– –	– –
2 00	8 07	20 55	12 37		13 03	.....	148	+ ..Sackville....	3 41		11 07	.....	16 00	15 42
2 24	8 33	21 17	12 58		13 28	.....	160	+ . Dorchester ...	3 18		10 43	.....	15 38	15 23
– –	8 39	– –	– –		13 34	.....	162	Upper Dorchester	– –		10 37	.....	– –	– –
2 42	8 50	21 31	– –		13 43	.....	167	+ Memramcook..	3 03		10 27	.....	15 23	– –
– –	9 06	– –	– –		13 59	.....	174	.Meadow Brook.	– –		10 11	.....	– –	– –
– –	9 18	21 55	– –	.....	14 09	.....	179	.**Painsec Junc.**	– –		10 00	.....	15 00	14 48
3 20	9 35	†22 10	13 50	**3**	14 25	**1**	186	ar. + **Moncton** lv.	2 25	**134**	†19 45	**2**	14 45	14 35
3 25	9 50	k22 30		†13 45	14 35	†18 05	186	lv. + **Moncton** ar.	2 20	22 00		9 25	14 35	13 45
3 52	10 17	22 58	.....	14 09	14 59	18 34	199	+ . Salisbury ...	1 54	21 33	.....	8 59	14 09	13 20
– –	10 26	23 08	.....	14 21	– –	18 44	204	.. River Glade ..	– –	21 24	.....	8 48	– –	– –
4 12	10 36	23 18	.....	14 32	15 17	18 55	209	+ **Petitcodiac**.	1 36	21 14	.....	8 38	13 51	13 03
4 22	10 46	23 30	.....	14 44	– –	19 07	215	... Anagance ...	1 26	21 02	.....	8 28	– –	– –
4 42	11 04	23 50	.....	15 05	– –	19 27	224	...Penobsquis...	1 07	20 44	.....	8 07	– –	– –
– –	11 12	24 00	**7**	– –	– –	19 36	229	.. Plumweseep ..	– –	20 35	**8**	7 58	– –	– –
4 57	11 18	24 07	†7 05	15 22	15 37	19 43	230	+ ... Sussex	24 53	20 29	19 05	7 52	13 07	12 22
5 05	11 27	24 18	7 15	15 32	– –	19 52	236	... Apohaqui ...	24 44	20 19	18 54	7 43	– –	– –
5 18	11 39	24 32	7 31	15 47	16 17	20 07	243	.....Norton.....	24 32	20 07	18 39	7 31	12 46	12 01
5 28	11 51	24 45	7 42	15 58	– –	20 20	248	... Bloomfield ...	24 22	– –	18 27	7 10	– –	– –
– –	11 54	24 46	7 46	– –	– –	20 24	249	... Passekeag ...	24 19	– –	18 24	7 05	– –	– –
5 40	12 02	24 54	7 55	16 09	16 35	20 35	253	+ . **Hampton** ...	24 12	19 45	18 15	6 53	12 26	11 41
5 43	– –	– –	7 59	– –	– –	20 38	255	.... Lakeside	24 09	– –	18 11	6 47	– –	– –
5 51	12 15	1 05	8 10	16 22	– –	20 48	259	. Nauwigewauk .	24 02	19 34	18 00	6 39	– –	– –
– –	– –	– –	8 13	– –	– –	20 51	260	.....Jubilee.....	24 00	– –	17 57	6 36	– –	– –
6 00	12 24	1 15	8 24	16 33	– –	21 00	263	...Quispamsis...	23 51	– –	17 47	6 29	– –	– –
6 07	12 32	1 23	8 34	16 40	17 00	21 08	267	+ ..Rothesay....	23 44	19 17	17 39	6 22	12 02	11 16
– –	12 35	1 25	8 39	16 44	– –	21 11	268	... Riverside ...	23 39	– –	17 35	6 17	– –	– –
– –	12 38	1 29	8 43	16 48	– –	21 16	270	... Torryburn ...	23 36	– –	17 31	6 14	– –	– –
– –	12 42	1 31	8 47	16 50	– –	21 19	271	... Brookville ...	23 33	– –	17 27	6 11	– –	– –
6 19	12 44	1 34	8 51	16 53	– –	21 23	272	.. Cold Brook ..	23 30	– –	17 23	6 08	– –	– –
†6 25	12 50	§1 40	9 00	17 00	17 15	21 30	275	ar. + **St. John**.lv.	†23 25	†19 00	†17 15	†6 00	†11 45	†11 00

(Column 85: Trains leave Truro †6 00, †21 15, arriving Halifax 8 45, 23 00. Column 18: ¶ Daily, except Monday; § Sunday only; & Saturday only.)

Train leaves Halifax for Truro †12 40. Lve. Hampton for St. John †6 50, †14 30. Lve. St. John for Hampton †13 15, †18 15. Lvs. Moncton for Oxford Junc. †18 10.

THROUGH CAR SERVICE.—Nos. 9 and 10—Sleeping Car Halifax and St. John. **Nos. 33 and 34**—Sleeping and Dining Cars Halifax and Moncton. **Nos. 85 and 86**—Parlor and Dining Cars Halifax and Sydney. **Nos. 133 and 134**—Sleeping Car Moncton and St. John. **Nos. 25 and 200**—Sleeping Car Moncton and St. John. Dining Car Truro and St. John. **Nos. 19 and 20**—Parlor Car between Halifax and North Sydney; Dining Car St. John.

DARTMOUTH BRANCH.

k21 30	†19 00	†15 25	†12 05	†7 25	†6 40	0	lve. + **Dartmouth** arr.	8 50	14 50	17 00	20 50	24 25	.....
21 55	19 25	15 55	12 35	7 55	7 05	11	+ .....Waverly.......	8 20	14 20	16 40	20 25	24 00	.....
22 00	19 30	16 05	12 45	8 00	7 10	13	arr.. **Windsor Jn**.lve.	†8 10	†14 10	†16 30	†20 20	†23 55	.....

POINT DU CHENE BRANCH.

....	†19 30	†17 00	†12 55	†8 00	†5 55	0	lv. + **Point du Chene**..ar.	10 45	14 40	15 30	18 55	23 15	....
....	19 50	17 07	13 00	8 05	6 00	2	+ ..... Shediac.......	10 40	14 35	15 25	18 50	23 09	....
....	20 04	17 17	13 09	8 17	6 12	6	...Dorchester Road...	10 28	14 23	15 13	18 38	22 58	....
....	20 20	17 30	13 20	8 30	6 25	11	.**Painsec Junction**.	10 15	14 10	15 00	18 25	22 45	....
....	20 45	18 20	13 35	8 45	6 45	19	arr. + **Moncton** ..lve.	†9 55	†13 50	†14 05	†18 20	†22 25	....

ST. CHARLES BRANCH.

.....	....	LEAVE]	[ARRIVE	.....
†17 35	0	+ **St. Charles Junction**.		6 00
18 25	13	.St. Jean Chrysostome.		5 10
18 40	17	ar. **Chaudiere Jn** .lv.		†5 00

NICOLET BRANCH.

.....	†19 30	0	lve. **St. Leonard Junc**.arr.	6 35	.....
.....	19 50	8	+ ... Ste. Monique.....	6 17	.....
.....	20 05	15	arr.. + **Nicolet**....lve.	†6 00	.....

PICTOU BRANCH.

....	.....	†21 00	†15 40	†10 30	†7 30	0	lve.. **New Glasgow**..arr.	7 50	11 05	15 55	19 45	.....	....
....	.....	21 15	16 05	11 00	7 45	2	..... **Stellarton**.....	7 30	10 40	15 35	19 30	.....	....
....	.....	21 24	16 14	11 10	7 55	5	+ .... Westville	7 20	10 31	15 25	19 20	.....	....
....	.....	21 37	16 27	11 25	8 10	10	...... Sylvester	7 05	10 17	15 10	19 00	.....	....
....	.....	21 50	16 40	11 40	8 25	14	....Brown's Point....	6 50	10 05	14 56	18 46	.....	....
....	.....	21 55	16 45	11 45	8 30	16	arr.. + **Pictou**....lve.	†6 45	†10 00	†14 50	†18 40	.....	....

OXFORD AND PUGWASH.

84	88	90	Mls	STATIONS.	83	87	89
†21 15	†14 30	†5 10	0	lv. + **Oxford Junc**..ar.	6 30	11 10	17 15
21 22	14 35	5 30	3	+ ......Oxford........	6 23	11 03	17 00
21 40	14 51	6 05	11	.....Conn's Mills.....	6 05	10 45	16 20
21 50	15 00	6 20	15	arr. + **Pugwash Junc**.lve.	5 55	10 35	16 05
22 00	15 10	6 35	21	arr. + **Pugwash** lve.	†5 40	10 25	15 50
.....	15 10	6 50	21	lve. + **Pugwash** arr.		10 25	15 40
.....	15 25	7 05	15	lve. **Pugwash Junc** arr		10 10	15 25
.....	15 43	7 22	23	+ ..... Wallace		10 02	14 59
.....	16 13	8 20	35	+ ..Tatamagouche....		9 31	14 16
.....	16 29	8 46	42	+ .....Denmark.......		9 17	13 57
.....	16 42	9 06	47	+ ....River John......		9 06	13 34
.....	17 02	9 29	55	+ ... Meadowville......		8 44	13 05
.....	17 14	9 43	60	+ .....Scotsburn.......		8 40	12 47
.....	17 30	10 05	67	.....Brown's Point.....		8 25	12 22
.....	17 35	10 10	69	arr... + **Pictou**....lve.		†8 20	†12 15

\+ Coupon stations.

FREDERICTON SECTION.

317	301	303	Mls	*June* 24, 1906.	302	304	330
†6 15	†17 00	†5 00	0	lve. + **Fredericton** ..arr.	12 05	16 30	.....
6 20	17 03	5 03	1	+ ..... Gibson........	12 02	16 23	21 30
6 30	17 10	5 20	3	+ ....Marysville......	11 54	16 06	†21 20
	18 17	6 52	26	..... Cross Creek	10 58	14 24	
.....	19 12	8 22	48	+ ....Boiestown	10 03	12 43	.....
.....	20 10	9 24	64	+ .... Doaktown	9 24	11 16	.....
305	21 10	10 54	88	+ .... Blackville......	8 25	9 24	**308**
†7 40	22 10	14 10	108	.**Chatham Junction**.	7 35	6 55	10 50
8 30	22 40	15 00	120	+ .... Chatham	6 50	[illegible]	10 00
8 45	22 25	15 20	125	arr. + **Loggieville**.lve.	†6 30	†4 45	†9 50

Additional Trains—Leave Fredericton for Marysville †11 15, †15 00, †18 25, †21 00. Returning, leave Marysville †8 00, †13 10, †18 05, †19 00. Leave Chatham Junction for Chatham †11 00, †12 55, †16 00; for Loggieville †24 30. Returning, leave Chatham †11 55, †15 10; Loggieville †3 00, †23 30.

PRINCE EDWARD ISLAND RAILWAY.

M. J. Butler, C. E., Deputy Minister of Ry. and Canals, Ottawa, Ont.
L. K. Jones, Secretary Railways and Canals, "
D. Pottinger, General Manager, Moncton, N.B.
E. Tiffin, General Traffic Manager, "
G. A. Sharp, Superintendent, Charlottetown, P.E.I.
W. T. Huggan, Accountant and Auditor, "

9	5-3	1-13	Mls.	*April* 16, 1906.	4-6	14-2	10
P M	P M	A M	.....	(*Atlantic time.*)	Noon	P M	A M
a5 05	†3 35	†8 20	0	lv. **Charlottetown**.ar.	12 15	9 25	10 00
5 30	3 52	8 35	5.3	..**Royalty Junction**..	12 00	9 10	9 41
5 47	4 07	8 47	9.9	.........Milton.........	11 45	8 57	9 26
6 01	4 19	8 56	13.4	........Colville........	11 33	8 47	9 14
6 28	4 42	9 14	19.9	..... Hunter River.....	11 12	8 30	8 48
6 48	4 57	9 26	24.4	...... Fredericton......	10 58	8 17	8 28
7 06	5 12	9 38	28.6	...... Bradalbane......	10 45	8 06	8 10
7 15	5 20	9 44	31.0	..**Emerald Junction**..	10 38	8 01	a8 00
8 55	†8 55	.....	11.6	arr. **Cape Traverse**.lve.	†7 05	.....	a7 05
P M	5 32	9 54	34.4	.... Freetown	10 27	7 51	A M
....	5 53	10 08	39.9	...... Kensington......	10 08	7 37	....
....	6 25	10 30	48.2	arr. ..Summerside.. lve.	9 35	7 15	....
....	7 20	11 00	48.2	lve. ..Summerside.. arr.	9 00	5 30	....
....	10 20	3 45	116.1	.... **Tignish**	†6 00	†12 55	....
....	P M	P M	.....	ARRIVE] [LEAVE	A M	Noon	....

Additional Trains—Leave Emerald Junction b8 00 a.m., arrive Summerside 9 10 a.m. Leave Summerside b1 15 p.m., arrive Emerald Junction 2 25 p.m.

CHARLOTTETOWN, SOURIS AND GEORGETOWN.

P M	Nos. 17-21	Ms.	*April* 16, 1906.	Nos. 18-22	P M
†3 20	†7 10 A M	0	lv. **Charlottetown** .ar.	8 50 A M	5 50
3 30	7 25 "	4.0	.......Sherwood.......	8 40 "	5 35
3 35	7 30 "	5.3	..**Royalty Junction**..	8 35 "	5 30
3 44	7 47 "	9.0	.... York	8 21 "	5 11
3 56	8 09 "	13.6	........Bedford........	8 09 "	4 53
4 03	8 20 "	16.5	........Tracadie........	8 01 "	4 42
4 20	8 42 A M	22.0	..**Mt. Stewart Junc**..	7 46 A M	4 20
5 07	9 48 A M	16.6	.......St. Peter's.......	6 59 A M	3 09
5 40	10 35 "	28.0	.......Bear River.......	6 28 "	2 26
5 47	10 44 "	30.4	..... New Zealand	6 21 "	2 18
6 10	11 15 A M	38.0	........**Souris**........	†6 00 A M	†1 50
4 27	8 55 A M	24.6	........Pisquid........	7 34 A M	3 55
4 45	9 22 "	31.3	.......St. Teresa.......	7 16 "	3 28
4 57	9 39 "	35.9	.........Perth.........	7 04 "	3 12
5 09	9 55 "	40.2	.... Cardigan	6 52 "	2 56
5 25	10 15 A M	46.2	arr.. **Georgetown** .lve.	†6 35 A M	†2 35

MURRAY HARBOR BRANCH.

.....	No. 23	Ms.	*April* 16, 1906.	No. 24	.....
.....	†3 10 P M	0	lv. **Charlottetown**..ar.	10 10 A M	.....
.....	3 43 "	7.4	...... Hazelbrook......	9 36 "	.....
.....	4 21 "	16.9	.....Vernon (Loop).....	8 58 "	.....
.....	4 50 "	16.6	..... Vernon River.....	8 30 "	.....
.....	6 03 "	36.3	..... Wood Island	7 17 "	.....
.....	6 30 "	43.7	..... Murray River.....	6 50 "	.....
.....	6 45 P M	47.8	ar. **Murray Harbor**.lv.	†6 35 A M	.....

QUEBEC & LAKE ST. JOHN RAILWAY.

Gaspard Le Moine, President.
William Hanson, 1st Vice-President.
J. T. Ross, 2d Vice-President.
J. G. Scott, General Manager.

Jas. Bain, Superintendent.
Alex. Hardy, Gen. Freight and Pas. Agt.
S. S. Oliver, Auditor.
Rob't Hunter, Paymaster.

A. E. Doucet, Chief Engineer.
General Offices—St. Andrew Street Terminus, Princess Louise Dock, Quebec.
E. B. Harris, Traveling Passenger Agent, No. 149 Broadway, Room 306, New York.

•11	•9	•7	•5	3	□13	▲1	Mls	*June* 17, 1906.	2	14	•16	4	•6	•8	•10	•12
P M	P M	P M	A M	P M	P M	A M	....	(*Eastern time.*)	A M	P M	P M	A M	P M	P M	P M	P M
§1 45	†6 20	†1 45	†10 00	†5 20	k10 00	†8 45	0	lve.. **Quebec**[1] ♁ arr.	†7 00	8 00	8 00	8 55	1 10	4 45	11 00	9 45
1 58	6 31	1 58	10 12	5 31	10 12	8 56	4	....Charlesbourg.. ♁	6 48	7 42	7 42	8 43	12 58	4 30	10 47	9 31
2 17	6 46	2 17	10 30	5 46	10 31	9 11	9	...Indian Lorette. ♁	6 35	7 26	7 26	8 30	12 45	4 14	10 31	9 12
2 37	7 01	2 37	10 48	6 01	10 49	9 27	17	......Valcartier... ♁	6 17	7 01	7 01	8 14	12 29	3 52	10 14	8 51
2 48	7 10	2 48	10 59	6 10	10 59	9 36	21	...St. Catherines...	6 07	6 45	6 45	8 05	12 20	3 41	10 05	8 40
3 05	7 25	3 05	11 15	6 26	11 03	9 52	23	..Lake St. Joseph ♁	6 02	6 26	6 26	7 49	†12 05	†3 25	†9 50	8 24
3 17	P M	P M	A M	6 37	11 15	10 03	28	... Lake Sergent. ..	5 48	6 05	6 05	7 38	Noon	P M	P M	8 11
3 24	....	....	....	6 42	11 22	10 08	30	....Bourg Louis....	5 41	5 55	5 55	7 33		....	....	8 05
3 35	....	....	....	6 50	11 32	10 16	34	+ ..St. Raymond.. ♁	5 30	5 44	5 44	†7 25	....	....	....	§7 55
				P M	12 18	10 55	50	......Perthuis.... ♁	4 42	4 57	4 47	A M	....	....	....	P M
					12 40	11 15	57	..**Riv. a Pierre Jn**[2]...	4 20	4 35	b4 25		....			
				....	2 07	12 24	85	...... Beaudet......	2 53	3 18	P M	....	....			
				....	2 28	12 44	93	.....Stadacona.....	2 32	2 59	....	....	....			
				....	3 07	1 18	107	....Triton Club....	1 53	2 27	....	....	....			
				....	3 40	1 55	112	.. ‖Lake Edward . ♁	1 40	2 15	....	....	....			
				....	4 40	2 45	134	..... Kiskisink ... ♁	12 35	12 47	....	....	....			
				....	5 49	3 43	160	...Lake Bouchette ♁	11 26	11 43	....	....	....			
				....	6 00	3 51	163	...... Dablon .... ♁	11 15	11 33	....	....	....			
				Sun	6 40	4 20	176	ar. + **Chambord Jn**. ♁ lv.	10 35	10 55	....	....	Sun.			
				⊡	7 10	4 50	188	+ ... **Roberval**... ♁	10 05	10 25	**20**	....	⊡			
				P M	§7 15	4 55	....	ar. **Hotel Roberval**.lv.	‡10 00	c10 20	P M	....	P M			
				§7 10	Sun.	†7 10	....	lv. **Hotel Roberval**.ar	9 00	A M	6 50	Sun	3 50			
				7 15	A M	7 15	188	..... **Roberval** ... ♁	8 55	....	6 45	A M	3 45			
				7 45	§6 50	7 45	176	**Chambord Junc** ♁	8 20	....	6 10	6 15	3 05			
				8 13	7 16	8 13	186	+ ..**St. Jerome**.. ♁	7 51	....	5 19	5 42	2 36			
				8 25	7 30	8 25	191	.....St. Gedeon... ♁	7 40	....	5 02	5 27	2 25			
				8 41	7 48	8 41	198	+ .. Hebertville .. ♁	7 26	....	4 39	5 06	2 11			
				9 26	8 40	9 26	217	..... Jonquiere ... ♁	6 44	....	3 35	4 07	1 29			
				9 55	9 10	9 55	227	+ ..**Chicoutimi**[3]. ♁	a6 15	....	c3 00	[illegible]	§1 00			
				P M	A M	P M	....	ARRIVE] [LEAVE	P M	....	P M	A M	P M			

CONNECTIONS. 1 With Canadian Pacific Ry.; Grand Trunk Ry.; Intercolonial Ry.; Quebec Central Ry.; Quebec Ry., Light & Power Co. and Richelieu & Ontario Navigation Co. 2 With Great Northern Ry. of Canada. 3 With Richelieu & Ontario Navigation Co. during season of navigation.

\+ Coupon stations; ♁ Telegraph stations.

† Daily, except Sunday.
‡ Daily, except Saturday.
§ Sunday only.
a Daily, except Saturday and Monday.
b Daily, except Sunday and Monday; on Wednesday and Saturday runs from La Tuque, leaving there 3 00 p.m.
c Monday only.
k Saturday only.
• First trip June 17, 1906.
□ Prior to June 17th lvs. Quebec *k*7 30 p.m.
▲ Prior to June 17th lvs. Quebec †8 10 a.m.
⊡ Runs July 8th to September 9th inclusive.
‖ Meals.

QUEBEC & LAKE ST. JOHN RAILWAY. The New Route to the FAR-FAMED SAGUENAY.

North American Transportation Co.

"BAIE DES CHALEURS ROUTE."

M. CONNOLLY, Prest. and Mgr. | M. P. CONNOLLY, Sec'y-Treas.
P. HUME, Chief Eng'r and Supt. | and Fht. and Pas. Agent.

General Offices—40 Dalhousie Street, Quebec, Canada.

MONTREAL-ST. JOHNS, NEWFOUNDLAND SERVICE.

Steamer *Restigouche*, E. C. Sears, Master, is intended to ply between **Montreal** and **St. Johns, N.F.**, during the season of navigation, sailing about every fourteen days from Montreal, calling at **Quebec, Summerside, Charlottetown, North Sydney** and **Sydney**. This steamer has superior passenger accommodations, is fitted with electric light and bells, hot and cold water baths, large commodious staterooms, with steam heat, and is first-class in every respect. For rates and other information, apply to the office as above.

ALBERTA RAILWAY & IRRIGATION CO.

E. T. GALT, President, Lethbridge, Alberta.
K. R. B. WODEHOUSE, Vice-President, London, England.
P. L. NAISMITH, Manager, Lethbridge, Alberta.
J. E. LETHBRIDGE, Auditor, "
C. A. MAGRATH, Land Commissioner, "
WALTER BARWICK, Counsel, Toronto, Ont.

No. 364	No. 2	Mls.	*November* 16, 190 ?	No. 1	No. 36	....
b7 30 A M	a7 30 A M	0	lve...**Lethbridge**..arr.	5 45 P M	11 00 P M	
8 38 "	7 38 "	1.5	...Montana Junction...	5 35 "	10 50 "	
8 25 A M	8 25 A M	19.0	arr.....**Stirling**....lve.	a4 50 P M	10 05 P M	
....	a9 05 A M	26.0	lve.... Raymond....arr.	4 30 P M	....	
....	9 45 "	37.0	........Magrath........	4 00 "	....	
....	10 25 "	48.0	....**Spring Coulee**....	3 25 "	....	
....	10 50 "	57.0	.... Raley.........	2 55 "	....	
....	11 20 A M	66.0	arr.....Cardston.....lve.	a2 30 P M	....	
8 30 A M	....	19.0	lve.....**Stirling**....arr.	....	10 00 P M	....
9 10 "	....	34.0	.....Tyrrell's Lake.....	....	9 20 "	....
9 35 "	....	42.0	.......Brunton.......	....	8 55 "	....
10 15 "	....	53.0	......Milk River......	....	8 25 "	....
11 05 A M	....	66.0	arr. **Sweet Grass (Coutts)** lve.	....	b7 45 P M	....

(*Mountain time.*)

a Monday, Wednesday and Friday.
b Tuesday, Thursday and Saturday.

Connections.—At Lethbridge—With Canadian Pacific Ry. for Kootenay points via the Crow's Nest Pass Branch and for all places east and west on the Main Line. At **Sweet Grass (Coutts)**—With Great Northern Ry. Line.

LAKE SUPERIOR TERMINAL & TRANSFER RAILWAY.

C. P. Brown, Superintendent, Superior, Wis.

Switching road. Located in Superior. Does a general switching business, also owns and operates the Union Passenger Station. Total mileage operated, 16 miles. *February*, 1906.

Casco Bay Steamboat Co.

CUSTOM HOUSE WHARF, PORTLAND, MAINE.

THE IDEAL RESORTS OF MAINE.

STEAMERS

Pilgrim, Forest Queen, Emita and Merryconeag,

Maintaining a Regular Service between **PORTLAND, ME.**, and the following Islands: **Forest City Landing (Peak's Island), Trefethen's Landing (Peak's Island), Evergreen Landing (Peak's Island), Cushing's Island, Little Diamond Island, Great Diamond Island and Ponce's Landing (Long Island).**

October, 1905. C. W. T. GODING, Gen. Mgr., Portland, Me.

CARILLON & GRENVILLE RAILROAD AND OTTAWA RIVER NAVIGATION COMPANY.

R. W. Shepherd, Managing Director, Montreal, Que.

The Carillon & Grenville R.R. is run during the season of navigation in connection with the Ottawa River Navigation Co. Steamers, and trains leave Carillon on arrival of steamers from Lachine †12 25 noon, arriving at Grenville (13 miles) 12 55 noon, connecting at Grenville with steamer for Ottawa. Returning, leaves Grenville †1 00 p.m., or on arrival of steamer from Ottawa, arriving at Carillon 1 25 p.m., connecting with steamer for Lachine and Montreal. *February*, 1906.

† Daily, except Sunday. *Eastern time.*

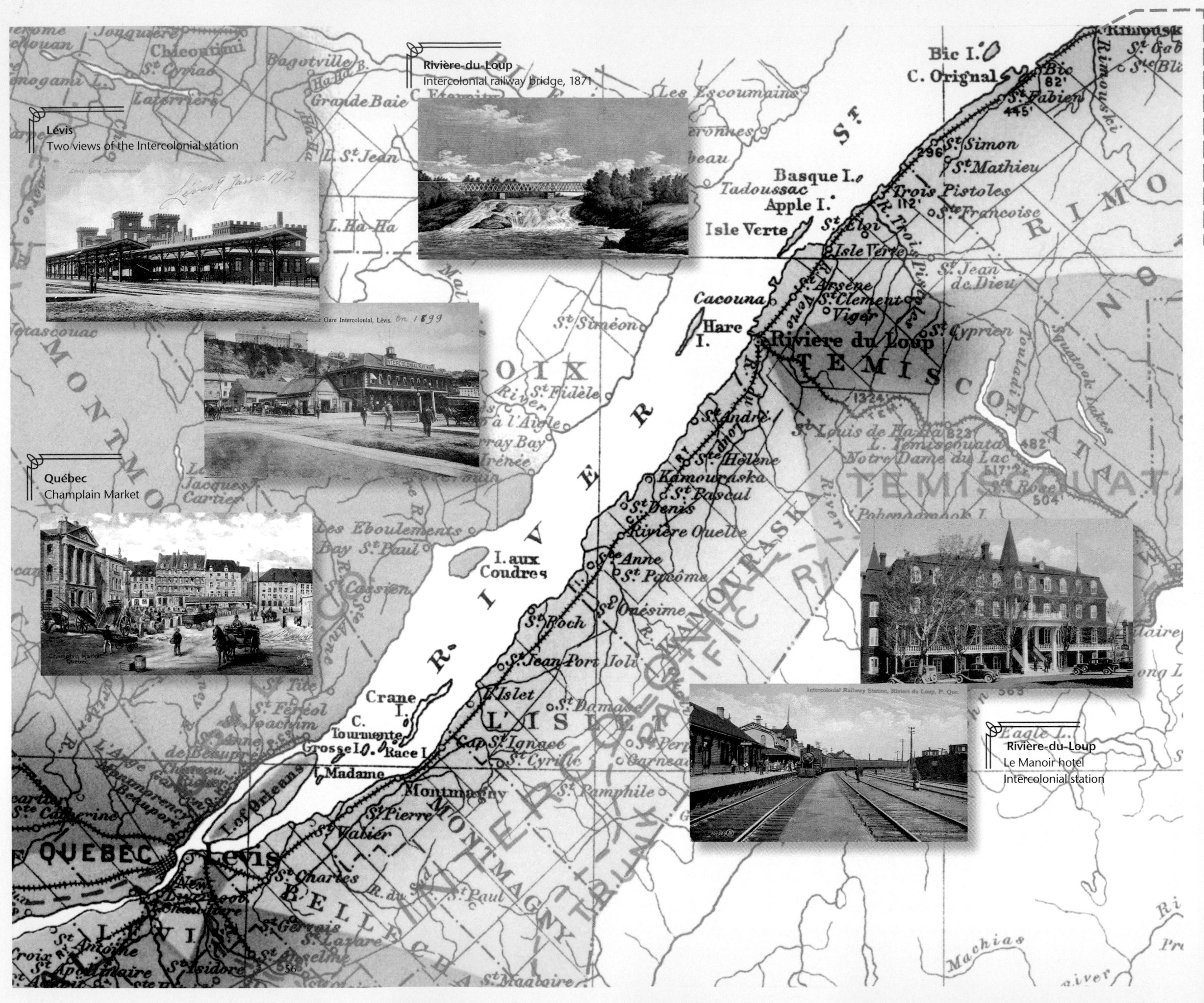

Lévis
Two views of the Intercolonial station

Rivière-du-Loup
Intercolonial railway bridge, 1871

Québec
Champlain Market

Rivière-du-Loup
Le Manoir hotel
Intercolonial station

Rimouski
Intercolonial Railway bridge

Dalhousie
Two views of the town, *c.*1910 and *c.*1920

Restigouche River

Campbellton
Chateau Restigouche hotel, *c.*1910

Bathurst
Main Street, 1940; pulp and paper mill, 1930s

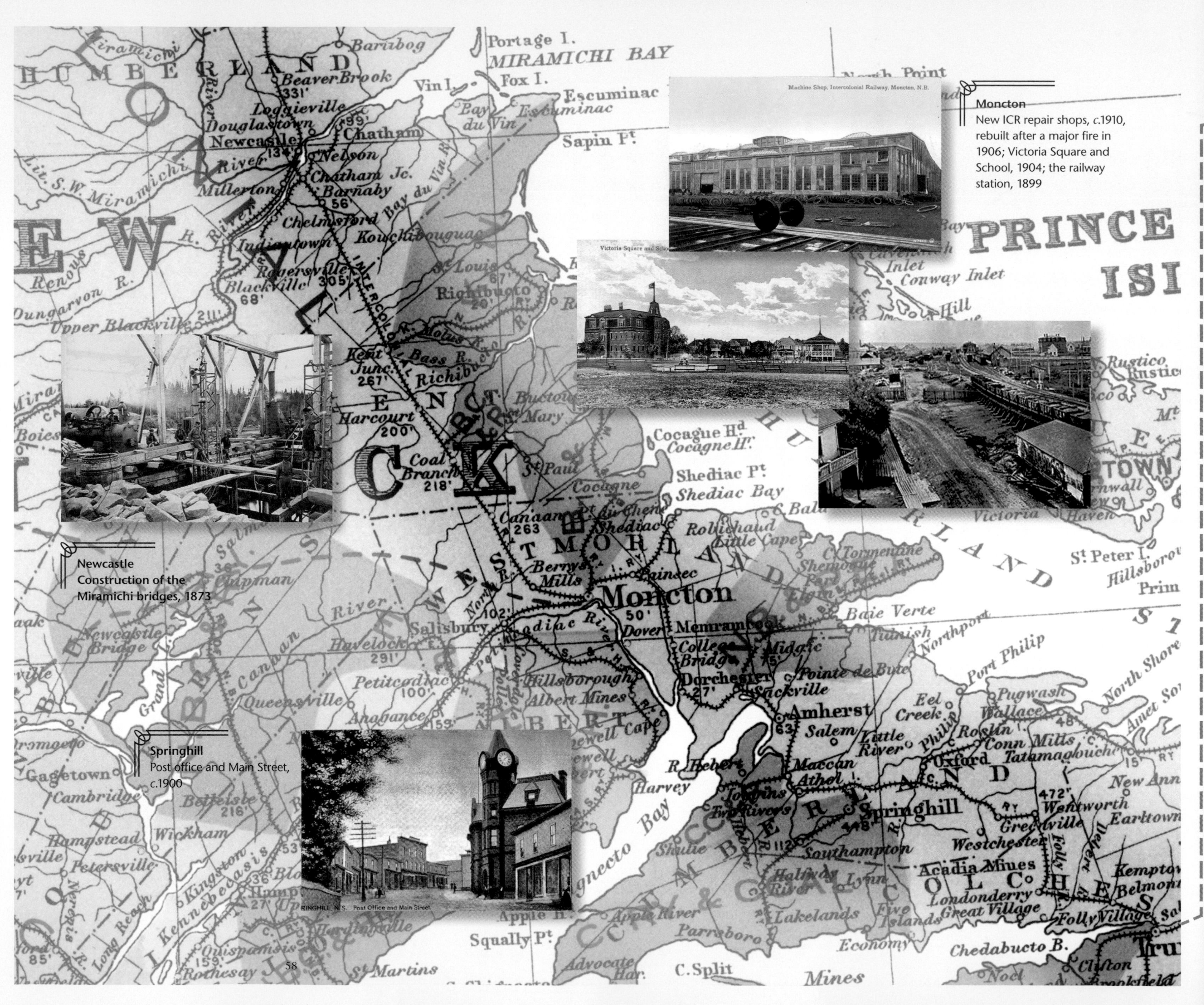

Moncton
New ICR repair shops, *c*.1910, rebuilt after a major fire in 1906; Victoria Square and School, 1904; the railway station, 1899

Newcastle
Construction of the Miramichi bridges, 1873

Springhill
Post office and Main Street, *c*.1900

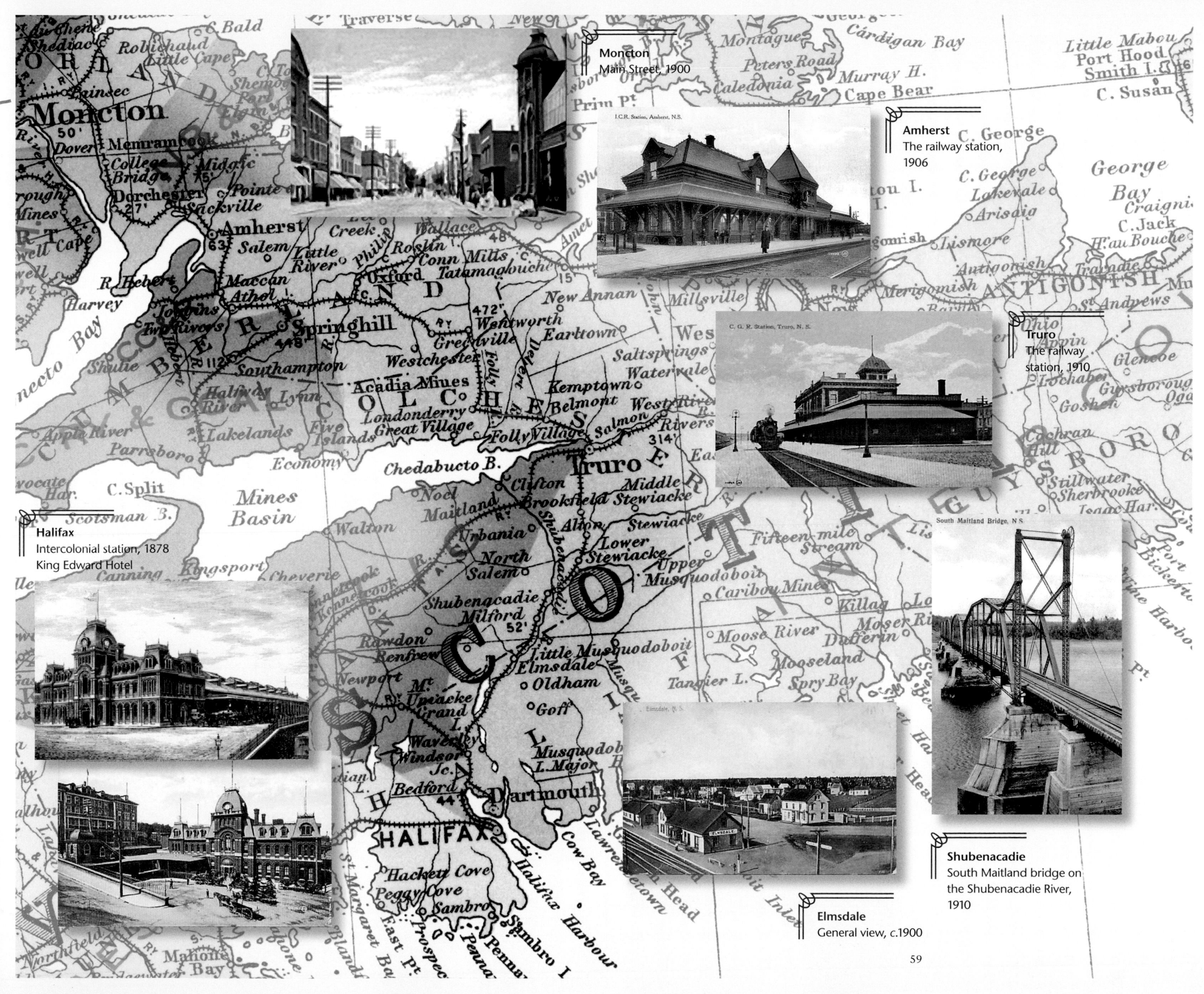

Moncton
Main Street, 1900

Amherst
The railway station, 1906

Truro
The railway station, 1910

Halifax
Intercolonial station, 1878
King Edward Hotel

Shubenacadie
South Maitland bridge on the Shubenacadie River, 1910

Elmsdale
General view, *c.*1900

THE PRINCE EDWARD ISLAND RAILWAY

The Winding Line

Georgetown station, PEI Railway, 1905 (top right).

Main Street, Montague, in 1900 (below).

There was a second eastern railway associated with Confederation—the Prince Edward Island Railway (PEIR). Island politicians chose not to join in the union of the British North American colonies in 1867, but when after 1870 the costs of constructing a railway threatened to bankrupt the small colony, they changed their minds. With the promise that the then fledgling Canadian government would take on the costs and further construction, on July 1, 1873 PEI became part of the Dominion of Canada.

In 1871, the colony had begun construction of a narrow gauge (3′ 6″ or 1.067 m) railway of "about 120 miles" from Casumpec Bay in the West to Georgetown in the East. The Canadian government completed the railway in 1875, adopting much of the winding route that was intended to serve a good deal of the island. The railway covered about 150 miles between Tignish and Georgetown, which are geographically only about ninety miles apart, with a branch to Souris. By 1910, the railway added an extension to the eastern tip of the island at Elmira, and between the capital Charlottetown and Murray Harbour. The railway stopped every few miles to meet the needs of the small, scattered, rural communities around the island. Apart from the scheduled stops, at other stations the station master could signal by flag that there were passengers or goods to be taken aboard; the trains would make unplanned halts at these "flag stop" stations. Despite all these efforts, the railway never covered its operating expenses, and freight and passenger traffic grew more slowly and remained much lighter than on other Canadian railways. Nevertheless, the road provided convenient overland transportation for many farmers to bring their goods to market, and introduced travellers to the beaches and seaside resorts of the north shore of Prince Edward Island.

In 1918 the PEIR was incorporated into the newly formed Canadian National Railways system.

In Gordon Woods, *c*.1900

North Wiltshire Embankment, 1898

North Wiltshire
Interior of the railway station, 1912

PEI Railway Locomotive No. 1

Charlottetown
Fire at the car shops, 1904

Murray Harbour
The railway station, *c*.1905

THE NOVA SCOTIA RAILWAY

TRACKS TO CANADA'S OCEAN PLAYGROUND

Nova Scotia saw some of the earliest steam locomotives in Canada, at the Albion Mines in Pictou County, and was also part of the first, halting experiments in government-owned railways, starting in the late 1840s. The three maritime provinces of Canada, New Brunswick and Nova Scotia all wanted an "Intercolonial" railway to link the colonies, and all three governments believed that it should be a government owned and operated line. However, the planned intercolonial railway scheme collapsed in 1852 when Britain refused financial support.

While the Province of Canada proceeded to support private construction with public financial assistance, Nova Scotia continued to promote public ownership as the only way to achieve a railway system. The government-run Nova Scotia Railway was opened in 1858 with two sections: one extended from Richmond (just north of the port of Halifax) to Windsor on the Bay of Fundy; the second ran from Richmond to Truro.

In 1867 the line was extended from Truro to Pictou, a port and important coal mining area on the Northumberland Straits opposite Prince Edward Island.

As originally proposed, the Nova Scotia Railway was to be built to link with the New Brunswick railway system, which consisted of the European and North American from Saint John to Shediac. The link was, in turn, envisaged as part of a much more ambitious scheme to connect the colonies of Nova Scotia and New Brunswick with the New England railway system. Although the Maritimes had a cultural affinity with the rest of British North America, they had much stronger business ties with New England. However, financing problems were insurmountable, and the line as a whole never materialized, although small sections were subsequently built.

In 1867, with the formation of the Dominion of Canada, the Nova Scotia Railway and the European and North American in New Brunswick were transferred to the new Dominion government and became components of the Intercolonial Railway.

Nova Scotia's railway heritage also includes the first "piggy back" service, when farmers could lead their horse-drawn wagons onto trains to go to market and back, as well as a named passenger train, *The Ocean Limited*, that has run since 1904 on the Intercolonial, though today's travellers will be reassured to know it has been substantially modernized.

A train leaving Yarmouth Wharf, 1910 (opposite).

Tatamagouche, Colchester County, 1894 (below left).

Dominion Atlantic Railway (DAR) train leaving Yarmouth for Halifax. This railway operated in western Nova Scotia, also running steamships and hotels, and limped on, mainly under CPR ownership, until 1994 (centre).

Canadian Government Railway station, Truro (below right).

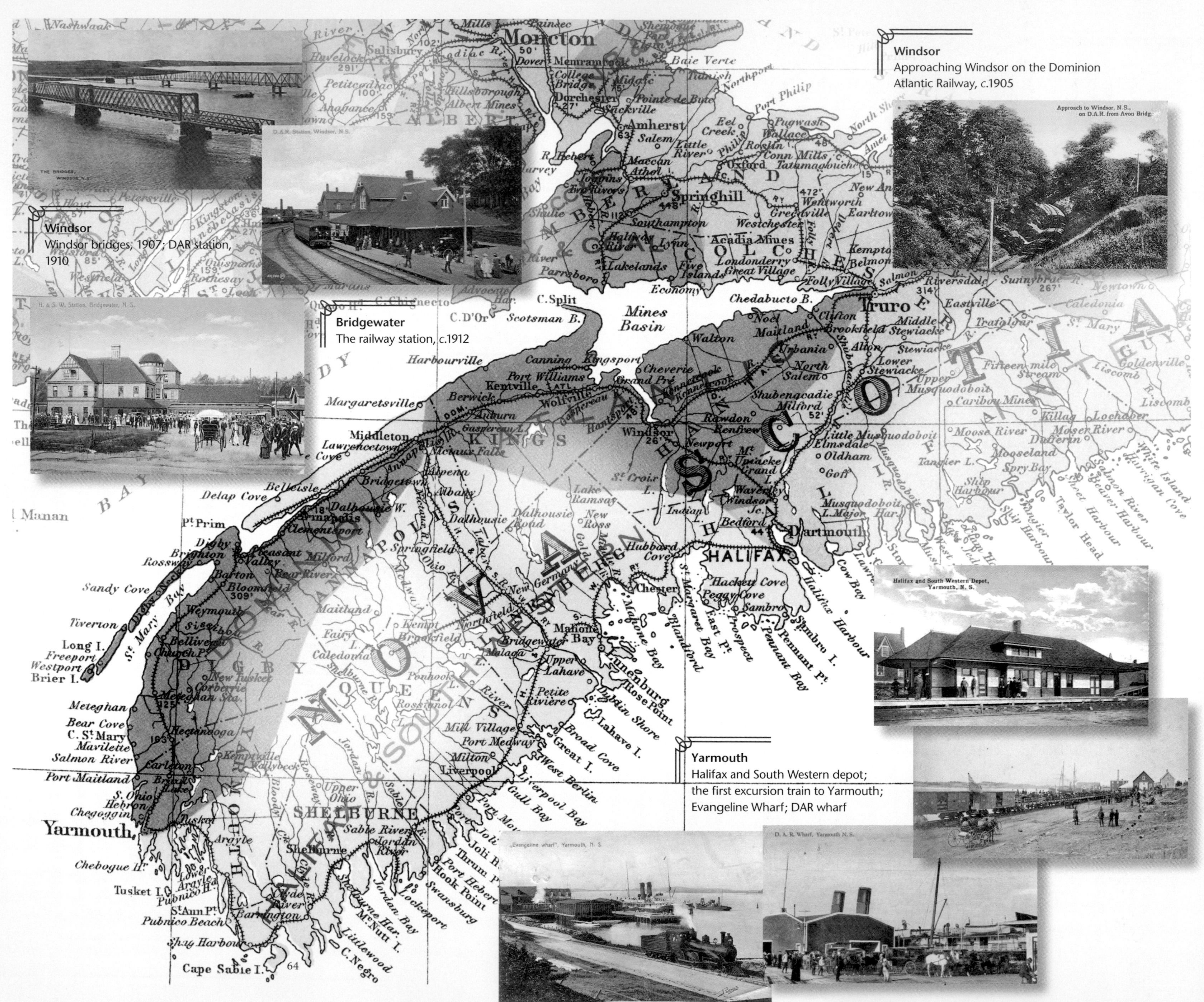

Windsor
Windsor bridges, 1907; DAR station, 1910

Windsor
Approaching Windsor on the Dominion Atlantic Railway, *c.*1905

Bridgewater
The railway station, *c.*1912

Yarmouth
Halifax and South Western depot; the first excursion train to Yarmouth; Evangeline Wharf; DAR wharf

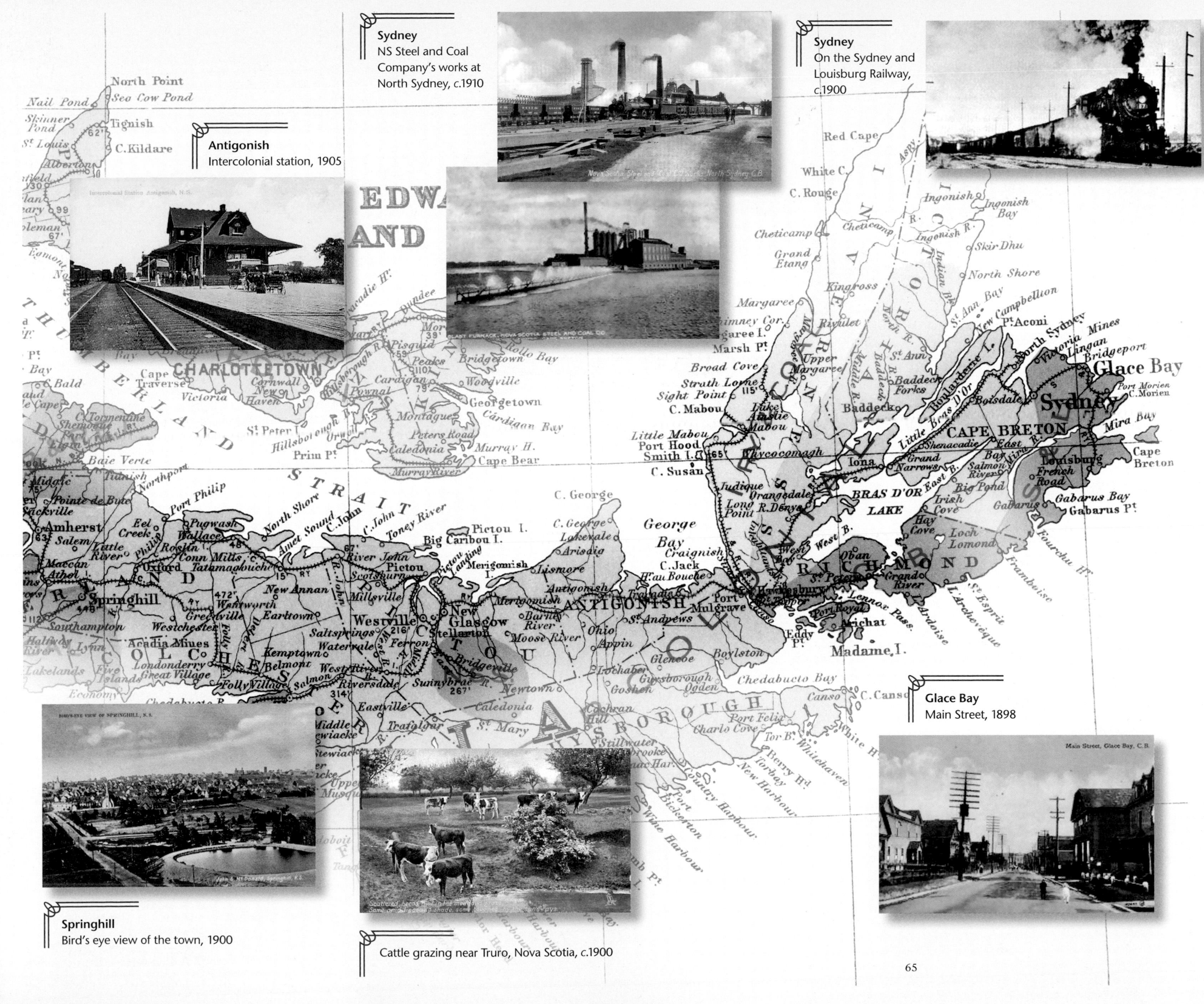

Sydney
NS Steel and Coal Company's works at North Sydney, *c.*1910

Sydney
On the Sydney and Louisburg Railway, *c.*1900

Antigonish
Intercolonial station, 1905

Glace Bay
Main Street, 1898

Springhill
Bird's eye view of the town, 1900

Cattle grazing near Truro, Nova Scotia, *c.*1900

THE NEWFOUNDLAND RAILWAY

HOME OF *THE NEWFIE BULLET*

Railway development came relatively late to Newfoundland. An ambitious government-funded trans-insular railway survey had been made in 1874, and in 1881 a private company started constructing a small system on the populous east coast Avalon Peninsula. Until then, the colony's small population (in 1891, the island had only 202,000 people) was scattered along the coast and was reached by coastal shipping.

The new line connected the capital and main city of St. John's to the settlements of Whitbourne and Harbour Grace. However, the company experienced financial problems and the colonial government acquired the line in 1886. During the 1890s the railway was completed across the island to Port aux Basques.

The government did not operate the railway but instead contracted with Robert Reid, a well-established Montréal contractor, to build and then operate the railway and ferry services for 10 years; in 1898 the agreement was extended to 50 years. He incorporated the Reid Newfoundland Company to manage the railway and steamship operations.

The railway track was unusual in Canada since in order to reduce construction costs it was built to a narrow gauge (the distance between the inside of the rails) of 3′ 6″ (1,067 mm), whereas the North American standard gauge is 4′ 8½″ (1.435 m). In 1988, when the system was abandoned, the 680 miles (1,090 km) of track made up the largest narrow gauge system in North America. While most of the once extensive narrow gauge lines in North America were abandoned or converted to standard gauge, the isolation of the Newfoundland system from the mainland systems preserved the gauge.

At the turn of the century the Reid Newfoundland Company provided the majority of coastal services in the colony. Two ferry routes connected the mainland with Newfoundland. In 1897 ferries began the run between Port aux Basques in the south and North Sydney, Nova Scotia (the shortest ferry route but the longest rail route), and, the following year, sailings were launched between Placentia, close to St. John's, and North Sydney.

The Reid Newfoundland Company, never particularly profitable, was repossessed by the government in 1923 and became the Newfoundland Railway. During the 1930s, the railway played a role in developing the fledgling transatlantic air service, for in 1936 the Canadian and British governments selected Gander, a station on the railway in the centre of the island railway, to serve as an airfield to refuel airliners for a

Sir Robert Gillespie Reid 1842–1908 (below).

Mr and Mrs Reid returning from their first trip across Newfoundland in 1898 (bottom).

The Newfie Bullet, 1938, painted by the late Wentworth Folkins and reproduced in *The Great Days of Canadian Steam*, published in 1988 (opposite).

The No. 2 Express leaving Port aux Basques, 1908 (above).

Newfoundland postage stamp, 1928 (right).

Section crew on a hand car near Port Blandford, *c.*1905, with Billy Best as the foreman (bottom right).

proposed transatlantic air service. Aviation fuel was received by rail through the port of Lewisporte. During World War II, Gander was a stop for the thousands of new fighter and bomber aircraft flown from factories in Canada and the United States to Britain. Gander remained a fuelling stop until the 1960s, when new long-range jets could fly directly between major North American and European airports.

World War II produced new traffic for the railway. The United States Navy constructed a base at Argentia and the United States Army established an air force base near Stephenville, both connected to the railway; the air base remained open until 1965.

In 1949, when the British colony of Newfoundland joined with Canada, the Canadian National Railways assumed operation of the railway. The infrastructure was upgraded and freight traffic increased to a level that justified introducing a train ferry to the mainland in 1968. This new service required that the standard gauge main line wheels had to be replaced with narrow gauge wheels when freight cars came to the island.

Despite these improvements, Newfoundland generated too little traffic to support a railway system, especially after the trans-insular highway from Port aux Basques to St. John's was completed in 1965 and introduced fierce new competition. The highway meant that the 547-mile (880-km) journey between the two points could be made by road in less than nine hours, whereas the cross-island passenger train had a twenty-three-hour schedule for the trip. This train was called *The Overland Limited* until 1950 when it was renamed the *Caribou*, and was colloquially known as "The Newfie Bullet." Despite the affection evident in its nickname, the train was cancelled in 1969.

In 1978 a federal commission recommended complete abandonment of the railway. Exactly ten years later the entire Newfoundland system was shut down. Newfoundland, Canada's newest province, became the first to lose all its rail facilities.

NEWFOUNDLAND AND QUEBEC CENTRAL TIMETABLES, 1906

REID NEWFOUNDLAND COMPANY.

	6	7	1	Mls	*February*, 1906.	2	6	8
		A M	P M		LEAVE / ARRIVE	A M		P M
		†8 30	*5 00	0	+ ....**St. John's**.... ♁	*11 00		9 30
		8 56	– –	7	......Dunnsmere......	– –		9 09
		9 00	5 25	8	..Western Junction ♁	10 35		9 04
		9 27	5 43	15	+ ......Topsail...... ♁	10 17		8 45
		9 55	6 03	22	+ ....Kelligrew's.... ♁	9 55		8 20
		10 39	6 38	33	+ .... Holyrood .... ♁	9 25		7 45
		10 59	6 58	39	+ .... Avondale .... ♁	9 07		7 28
	P M	11 30	7 15	44	+ **Brigus Junction** ♁	8 54	A M	7 15
	a8 15	12 10	b8 00	57	+ .. **Whitbourne** .. ♁	*8 15	7 45	†6 15
	9 18	Noon	8 49	73	.....Long Harbor.....	7 15	6 47	P M
	10 51		9 45	90	........Rantem........	6 16	5 36	
	10 43		9 55	92	......La Manche......	6 10	5 23	
	11 03		10 21	101	.....Arnold's Cove... ♁	5 42	4 50	
	11 35		10 36	105	...Come-by-Chance....	5 30	4 32	
	12 33		11 17	118	....Northern Bight....	4 51	3 44	
	e1 27		12 15	132	+ .. **Clarenville** .. ♁	4 07	2 51	
	1 37		12 25	136	.... Shoal Harbor	3 47	2 33	
	2 05		12 55	145	....Thorburn Lake....	3 17	1 47	
	2 50		a1 20	153	+ **Port Blandford** ♁	2 50	c1 20	
	3 38		2 05	167	......Terra Nova..... ♁	2 05	12 33	
	4 36		2 55	183	....Alexander Bay....	d1 17	11 37	
	5 08		3 23	192	+ ....Gambo....... ♁	12 53	11 04	
	5 55		4 05	206	+ ....Benton....... ♁	12 13	10 14	
	7 34		5 22	232	+ .....Glenwood..... ♁	11 00	8 42	
	8 12		6 05	245	+ **Notre Dame Jn** ♁	10 20	7 54	
	8 56		6 30	256	+ ... Norris Arm ... ♁	9 55	7 03	
	9 43		7 15	268	+ .. Bishop's Falls .. ♁	9 20	6 45	
	11 23		8 37	296	.... Badger Brook .. ♁	7 45	4 57	
	12 21		9 30	313	+ .Millertown Junc. ♁	6 55	4 00	
	1 05		10 10	327	.... Quarry ..... ♁	6 10	3 07	
	2 45		11 44	359	........Howley...... ♁	4 33	1 15	
	3 15		12 01	365	......Grand Lake..... ♁	4 15	12 46	
	6 00		2 15	404	+ ..Bay of Islands.. ♁	2 05	10 10	
	6 20		2 30	409	+ ...Birchy Cove... ♁	1 40	9 40	
	7 24		3 15	427	...... Howards .... ♁	12 55	8 37	
	7 35		3 24	430	.... Spruce Brook	12 41	8 26	
	8 10		3 50	439	....Harry's Brook....	12 15	7 51	
	9 03		4 30	453	.....Stephenville.....	11 35	6 54	
	9 21		4 45	459	..... Seal Rocks ... ♁	11 20	6 37	
	11 12		6 08	490	.... Crabbs ..... ♁	9 54	4 48	
	1 10		7 37	512	.... South Branch	8 23	2 50	
	1 50		8 00	529	+ ... Little River ... ♁	8 00	2 20	
	c3 00		a9 00	548	+ .**Port-Aux-Basques**. ♁	c7 00	e1 10	
	A M		P M	633	ar.. **North Sydney** lv.	A M	A M	

*Daily; †daily, except Sunday; *a* Monday, Wednesday and Friday; *b* Sunday, Tuesday and Thursday; *c* Sunday, Wednesday and Friday; *d* Monday, Thursday and Saturday; *e* Tuesday, Thursday and Saturday; *g* Tuesday, Wednesday and Friday.

STANDARD—*Newfoundland local time*, which is 30 minutes faster than *Intercolonial time*.

+ Coupon stations; ♁ Telegraph stations.

R. G. Reid, President.
W. D. Reid, V.-Prest. & Gen. Mgr.
H. D. Reid, Sec'y & Treasurer.
R. G. Reid, Jr., Gen. Supt.
G. H. Massey, Chief Engineer.

W. E. Hamilton, Gen. Pas. Agent.
D. Sutherland, Gen. Fht. Agent.
H. M'Niel, Auditor.
H. Crawford, Purchasing Agent.
F. Rioux, Superintendent.

General Offices—St. John's, Newfoundland.

BRIGUS BRANCH.

No. 3	No. 9	Mls	*February*, 1906.	No. 10	No. 4
†11 38 A M	d7 20 P M	0	lve...**Brigus Junction** ♁ arr.	8 40 A M	7 00 P M
12 15 Noon	7 58 "	11	............Brigus.......... ♁	8 03 "	6 15 "
12 45 Noon	8 21 "	18	........Clark's Beach........	7 39 "	5 35 "
1 00 P M	8 35 "	22	.........Bay Roberts....... ♁	7 25 "	5 20 "
1 20 "	8 44 "	24	........Spaniard's Bay........	7 16 "	4 59 "
1 40 "	8 53 "	26	............Tilton.......... ♁	7 07 "	4 37 "
2 00 "	9 12 "	32	........Harbor Grace...... ♁	6 48 "	4 17 "
2 30 P M	9 40 P M	39	arr......**Carbonear** ♁....lve.	d6 20 A M	†3 45 P M

PLACENTIA BRANCH.

	No. 7	Mls	*February*, 1906.	No. 8	
	†12 40 Noon	0	lve.....**Whitbourne** ♁...arr.	5 20 P M	
	2 09 P M	27	arr......**Placentia** ♁....lve.	†3 45 P M	

BROAD COVE BRANCH.

	No. 15	Mls	*February*, 1906.	No. 16	
	g8 00 P M	0	lve.....**Whitbourne** ♁...arr.	8 00 A M	
	8 30 "	10	.........Broad Cove....... ♁	7 28 "	
	9 02 "	22	.... Tilton .... ♁	7 00 "	
	9 40 P M	34	arr..... **Carbonear** ♁ ...lve.	g6 10 A M	

CONNECTIONS.

At **North Sydney** with the Intercolonial Ry. and via this line with the Canadian Pacific, Grand Trunk, Dominion Atlantic, Maine Central, Boston & Maine and all railway lines in Canada and the United States; also with the Canada and Plant Steamship Co., via Halifax.

Trains connect at **Lewisport** with steamer for Twillingate, Fogo, Tilt Cove, Pilleys Island and all points in Notre Dame Bay.

At **Placentia** for all parts of Placentia Bay, Burin Fortune, St. Lawrence, Lamaline, Fortune and Grand Bank, at **Port Blandford** with steamers for all points in Bonavista Bay and at **Clarenville** with steamers for all points in Trinity Bay. Navigation on Notre Dame, Bonavista and Trinity Bays closes on Dec. 31st each year and re-opens again on May 1st.

At **St. John's** with steamers for all points along the south and north coast and Labrador. At **St. John's** with all the steamers for London and Liverpool, Eng., and all European points, thus enabling tourists and travelers to reach all points in Newfoundland and Labrador.

"S.S. BRUCE"—PORT-AUX-BASQUES AND NORTH SYDNEY.

Mon. Wed. Fri.	9 00 P M	lv.. **Port-Aux-Basques** .ar.	5 30 A M	Wed. Fri. Sun.
Tue. Thu. Sat.	4 00 A M	ar.. **North Sydney** ..lv.	10 30 P M	Tue. Thu. Sat.

QUEBEC CENTRAL RAILWAY.

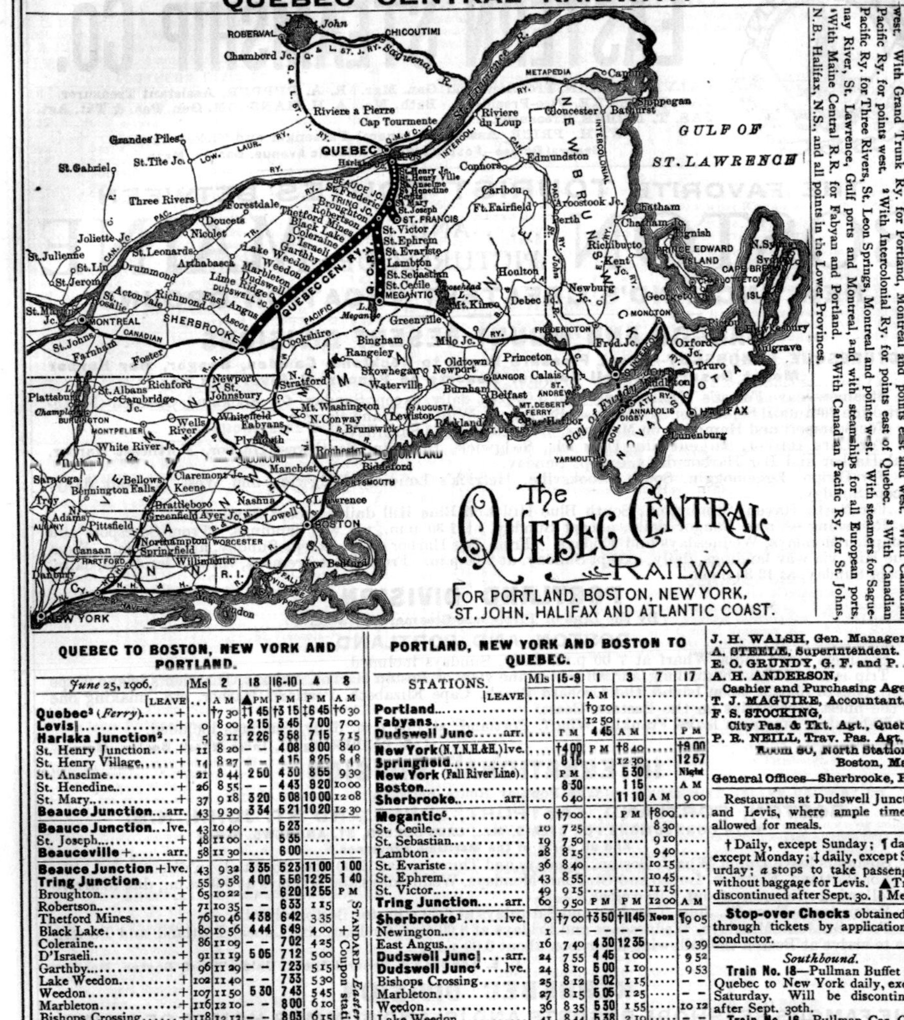

Connections.—[1]With Boston & Maine R.R. for Boston, New York, White Mountains, south and west. With Grand Trunk Ry. for Portland, Montreal and points east and west. With Canadian Pacific Ry. for points west. [2]With Intercolonial Ry. for points east of Quebec. [3]With Canadian Pacific Ry. for Three Rivers, St. Leon Springs, Montreal and points west. With steamers for Saguenay River, St. Lawrence, Gulf ports and Montreal, and with steamships for all European ports. [4]With Maine Central R.R. for Fabyan and Portland. [5]With Canadian Pacific Ry. for St. Johns, N.B., Halifax, N.S., and all points in the Lower Provinces.

QUEBEC TO BOSTON, NEW YORK AND PORTLAND.

June 25, 1906.	Ms	2	18	16-10	4	8
[LEAVE	...	A M	▲P M	P M	P M	A M
Quebec[3] (*Ferry*)......+	...	†7 30	‡1 45	†3 15	‡6 45	†6 30
Levis‖.............+	0	8 00	2 15	3 45	7 00	7 00
Harlaka Junction[2]....	5	8 11	2 26	3 58	7 15	7 15
St. Henry Junction.....+	11	8 20	– –	4 08	8 00	8 40
St. Henry Village......+	14	8 27	– –	4 15	8 25	8 48
St. Anselme..........+	21	8 44	2 50	4 30	8 55	9 30
St. Henedine.........+	26	8 55	– –	4 43	9 20	10 00
St. Mary.............+	37	9 18	3 20	5 08	10 00	12 08
Beauce Junction...arr.	43	9 30	3 34	5 21	10 20	12 30
Beauce Junction...lve.	43	10 40		5 23		
St. Joseph...........+	48	11 00		5 35		
Beauceville+......arr.	58	11 30		6 00		
Beauce Junction+lve.	43	9 32	3 35	5 23	11 00	1 00
Tring Junction......+	55	9 58	4 00	5 58	12 25	1 40
Broughton............+	65	10 22	– –	6 20	12 55	P M
Robertson............+	71	10 35	– –	6 33	1 15	
Thetford Mines.......+	76	10 46	4 38	6 42	3 35	
Black Lake...........+	80	10 56	4 44	6 49	4 00	
Coleraine............+	86	11 09	– –	7 02	4 25	
D'Israeli............+	91	11 19	5 05	7 12	5 00	
Garthby..............+	96	11 29	– –	7 23	5 15	
Lake Weedon.........+	102	11 40	– –	7 33	5 30	
Weedon..............+	107	11 50	5 30	7 43	5 45	
Marbleton............+	116	12 10	– –	8 00	6 10	
Bishops Crossing.....+	118	12 13	– –	8 03	6 15	
Dudswell Junc[4]+..arr.	119	12 15	5 49	8 05	6 25	
Dudswell Junc‖....lve.	119	12 20	5 50	8 25	7 00	
East Angus...........+	127	12 35	6 05	8 43	7 40	
Newington.............	142	1 13	6 38	9 18	8 50	
Sherbrooke[1]+.....arr.	143	1 15	6 40	9 20	8 55	P M
Tring Junction.....lve.	55	P M	P M	†6 00	A M	†2 15
St. Victor.............	66			6 25		2 50
St. Ephrem............	72			6 40		3 20
St. Evariste...........	79			7 00		3 50
Lambton..............	87			7 25		4 30
St. Sebastian..........	96			7 45		4 55
St. Cecile.............	105			8 18		5 48
Megantic[5].........arr.	115		P M	8 45	A M	6 10
Sherbrooke........lve.	...		‡6 50	†9 35	†11 30	P M
Boston..............	...			7 30	8 15	
New York (Fall River Line).	...		A M	A M	P M	
Springfield..........	...		3 10	7 10		
New York (N.Y.N.H.&H.) arr.	...	Noon	7 20	11 27		
Dudswell Junc.....lve.	...	12 35	A M	A M		
Fabyans.............	...	4 32				
Portland.............	...	7 45				
[ARRIVE	...	P M				

STANDARD—*Eastern time.* + Coupon stations.

PORTLAND, NEW YORK AND BOSTON TO QUEBEC.

STATIONS.	Mls	15-9	1	3	7	17
[LEAVE	....		A M			
Portland...........	....		†9 10			
Fabyans............	....		12 50			
Dudswell Junc.....arr.	....	P M	4 45	A M		P M
New York (N.Y.N.H.&H.) lve.	....	†4 00	P M	†8 40		†9 00
Springfield..........	....	8 16		12 30		12 57
New York (Fall River Line).	....	P M		5 30		Night
Boston..............	....	8 30		1 15		A M
Sherbrooke........arr.	....	6 40		11 10	A M	9 00
Megantic[5]...........	0	†7 00		P M	†8 00	
St. Cecile.............	10	7 25			8 30	
St. Sebastian..........	19	7 50			9 10	
Lambton..............	28	8 15			9 40	
St. Evariste...........	36	8 40			10 15	
St. Ephrem............	43	8 55			10 45	
St. Victor.............	49	9 15			11 15	
Tring Junction.....arr.	60	9 50	P M	P M	12 00	A M
Sherbrooke[1].......lve.	0	†7 00	†3 50	†11 45	Noon	¶9 05
Newington............	1	– –	– –	– –		– –
East Angus...........	16	7 40	4 30	12 35		9 39
Dudswell Junc‖....arr.	24	7 55	4 45	1 00		9 52
Dudswell Junc[4]....lve.	24	8 10	5 00	1 10		9 53
Bishops Crossing.......	25	8 12	5 02	1 15		– –
Marbleton.............	27	8 15	5 05	1 25		– –
Weedon...............	36	8 35	5 30	1 55		10 12
Lake Weedon..........	41	8 44	5 38	2 10		– –
Garthby...............	47	8 55	5 47	2 25		– –
D'Israeli	52	9 06	5 56	2 45		10 37
Coleraine.............	57	9 18	6 05	3 00		– –
Black Lake............	63	9 30	6 15	3 20		10 56
Thetford Mines........	67	9 39	6 23	3 35		11 04
Robertson.............	72	9 48	6 33	3 50		– –
Broughton.............	78	9 58	6 45	4 05	Noon	– –
Tring Junction.......	88	10 20	7 10	5 00	†12 35	11 40
Beauce Junction...arr.	100	10 36	7 25	5 25	1 00	11 55
Beauceville........lve.	115	†8 30	†6 25		†12 00	†8 30
St. Joseph............	105	9 00	6 55		12 30	9 00
Beauce Junction...arr.	100	10 37	7 26		1 30	11 56
Beauce Junction...lve.	100	10 37	7 26	5 45	1 30	11 56
St. Mary..............	106	10 50	7 38	6 00	2 10	12 08
St. Henedine..........	117	11 10	8 00	6 45	3 40	– –
St. Anselme...........	122	11 20	8 12	7 00	4 30	*a* –
St. Henry Village......	129	11 32	8 25	7 15	4 50	– –
St. Henry Junction.....	132	11 40	8 35	7 45	5 20	– –
Harlaka Junction[2]....	138	11 48	8 45	8 01	5 36	12 57
Levis‖.............arr.	143	12 00	8 58	8 20	5 50	1 10
Quebec[3].............	....	12 15	9 00	8 30	6 00	1 15
[ARRIVE	....	Noon	P M	A M	P M	P M

J. H. WALSH, Gen. Manager.
A. STEELE, Superintendent.
E. O. GRUNDY, G. F. and P. A.
A. H. ANDERSON, Cashier and Purchasing Agent.
T. J. MAGUIRE, Accountant.
F. S. STOCKING, City Pas. & Tkt. Agt., Quebec.
P. R. NEILL, Trav. Pas. Agt., Room 30, North Station, Boston, Mass.

General Offices—Sherbrooke, P.Q.

Restaurants at Dudswell Junction and Levis, where ample time is allowed for meals.

† Daily, except Sunday; ¶ daily, except Monday; ‡ daily, except Saturday; *a* stops to take passengers without baggage for Levis. ▲Train discontinued after Sept. 30. ‖ Meals.

Stop-over Checks obtained on through tickets by application to conductor.

Southbound.

Train No. 18—Pullman Buffet Car Quebec to New York daily, except Saturday. Will be discontinued after Sept. 30th.

Train No. 16—Pullman Car Quebec to Boston daily, except Sunday. On Sunday the Boston Pullman will go on No. 18.

Train No. 2—Through Pullman Drawing-room Buffet Car from Quebec to Portland, connecting with Pullman Drawing-room Car for Boston, via Dudswell Junction and Maine Central R.R.

Northbound.

Train No. 17—Pullman Buffet Car New York to Quebec. Will be discontinued Sept. 29th.

Train No. 15—Pullman Car Boston to Quebec daily, except Sunday. On Sunday the Boston Pullman will go on No. 17.

Train No. 1—Through Pullman Drawing-room Buffet Car from Portland to Quebec, via Maine Central R.R. and Dudswell Junction, except Sunday.

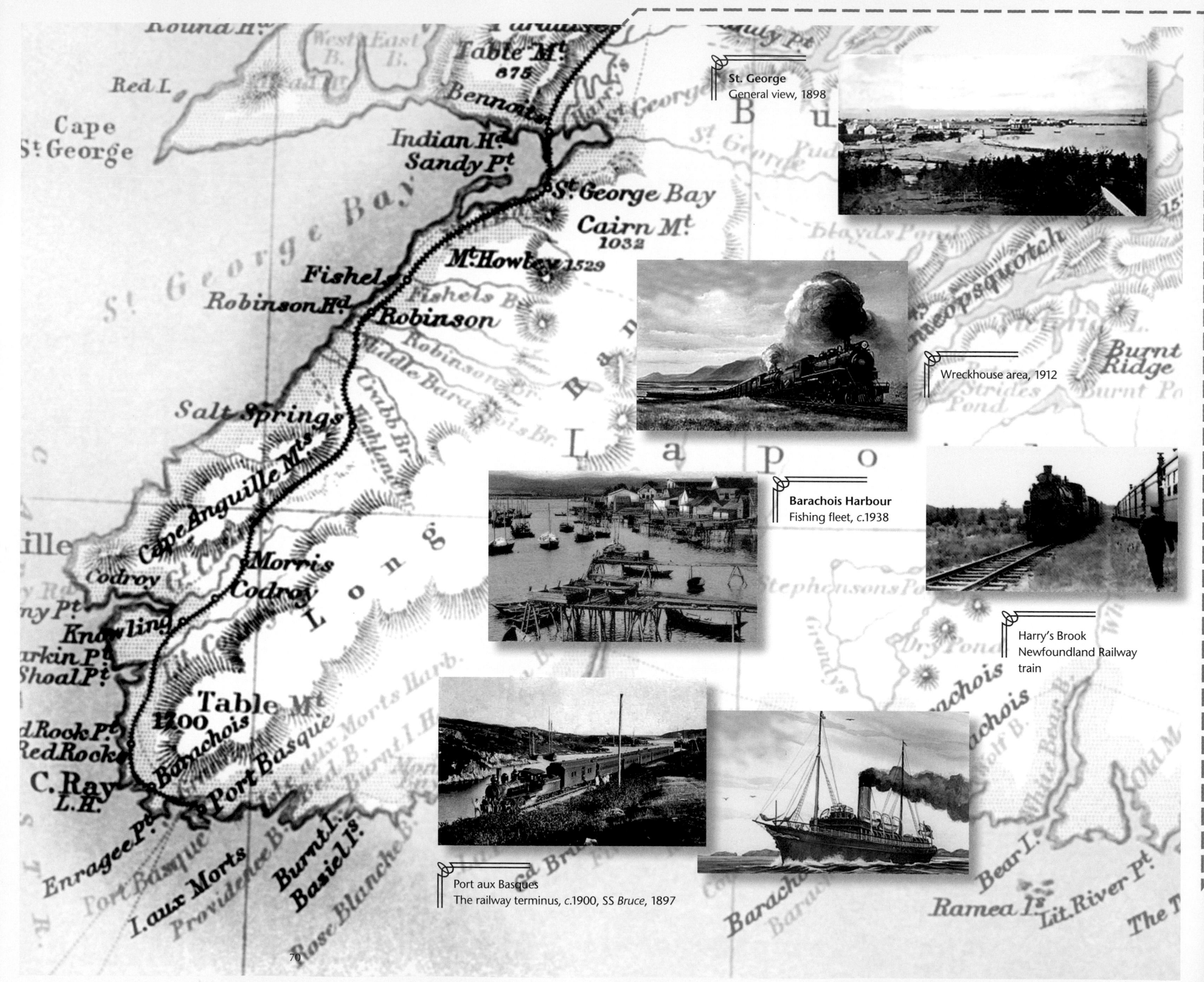

St. George
General view, 1898

Wreckhouse area, 1912

Barachois Harbour
Fishing fleet, *c.*1938

Harry's Brook
Newfoundland Railway train

Port aux Basques
The railway terminus, *c.*1900, SS *Bruce*, 1897

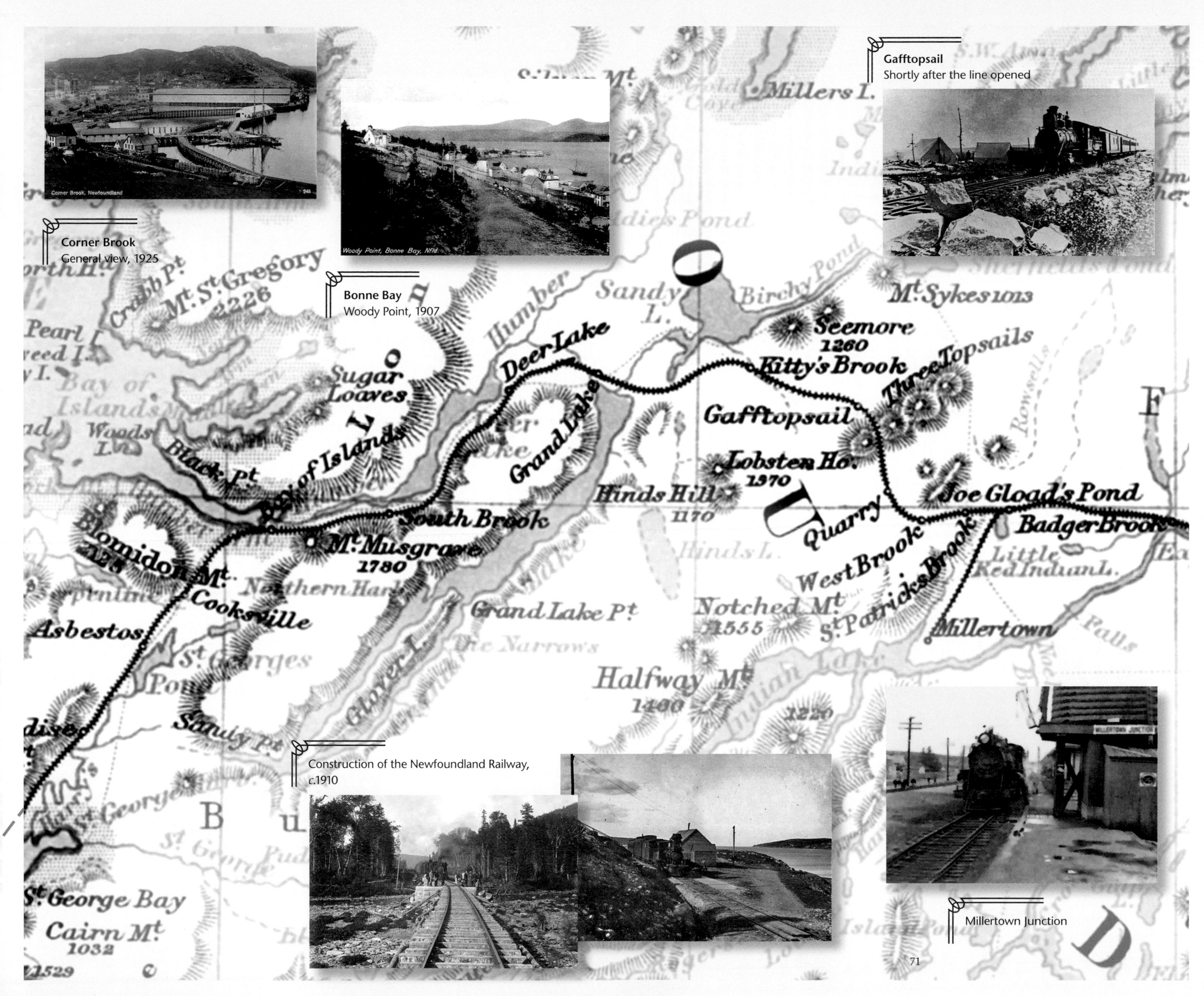

Corner Brook
General view, 1925

Bonne Bay
Woody Point, 1907

Gafftopsail
Shortly after the line opened

Construction of the Newfoundland Railway, *c.*1910

Millertown Junction

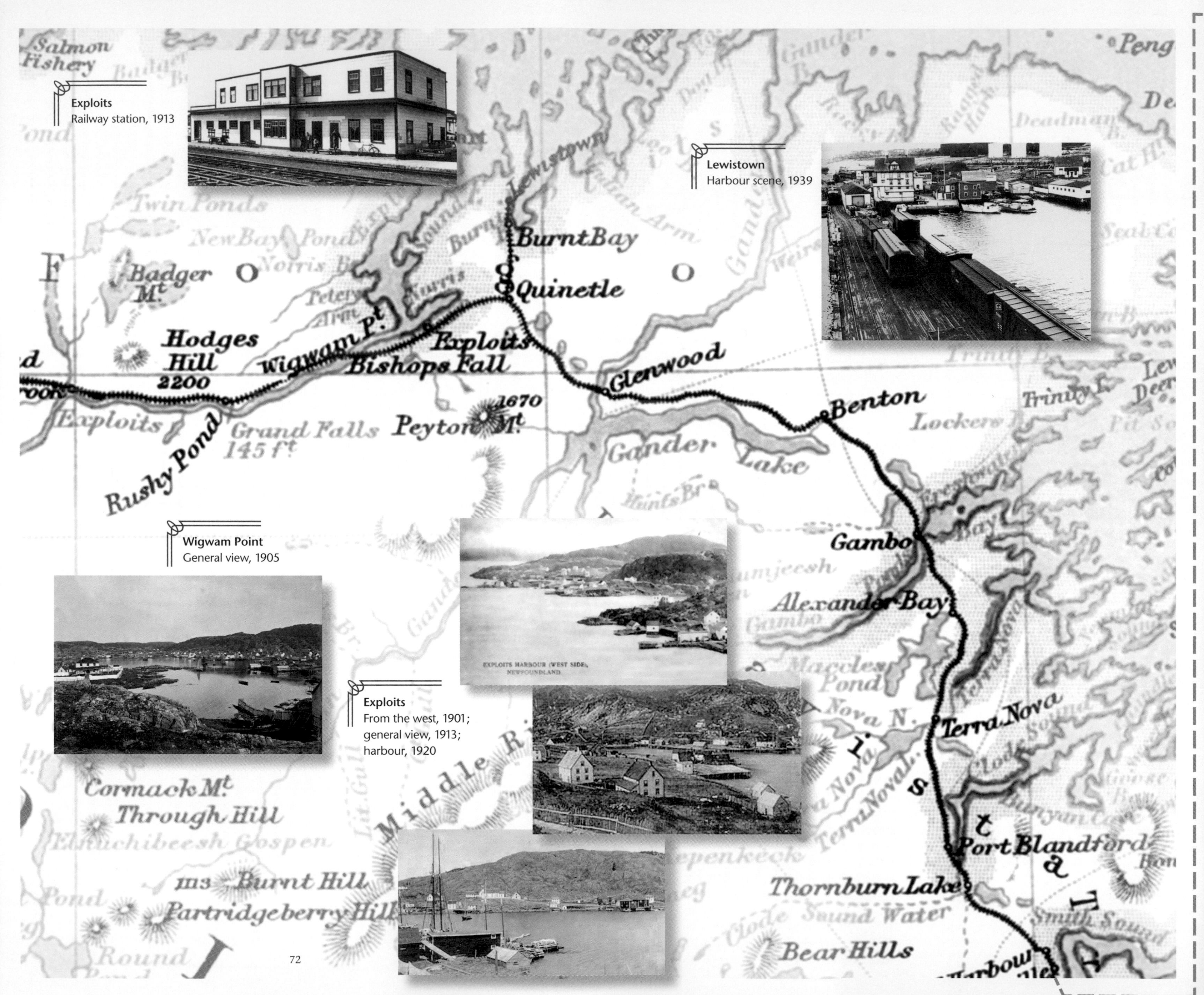

Exploits
Railway station, 1913

Lewistown
Harbour scene, 1939

Wigwam Point
General view, 1905

Exploits
From the west, 1901; general view, 1913; harbour, 1920

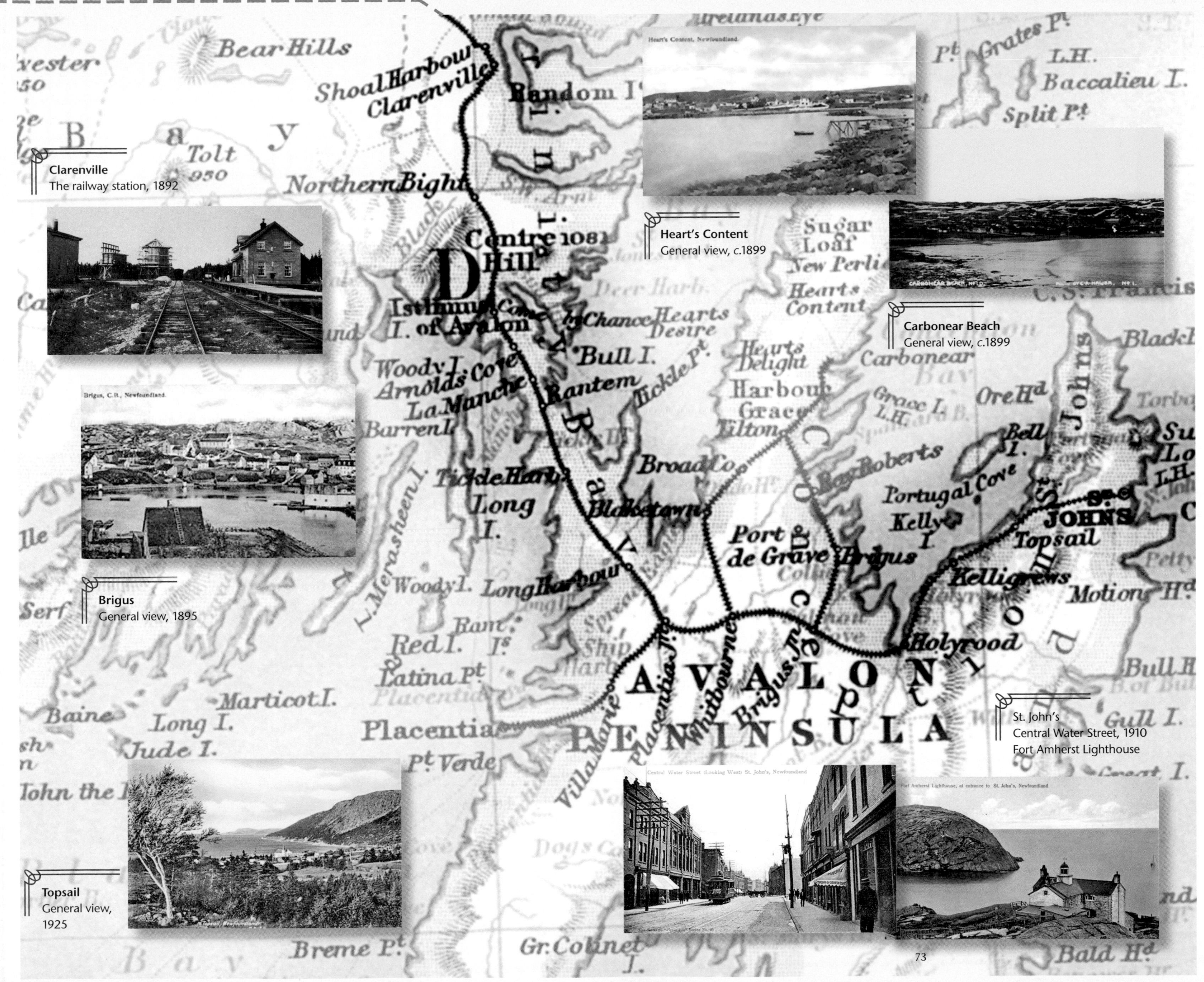

Clarenville
The railway station, 1892

Heart's Content
General view, *c.*1899

Carbonear Beach
General view, *c.*1899

Brigus
General view, 1895

Topsail
General view, 1925

St. John's
Central Water Street, 1910
Fort Amherst Lighthouse

THE ENTRANCE TO THE MOUNTAINS,
NEAR BANFF, ALBERTA.

THE CANADIAN PACIFIC RAILWAY

THE FIRST CANADIAN TRANSNATIONAL

Most Canadians think of their country as a unified whole. As recently as 150 years ago, however, this was not the case at all. Canada was divided as a nation and was also in danger of being assimilated by the United States. Before the construction of the transnational railway, Canada was separated into two distinctly different geographical and cultural areas, with vast swaths of prairie between them. To the East lay the industrially developed and well-populated provinces of Nova Scotia, New Brunswick, Québec and Ontario. Together, these four provinces formed the Federal Dominion of Canada. Even among these, there were divisions–the Maritime colonies were closer to Maine and Massachusetts than they were to Québec or Toronto, and had stronger trade relations with New England than with the rest of Canada. In fact, the people of the individual colonies had little communication with each other, and little in common aside from their status as British subjects.

To the West lay the rugged mountains and temperate coastline of British Columbia. Despite the physical barriers posed by the Rocky Mountains, the growing fur trade, several gold rushes, and the promises inherent in British Columbia's deep harbours and natural resources brought development to the coast. The government of the eastern provinces saw their future in a partnership with British Columbia, but as a condition of joining the Confederation of Canada the government of British Columbia insisted upon a Confederation-sponsored transportation link. Although the original proposal from British Columbia was only for a wagon road, the Conservative government of Prime Minister John A. Macdonald (1815–91) decided to "go the whole hog" and build a railway instead.

While the Canadian Pacific Railway (CPR) is primarily used for shipping freight today, for decades it was the primary form of passenger transportation across the continent, and was thus very closely associated with the development of Canada as a society and as a nation. The railway's logo, a beaver, was chosen both because it is a national symbol of Canada and because it represents hard work and persistence. A great deal of both were needed for Macdonald's ambitious venture to succeed.

Canadian railway history began back in 1836 with the opening of the Champlain and St. Lawrence Railroad. It was only after the establishment of the Canadian Pacific, however, that railroads became the economic backbone of Canada. With the possible exception of the Hudson's Bay Company, Canadian Pacific has been the most important single enterprise in shaping Canada's fate. The story of the CPR and the story of Canada as a nation are one story.

Not only did the construction of a coast-to-coast rail line in Canada meet the conditions set by the government of British Columbia, it facilitated the growth of industry in a way that a wagon road never could have done. The railway allowed the large-scale movement of raw materials from the West to the processing and distributing facilities of the East, as well as the transport of manufactured goods from the East to supply new populations in British Columbia (and the settlements dotting the track along the way), and thereby gave Canada the power to develop its industry without relying upon the United States.

When the railway construction began, many Canadians, including several of John A. Macdonald's own supporters, thought it was an unsound proposition. Here was a country of less than four million people–and less than four years old–building the longest and greatest of all railways to ever be built, and over some of

Cover of an 1893 CPR brochure (above).

"The entrance to the mountains, near Banff, Alberta," from *Rocky and Selkirk Mountains*, c.1900 (left).

The railway at Yale, BC, from *Picturesque Canada*, 1882 (above).

A three-headed monster with the faces of (left to right) Richard Angus, George Stephen, and Duncan McIntyre; cartoon by J.W. Bengough, editor of *Grip* (top right).

John A. Macdonald during his first term as Prime Minister (right).

the most difficult terrain imaginable. In order to avoid dipping its grade down below the national border into the United States, the Canadian government granted huge tracts of land to the railway across the Prairies. Macdonald originally proposed an ambitious construction schedule that would see a completed rail line by July 20, 1881, ten years from its inception. This schedule proved to be too ambitious, however, and several years were added to the timeline as construction moved ahead.

From the beginning, the railway project encountered many difficulties. Macdonald was caught with his proverbial pants down in a bribery scandal in 1873 involving the Canada Pacific Railway Company (a different company entirely from the similarly named Canada Pacific Railway, which went on to build the western sections of track). Macdonald was removed from office and replaced by Alexander Mackenzie of the Liberal party. He approved the construction of initial segments of the railway as a public project, which was poorly funded and supervised by the Department of Public Works. Under their inept auspices, the project quickly fell behind schedule—and stayed there.

In 1878, the tide turned back towards ambitious industrial growth when Macdonald returned to the office of prime minister. He soon directed that the railway should follow the path of the Thompson and Fraser rivers between Kamloops, British Columbia, and the intended terminus of the rail line in Port Moody, British Columbia. In 1879 the federal government contracted builder Andrew Onderdonk for the construction of a 128-mile (206 km) section of track between Yale, British Columbia and Savona's Ferry on Kamloops Lake. Onderdonk went on to build the track on both sides of this stretch.

THE COMPANY FORMS

In 1880, the Canadian Pacific Railway was formed by partners James J. Hill, Richard B. Angus, Duncan McIntyre, and George Stephen. Silent investors Norman Kittson and Donald A. Smith rounded out the Montréal-based conglomerate, which negotiated a deal with the Canadian

Hell's Gate, Fraser Canyon, from *Rocky and Selkirk Mountains* (left).

1883 poster published by the contractors Langdon, Shepard and Co. (below).

MEN WANTED!

A number of Men will be wanted by the undersigned during the grading season this year on west end of CANADIAN PACIFIC RAILWAY. Wages will be

$1.50 PER DAY,
BOARD $4.50 PER WEEK,

During the Summer Months for good, able-bodied, steady men.

Apply on the work at end of track, now near Cypress Hills, about 600 miles west of Winnipeg.

LANGDON, SHEPARD & CO.,
CONTRACTORS

END OF TRACK,
April 20th 1883

government to build the remaining section of railway. For the combined price of 25 million dollars and a land grant of 25 million acres, the Canadian Pacific Railway agreed to finish the plan originally set out nearly ten years before by John A. Macdonald. With a revised completion date of 1891, the CPR set to its task.

The CPR began growing west from its first spike at Bonfield, Ontario, where the Canada Central Railway extension ended. This line was owned by Duncan McIntyre, who amalgamated his railway with the CPR and joined the officers of the CPR. The CPR expansion was supervised by McIntyre and his contractor, James Worthington, although William Cornelius Van Horne (1843–1915) took over western construction in 1882, pledging to build 497 miles (800 km) of main line that year. Despite floods that delayed the start of construction, Van Horne completed the Thunder Bay branch west from Fort William in June of 1882. By the end of 1883 the railway had reached the Rockies, just 5 miles (8 km) east of Horse Pass. During the construction seasons of 1884 and 1885, crews worked on both the mountains in British Columbia and the north shore of Lake Superior.

Originally, the railway planners intended to take the CPR through the fertile North Saskatchewan River valley and across the Rockies through Yellowhead Pass. In order to compete with US rail, however, it was deemed favourable to run the line as close to the national border as possible.

Locomotive No. 217 on a bridge over the Sturgeon River west of Callander (below). This train was a Canada Central locomotive (No. 17) before it was taken over by CPR.

Soldiers being transported in CPR passenger cars (above).

Big Bear, the Cree leader who tried to defend First Nations' lands against encroachment by the railway, pictured in the centre of a photograph taken at Fort Pitt (above right).

As the CPR neared its goal, funding for construction ran low, so the Railway Relief Bill, which lent 22.5 million dollars to the CPR, was passed on January 31, 1884. This measure was unpopular among the Canadian public, which was skeptical about the solvency of the railway. The second North West Rebellion, however, did much to change that. The Métis, a group of French-speaking people descended from First Nations and French Canadian settlers, rose up against the Dominion of Canada in Saskatchewan. CPR trains quickly transported troops to the region, quashing the uprising and winning the appreciation and support of Canadians across the country. In the wake of the rebellion, the government loaned the CPR an additional five million dollars, allowing construction to reach completion.

Craigellachie: The Last Spike

The CPR finished its controversial, expensive, and ultimately successful project on November 7, 1885, when Donald Smith drove in the "Last Spike" at Craigellachie, British Columbia. The railway proved to be so lucrative that it paid off its government debts years ahead of schedule. It was the longest railway in the world at that time and had used one of the largest workforces of the day—five thousand horses, twelve thousand men, and three hundred dog sled teams. The first transcontinental passenger train departed from Montréal on June 28, 1886. The collection of two first-class coach cars, two "regular" sleeper cars, two emigrant sleeper cars (early railways nearly always used the term "emigrant" for immigrant), one second-class coach car, a dining car, a mail car, and two baggage cars rolled into Port Moody, British Columbia six days later on July 4. By the time this historic train reached the end of the line, however, the terminus had already been extended to the deep harbour port of "Gastown," which later became the city of Vancouver. Trains began running to the new terminus in 1887.

Mural at the entrance to The Last Spike Memorial at Craigellachie (right).

As construction wended its way through the Rockies, the CPR was also extending its reach to the East. Four days before the last spike was driven in at Craigellachie, the last spike of the Lake Superior section was driven in just west of Jackfish, Ontario. In the early 1880s the company launched a fleet of cargo ships on the Great Lakes. In 1884 the CPR acquired the Ontario and Québec Railway, and in 1888 opened a branch line connecting Sudbury, Ontario to Sault Ste. Marie, where the CPR linked to US railways and through them to CPR steamships. At the same time, construction began on a railway line from London, Ontario to the American border at Windsor; the line opened on June 12, 1890.

In 1890, CPR acquired a 990-year lease for the New Brunswick Railway, connecting the port of Saint John to points West. At the same time, the company built the International Railway of Maine between Saint John and Montréal. This linked the transnational rail system to a port that operated year-round. In 1895 the CPR bought the Toronto, Hamilton and Buffalo Railway, a link that gave the CPR the ability to ship goods from all over Canada for export to New York and, through New York, to the rest of the United States.

The CPR's greatest competitor was not a Canadian railway, but the Great Northern Railway in the United States. While the CPR ran its line as far south as practicable (or possible, at any rate), the GNR ran its line as far north as it could. Both to compete with the GNR and to access coal deposits in the Elk River valley, the CPR decided to build a second line in 1897 across southern British Columbia through Crowsnest Pass. The Crowsnest Pass line was financed by 3.6 million dollars of government aid as part of a deal that guaranteed a reduction in freight rates for grain products and other key commodities—an agreement which stayed in effect until 1983. After speedy construction, the line opened in 1899 between Lethbridge, Alberta and Nelson, British Columbia, with construction continuing through the early part of the twentieth century. In 1908, CPR opened a line connecting Sudbury to Toronto, creating a more direct route than had previously existed.

In the late nineteenth century the Canadian economy grew slowly but steadily, and throughout this time CPR trains continued to bring immigrant farmers to the West. Here farmers grew wheat on the land they had purchased from the CPR, which the railway then shipped to industrial mills in Ontario and Québec. CPR steamers then shipped the processed flour and other grain products across the Great Lakes and the Atlantic Ocean to international markets. In this way, Canada built a strong, commodities-based economy that stands in good stead even today.

The CPR took a comprehensive approach to attracting business to the railway. Not only did the company aggressively develop commodities trading and other industrial interests, it also had a huge part in developing tourism in Canada. Its measures ranged from offering attractive packages to European tourists, to building and running its own hotels, many of which went on to become famous Canadian landmarks. These buildings included Banff Springs Hotel, Chateau Lake Louise, the Chateau Frontenac in Québec City, the Royal York Hotel in Toronto, and the Hotel Vancouver. Incidentally, the company

Glacier Hotel and the Great Asulkan Glacier, from *Rocky and Selkirk Mountains* (above).

A CPR poster by Fred Gardner, *c.*1929 (below).

CANADIAN PACIFIC
INSIST ON TRAVELLING BY C.P.R.
FOR PARTICULARS AS TO RATES, SAILINGS & APPLY

Cover of a CP "Pacific Coast Tours" brochure from the early 1920s (above).

"*Trans-Canada Limited,*" a CP brochure cover, *c.*1917 (above right).

contributed towards the development of poster art, as it hired artists to travel the line and paint the natural wonders they saw for advertisements and promotional posters.

Beginning in 1882, the CPR also ran a telegraph and telephone service as a side-business, consolidating construction by building and maintaining pole lines along the tracks. This arm of the business lasted well into the 1930s, when the CPR's Communications Department provided stock market ticker quotations and a news wire.

FROM TRAINS TO SHIPS

As the twentieth century progressed, the CPR became an industry leader in water transportation, buying and operating steamship and ferry services throughout British Columbia. Canadian Pacific Ocean Services provided sea transport all the way from Britain via Canada to Hong Kong, with hotels en route. Inland, CPR operated rail ferries and freight barges in several locations across Canada, especially in British Columbia and across the Great Lakes. In 1901, the company acquired the Canadian Pacific Navigation Company with a fleet of ships serving seventy-two ports along the coast of mainland British Columbia and Vancouver Island.

The company also built its own steam locomotives, expanding business to sell locomotives to other railways. A separate department of the railway operated the sleeping, dining, and parlour cars. Unlike most American railways, the CPR manufactured its own luxury cars in order to maximize both customer experience and profit. This department also ran the news service, which sold drinks, snacks, and other amenities such as playing cards aboard the trains. This was a source of food for those passengers who could not afford the highly-priced dining cars. The news service also operated lunch counters in many train stations and even some dining rooms in larger stations.

A CP poster by Barrilal, *c.*1930 (right).

Other streams of revenue developed by the CPR included the Dominion Express Company, which specialized in very quick and fairly inexpensive transport of time-sensitive goods such as dairy products, seafood, flowers, and livestock. The express service was also used for transporting money and valuables. At many locations, express trains were serviced at a separate freight house facility next to the CPR station. Not only did the CPR have a monopoly on grain transportation, the company also specialized in "silk trains" by shipping cocoons from the Orient to

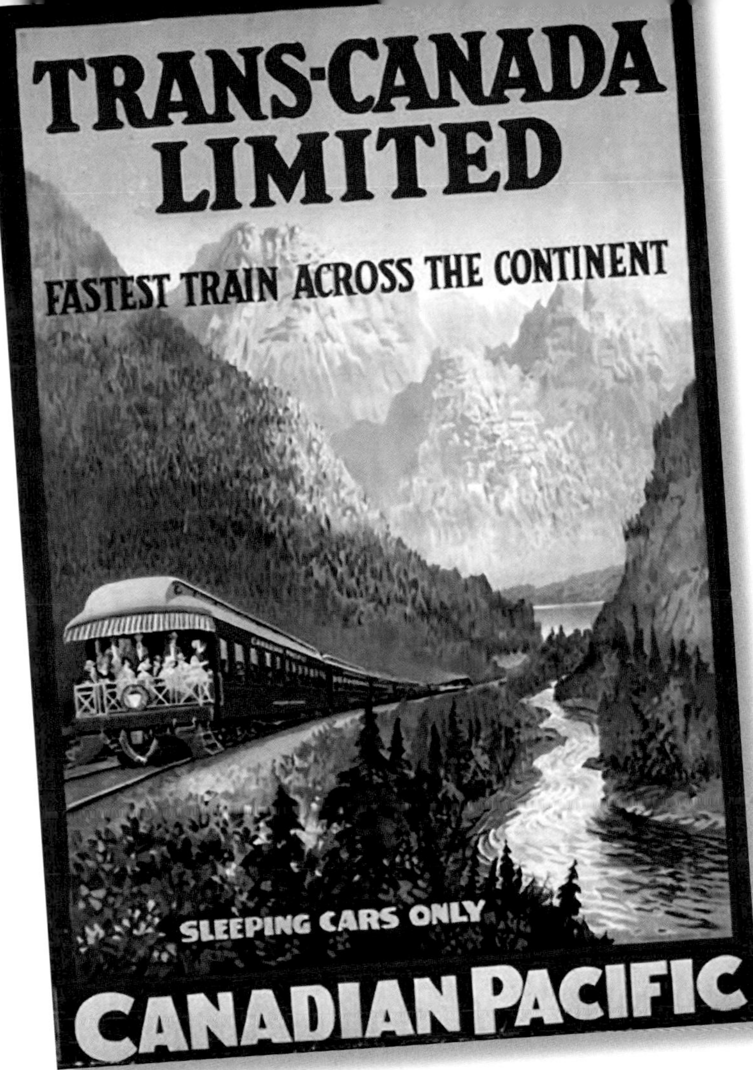

Vancouver by sea, then transporting them by train to manufacturers in New Jersey and New York. Each silk train carried several million dollars worth of silk. These trains travelled with their own armed guards and took priority over all other trains on the tracks—even the Royal Train of 1939, which took British monarchs King George VI and Queen Elizabeth on a rail tour of Canada.

The CPR continued to acquire smaller railways in the early twentieth century. On January 3, 1912 the company signed a long-term lease for the Dominion Atlantic Railway through western Nova Scotia, thus creating a link to the Atlantic port in Halifax—although the CPR still needed to use the CNR to link railcars from this line to their main tracks. The DAR also operated ferry services for passengers and cargo across the Bay of Fundy from Digby, Nova Scotia to the CPR terminal at Saint John, New Brunswick. DAR steamships provided transport for passengers and cargo from Yarmouth, Nova Scotia to ports in Boston and New York. On December 14, 1912, CPR acquired the Quebec Central Railway. Also in 1912 it purchased the Esquimalt and Nanaimo Railway on Vancouver Island, connecting to the mainland railway by railcar ferry.

The importance of the CPR as a shipping link increased in 1914, when the opening of the Panama Canal created a continuously flowing cycle of trade through the Americas. Around this time, the CPR extended its influence by purchasing additional lines in Canada and the United States and by improving the main line, with innovations such as the spiral tunnels at Kicking Horse Pass, the Connaught Tunnel, and the Lethbridge viaduct.

During World War I, the CPR managed to stay in the black, while all its competitors struggled, by using its power and resources to support the war effort. The company's trains transported troops and resources across the country, it sent ships to war, and it produced tanks in the locomotive-constructing facilities. After the war, the Canadian government merged several bankrupt railways into Canadian National Railways—which then became the main competitor for CPR business, albeit a minor one.

"*Trans-Canada Limited,*" a famous CP brochure cover from 1915 (left).

Building the Lethbridge Viaduct, completed in 1909. This CPR bridge is the longest and highest trestle bridge in the world, reaching 5,328 feet (1.6km) in length and 314 feet (96 metres) in height (above).

THE PRAIRIE LINE

The Granary of the World

SAMPLE
No. 1 HARD WHEAT
(RED FYFE),
FROM THE
CANADIAN NORTH-WEST,
ALONG THE LINE OF THE
CANADIAN PACIFIC RAILWAY,
On Land extending from 400 to 800 miles
West of Winnipeg, Manitoba.

The Canadian Pacific Railway raced across the Prairies, laying 418 miles (673 km) of main line track in 1882 and building all the way to the Alberta–British Columbia border by the end of 1883. One of the major obstacles to construction across the Prairies was conflict with the natives of the area. CPR rails crossed through First Nations' territory in Manitoba without trouble, but once they began building tracks on the plains, expeditions of warriors, often mounted and in warpaint, began to challenge the construction. (It is important to note that the CPR was in fact breaking already-signed government treaties with the tribes by building on this land.)

Famous among these protestors was the Cree chief Piapot, who often boasted that he would halt the construction of the CPR—and nearly succeeded in doing so. He and his warriors employed a number of creative tactics: they pulled out survey pegs, took and hid rails, and pitched camps across the route of the railbed. Ultimately, an anticlimactic standoff between the North-West Mounted Police and the warriors ended in an uneasy success for the CPR. As tracks were laid on Blackfeet land, Blackfeet warriors also tore up rails. With the help of their cautious chief Crowfoot, agreement to continue construction was reached. Crowfoot received a lifetime train pass in exchange for his cooperation.

The arid land of the Prairies that the tracks traversed needed settlers in order to be financially productive for the railway. To achieve this end, the Canadian government instituted the North-West Mounted Police (anticipating a need to keep law and order in the region) and sponsored the Dominion Lands Act of 1872. The Lands Act encouraged immigrants to settle in the Prairie provinces of Alberta, Saskatchewan and Manitoba, especially in the dry, treeless area known as Palliser's Triangle that spans southern Alberta and Saskatchewan. This area was originally considered an agricultural wasteland. In the late 1860s, however, government official John Macoun mounted an argument that wheat could be grown successfully in the region, and advertised it as agricultural land to immigrant farmers. Palliser's Triangle was also attractive to ranchers, as the grassy land supported grazing. By 1912, however, much of the land was overgrazed.

Under the Lands Act, homesteaders were allowed to purchase 160 acres (65 hectares) of farmland for only ten dollars. For an additional ten dollars, farmers could double their land holdings to 320 acres (130 hectares). Given the quality of the soil and scarcity of rainfall, this double amount was often necessary in order for a farmer to turn a profit. The development of specifically Canadian varieties of wheat, such as Red Fife, eventually allowed agriculture to take hold in this enormous and previously unfarmed area.

Three million acres of the CPR's original 25-million-acre land grant in southern Alberta were particularly dry during a critical part of the grain-growing season. Determined to make profit from all of its land, CPR built 1,330 miles (2,140 km) of irrigation canals, a two-mile-long (3.2 km) concrete aqueduct at Brooks, and a huge dam at Bassano, Alberta. After this infrastructure was laid in place, the company set up twenty-four separate colonies with a total of sixty-two ready-made farms, including barns, houses, sheds, fences, and pre-ploughed fields to create turnkey operations for new settlers. For those

CPR line construction in central Manitoba, showing the large team of workers involved in lifting the wood off the train platform and measuring out its exact positioning on the ground.

who wished to farm but could not afford to buy, the CPR loaned money, and in bad crop years, the company deferred farm payments. Despite an initial shortfall of $14 million, the CPR's extensive measures to settle the Prairies provided a long-term, stable population of producers and consumers who ultimately supported the success of the railway.

The CPR drew upon a couple of large populations for settlement of the Prairies. First, the company constructed an attractive immigration package for Europeans. A typical package included passage from Europe to Halifax on a CP steamer, a railway trip from Halifax to the Prairies, and acreage for farming wheat at the destination. The newly arrived farmers grew grain on the land they received from CPR, then sent it east for processing on CPR trains. Secondly, the CPR enticed Canadians from the East. The advantages of Prairie life were plastered on posters across Ontario and Québec—even on the sides of the trains themselves, as bilingual advertisements enticed Canadians to push west. At the time, many Canadians were leaving the farms of eastern Canada for industrialized New England in the United States, so the CPR's initiatives helped to keep them in Canada. In fact, the CPR worked to reverse the trend of attrition by bringing settlers north from the United States. In the first few decades of settling the Prairies, the company also ran harvester excursion trains with special, low-rate fares to bring seasonal workers to Alberta and Saskatchewan to harvest what their advertising materials called "the granary of the world."

Thanks in large part to the CPR, Canada's population grew by one-third in the first decade of the twentieth century, from 5.3 million in 1901 to 7.2 million in 1911. Nearly a million people settled on the Prairies in this time frame, tripling the population of the area. Saskatchewan wheat yields grew eleven-fold, from a half million acres to 5.5 million acres. The CPR pushed agriculture in the area to branch beyond wheat by setting up experimental farms, encouraging livestock farming, and building a sugar beet factory. Palliser's Triangle produced high yields for several decades, but between dry conditions and inadequate agricultural practices, the area turned into a dust bowl in the 1930s, contributing to Canada's Great Depression.

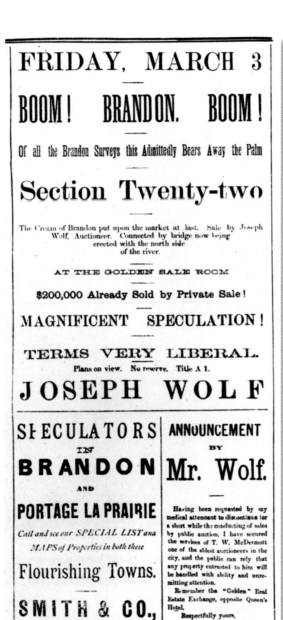

FRIDAY, MARCH 3

BOOM! BRANDON. BOOM!

Of all the Brandon Surveys this Admittedly Bears Away the Palm

Section Twenty-two

The Cream of Brandon put upon the market at last. Sale by Joseph Wolf, Auctioneer. Connected by bridge now being erected with the north side of the river.

AT THE GOLDEN SALE ROOM

$200,000 Already Sold by Private Sale!

MAGNIFICENT SPECULATION!

TERMS VERY LIBERAL.

Plans on view. No reserve. Title A 1.

JOSEPH WOLF

SPECULATORS IN BRANDON AND PORTAGE LA PRAIRIE

Call and see our SPECIAL LIST and MAPS of Properties in both these

Flourishing Towns.

SMITH & CO.,

Real Estate Agents and Conveyancers,

ANNOUNCEMENT BY Mr. Wolf.

Having been requested by my medical attendant to discontinue for a short while the conducting of sales by public auction, I have secured the services of T. W. McDermott one of the ablest auctioneers in the city, and the public can rely that any property entrusted to him will be handled with ability and unremitting attention.

Remember the "Golden" Real Estate Exchange, opposite Queen's Hotel.

Respectfully yours,

JOSEPH WOLF.

Prairie land boom advertisements from Winnipeg newspapers in 1881 and 1882.

REGINA

A Town Built by the Railway

The capital of the Province of Saskatchewan, Regina lies 360 miles (580 km) west of Winnipeg and 460 miles (740 km) east of Calgary. Regina falls within the Assiniboine region, a patchwork of treeless plains that comprise archetypal prairie. Before colonization, buffalo hunters frequented a camping site next to the small creek which flows through modern-day Regina; the site was called Wascana in Cree, meaning "pile of bones," after the buffalo bones that accumulated there. Before railway construction it was just a small trading post, then, when the CPR reached Wascana in 1882, the settlement became the capital of the Northwest Territories. Its name was changed to Regina in honour of Queen Victoria, i.e. Victoria Regina. The following year, Regina was selected to be the headquarters of the newly formed North-West Mounted Police.

The Regina area had its challenges, not least of which was the weather. Winter temperatures of around -40 degrees Celsius are not unusual; then, when the prairie thaws in the spring, it turns into a vast sea of mud. On the other end of the scale, summers can see humid days with temperatures of 40 degrees or more. Wascana Creek, the only defining feature of the landscape, was a small spring run-off. Making the most of what they had, early planners dammed the creek and created a watering hole, which the CPR used to water the stock it transported on livestock trains. The lake also originally provided water for the new legislative building nearby, although within a few years it was converted to recreational uses, such as canoeing and sailing. Wascana Lake stands in the middle of a green park of over a thousand acres, making it a perfect oasis for the day visitor.

Regina City Hall, 1908 (centre).

Regina in the early 1890s. Nicholas Flood Darwin started his newspaper business, The Leader Company, in 1883 (below).

Lake water was used to cool nearby power plant machinery in the nineteenth century. The warmed water that was returned to the lake had the effect of creating a year-round ice-free zone. As a result, many species of migratory birds began to stay on the lake throughout the winter. Today, that part of the lake is a waterfowl sanctuary.

The area was nearly perfectly flat, allowing for a well-planned and essentially square-shaped town. Regina grew rapidly, reaching a population of 30,000 by 1911, just 30 years after its inception as a trade and administrative centre. The railway in Regina allowed colonists to travel to Saskatoon, 149 miles (240 km) to the northwest. Regina also became the hub for smaller settlements in the area, including Moose Jaw, Weyburn, Yorkton, Melville, and Estevan. The original railway junction is still the hub of Regina today. In 1912 a cyclone (another liability of the Prairies) destroyed much of Regina; thanks in part to the CPR, however, the town was quickly rebuilt.

Over time, Regina became a vital trading centre. Buffalo bones and hides were shipped to the East while manufactured goods were shipped West. A branch line to Saskatoon built in 1890 turned Regina into a key distribution point. In 1905, the city of 6,000 residents became the capital of the newly formed province of Saskatchewan. One of the most important factors in Regina's growth was the establishment of the North-West Mounted Police, a force that focused heavily on the control of social vices. At the end of 1882, the CPR's Van Horne wrote to the NWMP Commissioner at Regina, Lieutenant-Colonel Irvine, "... without the assistance of the officers and men of the splendid force under your command it would have been impossible to have accomplished as much as we did. On no great work within my knowledge, where so many men have been employed, has such perfect order prevailed."

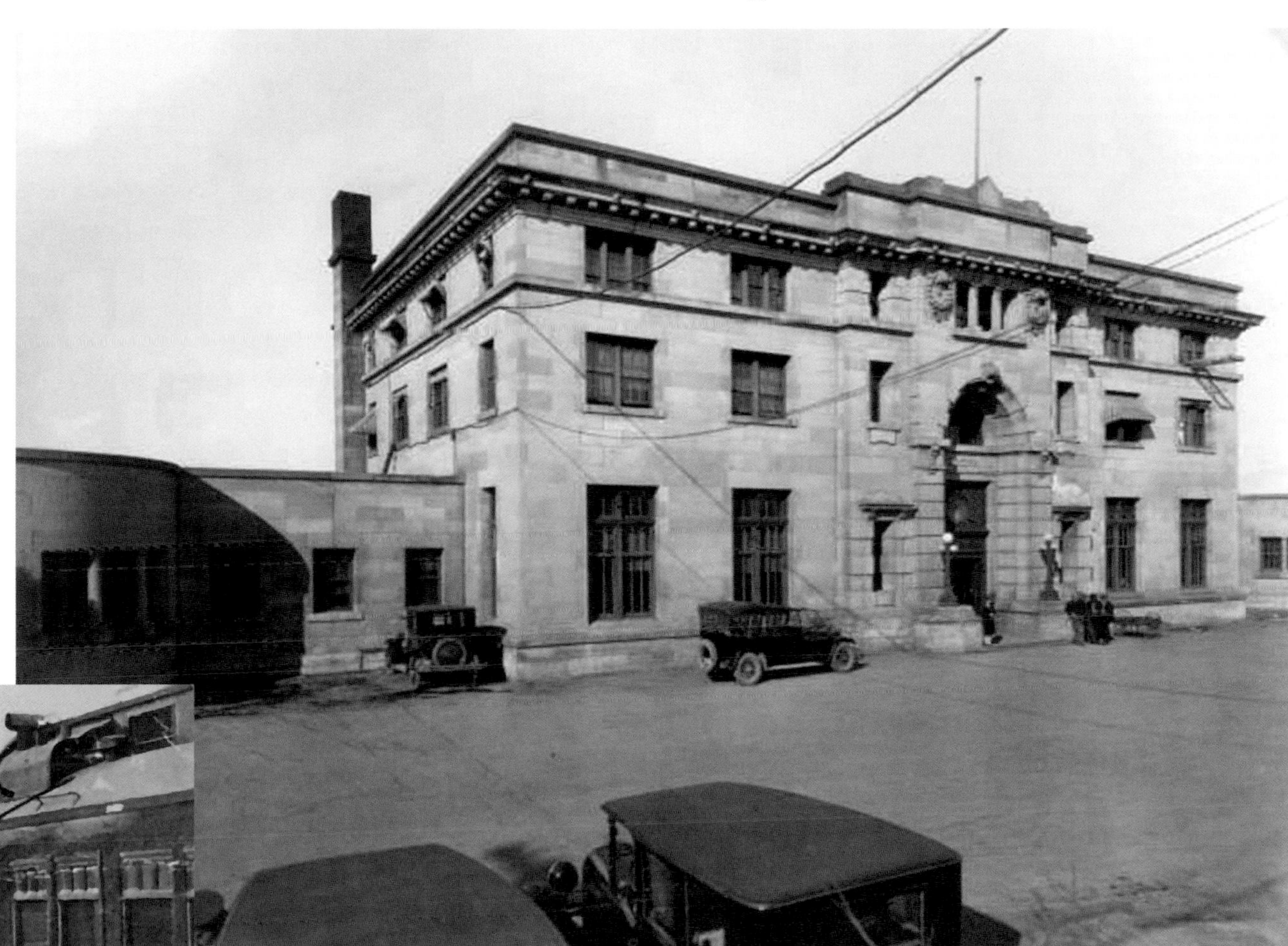

Regina Union station, 1911 (above).

Passengers at Regina Station, *c.*1903 (left).

KICKING HORSE PASS

Over the Big Hill

The CPR's western route was the most challenging known in railway history. One of the highlights of the immensely difficult terrain it traversed was the spectacular Kicking Horse Pass over Mount Stephen, nicknamed "The Big Hill." At an elevation of more than 5,000 feet (1,627 m), Kicking Horse Pass lies on the Continental Divide as well as the Alberta–British Columbia border.

Kicking Horse Pass was first explored by an expedition led by Captain John Palliser in 1858. Both the pass and the adjacent Kicking Horse River were named in honour of expedition member James Hector, a naturalist, geologist, and surgeon, who was kicked by his horse at the site of the pass. From the CPR's perspective, the route cut several hours off the Yellowhead Pass crossing to the north. Initially, blasting a tunnel through the mountain seemed impossible—it was 1,410 feet from one side to the other. So the CPR chose to build an eight-mile-long track over the mountain on a "temporary" basis. The railway line descended from the high-mountain Wapta Lake to the Kicking Horse River below, then rose to meet the original route. These temporary tracks remained in use for 25 years, until they were replaced with the spiral tunnels in 1909. In order to navigate the pass, the tracks had to make a steep crossing of the Continental Divide with a gradient of 4.5 per cent—more than double the recommended angle for trains at the time—and an impressive slope even today.

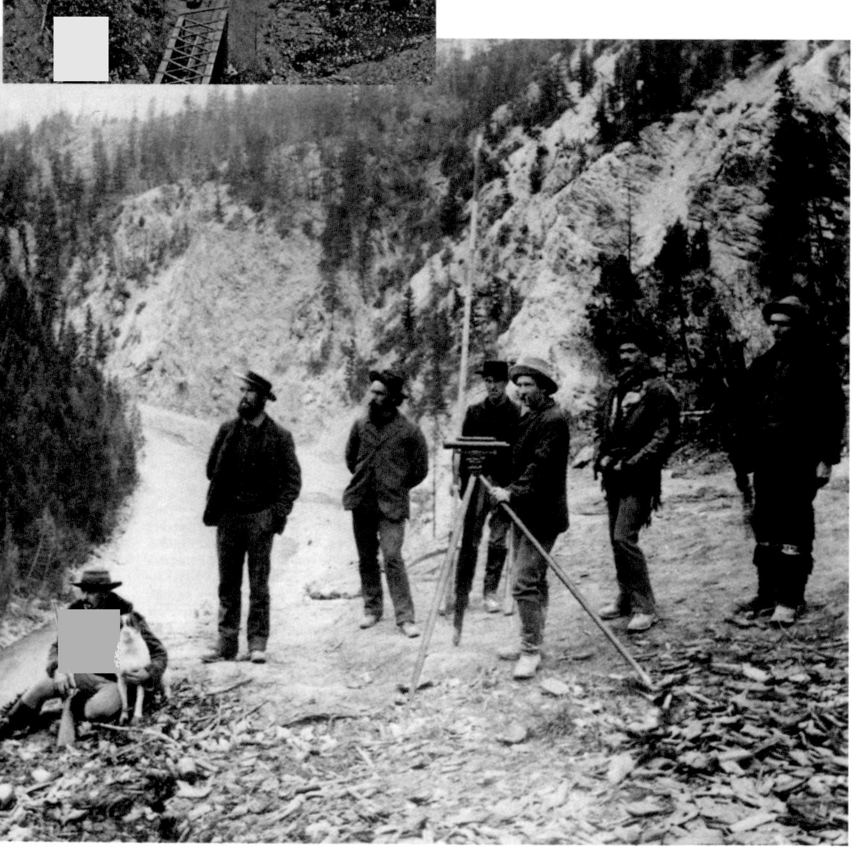

Because the route was so difficult, construction was slow. In 1882, the CPR sought to increase the rate of progress by hiring railway executive William Cornelius Van Horne to oversee the process. Despite a season of severe flooding, 417 miles (671 km) of track were laid that year. By the beginning of 1884, tracks had extended through Winnipeg to the eastern side of the Rockies, and throughout that year and the next, construction winnowed its way up into the mountains.

The many safety problems and precautions on and around Kicking Horse Pass required large crews of railway workers to be on site every time a train came through. To house both employees and additional locomotives, the CPR developed the town of Field, British Columbia—named after C.W. Field, a Chicago businessman. CPR work crews installed a series of three safety switches, each leading to a short spur with a sharp reverse upgrade. The standard policy was for each switchman to keep his switch turned to the uphill position until he was confident that the train barrelling down the mountain towards him was, in fact, in control. The strictly observed speed limits for descending trains were very low; six miles an hour for freight trains, and eight miles an hour for the lighter and easier to control passenger trains.

Since the standard steam locomotive of the time, the 4–4–0, did not have enough power to make it over Kicking Horse Pass, the CPR contracted with Baldwin Locomotive Works of Pennsylvania to build "pusher" engines, known as 2–8–0s. In 1887, however, the railway company began producing their own locomotives, going on to become a major producer of the 2–8–0 as ambition pushed technology, which in turn promoted ambition.

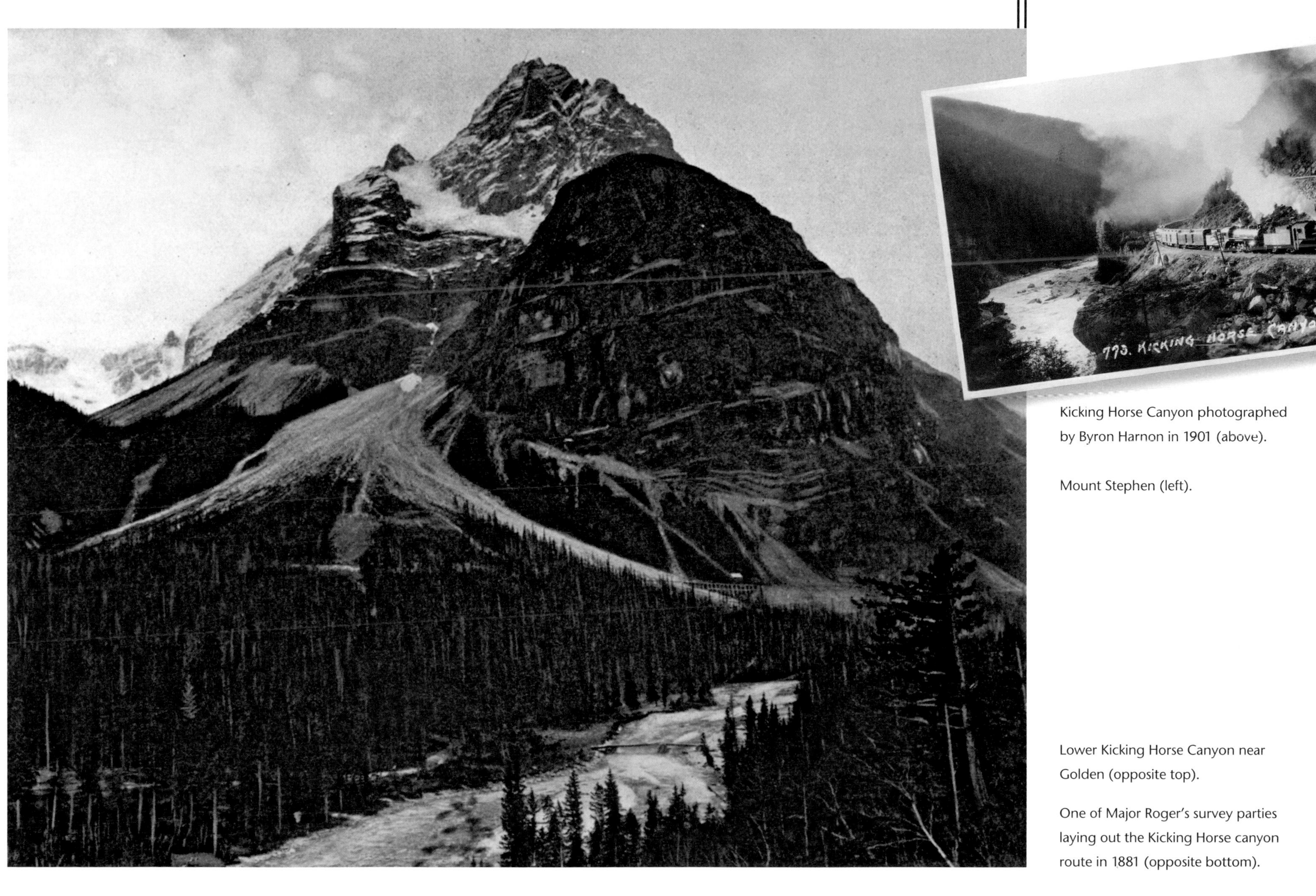

Kicking Horse Canyon photographed by Byron Harnon in 1901 (above).

Mount Stephen (left).

Lower Kicking Horse Canyon near Golden (opposite top).

One of Major Roger's survey parties laying out the Kicking Horse canyon route in 1881 (opposite bottom).

THROUGH THE SELKIRKS

The Connaught Tunnel

Today the Selkirk Mountains lie within Glacier National Park in British Columbia, but when the CPR first decided to route the railway through the Selkirks they were a largely unexplored, mysterious wilderness. Simply surveying the region was incredibly challenging work. The CPR hired a man who was up to the job—Major Albert Bowman Rogers of the United States Cavalry. Rather than accept pay for his work locating the pass, Rogers negotiated a deal with the railway that included a $5,000 bonus for his success and the honour of having the pass named after him.

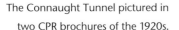

The Connaught Tunnel pictured in two CPR brochures of the 1920s.

Rogers prepared for the job by studying the reports from earlier surveyors of the Selkirks. He paid particular attention to the writings of Walter Moberly, who had looked for a pass in 1865, and whose assistant, Albert Perry, identified the area of Rogers Pass as a strong possibility for the route. Rogers' first attempt to find the pass in May of 1882 was a failure—the expedition ran out of provisions and had to turn around eighteen miles short of their intended goal. They tried again in July, identified and mapped the pass, and informed the CPR of their results. Two years later, construction began over the pass. It was completed in 1885, and Major Rogers was so proud of his accomplishment that he did not cash his payment cheque, choosing to frame it for display instead. Only when CPR president William Van Horne gave him a souvenir gold watch as a replacement did Rogers take his payment to the bank.

The line over Rogers Pass includes some of the largest railway bridges in Canada. It also includes a series of loops on the west side of the pass—a necessity for negotiating the steep incline of the mountainside, as well as for avoiding the worst of the avalanche areas. Winter snowfall in Rogers Pass averages 32 feet (10 metres) a year, and avalanches were a constant concern in colder months.

After completing construction, the CPR shut down the track for the winter to observe avalanche activity. As a result of the company's observations, the following year it built thirty-one snowsheds along a four-mile-long section of track on Rogers Pass to divert avalanche activity, but with only partial success. In 1899, an avalanche destroyed a train station at the pass, killing eight people, while in 1910 workers clearing snow off the tracks were caught in an avalanche that killed sixty-two people. It was these two tragedies that fuelled the construction of a new tunnel, the Connaught Tunnel. Built by Foley Bros. Welch and Stewart between 1913 and 1916, the Connaught Tunnel construction employed more than three hundred workers and cost 5.5 million dollars. The end result was an impressive five-mile-long (8 km) tunnel with a mild gradient of .95 per cent and a clear sightline from start to finish.

The Great Glacier of the Selkirks, from *Through Mountains and Canyons*, published by Notman & Son, Montréal, in 1902.

THE SPIRAL TUNNELS

Piercing the Mountains

Despite all the safety precautions and additional crew members, many spectacular and tragic accidents occurred on Kicking Horse Pass. Plummeting profits and bad publicity drove the CPR to seek a permanent solution; John Edward Schwitzer (1870–1911), senior engineer for the CPR, eventually found one.

At first Schwitzer considered reducing the gradient of the tracks by extending them to the south side of the river valley, which would make for a longer track and a gentler gradient. He also considered extending the route in a northwards loop across both sides of the valley, but was put off by the safety hazards posed by avalanches and landslips on the north side of the valley. Inspired by spiral tunnels in Europe, he decided in 1906 to begin construction on a similar plan for Kicking Horse Pass. To build the tunnels, the CPR hired the company MacDonnell, Gzowski and Company, which employed 1,000 men on the job at an ultimate cost of around 1.5 million dollars. The tunnels opened to traffic on September 1, 1909.

There were two distinct tunnels in the new arrangement, each of which pierced the valley wall, then curved in a three-quarters circle (270 degrees) inside the mountain. The higher of the two tunnels, Tunnel Number One, ran under Cathedral Mountain for a thousand yards to the south of the original tracks. The tracks emerged from Tunnel Number One 50 feet (15 metres) below the entrance and ran in the opposite direction. They then crossed the Kicking Horse River and pierced into the side of Mount Ogden in Tunnel Number Two. Slightly shorter than Number One, the second tunnel also descended about 50 feet (15 metres). When trains left Number Two they were facing in the original direction again. The use of the spiral tunnels doubled the length of the track over the pass, therefore reducing the gradient to the recommended 2.2 per cent. Despite the changes, the CPR still found it prudent to use the sturdy 2–8–0 engines to power trains up and over the pass.

J.E. Schwitzer also supervised the construction of the Lethbridge Viaduct. At a length of one mile (1.7 km), and rising more than 312 feet (95 metres) above the valley floor, the viaduct provided a direct route from Lethbridge to Macleod and cut 5 miles (8 km) of track off the route. The structure, supported by 33 steel towers resting on concrete pedestals, is the longest and highest railway bridge of its kind in Canada. The Lethbridge Viaduct opened for service in November 1909, three months after the Spiral Tunnels opened. The success of the Spiral Tunnels and Lethbridge Viaduct engineering projects earned Schwitzer the title of Chief Engineer of the CPR in January 1911, although unfortunately he died of complications from pneumonia three weeks after this appointment. His name is commemorated in a railway junction near Souris, Manitoba.

Two track-level photographs by Byron Harman, taken in 1900 (below).

New grade reduction showing Mount Stephen and Kicking Horse River, from *Rocky and Selkirk Mountains* (right).

A 1906 CP souvenir poster of the Spiral Tunnels.

PACIFIC RY.—Trans-Continental Route and Soo and South Shore Lines.

For Parlor, Sleeping and Dining Car Service, and Explanation of Reference Marks, see page 592.

				1	Mls	May 6, 1906.	2	96	8	78	82
		A M	A M	P M		LVE.] E. time. [ARR.	A M	P M	P M		
		*10 00	*10 00	8 30		Boston	7 30	*8 15	*8 15		
		†9 10	†9 10	9 00		Portland (M. Cent.)	8 05	†7 45	†7 45		
		A M	A M	P M		LVE.] E. time. [ARR.	A M	P M	P M		
		7 50	7 50	7 30		New York (N. Y. C.)	8 56	10 21	10 21		
		A M	A M	A M		LVE.] A. time. [ARR.	P M	P M	P M		
		†8 10	†8 10	†8 10		Halifax (I. C.)	8 45	8 45	8 45		
		P M	P M	P M		LVE.] [ARR.	A M	A M	A M		
		†5 40	†5 40	†5 40		+ St. John (C. P.)	11 20	11 20	11 20		
P M		P M	P M	P M		LVE.] E. time. [ARR.	A M	P M	P M	A M	
*11 30		*2 00	*2 00	*11 30		+ Quebec	6 30	†2 55	†2 55	6 30	
A M		P M	P M	A M		lv. + Montreal ... ar.	P M	A M	A M	P M	
†9 40		*10 15	*9 40	*9 40	0	Windsor St.	*6 30	7 00	*8 00	6 30	
P M		P M	P M	A M		LVE.] [ARR.	P M	A M	A M	P M	
†2 10		†2 10	†2 10	†7 30		+ Prescott	†5 00	†9 50	†9 50	†5 00	
P M	A M	A M	A M	P M		LVE.] [ARR.	P M	A M	A M	A M	P M
†5 00	†8 40	*1 42	*1 10	*1 15	116	+ Ottawa	*3 00	*3 30	*4 20	†11 10	†5 57
†2 40	†7 15	†6 30	†6 30	†7 15		+ Brockville	*9 30	†1 00	†1 00	†2 15	†9 30
P M	A M	A M	A M	P M		LVE.] [ARR.	P M	A M	A M	A M	P M
†5 55	†9 34	*2 30	*1 58	*2 15	144	+ Carleton Jn	2 00	2 25	3 20	10 20	5 06
6 10	9 48	2 45	– –	2 30	151	Almonte	1 42	– –	3 04	10 05	4 50
6 25	10 06	– –	– –	– –	160	Pakenham	– –	– –	– –	9 46	4 32
6 39	10 20	3 17	– –	3 02	168	Arnprior	1 11	– –	2 25	9 30	4 16
6 50	10 31	– –	– –	– –	173	Sand Point	– –	– –	– –	9 17	4 03
7 15	11 02	3 56	3 20	3 40	186	+ Renfrew	12 36	1 10	1 52	8 54	3 40
7 33	11 20	– –	– –	– –	195	Haley's	– –	– –	– –	8 37	3 18
7 48	11 32	4 25	– –	4 09	202	Cobden	12 07	– –	1 22	8 24	3 05
8 25	12 10	4 56	4 25	4 45	221	+ Pembroke	11 35	12 17	12 53	†7 50	2 30
P M	12 50	5 40	5 20	5 30	243	Chalk River	10 55	11 45	12 15	A M	†1 50
	Noon	– –	– –	5 38	248	Wylie	10 38	– –	– –		P M
		6 06	– –	– –	258	Moorlake	10 21	– –	– –		
		– –	– –	6 21	267	Mackey	10 02	– –	– –		
		– –	– –	6 29	271	Rockcliffe	9 54	– –	– –		
		– –	– –	6 48	281	Bissett	9 35	– –	– –		
		7 09	– –	7 13	294	Deux Rivieres	9 10	– –	10 34		
		7 48	7 22	7 53	315	Mattawa	8 33	9 30	10 00		
		– –	– –	8 30	334	Rutherglen	7 57	– –	– –		
		8 36	– –	8 46	341	Bonfield	7 38	– –	9 05		
		9 15	9 00	9 25	360	ar. + North Bay lv.	6 55	8 10	8 30		
			*1 30	*1 15		lv. + Detroit .. ar.	2 55	3 10			
			†5 00	†8 15		+ St. Thomas	8 20	11 55			
			P M	A M		LVE.] [ARR.	P M	A M			
		P M	P M	P M		LVE.] [ARR.	P M	A M	A M		
		*11 30	*11 30	*1 45		Toronto	2 55	7 00	*7 00		
	117	8 35	8 35	9 40		arr. North Bay lve.	*6 45	*8 50	*8 50		118
	P M	A M	A M	P M		LVE.] [ARR.	A M	P M	P M		P M
	*2 00	9 30	9 50	10 05	360	+ North Bay	6 30	7 45	8 12		10 00
	2 30	△ –	10 07	– –	370	Beaucage	– –	7 24	□ –		9 18
	3 08	△ –	10 29	10 41	384	Sturgeon Falls	5 54	6 59	□ –		8 33
	3 45	△ –	10 51	10 58	394	Verner	5 34	6 34	□ –		8 01
73	4 41	△ –	11 28	11 31	416	Markstay	4 58	5 52	□ –	74	6 38
P M	6 40	11 53	12 16	12 16	440	ar. Sudbury lv.	4 15	5 05	*5 50	A M	*4 35
†5 15	P M	11 58			440	lv. Sudbury .. ar.			5 45	11 00	P M
5 48		– –			451	Naughton			– –	10 39	
6 00		– –			458	White Fish			– –	10 26	
7 02		1 32			488	Webbwood			4 21	9 23	
7 34	9	– –			506	Walford			– –	8 44	10
7 56	A M	2 22			517	Cutler			3 25	8 23	P M
8 35	†8 00	2 54			535	Algoma			2 54	†7 45	7 20
P M	8 38	– –			552	Dean Lake			– –	A M	6 43
	9 19	4 02			573	Thessalon			1 39		6 04
	9 54	4 36			591	Desbarats			1 04		5 29
	10 21	– –			604	Ekoba			– –		5 02
	10 50	5 36			619	+ Sault (Can.)			12 16		†4 30
	11 10	5 52			622	Ste Marie (Mich.)			*11 59		†4 00
	A M	P M				(Eastern time.)			A M		P M
	10 10	4 52				(Central time.)			*10 59		†3 00
	A M	P M				(Soo Line.)			A M		P M
		5 12			622	lv. + S. Ste. M., Mich. ar.			10 30		
		9 50			773	arr. Gladstone. lve.			5 55		
		11 35			826	arr. Pembine .. lve.			4 17		
		P M				ARR.] [LVE.			A M		
		8 45			1106	St. Paul			7 20		
		9 30			1106	Minneapolis			*6 35		
		A M				ARR.] [LVE.			P M		
		P M				(D. S. S. & A. Ry.)			A M		
		10 50			787	ar. Marquette. lv.			5 00		
					812	Republic					
		A M				ARR.] [LVE.			P M		
		5 40			874	ar. Houghton. lv.			10 20		
	75	8 55			1037	Duluth			*6 20	76	
	Noon	A M				ARR.] [LVE.			P M	P M	
	†12 36		12 16	12 15	440	lve. Sudbury arr.	4 15	5 05		4 40	
	1 05		– –	– –	452	Chelmsford	– –	) –		4 10	
	1 17		– –	– –	458	Larchwood	– –	) –		3 56	
	2 05		1 45	1 35	475	arr. Cartier lve.	3 10	3 55		†3 15	
	P M		1 50	1 45	475	lve. Cartier .. arr.	3 05	3 50		P M	
			2 11	– –	486	Stralak	– –	3 24			
			2 28	– –	495	Pogamasing	– –	3 05			
			3 32	– –	529	Bisco	– –	1 52			
			4 29	– –	561	Woman River	– –	12 49			
			5 34	– –	596	Nemegos	– –	11 38			
			6 15	6 20	612	Chapleau	10 55	11 05			
			7 34	7 43	658	Dalton	9 14	– –			
			8 03	– –	672	Missanabie	8 48	– –			
			9 49	– –	724	Amyot	7 15	– –			
			10 30	10 35	744	White River	*6 40	*6 45			
			P M	A M		ARR.] [LVE.	P M	A M			

75	75	75	97	1	Mls	June 17, 1906.	2	96	72	76	76
			P M	A M		LVE.] [ARR.	P M	A M			
			*10 35	*10 45	744	White River	6 30	6 35			
			– –	11 14	760	Bremner	6 00	– –			
			– –	– –	784	Cache	– –	– –			
			– –	– –	794	Melgund	– –	– –			
			– –	12 25	800	Heron Bay	4 45	– –			
			– –	1 05	819	Coldwell	4 10	– –			
			– –	1 56	844	Jack Fish	3 20	– –			
			2 40	2 57	863	Schreiber	2 45	2 50			
			– –	3 27	877	Rossport	1 58	– –			
			4 40	5 08	926	Nipigon	12 34	12 39			
			– –	5 41	944	Wolf	12 04	– –			
			– –	6 14	959	Pearl	11 38	– –			
			6 48	7 28	992	+ Port Arthur	10 35	10 40			
			7 00	7 40	995	+ Ft. William	10 25	10 30			
						ar. Eastern time .. lv.					
						lv. Central time .. ar.					
	†7 30		*6 20	*19 00	995	Fort William	9 05	21 10		18 00	
	9 35		7 10	– –	1019	Kaministikwia	– –	20 15		16 20	
	12 00		8 17	– –	1049	Dexter	– –	19 19		14 30	
	13 10		8 50	– –	1067	Savanne	– –	18 46		13 10	
	14 00		9 13	– –	1080	Upsala	– –	18 25		12 00	
	14 20		– –	– –	1085	Carlstadt	– –	– –		11 35	
	15 50		10 04	– –	1108	English	– –	17 35		10 04	
	16 15		– –	– –	1114	Martin	– –	– –		9 40	
	17 02		10 37	– –	1126	Bonheur	– –	17 02		9 00	
	18 00		11 10	23 40	1144	ar. Ignace lv.	4 25	16 30		†8 00	
						LVE.] [ARR.					
		†7 30	11 20	23 50	1144	Ignace	4 15	16 20	18 30		
		8 10	– –	– –	1159	Raleigh	– –	– –	17 35		
		8 40	12 12	– –	1172	Tache	– –	15 27	16 45		
		12 15	13 50	– –	1224	Eagle	– –	13 50	12 15		
		13 05	14 10	– –	1234	Vermilion	– –	13 33	11 10		
		14 10	– –	– –	1248	Parry	– –	– –	10 10		
		17 10	– –	– –	1281	Margach	– –	– –	8 05		
		18 00	15 50	4 15	1289	ar. Kenora lv.	23 50	11 55	†7 30		
						LVE.] [ARR.					
†8 00			16 00	4 25	1289	Kenora	23 40	11 45			18 30
8 15			16 08	4 33	1292	Keewatin	23 32	11 36			18 15
10 05			17 08	– –	1321	Ingolf	– –	10 40			16 30
12 15			17 52	– –	1341	Rennie	– –	10 00			15 00
14 00			18 30	6 42	1361	Whitemouth	21 27	9 23			13 05
15 10			19 02	– –	1377	Molson	– –	8 54			11 5[illegible]
15 55			19 22	– –	1387	Beausejour	20 45	8 36			11 1[illegible]
16 55			19 52	7 46	1401	Selkirk	20 20	8 10			10 0[illegible]
17 55			– –	8 14	1414	Birds Hill	19 51	– –			8 5[illegible]
18 30			20 40	8 30	1422	ar. + Winnipeg lv.	19 35	7 20			†8 0[illegible]
	7	5				LVE.] [ARR.			6	8	
	†8 40	†16 50	21 40	9 15	1422	+ Winnipeg	18 45	6 45	12 15	17 35	
	u –	17 06	– –	– –	1430	Bergen	18 25	– –	11 57	u –	
	u –	17 20	– –	9 46	1437	Rosser	18 10	– –	11 42	u –	
	u –	17 46	– –	10 10	1451	Marquette	17 46	– –	11 16	u –	
	u –	17 58	– –	10 22	1457	Reaburn	17 34	– –	11 04	u –	
	u –	18 09	– –	10 33	1463	Poplar Point	17 23	– –	10 53	u –	
	10 25	18 40	23 14	11 10	1478	+ Portage la Prairie	16 52	5 05	10 25	†15 55	
		18 54	– –	11 28	1486	Burnside	16 29	– –	10 03		
		19 06	– –	11 46	1493	Bagot	16 15	– –	9 49		
		19 18	– –	12 00	1500	MacGregor	16 03	– –	9 37		
		19 31	– –	12 15	1507	Austin	15 49	– –	9 23		
		19 53	– –	12 40	1515	Sidney	15 33	– –	9 10		
		20 17	24 45	13 08	1528	Carberry	15 09	3 32	8 49		
		20 35	– –	– –	1536	Sewell	– –	– –	8 33		
		20 50	– –	13 43	1544	Douglas	14 35	– –	8 20		
		21 02	– –	13 55	1549	Chater	– –	– –	8 10		
3		21 15	1 40	14 10	1555	ar. + Brandon. lv.	14 10	2 40	†8 00		
†7 30			1 50	14 25	1555	lv. Brandon ar.	13 55	2 30			
7 50			– –	14 45	1563	Kemnay	– –	– –			
8 05			– –	15 00	1571	Alexander	13 24	– –			
8 23			– –	15 25	1580	Griswold	13 05	– –			
8 37			– –	15 37	1587	Oak Lake	12 50	– –			
9 07			– –	16 10	1603	Virden	12 18	– –			
9 38			4 03	16 52	1619	Elkhorn	11 45	24 37			
9 54			4 18	17 10	1626	Kirkella	11 30	24 23			
10 09			– –	17 25	1634	Fleming	11 13	– –			
10 24			– –	17 44	1642	Moosomin	10 57	– –			
11 00			– –	18 15	1658	Wapella	10 22	– –			
11 33			– –	18 45	1672	Whitewood	9 54	– –			
12 05			6 20	19 15		ar. .C. time.. lv.	9 25	22 35			
		3			1687	Broadview			4		
		†11 15	5 30	18 25		lv. .M. time.. ar.	8 15	21 25	12 40		
		11 30	– –	– –	1695	Oakshela	– –	– –	12 26		
		11 45	6 10	18 55	1703	Grenfell	– –	20 50	12 12		
		12 17	6 47	19 29	1718	Wolseley	– –	20 18	11 41		
		12 55	7 35	20 10	1738	Indian Head	– –	19 27	11 03		
		13 22	8 03	20 36	1748	Qu'Appelle	– –	19 03	10 45		
		14 25	9 17	21 47	1780	+ Regina	– –	17 50	9 40		
		15 02	9 55	– –	1797	Pense	– –	17 10	8 56		
		15 45	10 35	– –	1815	Pasqua	4 15	16 30	8 20		
			*9 25	*20 00	0	lv. St. Paul .. ar.	10 25	18 40			
			10 05	20 40	0	Minneapolis	9 45	18 00			
			5 20	17 20	550	+ Portal	12 30	23 30			
			10 20	22 20	711	Pasqua	4 30	16 45			
			10 35	22 35	717	ar. + Moose Jaw. lv.	*4 00	*16 15			
		16 00	11 25	*23 30	1821	lv. Moose Jaw ar.	*3 45	15 55	†8 05		
			11 57	– –	1838	Caron	– –	15 23			
			12 38	– –	1856	ar. Parkbeg .. lv.	– –	*14 51			

Varcoe Br.—Train lvs. **MacGregor** ƒ12 10, arr. at Varcoe (54.9 m.) 14 10, Rapid City (67.4 m.) 14 45. Lvs. Rapid City ƒ13 20, Varcoe ƒ13 55, arr. at MacGregor 15 55.

Continued on following page.

Teulon Br.—Train lv. **Winnipeg** †17 30, ar. Teulon (40 m.) 19 30. Lv. Teulon †6 50, ar. Winnipeg 9 00. Trains lv. Winnipeg †11 25, †17 00, ar. Stonewall 11 40, 18 15. Lv. Stonewall †8 15, †14 20, ar. Winnipeg 9 00, 15 35.

Eastern time is adopted on lines east of Fort William, Detroit and Sault Ste. Marie and west of Vanceboro, Me.

CANADIAN PACIFIC RAILWAY.

For Parlor, Sleeping and Dining Car Service and Explanation of Reference Marks, see page 592.

TRANS-CONTINENTAL ROUTE.—Continued.

3	97	1	Mls	June 17, 1906.	2	98	41
	*12 38	– –	1856	lve. Parkbeg .. arr.	– –	14 51	
	13 22	– –	1875	Chaplin	– –	14 15	
	14 50	– –	1912	Rush Lake	– –	13 00	
	15 25	– –	1926	Aikins	– –	12 28	
	15 50	*3 25	1932	Swift Current	24 20	12 15	
	17 08	– –	1967	Gull Lake	– –	10 54	
	19 00	5 59	2018	Maple Creek	21 30	9 08	
	19 44	– –	2037	Forres	– –	8 29	
	20 13	– –	2049	Walsh	– –	8 02	
	20 36	7 13	2060	Irvine	20 14	7 40	
	21 06	– –	2074	Coleridge	– –	7 05	
	21 18	7 47	2076	Dunmore Junc	– –	6 59	
	21 50	8 20	2082	Medicine Hat	19 25	6 45	
	– –	8 40	2089	Stair	18 49	– –	
	– –	8 55	2096	Bowell	18 37	– –	
	– –	9 35	2117	Langevin	17 56	– –	
	– –	10 10	2134	Tilley	17 22	– –	
	– –	10 55	2154	Cassils	16 46	– –	
	– –	11 30	2171	Lathom	16 15	– –	
	1 50	12 47	2206	Gleichen	15 10	2 37	
	– –	13 35	2227	Strathmore	14 31	– –	
	– –	14 05	2241	Langdon	14 05	– –	
	4 05	15 15	2262	+ Calgary	13 20	24 55	
	– –	16 12	2284	Cochrane	12 13	– –	
	– –	16 36	2295	Radnor	11 53	– –	
	– –	16 57	2303	Morley	11 37	– –	
	– –	17 27	2316	Kananaskis	11 15	– –	
	– –	17 45	2324	The Gap	11 00	– –	
	– –	17 58	2329	Canmore	10 50	– –	
	– –	18 28	2342	Bankhead	10 26	– –	
	7 20	18 40	2343	+ Banff	10 20	22 05	
	– –	19 15	2360	Castle Mountain	9 45	– –	
	8 45	19 55		arr. M. time .. lve.	9 15	20 55	
			2378	Laggan			
	8 00	19 05		lve. P. time .. arr.	8 00	19 40	
	8 17	19 20	2384	Stephen	– –	– –	
	8 30	19 35	2386	Hector	– –	19 10	
	9 30	20 32	2394	Field	6 35	18 10	
	10 05	– –	2409	Leanchoil	– –	16 53	
	10 26	21 24	2417	Palliser	– –	16 24	
	11 07	22 00	2429	Golden	4 32	15 32	
	11 45	– –	2446	Donald	– –	14 55	
	12 18	23 07	2458	Beavermouth	3 32	14 23	
	14 08	– –	2479	Roger's Pass	– –	13 13	
	14 55	24 57	2482	Glacier	2 22	12 55	
	15 52	– –	2497	Illecillewaet	– –	11 02	
	16 22	– –	2504	Albert Canyon	– –	10 31	
	16 49	– –	2514	Twin Butte	– –	9 57	
	17 45	3 10	2525	+ Revelstoke	23 45	9 25	
	20 01	5 11	2570	Sicamous Junc	21 36	7 10	
	20 55	5 56	2588	Salmon Arm	20 55	6 23	
	21 48	6 50	2594	Notch Hill	20 15	5 49	
	22 35	7 34	2620	Shuswap	19 30	5 06	
	23 09	8 06	2636	Ducks	18 56	4 32	
	23 55	8 55	2654	Kamloops	18 25	4 00	
	– –	10 00	2679	Savonas	17 09	– –	
	1 50	10 51	2701	Ashcroft	16 17	1 50	
	2 56	11 51	2726	Spence's Bridge	15 22	24 48	
	3 57	12 54	2748	Lytton	14 25	23 43	
	– –	13 42	2764	Keefers	13 42	– –	
	5 35	14 22	2775	North Bend	13 05	22 30	
	6 55	15 36	2802	Yale	11 45	21 08	
	– –	16 05	2815	Hope	11 15	– –	
	– –	16 22	2823	Ruby Creek	10 55	– –	
	7 58	16 42	2834	Agassiz	10 33	20 00	
	8 16	17 02	2843	Harrison Mills	10 13	19 42	
	– –	17 22	2852	Nicomen	9 55	– –	
	8 55	17 42	2862	arr. Mission Junc. lve.	9 35	19 03	
	10 05		2872	arr. .. + Sumas .... lve.		*17 53	
	11 10		2895	arr. .. Bellingham .. lve.		16 25	
	13 40		2960	arr. .. Snohomish .. lve.		14 30	
	15 25		2998	arr. ... Seattle ... lve.		12 35	
	17 45		3039	arr. ... Tacoma ... lve		10 55	
	22 55		3183	arr. .. Portland .. lve.		*23 45	
*19 03	9 10	17 40	2862	lve. .Mission Jn. .arr.	9 35	18 53	8 50
19 54	10 05	18 40	2887	ar. + Westminster Jn. lv.	8 43	17 57	7 55
20 20	10 30	19 10	2896	ar. Westminster lv.	*7 25	*17 20	*7 25
*19 25	*9 35	*17 20	2896	lve. Westminster. arr.	9 15	19 10	9 15
19 59	10 05	18 45	2887	lve. Westminster Jn. arr.	8 38	17 52	7 50
20 09	10 15	18 54	2892	arr. Port Moody lve.	8 28	17 42	7 40
20 43	10 45	19 25	2904	ar. + Vancouver . lv.	*8 00	*17 15	*7 10
	17 00		2988	ar. + Victoria, B. C. lv.	b1 00	*7 30	

VANCOUVER AND PORTLAND, ORE.

Exp.	STATIONS.	Exp.
*7 10	lve. .. + Vancouver. arr.	20 43
*7 25	lve. Westminster. arr.	20 20
8 50	arr. .. Mission Jn. .. arr.	18 43
10 05	Sumas City	17 53
15 25	Seattle	12 35
17 40	Tacoma	10 55
22 55	arr. .. Portland ... lve.	*23 45

Eganville Branch.—Trains leave Renfrew †11 07 a.m., †7 22 p.m., arrive Eganville (23 miles) 12 25 noon, 8 40 p.m. Returning, leave Eganville †7 20 a.m., †2 00 p.m., arrive Renfrew 8 33 a.m., 3 10 p.m.

Pheasant Hills Branch.—Train lvs. Kirkella ƒ11 35, arr. Strassburg (2[illegible]5 miles) 19 30. Ret'g, lvs. Strassburg ƒ7 15, arr. Kirkella 15 35.

ROSSLAND BRANCH.

64	62	Mls	May 6, 1906.	61	63
			LEAVE] [ARRIVE		
*20 50		0	... West Robson		21 00
20 55	†9 25	2	Castlegar Junction	9 15	20 55
21 26	10 10	12	China Creek	8 44	20 06
21 52	10 55	21	arr. Smelter Jn lve.	8 20	19 40
	11 15	23	arr. .... Trail .... lve.		*19 20
19 20	†10 45	23	lve. .... Trail ... arr.		19 55
21 52	11 05	21	lve. .Smelter Jn. .arr.	8 20	19 40
22 20	11 33	28	Tiger	7 55	19 09
22 25	11 40	29	Crown Point	7 50	19 03
22 50	12 15	33	arr. ... Rossland .lve.	†7 30	*18 40

BOUNDARY BRANCH.

May 6, 1906.

41	Mls		42
†9 30	0	lv. West Robson ar.	20 35
13 07	67	Grand Forks	16 54
14 00	81	Eholt Junction	16 05
15 00	91	arr. .. Phoenix .lve.	†15 15
15 00	90	arr. .. Midway .. lve.	†15 10

MINIOTA BRANCH.

33	149	143	153	Ms	June 17, 1906.	154	150	144	34
	j7 00	f7 00	†14 30	0	lve. + Brandon .arr.	11 15	17 10	17 10	
	7 30	7 25	14 50	6	Chater	11 00	16 55	16 55	
		11 55		56	arr. ... Lenore ... lve.			f13 00	
f14 45	9 40		16 40	37	Rapid City	9 05	j14 50		13 20
16 55			19 50	77	arr. ... Miniota .lve.	†6 00			j11 10

WALTHAM BRANCH.

113	117	Mls.	May 6, 1906.	112	114
P M	A M		LEAVE] [ARRIVE	A M	P M
†5 10	†6 45	0	+ Ottawa (U. D.)	9 35	6 15
5 20	7 05	2.0	Hull (C. P. Station)	9 25	6 05
5 40	7 45	9.6	Aylmer	9 05	5 40
5 55	8 10	17.3	Breckenridge	8 51	5 10
6 05	8 25	23.1	Eardley	8 41	4 55
6 09	8 37	24.9	Parker	8 37	4 50
6 17	8 49	28.8	Mohr	8 28	4 40
6 26	9 05	32.7	Quio	8 20	4 30
6 34	9 20	35.8	Wyman	8 09	4 10
6 46	9 40	39.9	Maryland	7 58	3 56
6 53	9 55	42.6	McKee	7 50	3 42
7 02	10 20	46.4	Shawville	7 42	3 30
7 20	10 42	53.7	Moorehead	7 24	2 55
7 28	11 07	57.6	Campbell's Bay	7 14	2 40
8 01	11 47	68.9	Fort Coulonge	6 47	2 00
8 05	11 50	69.9	Davidson	6 40	1 50
8 19	12 12	76.4	Mellon	6 28	1 30
8 30	12 30	80.4	Waltham	†6 20	†1 20
P M	Noon		ARRIVE] [LEAVE	A M	P M

Lindsay Branch.—Trains leave Burketon Junction †10 55 a.m., †6 50 p.m., arrive Bobcaygeon (39 miles) 12 25 noon, 8 00 p.m. Returning, leave Bobcaygeon †7 40 a.m., †4 30 p.m., arrive Burketon Junction 8 50 a.m., 6 00 p.m. *May* 6, 1906.

Lac du Bonnet Branch.—Train leaves Molson x9 15, arriving Lac du Bonnet (22 miles) 11 00. Returning, leaves Lac du Bonnet x13 30, arriving Molson 15 10. *June* 17, 1906.

Lacombe Branch.—Lvs. Lacombe †13 00, arr. Stettler (51 miles) 16 30. Lvs. Stettler †7 15, arr. Lacombe 11 00.

Wetaskiwin Br.—Leaves Wetaskiwin †14 30, arr. Daysland (51 m.) 18 40. Lvs. Daysland †5 45, arr. Wetaskiwin 9 35.

MANIWAKI BRANCH.

101	103	107	Ms.	May 6, 1906.	102	108	104
P M	P M	A M		LEAVE] [ARRIVE	A M	P M	P M
†5 00	k1 30	a7 20	0	+ ... Ottawa (U. D.)	8 50	7 45	9 15
5 05	1 35	7 33	2.0	Hull (C. P. Station)	8 41	7 30	9 05
5 15	1 46	7 57	4.7	Ironside	8 31	7 15	8 56
5 26	1 57	8 22	7.9	Chelsea	8 22	7 05	8 47
5 39	2 09	8 35	11.7	Kirk's Ferry	8 11	6 45	8 36
5 48	2 18	8 46	15.4	Cascades	8 02	6 35	8 27
6 06	2 36	9 25	21.2	Wakefield	7 45	6 06	8 10
6 16	2 46	9 40	24.4	North Wakefield	7 35	5 50	8 02
6 26	2 56	9 55	29.5	Farrellton	7 25	5 32	7 50
6 44	3 14	10 20	34.7	Low	7 13	5 10	7 40
7 00	3 25	10 40	40.8	Venosta	6 57	4 50	7 27
7 14	3 39	11 00	46.8	Kazubazua	6 45	4 30	7 14
7 20	3 48	11 07	48.5	Aylwin	6 38	4 22	7 08
7 45	4 13	11 45	59.1	Gracefield	6 15	3 50	6 40
8 05	4 38	12 07	67.0	Blue Sea	5 50	3 15	6 15
8 15	4 48	12 30	71.5	Burbidge	5 40	3 00	6 05
8 45	5 13	1 20	82.1	Maniwaki	†5 15	a2 25	k5 40
P M	P M	P M		ARRIVE] [LEAVE	A M	P M	P M

Sunday Trains—Lvs. Ottawa §9 00 a.m., arr. Maniwaki 12 25 noon. Lvs. Maniwaki §6 00 p.m., arr. Ottawa 9 35 p.m.

NAKUSP AND SLOCAN BRANCH.

52	Mls	STATIONS.	51
†14 20	0	lve. ... Nakusp ... arr.	12 15
16 48	28	Rosebery	9 50
17 13	32	Denver Canyon	9 14
18 20	40	arr. ... Sandon ... lve.	†8 20

Lardo Branch.—Train leaves Lardo ƒ13 00, arriving Gerrard (33 miles) 14 30. Returning, leaves Gerrard ƒ9 40, arriving Lardo 11 15.

COLUMBIA AND KOOTENAY BRANCH.

45	43	41	Mls	STATIONS.	42	44	46
*19 15	†9 10	†8 10	0	lve. ... + Nelson ... arr.	22 05	16 30	10 37
20 35		9 25	28	Castlegar Junction	20 55		†9 22
20 40		9 30	30	arr. ... West Robson . lve.	*20 45		
	12 00		44	arr. ... Slocan City ... lve.		†13 45	

ARROW LAKE BR.

22	M		23
*9 20	0	lve. . + Revelstoke . arr.	17 10
10 40	28	arr. ... Arrowhead . lve.	*15 45

EDMONTON BRANCH.

13	Mls	May 6, 1906.	14
*7 45	0	lve. ... + Calgary . arr.	16 05
7 50	2	Calgary Junction	16 00
9 21	41	Carstairs	14 30
10 45	77	Innisfail	13 02
11 40	95	Red Deer	12 15
12 33	114	Lacombe	11 20
14 00	152	Wetaskiwin	9 50
14 50	174	Leduc	8 59
15 30	192	arr. ... Strathcona . lve.	†8 20
		(South Edmonton)	

Additional Trains—Lvs. Calgary †15 15, arr. Strathcona 22 45. Lvs. Strathcona *16 00, arrives Calgary 23 30.

CROWSNEST BRANCH.

5	Ms	May 6, 1906.	6
		LEAVE] [ARRIVE	
*20 50		Medicine Hat	6 00
21 25	0	lve. .. Dunmore Junc. arr.	5 47
23 25	55	Grassy Lake	3 41
24 26	81	Woodpecker	2 46
1 25	107	arr. + Lethbridge . lve.	1 40
3 15	143	Macleod	23 40
4 25	172	Pincher	22 23
5 33	197	Frank	21 18
6 23	212	Crowsnest	20 30
7 48	248	Fernie	18 29
10 25	311	Cranbrook	15 40
11 26	333	Aldridge	14 28
12 05	352	Yahk	13 42
12 51	366	Kitchener	12 51
14 00	394	Kootenay Landing	*11 20
		ARRIVE] [LEAVE	

Train leaves Lethbridge †6 45, arr. Macleod 8 50. Lvs. Macleod †14 05, arr. Lethbridge 16 30.

Okanagan Branch.—Train leaves Sicamous Junction †7 30 for Enderby (23 miles), Larkin (38 miles), arriving at Okanagan Landing (51 miles) 10 50. Returning, leaves Okanagan Landing †13 40, arriving Sicamous Junction 18 00. *May* 6, 1906.

Kimberly Branch.—Train leaves Cranbrook †7 30, arriving Kimberly (19 miles) 10 30. Returning, leaves Kimberly †11 30, arriving at Cranbrook 15 10.

THROUGH CAR SERVICE.

WESTBOUND.

No. 1—IMPERIAL LIMITED—Daily. Has Colonist and First Class Coaches and Sleeping Car Montreal to Vancouver. Sleeping Car from Toronto to Winnipeg daily, via North Bay. Tourist Car Montreal to Vancouver, Sunday, Monday and Thursday; Toronto to Vancouver, Tuesday, Wednesday, Friday and Saturday; Winnipeg to Vancouver, daily. Sleeping Car St. Paul to Banff. Sleeping Car Ft. William to Winnipeg daily. Sleeping Car St. Paul to Winnipeg, via Emerson. Dining Car Montreal to Laggan and Revelstoke to Vancouver.

No. 97—PACIFIC EXPRESS—Daily. Has First Class Coach, Sleeping Car and Colonist Car Montreal to Vancouver. Sleeping Car Winnipeg to Calgary and Strathcona. Tourist Cars for Vancouver leave Boston Wednesday, Montreal Tuesday, Wednesday, Friday and Saturday, Toronto Sunday, Monday and Thursday. Sleeping and Tourist Car St. Paul to Seattle, via Soo Pacific Route. Sleeping Car Arrowhead to Vancouver. Dining Cars Montreal to Laggan and Revelstoke to Vancouver.

No. 3—EXPRESS—Leaving Montreal week-days has First and Second Class Coaches to Detroit. First Class Coach and Sleeping Car to Chicago daily. From Toronto, has Coaches and Sleeping Car to Detroit daily. Sleeper and Coach Toronto to Chic. daily. Cafe Car Montreal to Toronto.

No. 5—CHICAGO EXPRESS—Daily. Has First and Second Class Coaches Montreal to Detroit and Sleeping Cars Montreal to Toronto and Chicago, and Ottawa to Toronto. Through Tourist Sleeper Boston to Chicago Tuesday. Cafe Car Toronto to Detroit. Dining Car west of Detroit.

No. 7—ST. PAUL, MINNEAPOLIS AND DULUTH EXPRESS—Daily. Sleeping Car Montreal to Ottawa (passengers may remain in car until 9 00 a.m.). Has First and Second Class Coaches and Sleeping Car Montreal to St. Paul and Minneapolis and to Duluth, via Marquette Route. Sleeping Car Boston to St. Paul and Minneapolis. Dining Cars en route.

No. 9—HALIFAX EXPRESS—Leaving Montreal daily, except Saturday, has First and Second Class Coaches and Sleeping Car to St. John, N.B., and Halifax, N.S. Sleeping Car Montreal to St. Andrews Tuesday, Wednesday, Thursday and Friday till July 13th, and after July 14th, Tuesday and Friday only. Dining Car Mattawamkeag to Truro.

No. 11—BOSTON EXPRESS—Leaving Montreal daily, has First and Second Class Coaches to Boston, and Sleeping Car from St. Paul and Minneapolis to Boston. Cafe Car Montreal to Boston. Parlor Car Montreal to Old Orchard and Portland. Parlor Car Boston to St. John.

No. 10—NEW ENGLAND EXPRESS—Leaving Montreal daily, has First and Second Class Coaches and Sleeping Cars to Boston. Sleeping Car Montreal to Old Orchard and Portland. Composite First Class Coach and Sleeping Car to Springfield daily, except Sunday. Tourist Sleeper leaves Chicago Friday and Toronto Saturday for Boston.

No. 12—Express from St. John, N.B., daily, except Sunday, has First and Second Class Coaches and Pullman Sleeping Car to Boston. Dining Car Truro to Vanceboro.

No. 13—Through Sleeper and Diner St. Paul to Winnipeg, via Minneapolis, St. Paul & Sault Ste. Marie Ry.

No. 30—Leaving New York (N. Y. C.) daily at 8 00 p.m., has Sleeping Car for Toronto. Parlor and Dining Car Buffalo to Toronto.

No. 40—Leaving Quebec daily, has First and Second Class Coaches and Sleeping Car for Montreal.

CAFE CARS on Nos. 7 and 8 Winnipeg and Yorkton; 17 and 18 Winnipeg and Deloraine; 55 and 56 Prince Albert Branch.

EASTBOUND.

No. 2—IMPERIAL LIMITED—Daily. Has Colonist and First Class Coaches and Sleeper Vancouver to Montreal. Sleeping Car from Strathcona to Winnipeg leaves Calgary except Monday; from Calgary to Winnipeg Mondays, and Winnipeg to Toronto daily, via North Bay. Tourist Cars from Vancouver for Montreal Mon., Wed. and Fri.; for Toronto Sun., Tues., Thur. and Sat. Dining Cars Vancouver to Revelstoke and Laggan to Montreal. Sleeper Banff to St. Paul daily, via Soo Pacific Route. Sleeper Winnipeg to Ft. William daily.

No. 96—ATLANTIC EXPRESS—Daily. Has Coach, Colonist Car and Sleeper Vancouver to Montreal. Sleeper and Tourist Car Seattle to St. Paul, via Soo Pac. Route. Sleeper Vancouver to Arrowhead and Strathcona and Calgary to Winnipeg. Tourist Sleeper Vancouver for Toronto on Mon., Wed. and Fri., for Montreal Sun., Tues., Thur. and Sat., for Boston Thur. Sleeper from Winnipeg to St. Paul, via Emerson, daily. Dining Cars Vancouver to Revelstoke and Laggan to Montreal.

No. 4—EXPRESS—Leaving Chicago (Wab. R.R.) at 3 00 p.m. has Sleeping Car and Coach to Toronto daily, to Montreal daily, except Sat. Through Tourist Sleepers Chicago to Boston Fri. From Detroit has Sleeping Car and First and Second Class Coaches daily for Toronto, running through to Montreal daily, except Sun., with Cafe Car Toronto to Montreal. Dining Car west of Detroit. Parlor Car St. John to Boston.

No. 6—MONTREAL EXPRESS—Leaving Chicago (Wabash R.R.) at 10 32 p.m. has Sleeping Cars to Montreal daily, and First Class Coach to Toronto daily. From Detroit has First and Second Class Coaches and Sleeper to Montreal daily. Sleeping Cars Toronto to Montreal and Ottawa. Cafe Car Detroit to Toronto.

No. 8—MONTREAL AND BOSTON EXPRESS—Daily. Sleeping Car Ottawa to Montreal (open at 9 00 p.m.) Has First and Second Class Coaches Minneapolis and St. Paul to Montreal. Sleeping Car to Montreal and Boston. Sleeping Car from Duluth to Montreal, via Marquette Route. Sleeping Car St. Paul and Minneapolis to Boston. Dining Cars.

No. 10—HALIFAX EXPRESS—Leaving Halifax and St. John, N.B., daily, except Sunday, has First and Second Class Coaches and Sleeping Car to Montreal. Sleeping Car St. Andrews to Montreal Wednesday, Thursday, Friday and Monday to July 13th, inclusive, and after July 14th, Monday and Wednesday only. Dining Car Truro to Mattawamkeag.

No. 12—NEW ENGLAND EXPRESS—Leaving Boston daily, has First and Second Class Coaches with Sleeping Car to Montreal. Sleeping Car Portland and Old Orchard to Montreal. Composite First Class Coach and Sleeping Car Springfield to Montreal, except Sunday.

No. 14—Through Sleeper and Diner Winnipeg to St. Paul, via Minneapolis, St. Paul & Sault Ste. Marie Ry.

No. 16—BOSTON EXPRESS—Leaving Boston daily, has First and Second Class Coaches and Cafe Car to Montreal, and Sleeping Car to Montreal, St. Paul and Minneapolis. Parlor Car Portland and Old Orchard to Montreal. Tourist Sleeper for Chicago Tuesday.

No. 9—Express from Boston daily, except Saturday, has Pullman Sleeping Car to St. Johns, N.B., First and Second Class Coaches and Dining Car Vanceboro to Truro.

No. 35—Leaving Toronto daily, has Sleeping Car for New York, via N. Y. C. Parlor and Dining Car Toronto to Buffalo.

No. 39—Leaving Montreal daily, has First and Second Class Coaches and Sleeping Car for Quebec.

PARLOR CARS are run on Trains Nos. 1, 2, 23, 24, 35, 36, 37 and 38 between Ottawa and Montreal; on Nos. 41, 54 (Cafe), 58 and 63 between Quebec and Montreal; on Nos. 77 and 80 between Ottawa and Brockville; on Nos. 27, 29, 34 and 38 between Toronto, Hamilton and Buffalo; on Nos. 3 and 4 between Vancouver and Seattle; on Nos. 41 and 42 between Nelson and Midway, B.C.; on Nos. 9 and 10 between Calgary and Edmonton.

PACIFIC COAST STEAMSHIP CONNECTIONS.

Leave **VANCOUVER**—C. P. Ry. Co.'s B. C. Coast Service Steamers for **Skagway**, connecting with W. P. & Y. Ry. for points in Alaska and Yukon Territory. S.S. *Princess Beatrice* or *May* 11 00 p.m., July 1st, 7th, 13th, 17th, 25th and 31st. **For Nanaimo**—Week-days only, on arrival of Transcontinental Trains. From Nanaimo 7 00 a.m. daily, except Sat. and Sun., Sat. only 8 00 a.m., connecting with Transcontinental Trains.

Leave **VICTORIA**—C.P.Ry.Co.'s B.C. Coast Service Steamers for Seattle—S.S. *Victoria* 1 00 p.m., except Thursday. From Seattle, 12 00 night, except Thursday.

C. P. Ry. Co.'s B. C. Coast Service Steamers for **Skagway**, connecting there with the White Pass & Yukon Ry., for all points in Alaska and the Yukon Territory. S.S. *Princess Beatrice* or *May* 11 00 p.m., July 6th, 12th, 16th, 24th and 30th.

C. P. Ry. Co.'s B. C. Coast Service Steamers for Port Simpson, Naas, etc.—S.S. *Tees* 11 00 p.m., 1st and 15th of each month (Vancouver 2 00 p.m. 2d and 16th of each month) for Surf Inlet, Skeena River, Port Simpson, Naas and intermediate points. Calls at Skidegate trip of 1st and at Bella Coola trip of 15th.

C. P. Ry. Co.'s B. C. Coast Service Steamers for Ahouset, Quatsino, Cape Scott, etc.—S.S. *Queen City* 11 00 p.m., 1st, 7th, 14th and 20th of each month for Ahouset and way ports, 7th and 20th of each month for Quatsino, 20th of each month for Cape Scott and way ports.

BRITISH COLUMBIA LAKE AND RIVER SERVICE.

COLUMBIA AND KOOTENAY STEAMER LINES.

ARROW LAKE AND COLUMBIA RIVER ROUTE.
Steamers "Rossland," "Kootenay" and "Minto."

*9 20 A M	Miles 0	lve. **Revelstoke**...(*C. P. Ry.*) arr.	5 10 P M	....
10 55 A M	" 28	lve. **Arrowhead**....(*Steamer*) arr.	3 25 P M	....
1 45 P M	" 64	arr........... **Nakusp**........... lve.	12 25 Noon	....
8 35 P M	" 152	arr........... **Robson**........... lve.	*11 00 P M	....

SLOCAN LAKE ROUTE.—Steamer "Slocan."—Steamer leaves Rosebery †10 15 a.m., †4 50 p.m. for New Denver, Silverton and Enterprise, arriving Slocan City 1 00, 7 40 p.m. Returning, leaves Slocan City †6 30 a.m., †2 00 p.m. for Enterprise, Silverton and New Denver, arriving Rosebery 9 30 a.m., 4 00 p.m.

KOOTENAY LAKE—Kaslo Route.—Steamer "Kokanee."

....	†8 00 A M	lve.......... **Nelson** .... arr.	3 15 P M	6 25 P M
....	11 20 A M	arr.......... **Kaslo** .... lve.	j12 15 Noon	f3 00 P M

OKANAGAN LAKE.—Steamer "Aberdeen."—Steamer leaves Okanagan Landing *f* 11 00 a.m., arriving Kelowna 2 30 p.m., Penticton 6 10 p.m. Returning, leaves Penticton *j* 6 00 a.m., calling at Kelowna 9 30 a.m., arriving Okanagan Landing 1 00 p.m.

KOOTENAY LAKE—Lardo Route.—Steamer "Kokanee."—Leaves Kaslo *f* 11 30 a.m., arriving Lardo 12 50 noon. Leaves Lardo *f* 1 30 p.m., arrives Kaslo 2 50 p.m.

CROWSNEST ROUTE.—Steamer "Moyie."—Leaves Nelson *4 30 a.m., arriving **Kootenay Landing** 10 00 a.m. Returning, leaves Kootenay Landing *1 00 p.m., arriving Nelson 6 10 p.m.

TROUT LAKE ROUTE.—Steamer "Procter."—Leaves Trout Lake City *f* 7 30 a.m., arrives **Gerrard** 9 30 a.m. Leaves Gerrard *f* 2 45 p.m., arrives Trout Lake City 4 45 p.m.

Connections.—At Kootenay Landing and Arrowhead with Canadian Pacific Ry. steamers to Kootenay points.

STANDARD TIME—*Atlantic time.*—East of Vanceboro, Me. *Eastern time.*—Vanceboro, Me., to Fort William, Sault Ste. Marie and Detroit. *Central time.*—Fort William to Broadview, including Manitoba branches. *Mountain time.*—Broadview to Laggan and branches. *Pacific time.*—Laggan to Vancouver and branches. ● Daily, except Friday. ‖ Meal stations. + Coupon stations; ♁ Telegraph stations.

Explanation of Reference Marks.—* Daily; †daily, except Sunday; ‡daily, except Saturday; ¶daily, except Monday; § Sunday only; *a* daily, except Saturday and Sunday; *b* Friday only; *c* Tuesday and Friday; *d* stops to take on for Detroit and west; *e* stops to let off from Montreal or beyond; *f* Monday, Wednesday and Friday; *g* stops to take on for Toronto or beyond; *h* stops to let off from Toronto or beyond; *i* Monday only; *j* Tuesday, Thursday and Saturday; *k* Saturday only; *l* stops to let off from Detroit and west; *m* daily, except Sunday and Monday; *n* stops to let off from Toronto and points east only; *o* Tuesday and Thursday; *p* stops to let off from west of Chatham and to take on for Toronto and points east only; *q* Saturday and Sunday only; *r* stops to let off from west of Streetsville Junction; *s* stops Sunday only; *t* stops to take for points beyond Mattawamkeag; *u* stops for passengers to and from points north of Portage la Prairie; *v* stops to take passengers for west of Fredericton Junction; *w* Sunday, Tuesday and Thursday; *x* Monday, Wednesday and Saturday; *y* stops Saturday only; □ Stops to leave passengers from points on Soo Branch and points west. △ Stops to take passengers on Soo Branch and points west of Sault Ste. Marie only. ❩ Stops to leave passengers from points beyond Cartier. ■ Will commence running Monday, July 2d, and be discontinued after Saturday, September 15th.

For Parlor, Sleeping and Dining Car Service and Explanation of Reference Marks, see page 592.

Commencing May 6, 1906.

No. 97 Pacific Express.	No. 1 Imperial Limited.	STATIONS	No. 2 Imperial Limited.	No. 96 Atlantic Express.
9 40 P M	9 40 A M	lve....**Montreal**...arr.	6 30 P M	7 00 A M
1 10 A M	1 15 P M	........**Ottawa**........	3 10 P M	3 40 A M
3 20 A M	3 40 P M	.......**Renfrew**.......	12 36 Noon	1 10 A M
9 00 A M	9 25 P M	arr...**North Bay**..lve.	6 55 A M	8 10 P M
11 30 P M	1 45 P M	lve.....**Toronto**....arr.	2 55 P M	7 00 A M
8 35 A M	9 40 P M	arr...**North Bay**..lve.	6 45 A M	8 50 P M
9 50 A M	10 05 P M	lve...**North Bay**..arr.	6 30 A M	7 45 P M
12 16 Noon	12 15 Night	lve.....**Sudbury**....lve.	4 15 A M	5 05 P M
7 00 A M	7 40 P M	arr. (Eastern time.) **Ft. William** lve.	10 25 A M	10 30 P M
....	....		....	....
6 20	19 00	lve. (Central time.) **Ft. William** arr.	9 05	21 10
16 00	4 25	........**Kenora**........	23 50	11 55
20 40	8 30	arr. **Winnipeg** lve.	19 35	7 20
21 40	9 15	lve. **Winnipeg** arr.	18 45	6 45
1 40	14 10	arr. **Brandon** lve.	14 10	2 40
1 50	14 25	lve. **Brandon** arr.	13 55	2 30
9 17	21 47	.**Regina** (Mountain time.).	5 22	17 50
11 25	23 30	lve...**Moose Jaw**..lve.	4 00	16 15
21 50	8 20	lve..**Medicine Hat**.lve.	19 25	6 45
4 05	15 15	........**Calgary**........	13 20	24 55
7 20	18 40	........**Banff**........	10 20	22 05
8 00	19 05	........**Laggan**........	9 15	20 55
9 30	20 32	........**Field**........	6 35	18 10
14 55	24 57	........**Glacier**........	2 22	12 55
17 45	3 10	......**Revelstoke**......	23 45	0 25
5 25	14 12	arr. **North Bend** lve.	13 05	22 30
5 35	14 22	lve. **North Bend** arr.	12 55	22 20
10 45	19 25	arr...**Vancouver**..lve.	8 00	17 15

TWO THROUGH EXPRESS TRAINS

EVERY DAY, EACH WAY, BETWEEN

Montreal, Ottawa, Toronto and Vancouver

COMMENCING MAY 6, 1906.

WESTBOUND—The "Imperial Limited"—The Pacific Express.
EASTBOUND—The "Imperial Limited"—The Atlantic Express.

† Daily, except Sunday; ‡ daily, except Saturday; ¶ daily, except Monday.

CANADIAN PACIFIC RAILWAY CO'S ROYAL MAIL STEAMSHIP LINES.

ATLANTIC SERVICE.—Montreal and Liverpool, via Quebec.

NAME OF STEAMSHIP.	Intended Sailings from Montreal.	NAME OF STEAMSHIP.	Intended Sailings from Liverpool.
Lake Manitoba	Thursday......June 14, 1906.	Empress of Britain	Saturday......June 9, 1906.
Empress of Britain	Saturday......June 23, 1906.	Lake Champlain	Tuesday......June 12, 1906.
Lake Champlain	Saturday......June 30, 1906.	Empress of Ireland	Saturday......June 23, 1906.
Empress of Ireland	Saturday......July 7, 1906.	Lake Erie	Tuesday......June 26, 1906.
Lake Erie	Thursday......July 12, 1906.	Empress of Britain	Saturday......July 7, 1906.
Empress of Britain	Saturday......July 21, 1906.	Lake Manitoba	Tuesday......July 10, 1906.

ROYAL MAIL STEAMSHIP SERVICE.—JAPAN AND CHINA.

INTENDED SAILINGS—EASTBOUND.						NAME OF STEAMSHIP.	INTENDED SAILINGS—WESTBOUND.					
Hong Kong. Wednesday.	Shanghai (Woosung).	Nagasaki.	Kobe.	Yokohama.	Vancouver.		Vancouver. Monday.	Yokohama	Kobe.	Nagasaki.	Shanghai (Woosung).	Hong Kong.
Dep.	Arr.	Arr.	Arr.	Arr.	Arr.		Dep. 12 45	Arr.	Arr.	Arr.	Arr.	Arr.
1906	1906	1906	1906	1906	1906		1906	1906	1906	1906	1906	1906
May 2	May 5	May 7	May 9	May 11	May 26	....Monteagle....	June 4	June 20	June 22	June 24	June 26	June 30
May 9	May 11	May 14	May 15	May 18	May 30	Empress of Japan	June 11	June 25	June 26	June 28	June 30	July 3
May 23	May 26	May 28	May 30	June 2	June 16	......Tartar......	June 25	July 14	July 16	July 18	July 20	July 24
May 30	June 1	June 4	June 5	June 8	June 20	Empress of China	July 2	July 16	July 17	July 19	July 21	July 24
June 20	June 22	June 25	June 26	June 29	July 11	Empress of India	July 23	Aug. 6	Aug. 7	Aug. 9	Aug. 11	Aug. 14
June 27	June 30	July 2	July 4	July 7	July 21	.....Athenian.....	July 30	Aug. 18	Aug. 20	Aug. 22	Aug. 24	Aug. 28
July 11	July 13	July 16	July 17	July 20	Aug. 1	Empress of Japan	Aug. 13	Aug. 27	Aug. 28	Aug. 30	Sept. 1	Sept. 4
July 18	July 21	July 23	July 25	July 28	Aug. 11	....Monteagle....	Aug. 20	Sept. 5	Sept. 7	Sept. 9	Sept. 11	Sept. 15
Aug. 1	Aug. 3	Aug. 6	Aug. 7	Aug. 10	Aug. 22	Empress of China	Sept. 3	Sept. 17	Sept. 18	Sept. 20	Sept. 22	Sept. 25
Aug. 8	Aug. 11	Aug. 13	Aug. 15	Aug. 18	Sept. 1	......Tartar......	Sept. 17	Oct. 6	Oct. 8	Oct. 10	Oct. 12	Oct. 16

Steamships for Japan leave Vancouver on arrival of Canadian Pacific Ry. "Pacific Limited" and (except Athenian and Tartar), call at Victoria, B.C., to embark passengers, and returning to land passengers. Athenian and Tartar do not carry first-class passengers. Steamers sail frequently from **Hong Kong** to **Manila, Philippine Islands,** and passengers by this line, transfer at **Hong Kong** to **Manila** steamers. Steamships may leave intermediate ports (Yokohama, Kobe, Nagasaki and Shanghai) in advance of the dates given in the time-table. The usual stay at intermediate ports is: Yokohama, 24 hours; Kobe, 12 hours; Nagasaki, 10 hours; Shanghai, 12 to 24 hours, according to tide. These periods may be reduced or increased according to circumstances. Passengers should ascertain from company's agents at those ports the exact hours of departure.

CANADIAN-AUSTRALIAN ROYAL MAIL STEAMSHIP SERVICE.

Intended Sailings. Southbound.	Vancouver.	Honolulu, H. I.	Suva, Fiji.	Brisbane.		Sydney, N. S. W.
	▲	Dep.	Dep.	Arr.	Dep.	Arr.
Name of Steamship.	1906	1906	1906	1906	1906	1906
Maheno......	May 25	June 2	June 12	June 17	June 18	June 19
Miowera.....	June 22	June 30	July 10	July 15	July 16	July 17
Aorangi......	July 20	July 28	Aug. 7	Aug. 12	Aug. 13	Aug. 14

Intended Sailings. Northbound.	Sydney, N. S. W.	Brisbane.		Suva, Fiji.	Honolulu, H. I.	Vancouver.
	Dep.	Arr.	Dep.	Dep.	Arr.	Arr.
Name of Steamship.	1906	1906	1906	1906	1906	1906
Miowera.....	May 14	May 16	May 17	May 22	May 30	June 7
Aorangi......	June 11	June 13	June 14	June 19	June 27	July 5
Maheno......	July 9	July 11	July 12	July 17	July 25	Aug. 2

▲ Steamships leave Vancouver on arrival of C. P. Pacific Limited.

Steamships call at Victoria, B.C., both ways. Passengers can ascertain from commanders of ships the time allowed at intermediate ports. Passengers for New Zealand points will be forwarded via Sydney.

From points west of Chicago, Sault Ste. Marie and Port Arthur berths can be secured from Assistant General Passenger Agent, Vancouver; east of those points from the General Passenger Agent, Montreal, through any Canadian Pacific Ry. Agent.

UPPER LAKES SERVICE.—Lakes Huron and Superior.

EXPRESS STEAMSHIPS "ALBERTA," "ATHABASCA" AND "MANITOBA."

(STANDARD—*Eastern time.*)

Intended Sailings—Westbound.

Ports of Call.	Mls	Time.	Days.		
Toronto (via C. P. Express Train)..lve.	0	1 50 P M	Tues.	Thu.	Sat.
Owen Sound " " ..arr.	122	5 40 P M	Tues.	Thu.	Sat.
Owen Sound..........lve.	122	5 50 P M	Tues.	Thu.	Sat.
Sault Ste. Marie..........arr.	397	1 00 P M	Wed.	Fri.	Sun.
Port Arthur..........arr.	672	11 00 A M	Thu.	Sat.	Mon.
Fort William..........arr	677	12 00 Noon	Thu.	Sat.	Mon.

Intended Sailings—Eastbound.

Ports of Call.	Mls	Time.	Days.		
Fort William..........lve.	0	10 30 A M	Fri.	Sun.	Tues.
Port Arthur..........lve.	5	11 00 A M	Fri.	Sun.	Tues.
Sault Ste. Marie..........arr.	280	12 30 Noon	Sat.	Mon.	Wed.
Owen Sound..........arr.	555	8 30 A M	Sun.	Tues.	Thu.
Owen Sound (via C. P. Exp. Train)..lve.	555	9 00 A M	Sun.	Tues.	Thu.
Toronto.... " " ..arr.	677	12 55 Noon	Sun.	Tues.	Thu.

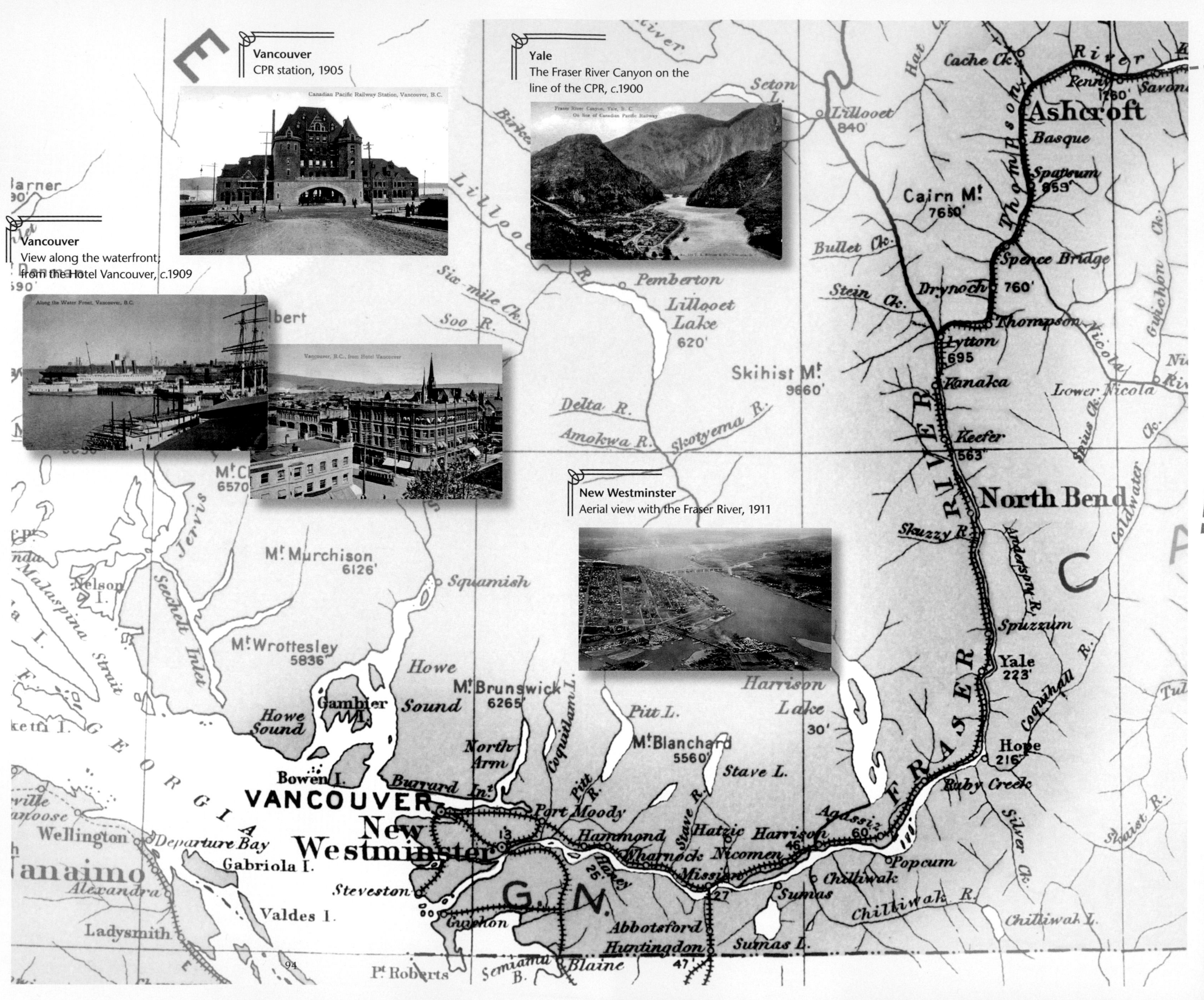

Vancouver
CPR station, 1905

Yale
The Fraser River Canyon on the line of the CPR, *c*.1900

Vancouver
View along the waterfront; from the Hotel Vancouver, *c*.1909

New Westminster
Aerial view with the Fraser River, 1911

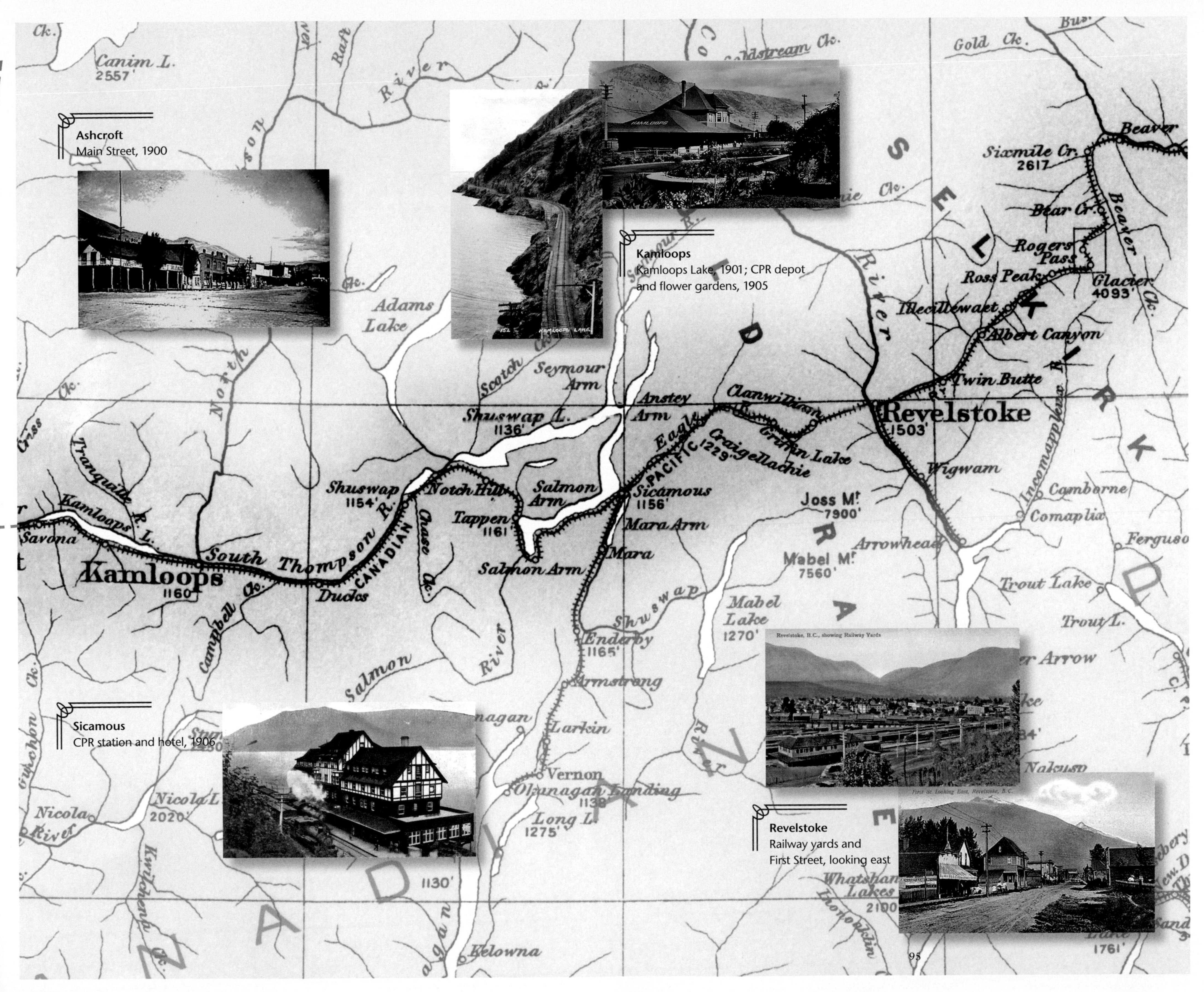

Ashcroft
Main Street, 1900

Kamloops
Kamloops Lake, 1901; CPR depot and flower gardens, 1905

Sicamous
CPR station and hotel, 1906

Revelstoke
Railway yards and First Street, looking east

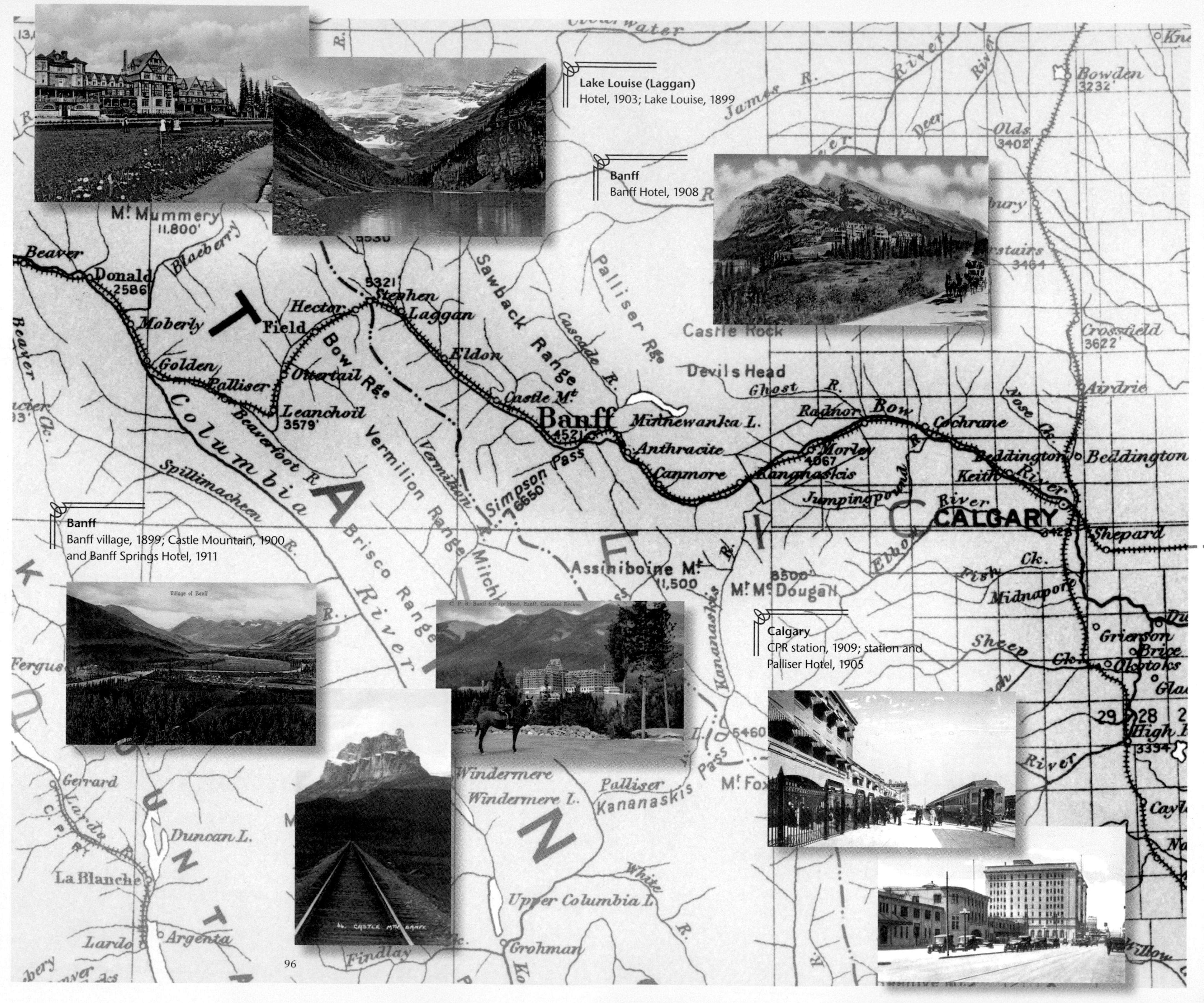

Lake Louise (Laggan)
Hotel, 1903; Lake Louise, 1899

Banff
Banff Hotel, 1908

Banff
Banff village, 1899; Castle Mountain, 1900
and Banff Springs Hotel, 1911

Calgary
CPR station, 1909; station and
Palliser Hotel, 1905

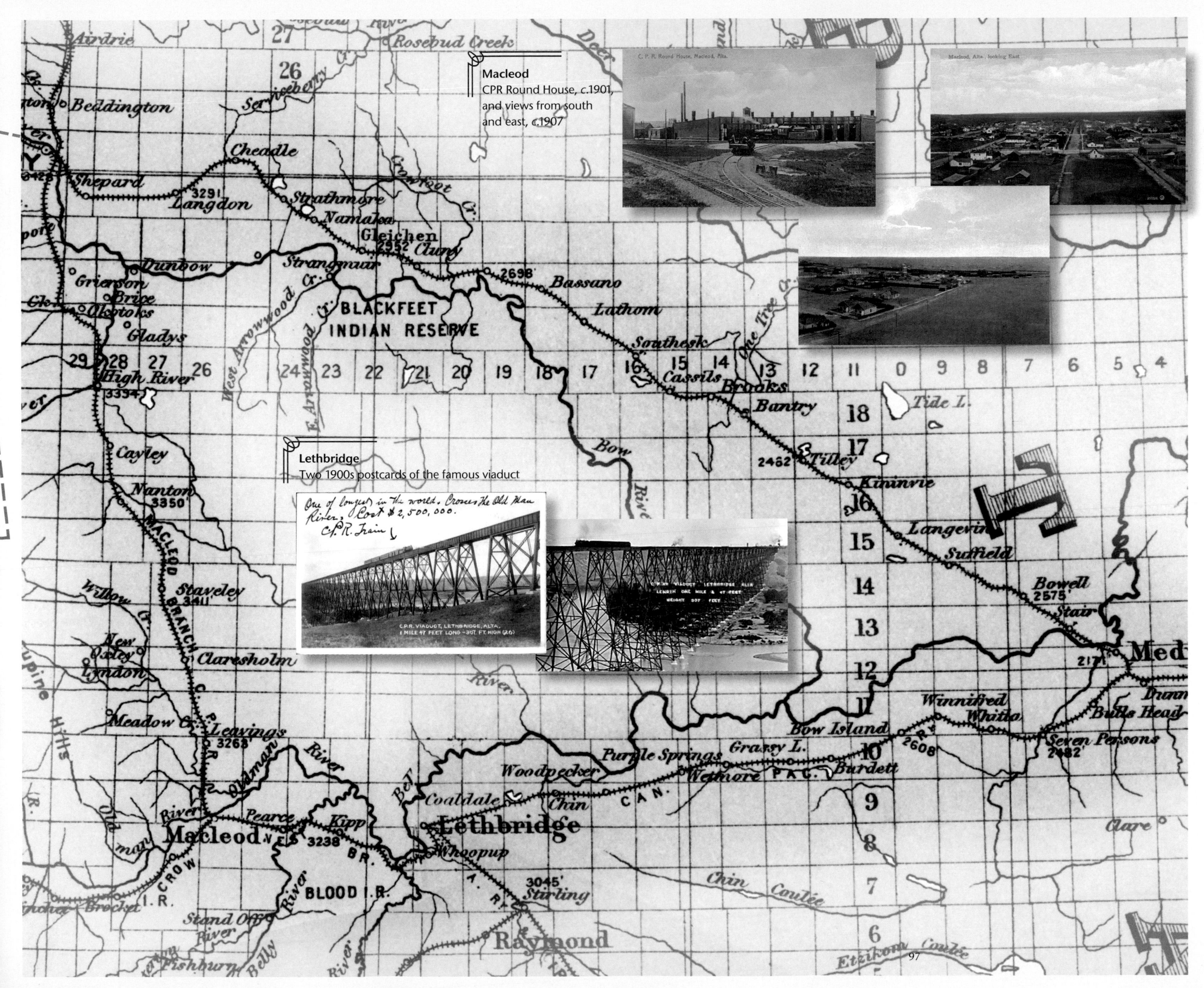

Macleod
CPR Round House, *c.*1901, and views from south and east, *c.*1907

Lethbridge
Two 1900s postcards of the famous viaduct

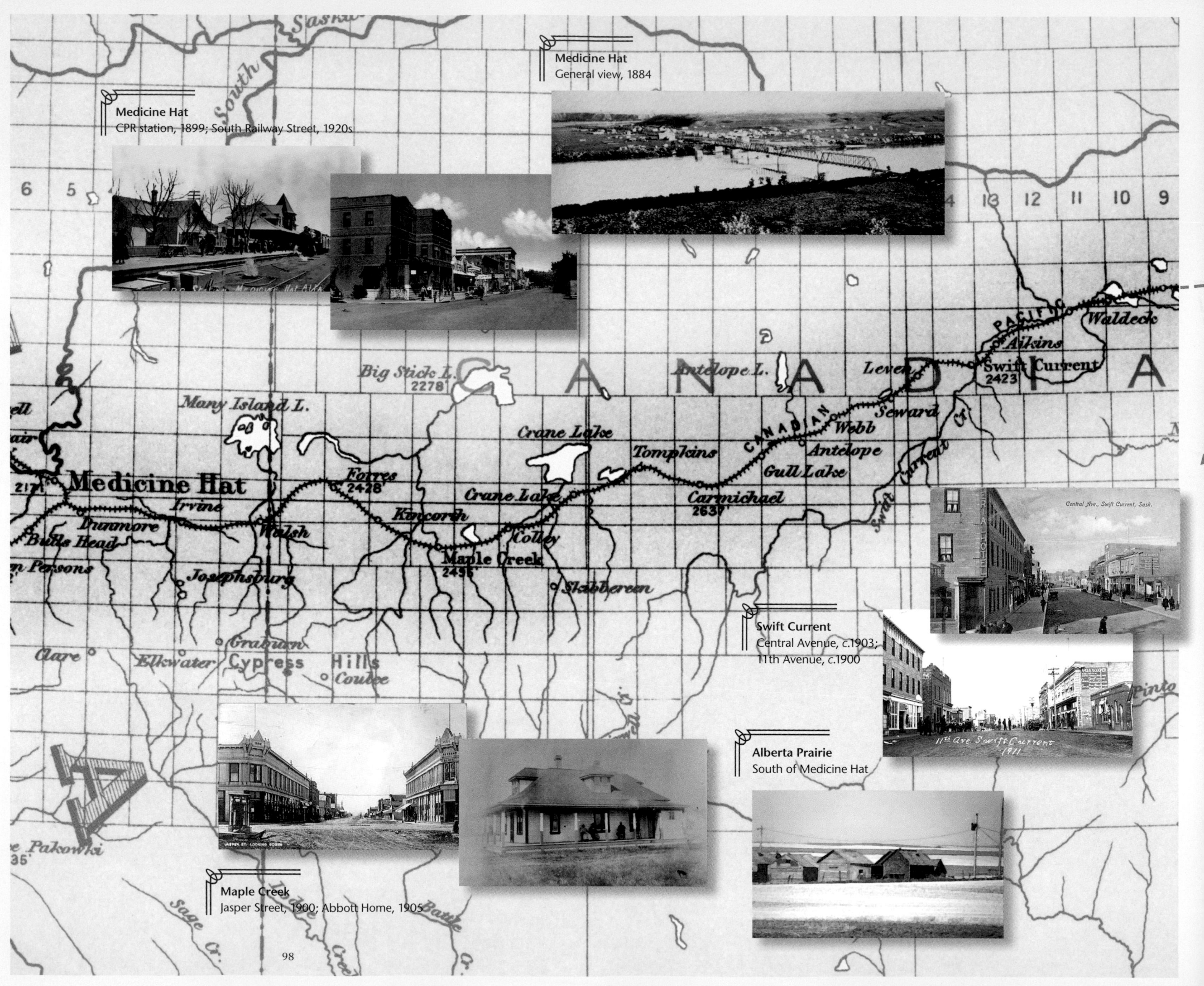

Medicine Hat
CPR station, 1899; South Railway Street, 1920s

Medicine Hat
General view, 1884

Swift Current
Central Avenue, *c.*1903; 11th Avenue, *c.*1900

Alberta Prairie
South of Medicine Hat

Maple Creek
Jasper Street, 1900; Abbott Home, 1905

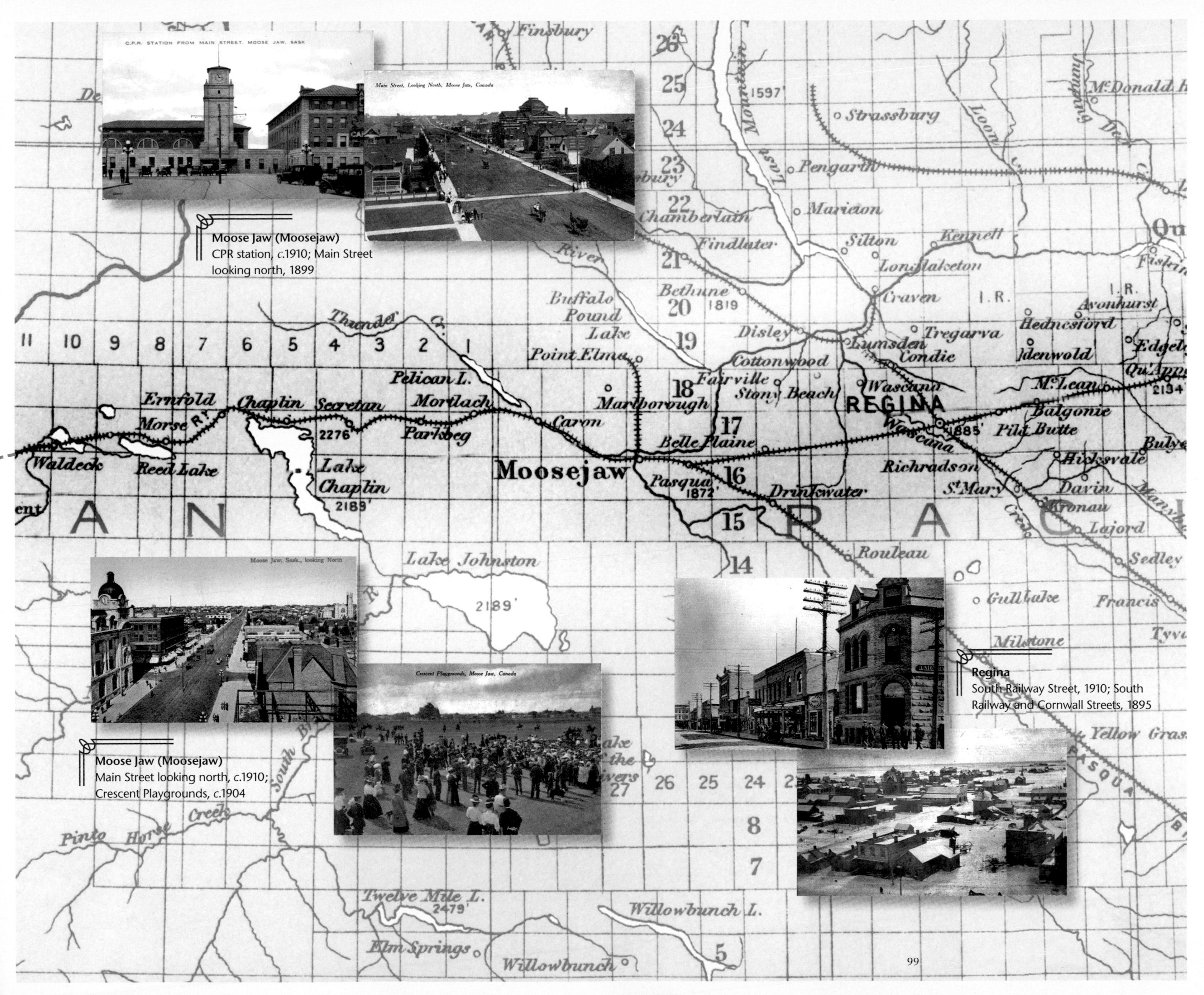

Moose Jaw (Moosejaw)
CPR station, *c.*1910; Main Street looking north, 1899

Moose Jaw (Moosejaw)
Main Street looking north, *c.*1910; Crescent Playgrounds, *c.*1904

Regina
South Railway Street, 1910; South Railway and Cornwall Streets, 1895

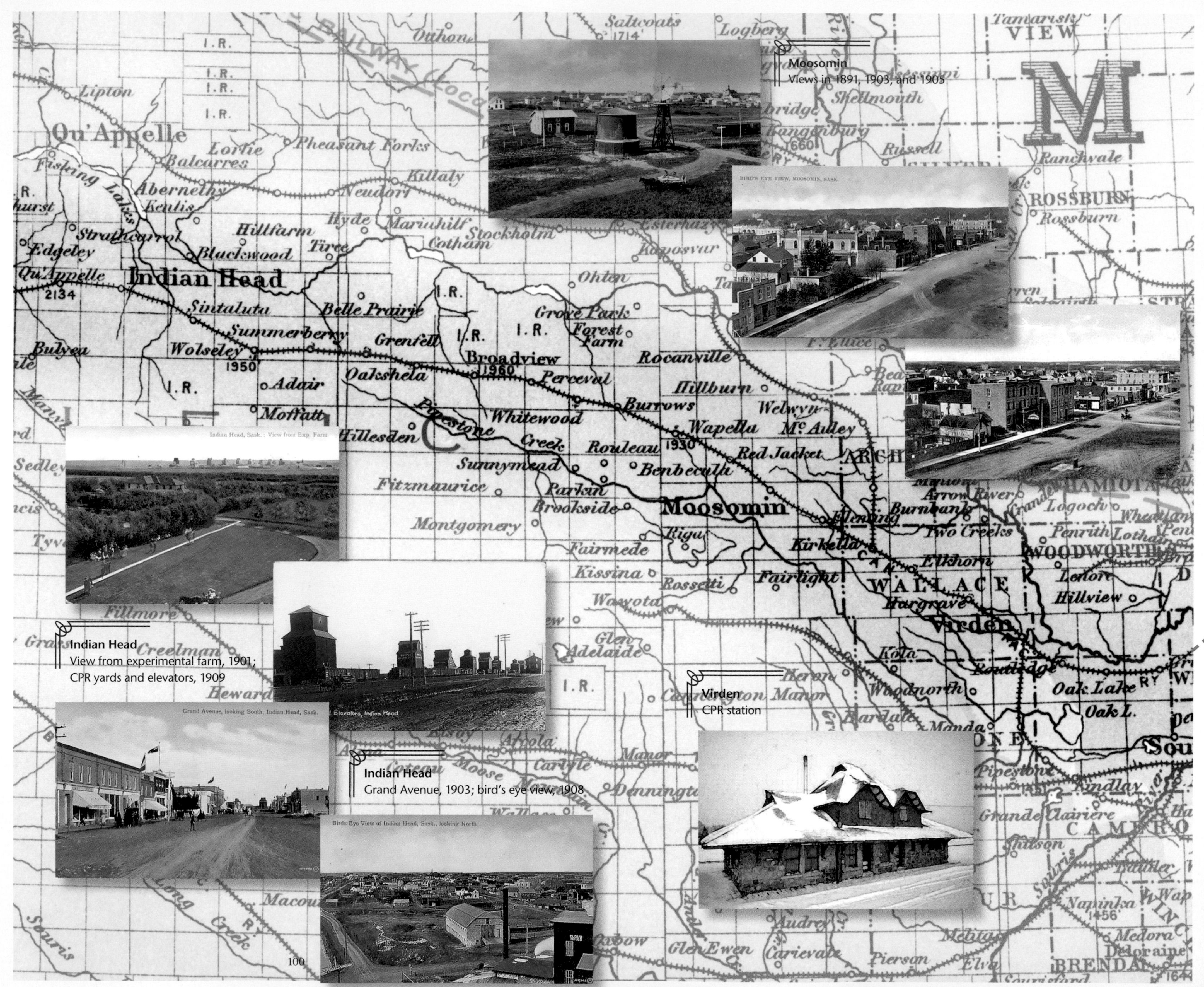

Moosomin
Views in 1891, 1903, and 1905

Indian Head
View from experimental farm, 1901;
CPR yards and elevators, 1909

Indian Head
Grand Avenue, 1903; bird's eye view, 1908

Virden
CPR station

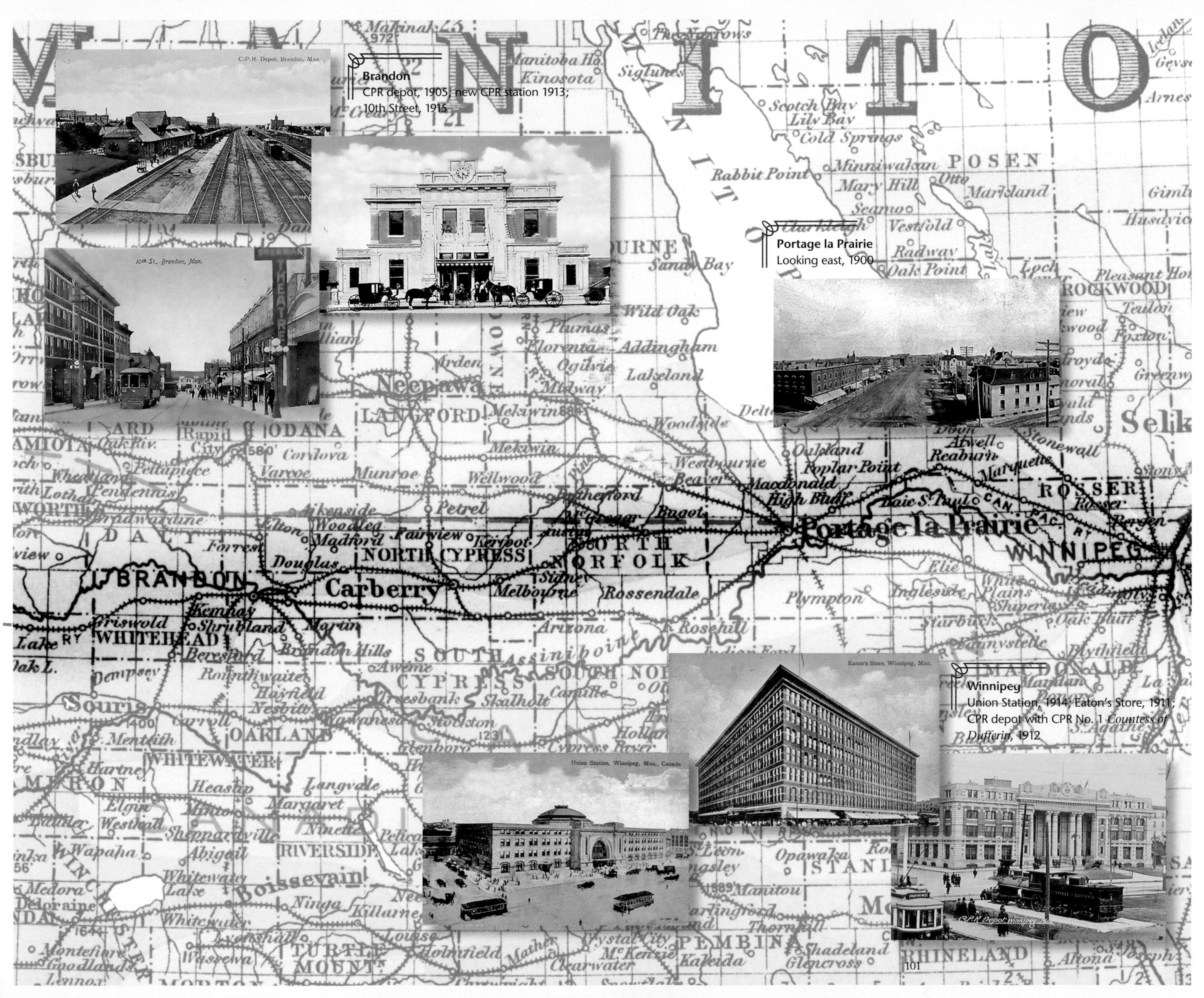

Brandon
CPR depot, 1905; new CPR station 1913; 10th Street, 1915

Portage la Prairie
Looking east, 1900

Winnipeg
Union Station, 1914; Eaton's Store, 1911; CPR depot with CPR No. 1 *Countess of Dufferin*, 1912

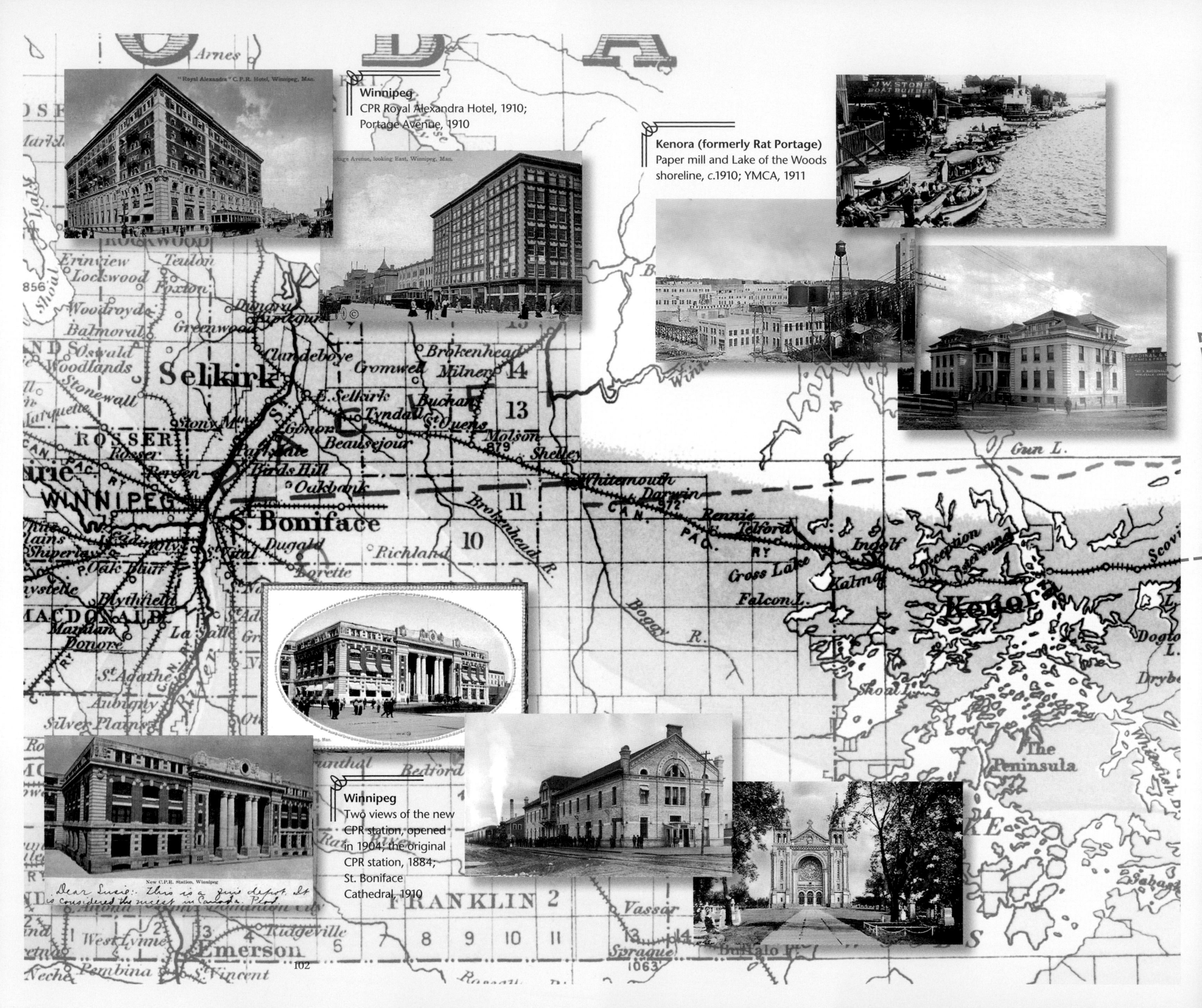

Winnipeg
CPR Royal Alexandra Hotel, 1910;
Portage Avenue, 1910

Kenora (formerly Rat Portage)
Paper mill and Lake of the Woods shoreline, c.1910; YMCA, 1911

Winnipeg
Two views of the new CPR station, opened in 1904; the original CPR station, 1884; St. Boniface Cathedral, 1910

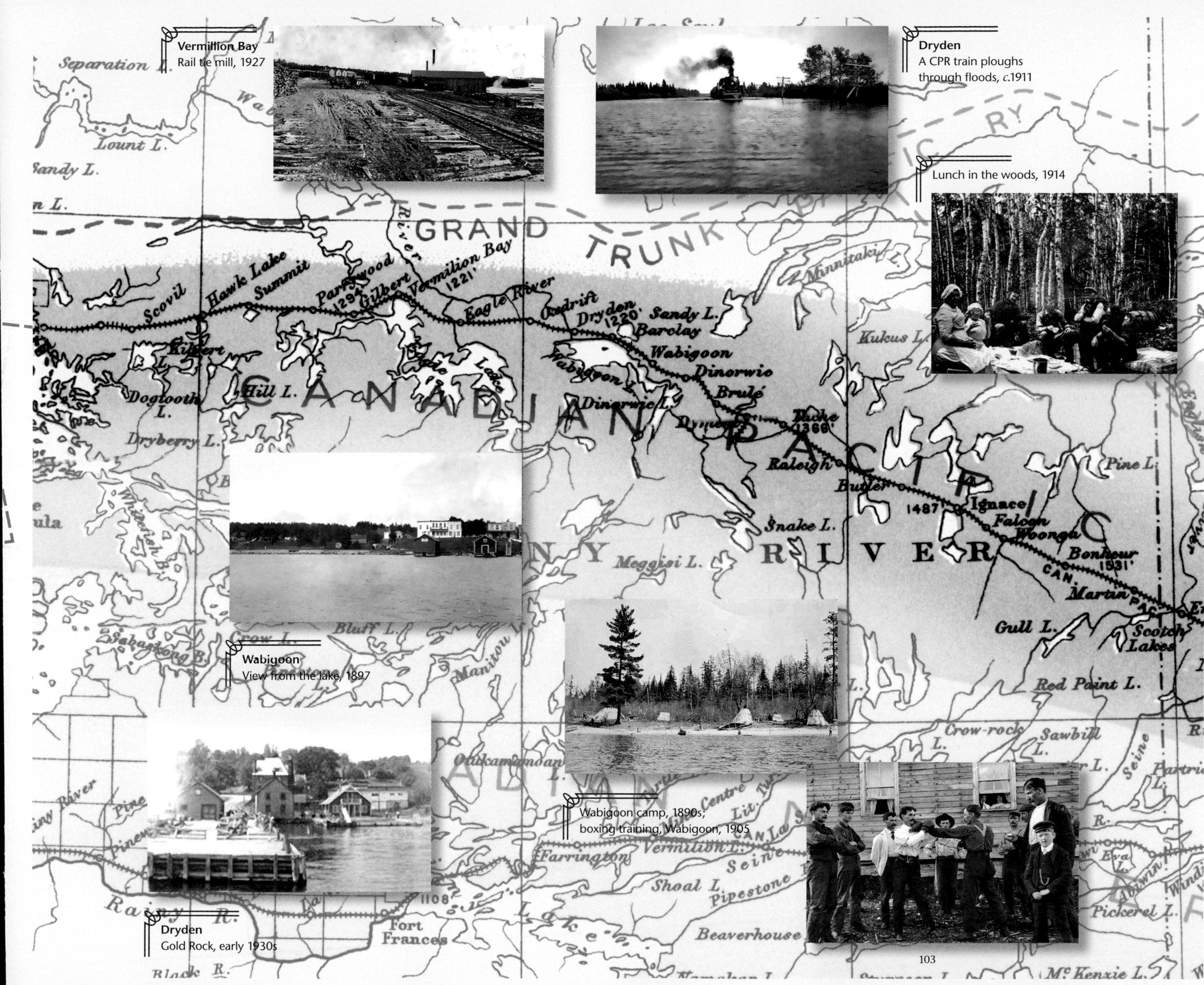

Vermillion Bay
Rail tie mill, 1927

Dryden
A CPR train ploughs through floods, *c.*1911

Lunch in the woods, 1914

Wabigoon
View from the lake, 1897

Wabigoon camp, 1890s;
boxing training, Wabigoon, 1905

Dryden
Gold Rock, early 1930s

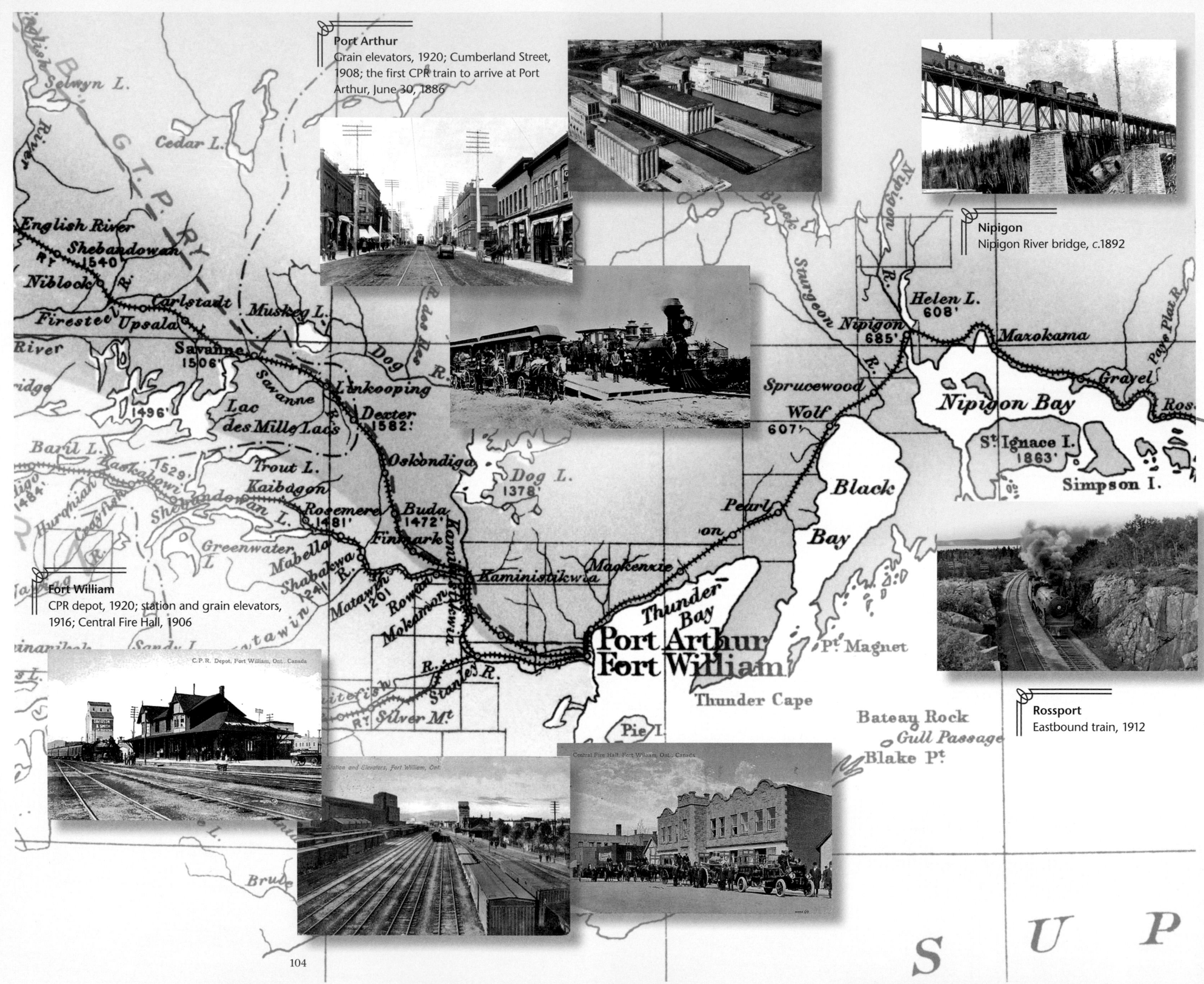

Port Arthur
Grain elevators, 1920; Cumberland Street, 1908; the first CPR train to arrive at Port Arthur, June 30, 1886

Nipigon
Nipigon River bridge, *c.*1892

Fort William
CPR depot, 1920; station and grain elevators, 1916; Central Fire Hall, 1906

Rossport
Eastbound train, 1912

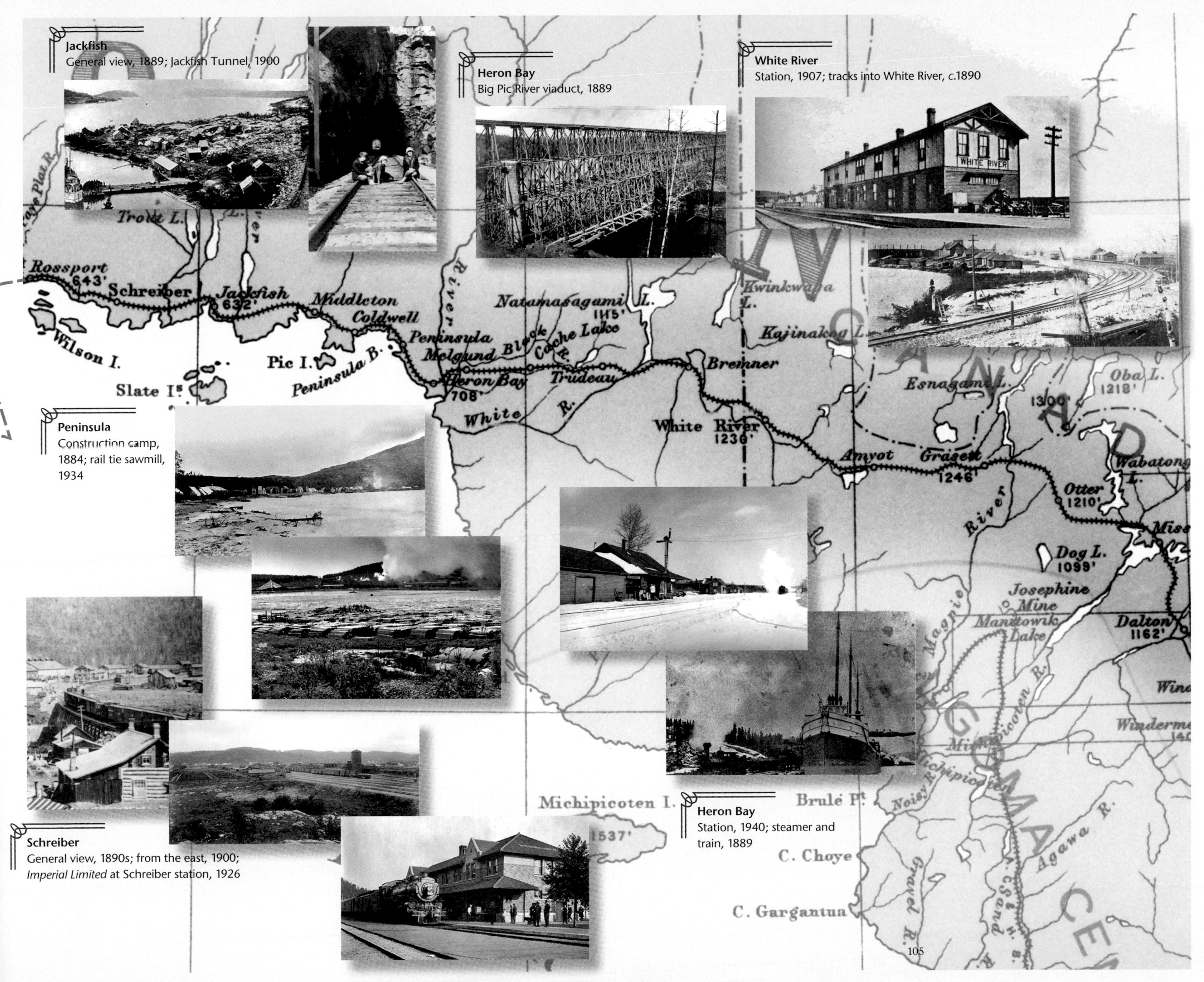

Jackfish
General view, 1889; Jackfish Tunnel, 1900

Heron Bay
Big Pic River viaduct, 1889

White River
Station, 1907; tracks into White River, *c*.1890

Peninsula
Construction camp, 1884; rail tie sawmill, 1934

Schreiber
General view, 1890s; from the east, 1900; *Imperial Limited* at Schreiber station, 1926

Heron Bay
Station, 1940; steamer and train, 1889

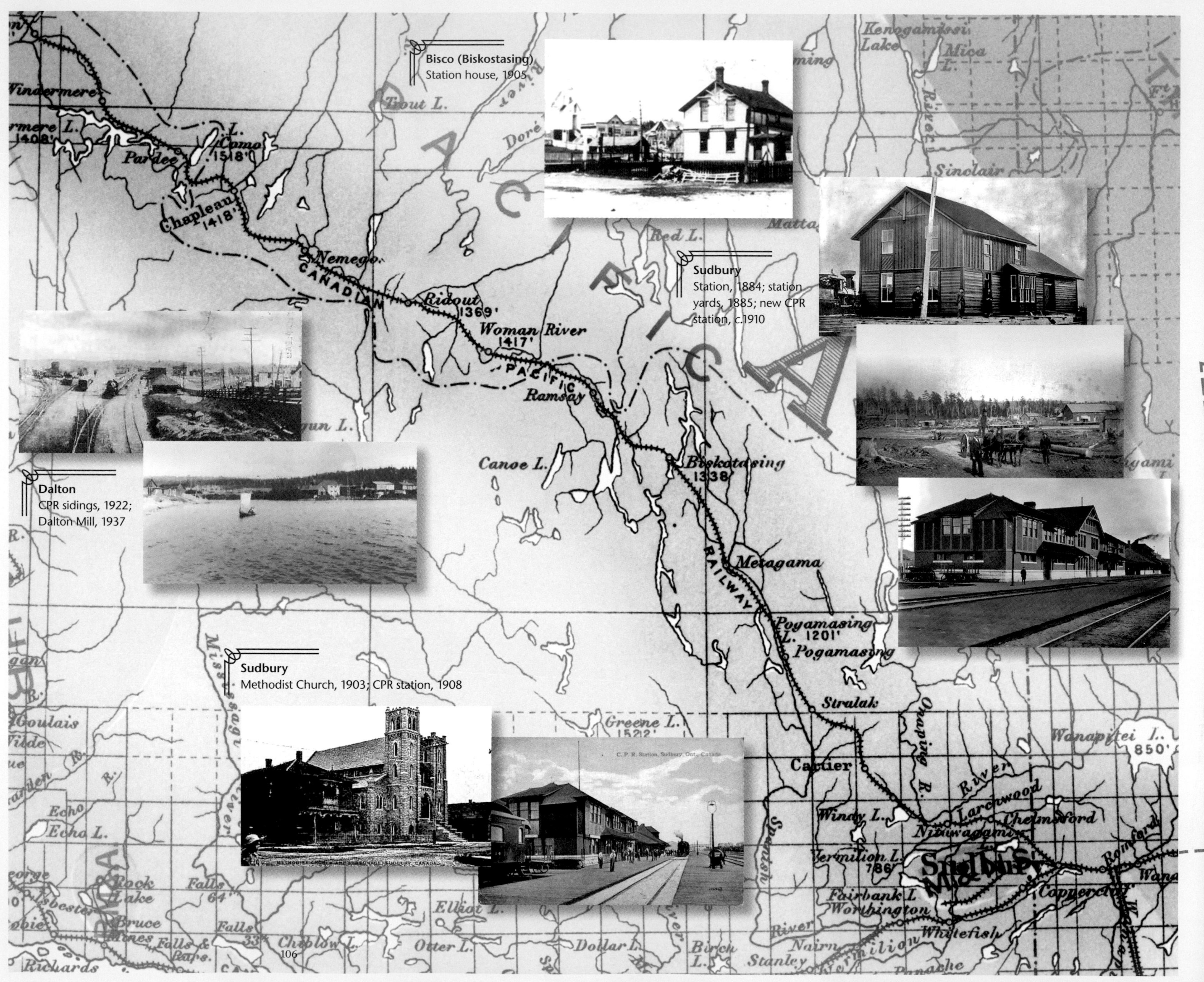

Bisco (Biskostasing)
Station house, 1905

Sudbury
Station, 1884; station yards, 1885; new CPR station, c.1910

Dalton
CPR sidings, 1922; Dalton Mill, 1937

Sudbury
Methodist Church, 1903; CPR station, 1908

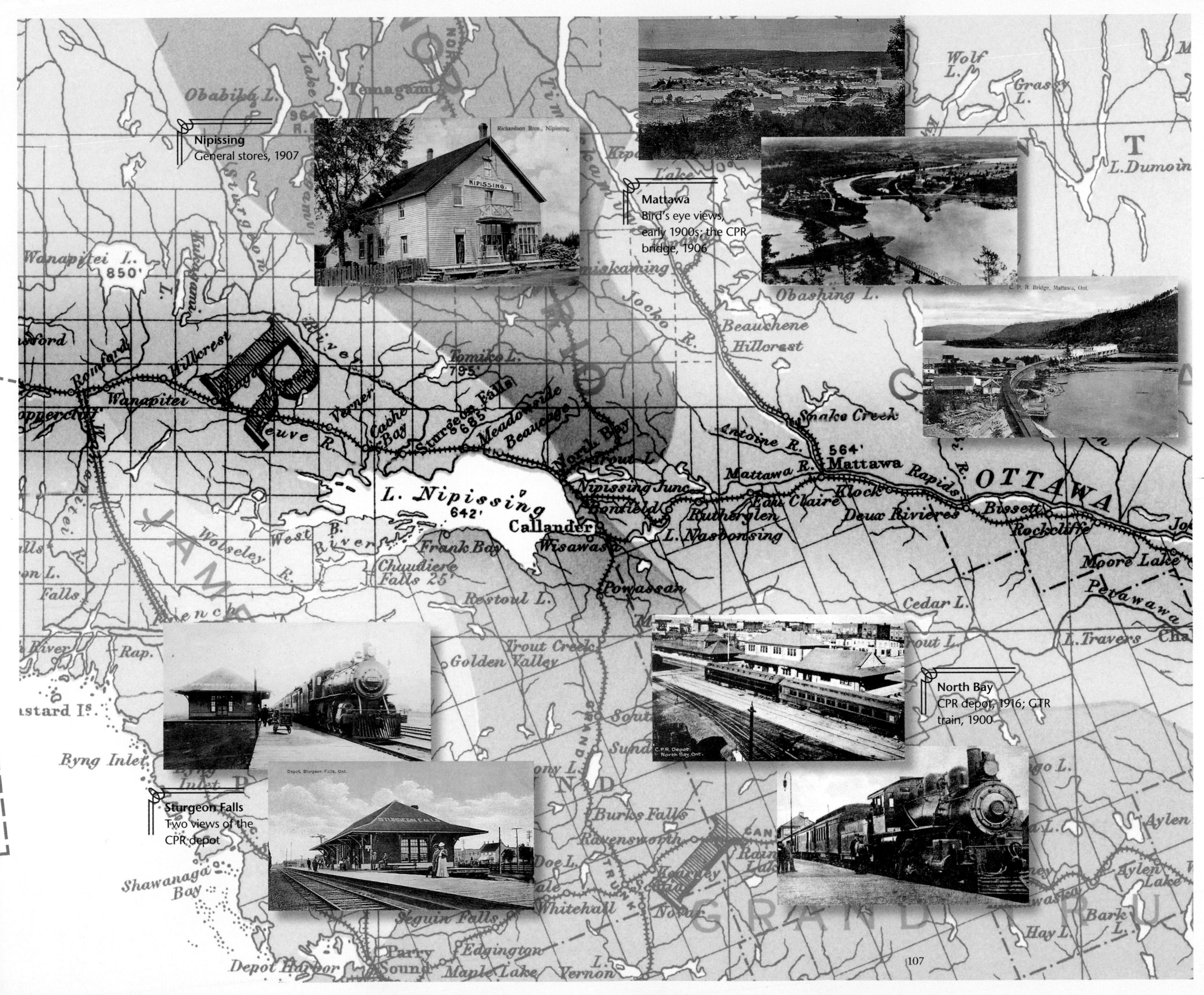

Nipissing
General stores, 1907

Mattawa
Bird's eye views, early 1900s; the CPR bridge, 1906

North Bay
CPR depot, 1916; GTR train, 1900

Sturgeon Falls
Two views of the CPR depot

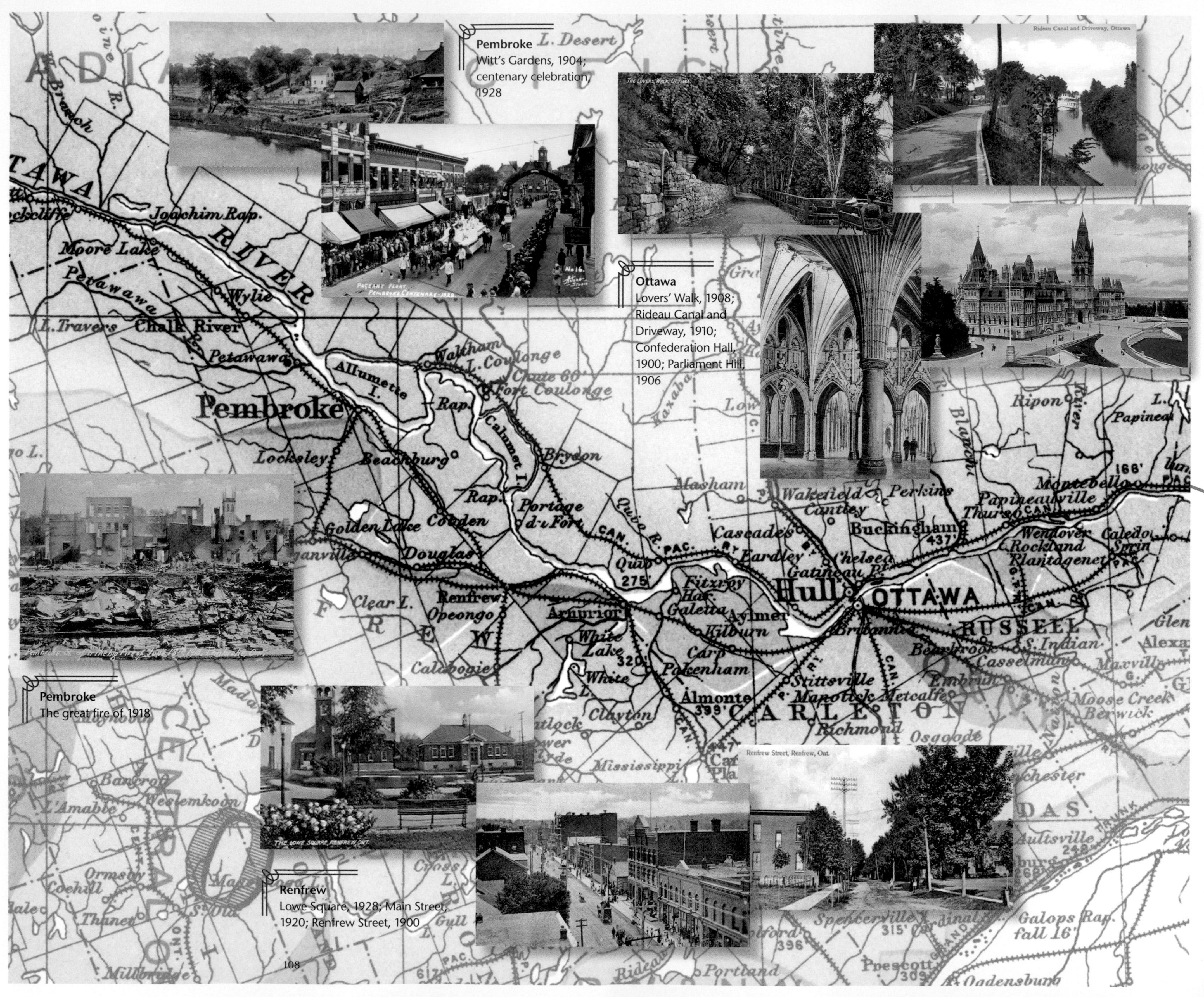

Pembroke
Witt's Gardens, 1904; centenary celebration, 1928

Ottawa
Lovers' Walk, 1908; Rideau Canal and Driveway, 1910; Confederation Hall, 1900; Parliament Hill, 1906

Pembroke
The great fire of 1918

Renfrew
Lowe Square, 1928; Main Street, 1920; Renfrew Street, 1900

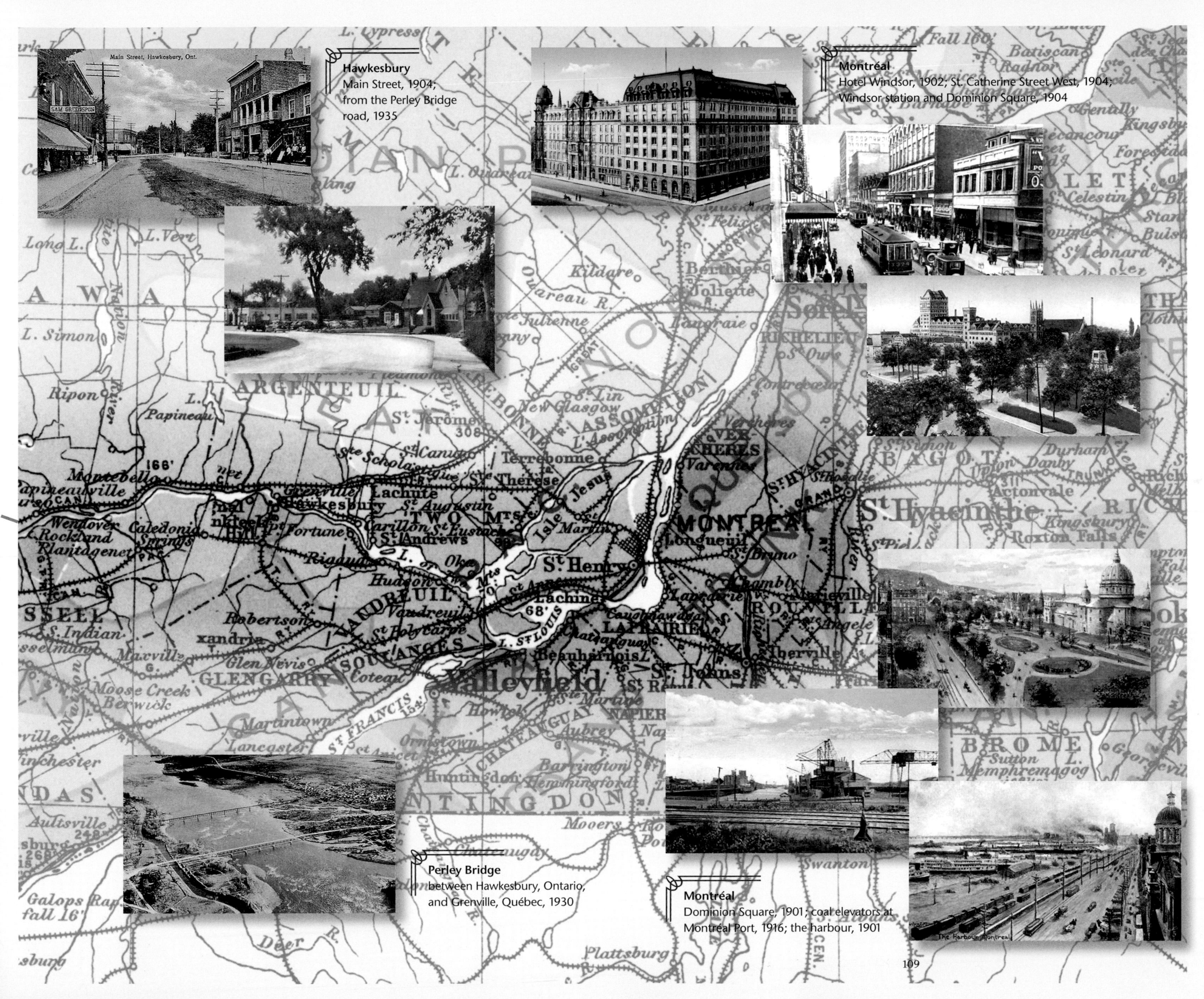

Hawkesbury
Main Street, 1904; from the Perley Bridge road, 1935

Montréal
Hotel Windsor, 1902; St. Catherine Street West, 1904; Windsor station and Dominion Square, 1904

Perley Bridge
between Hawkesbury, Ontario, and Grenville, Québec, 1930

Montréal
Dominion Square, 1901; coal elevators at Montréal Port, 1916; the harbour, 1901

THE NATIONAL TRANSCONTINENTAL RAILWAY

THE DIRECT ALTERNATIVE

Until 1915 the Canadian Pacific provided the only all-Canadian line from the Pacific coast to eastern Canada. This traffic monopoly was becoming increasingly unpopular with western farmers, as can be seen by the efforts to build a railway to Hudson Bay. Moreover, it seemed that the CPR was about to exceed its capacity to carry grain from the Prairies to eastern Canada.

Not surprisingly, the Dominion government was interested in promoting construction of a second, competing transcontinental line. At the beginning of the twentieth century, the Canadian Northern had built an extensive railway network in the prairie provinces. Meanwhile, the Grand Trunk Railway had an old and established network in eastern Canada. Logic dictated that these two lines should cooperate to build a single trans-Canada railway, but the two companies were not in a cooperative mood. Thus Canada got two new transcontinental lines when one would have been more than adequate.

In the 1870s the Dominion government had approached the Grand Trunk about the possibility of building a railway through to the Pacific, but the company decided that the project was not economically viable. However, by 1900 the situation changed and it was obvious that the Prairies now offered considerable traffic in both people and freight. The Grank Trunk wanted access to this potential business. The company proposed to enter the Canadian prairies via an inexpensive route through Chicago, thinking that an all-Canadian line north of Lake Superior would be both expensive to build and would not generate much traffic.

To the Dominion government, however, the United States link was politically unacceptable. A compromise was reached by which the Grand Trunk created a subsidiary, the Grand Trunk Pacific, to build between Winnipeg and the Pacific Ocean, while the Dominion government would build the unprofitable eastern section from the Maritime provinces to Winnipeg. The eastern line, known as the National Transcontinental Railway, was to be leased upon completion by the Grand Trunk Pacific. The Grand Trunk Pacific surveys began in 1903 and the main line from Winnipeg to Prince Rupert on the Pacific coast was completed in 1914. The National Transcontinental was completed the next year.

By 1900 an efficient grain handling system had evolved in Canada. Grain was carried by rail from storage elevators located along the prairie rail network to the ports of Port Arthur and Fort William (today Thunder Bay) on the western shore of Lake Superior. From there the grain was carried by lake boats through the Great Lakes to Montréal harbour where it was transhipped into ocean-going vessels for export to Europe. During the winter, grain was carried by rail to ice-free ocean ports at Halifax and Saint John.

An important premise for the construction of the National Transcontinental was that the railway could economically haul grain from Winnipeg to Québec City. But, since interior

Building a bridge on the National Transcontinental Railway, *c.*1910 (left).

NTR standard sections for cuttings and embankments (below left).

Culvert construction on the National Transcontinental Railway, Ontario, Sunday Lake, 1908 (left).

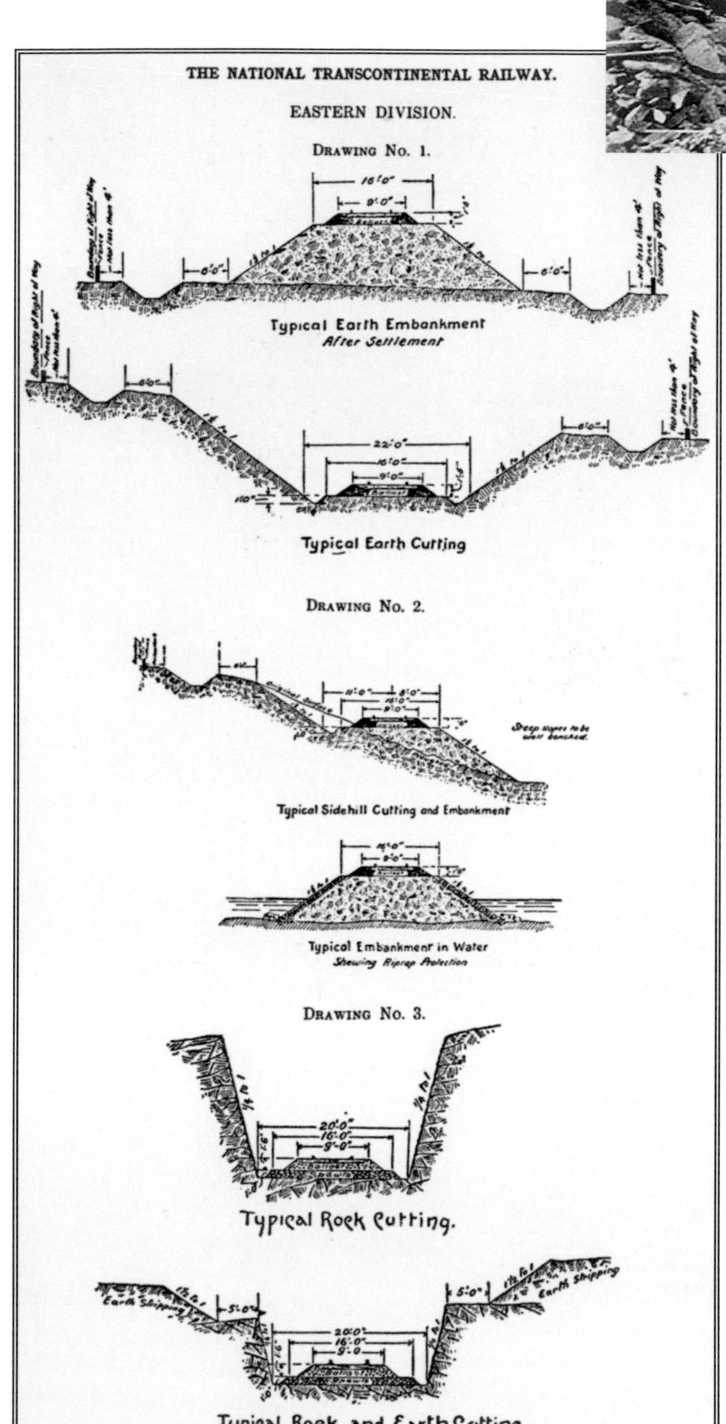

water transport was cheap and overland transport required investment in a vast infrastructure of grain elevators, harbours and rail yards, it is difficult to understand how anyone could believe that western grain could be hauled economically entirely by rail to Québec City, let alone to Halifax.

The National Transcontinental route was located to provide the shortest distance between Winnipeg and Québec City without regard to the traffic potential of the intervening country. This type of route is called a "bridge line" in which populous, traffic-generating areas are connected, or bridged, by a section of non-traffic-bearing track. Such bridge lines are not uncommon but have rarely occurred on the scale of the National Transcontinental.

The route of the National Transcontinental can be divided into two sections. One extended from Moncton, New Brunswick (the eastern terminal of the line) to Québec City. The second ran from Québec City to Winnipeg, the western terminus.

At Moncton the railway obtained rights to operate trains over tracks of the Intercolonial Railway to ocean ports at Saint John, New Brunswick, and Halifax, Nova Scotia. From Moncton the railway proceeded westward through the centre of the province and then headed northward, skirting the border with Maine. This route had been considered for the Intercolonial railway almost forty years earlier. At that time the route was rejected because of the inability to protect the line in case of war with the United States. This was not a risk by 1900.

The land was well settled and did not present many construction problems. One exception was the 3,920-foot (1,195-metre) viaduct over the Little Salmon River in New Brunswick.

Along the St. Lawrence River the railway ran parallel to, but some miles inland from, the Intercolonial Railway which hugged the shoreline. The National Transcontinental carefully chose better grades and alignments than the older Intercolonial, permitting the newer railway to run heavier trains.

Québec City was by far the largest and most important city on the National Transcontinental, and construction of the railway was the culmination of over thirty years of effort to improve the rail service at the port. Québec was at the end-of-the-line of the Canadian rail network, but most traffic passed through the port of Montréal. Throughout the 1870s, the Québec City commercial community believed that its port was the logical eastern terminus of the Canadian Pacific Railway. However, in 1882 the incorporation of the CPR ended any thoughts of Québec City being the eastern terminus – it would be Montréal.

An added aggravation felt by Québec City was that although the city was on the north shore of the St. Lawrence, the Grand Trunk and later Intercolonial terminals were on the south bank in Lévis. Although the Grand Trunk wharf could handle ocean vessels, most freight and passengers were landed at Québec and had to be ferried across the river. Québec's real opportunity to obtain good rail connections finally came in 1903 when the Liberal government announced that it would construct a second transcontinental railway passing through Québec City and avoiding Montréal. As a separate activity, the Dominion government began work in 1900 on a railway bridge across the St. Lawrence River.

From Québec, the National Transcontinental route ran northward for about 120 miles (200 km) to the settled Lac Saint-Jean region. After that, the country was undeveloped, although some of its economic potential was known.

The railway bisected the "clay belt" that extended from Barraute, Québec, to Cochrane, Ontario. This soil and climate supported agriculture, but until construction of the National Transcontinental the area was far too isolated to be attractive for settlement. The Québec government started to encourage settlement about 1910, followed by the Ontario government after World War I.

The potential mineral wealth of northern Québec was recognized at the time of construction of the National Transcontinental, but large-scale mining did not begin until after World War I. In 1928 the first of several rail lines was constructed into the gold and copper district of Rouyn-Noranda.

The only rail connection in Ontario between the National Transcontinental and populous southern Ontario was provided at Cochrane. Here, the railway obtained trackage rights over the Temiskaming and Northern Ontario Railway to North Bay where a connection was made with the parent Grand Trunk Railway.

The importance of the grain trade in promoting railway construction cannot be underestimated. The Grand Trunk Pacific's main line across the Prairies from Winnipeg to Edmonton was finished in 1909. The connecting line built by the National Transcontinental was not completed for another six years. Rather than lose the lucrative grain traffic, the Grand Trunk Pacific built a line in 1910 from Sioux Lookout on the completed section of the National Transcontinental to Fort William on Lake Superior, specifically to carry grain to lake boats.

The Union Station at Winnipeg was built by the Canadian Northern in 1911. Despite being fierce competitors, the station was also used by the Grand Trunk Pacific and National Transcontinental. The station is still used today by VIA Rail.

When completed, the National Transcontinental was one of the best built railways in North America. One has to question why it was built, given the limited traffic that was anticipated. For example, the railway's Transcona shops at Winnipeg, completed in 1911, were among the best equipped in North America. The facility could build 50 and repair 225 locomotives per year—twice the required needs of the line. Similar overcapacity existed in the other shops in the complex.

The normal practice was to build a line cheaply and then increase traffic capacity as needed. For example, the immense Little Salmon River trestle, mentioned earlier, could have been built substantially cheaper if a shorter bridge had been constructed with steeper grades at each end. Even though an extra locomotive would have been needed for this section of track, the operating cost of the service would have been more than offset by the savings on a cheaper river crossing.

Not only over-built, the National Transcontinental also suffered from poor management, irregular contracting, and construction problems, all of which vastly inflated its cost. In the end the final bill was $160 million, up from an original estimate of $62 million. In 1911, four years before the railway was even completed, the Dominion government established an investigating committee to determine why construction had been so expensive.

As the cost of construction rose, the Grand Trunk Pacific Railway refused to lease such an expensive railway. Effectively bankrupt, the Grand Trunk Pacific quite simply could not afford it. After all, by 1915, economic conditions in Canada were far different from when the line was first proposed fifteen years earlier; the country had experienced an economic downturn in 1913 and the following year the war started.

In 1915 the National Transcontinental was turned over to the Canadian government and folded into the federally owned Canadian Government Railways. This was then transformed at the end of 1918 into the Canadian National Railways, set up by the federal government to operate all its various railways. In July 1920 the Grand Trunk Pacific was nationalized and added to the Canadian National, although the Grand Trunk itself was not merged into the Canadian National until January 1923.

Significant portions of the National Transcontinental exist today. It forms part of the main line between Manitoba and Ontario and through New Brunswick, and sections are still used to service the mining and timber operations in northern Ontario and Québec. But the best built railway in Canada was never called upon to handle the traffic for which it had been designed.

Decorative emblem depicting Canada as an international provider of grain, from *Canada,* published in 1905.

THE QUEBEC BRIDGE

Crossing the St. Lawrence

A bridge over the St. Lawrence River at Québec City was first mooted in 1852, and again in 1867, 1882, and 1884. Successfully constructing a railway bridge at this location faced two major hurdles, one technical and the other commercial.

The technical challenge was the depth—not the width—of the river at Québec. At the bridge location, it is 183 feet (56 m) deep. Long railway bridges had been built in the 1850s, but they relied on short-span structures resting on river piers. Bridge piers could not be constructed in such deep water as at Québec. Instead, a single, very long span bridge would be necessary.

The lack of rail traffic was the commercial problem. If sufficient traffic had existed, a railway car ferry service would have been established long before the bridge was finally completed. The Grand Trunk Railway with its terminus in Lévis, opposite Québec, had no need for such a service. Only one ferry proposal was seriously explored in 1879–85, but nothing came of the scheme since the volume of traffic was not great enough.

The Québec Bridge Company was incorporated in 1887, beginning a thirty-year odyssey of design, construction, failure, and finally completion of the bridge. In 1898 the Dominion government approved a bridge design for a crossing at the narrowest part of the river at Ste-Foy, just upstream from Québec.

The bridge was designed as a daring, lightweight cantilever structure with a span of 1,800 feet (549 m). This design was well suited for long-span bridges that could support the weight of heavy trains. The most famous cantilever bridge is that over the Firth of Forth in Scotland, which consists of four main spans, the longest of which is 1,700 feet (520 m).

Work began in October 1900, with construction supervised by Theodore Cooper of New York City, the leading American bridge engineer of the era. The steel superstructure was built by the well-known Phoenix Bridge Company of Phoenixville, Pennsylvania, but the company and Cooper did not share a good working relationship, leading to a tragic series of errors.

Mistakes in the preliminary calculations produced a design that could not support the weight of the bridge structure, let alone the weight of a train. It was inevitable that the bridge would collapse before it was finished. The erection of steel work began on July 22, 1905, with completion promised by December 31, 1908. However visible deformations in the steelwork on the south end of the bridge started to appear in June 1907. These were reported to Cooper by his on-site inspector.

The Phoenix Bridge Company ignored the concerns raised by field engineers, and similarly Cooper did not believe that the bridge was in urgent danger. Only when the deformations increased did he telegraph the Phoenix Bridge Company on August 29, 1907 to stop work until the design was re-assessed. It was too late. At 5.30p.m. of that same day the south span collapsed, with a loss of seventy-five of the eighty-six workers on the bridge at the time.

Of the victims, thirty-three were Mohawk steelworkers from the Kahnawake reserve near Montréal. The Kahnawake Mohawks had a reputation as skilled high-steel workers, and many had been employed on the bridge.

Québec Bridge, May 1947 (below).

A postcard of 1907, which was widely distributed after the accident (right).

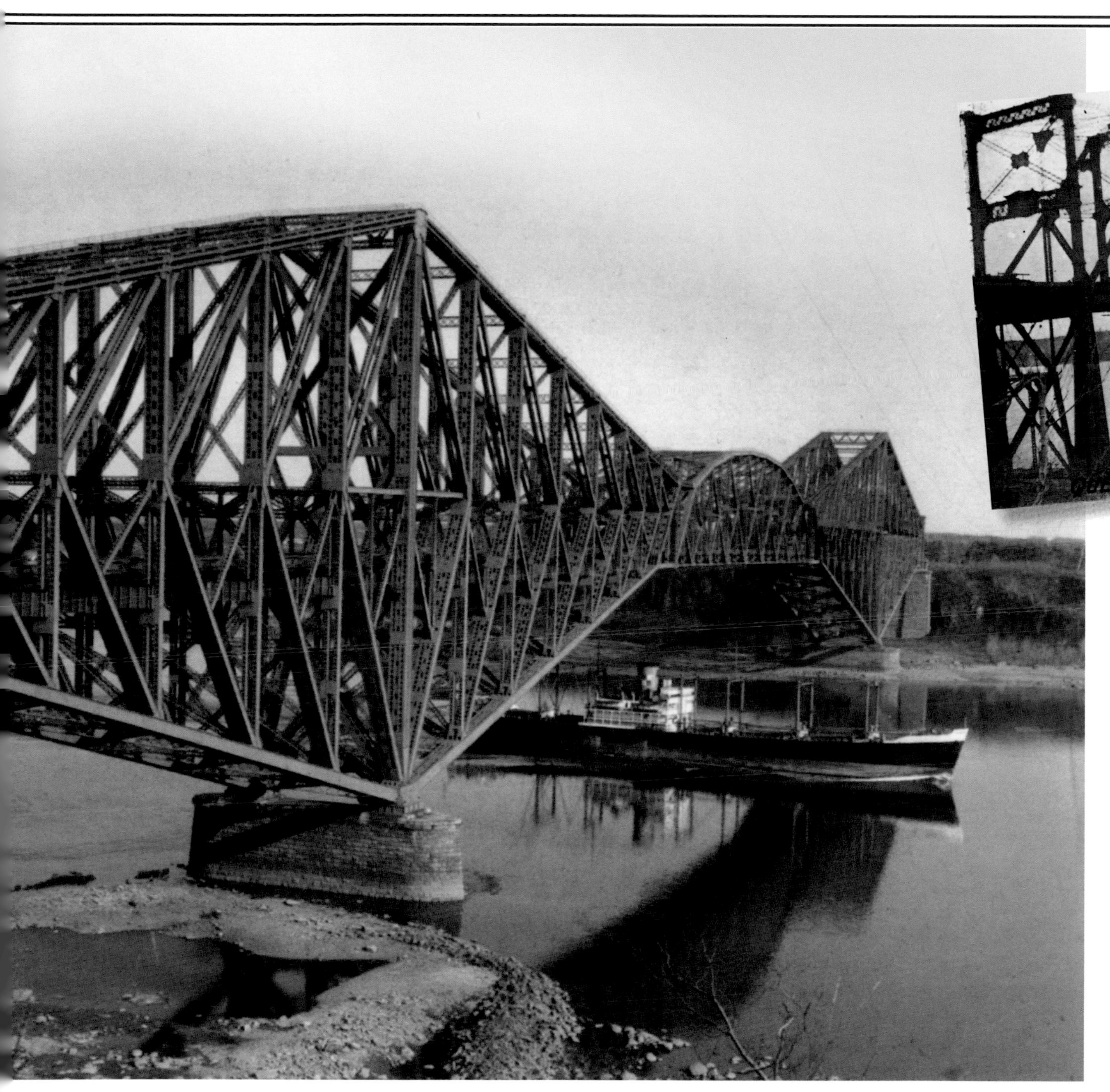

Collapse of the span and subsequent delays in construction did finally lead to train ferry operations. In 1907 the Grand Trunk commenced a service, followed by the National Transcontinental Railway in 1915. Both ended when the bridge finally opened.

In 1908 the Dominion government took over the bridge company's assets since the crossing was now part of the National Transcontinental Railway scheme. A new design was prepared–also based on the cantilever principle–but much more massive than the 1898 design. Construction began in 1910 and proceeded uneventfully. Then, on September 11, 1916, the centre span fell into the river while being raised into position, and thirteen workers died, although this accident was caused by a technical failure in the hoisting equipment rather than a design flaw. The bridge was finally opened to rail traffic on December 3, 1919 and is still used today by the Canadian National Railway and as a highway crossing of the river.

THE LONGLAC–NAKINA CUTOFF

Merging the Lines

In 1915 the Canadian Northern and National Transcontinental Railways were finishing their lines across northern Ontario. The National Transcontinental track ran in a general east–west direction far north of Lake Superior, whereas the Canadian Northern served the port of Fort William (today Thunder Bay) on the lake before running northeast to avoid the difficult topography along the Lake Superior shore. The two companies had no physical connection between Winnipeg and Québec City.

The economic wisdom of building two competing main line railways through the largely undeveloped region of northern Ontario had been questioned prior to their construction, since the region would not generate business for either company. The need to eliminate this costly duplication could not be avoided when the two railways were folded into the Canadian National Railways in 1917.

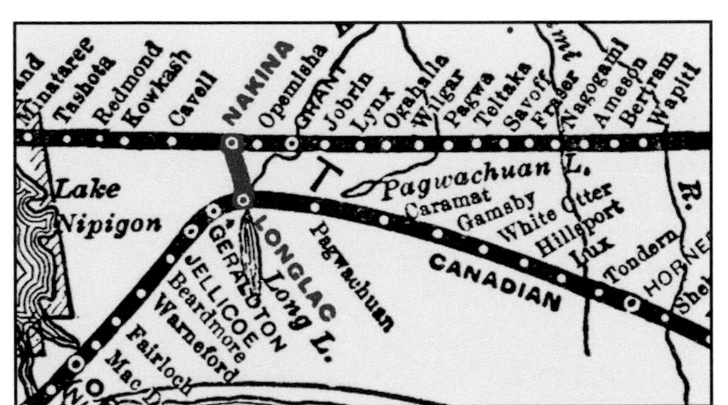

The cutoff shown on the standard Canadian National railways timetable map; this one dating from 1943.

The solution was to build a connecting line in 1923 between the two closest points on the rival lines—Longlac on the Canadian Northern about 199 miles (320 km) west of Thunder Bay, and Nakina about 30 miles (45 km) further north on the National Transcontinental.

The main transcontinental line then became the former National Transcontinental between Winnipeg and Nakina, and the Canadian Northern from Longlac to southern Ontario and Québec. The line east of Nakina was retained as a secondary line for local businesses, and survived until 1986 when a 122-mile (195-km) section east of Nakina was abandoned. The line west of Longlac was also retained as a secondary main line to Thunder Bay, and is still in service today.

An added expense was the need to build a new division point at Nakina (a service centre that provided facilities for changing train crews and maintaining locomotives), since the original division point for this section of National Transcontinental track had been built in 1913 at Grant, 16 miles (26 km) east of Nakina. Grant, along with its shops, hotels, and service yard, was later abandoned.

In contrast, Nakina and Longlac both benefited from the railways and became thriving towns with timber and pulping businesses, offering themselves as "gateways" to the leisure facilities of the Ontario wilderness. The two lines across northern Ontario formed the longest operational challenge that the Canadian National had had to confront, but it was by no means the only route duplication that the new railway entity had to resolve. Problems extended from the Québec–New Brunswick border to the Rocky Mountains, and it took fifteen years to meld the networks into a unified operation.

Some problem areas were quite short, as in merging the parallel Canadian Northern and National Transcontinental lines entering Québec City into a single trunk line, and there was relatively less duplicate track in western Canada, where the Canadian Northern had built an extensive system of main lines and branch lines, but the Grand Trunk Pacific had not had time to build much more than its main line.

In 1917 parts of the two lines in the West were combined into a single track, and the salvaged rail was shipped to France to replace track destroyed by World War I. From Tête Jaune on the Fraser River in British Columbia the Canadian Northern line swung southward to Vancouver, while the Grand Trunk headed northwest to Prince Rupert on the Pacific coast. Almost eighty years later some of the abandoned route in the Yellowhead Pass was rebuilt as part of a double-tracking program that the Canadian National undertook in the 1990s.

764 ENGINEERING NEWS-RECORD Vol. 92, No. 18

arising from the diversion of water from Black River for the operation of the canal system of the state. It has an area of about 2,757 acres, an effective depth of about 10 ft. and a capacity of 900,000,000 cu.ft. The present dam consists of an earth embankment 500 ft. long and 35 ft. high, a concrete spillway section 200 ft. long and 20 ft. high, separated from the embankment by a small knoll of granitic rock. The spillway is founded on rock and the embankment partly on rock and partly on glacial hardpan. The outlet works consist of four 48-in. circular sluice gates which discharge into a tunnel around the south end of the spillway.

Plans for the enlargement of the reservoir call for raising the dam 19 ft. to increase the permanent area to 6,715 acres and the capacity to 4,500,000,000 cu.ft. In increasing the height of the embankment the upstream slope will be reduced from a one on two slope to a one on two and one-half slope. The height of the concrete spillway will be increased 17 ft. and it will be provided with 2-ft. flash-boards. The increase in water level will necessitate the construction of a second earth embankment 300 ft. long and 20 ft. high and of a second or auxiliary spillway 200 ft. long across two valleys south of the present structure. The auxiliary spillway will consist essentially of a concrete cutoff wall built in a trench across the valleys at a point where ground lines correspond approximately to the flow line of the reservoir. It will also be provided with 2-ft. flash-boards and its length added to that at the main spillway will make possible the discharge of the assumed maximum flood flow of 6,600 sec.-ft. and keep the flood height within the limits of the flow line of the reservoir. The new outlet works will consist of a series of five sluice gates, ranging in size from 24x24 in. to 48x48 in., set in gate wells at the south end of the spillway. Owing to the necessity of keeping the present reservoir in operation during the period of reconstruction the construction of entirely new outlets was decided upon. When the new ones are built the old ones will be plugged with concrete and the outlet tunnel will be abandoned.

Auxiliary work will include raising about 1½ miles of the New York Central track where it crosses the reservoir, the building of a new bridge across the south branch of Beaver River and the clearing of the 4,000 acres of land flooded at the increased height. The law requires the clearing of all land below the flood flow line. The timber on the 3,000 acres of state land to be cleared was sold in August, 1923, and it is expected that the lumbering operations will be completed by the fall of this year and that the entire work of enlarging the reservoir will be completed before the spring flood in 1925.

A contract for the raising and rebuilding of the dam and spillway was awarded to Scott Brothers Construction Co. in December, 1923.

Canadian National Railways Complete Longlac-Nakina Cutoff

A CUTOFF that is unique in railway development has recently been completed by the Canadian National Railways. Its construction was made possible through the consolidation of the National Transcontinental Ry. and the Canadian Northern Ry. into the National Railways, thus giving the National Railways two through lines from eastern Canada to Winnipeg. The accompanying map shows the peculiar relation of these two transcontinental railways in the territory north of Lake Superior.

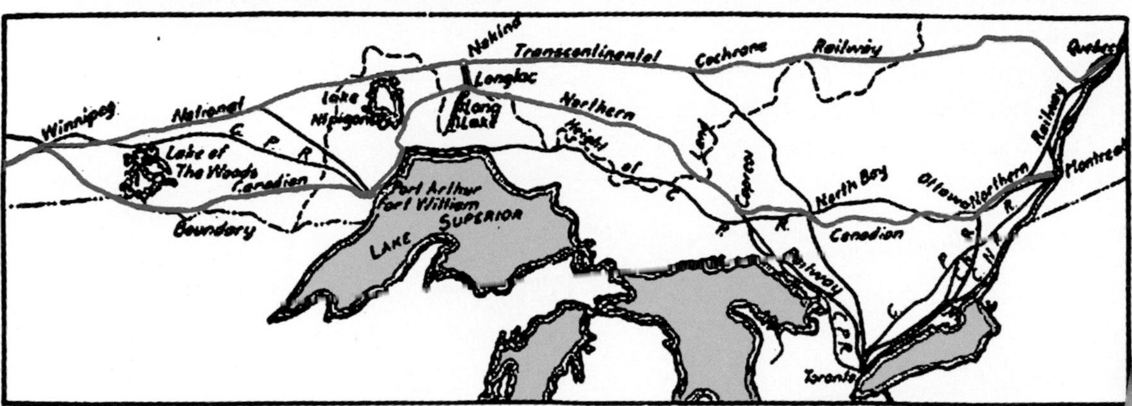

CANADIAN NATIONAL RY. THROUGH LINES FROM EASTERN CANADA TO WINNIPEG

The National Transcontinental, running in an almost straight line from Quebec to Winnipeg through the comparatively flat land of the clay belt north of the height of land passes north of Lake Nipigon while the Canadian Northern, also taking advantage of the clay country north of the height of land passed to the north of Long Lake and then turned south down the Nipigon River to Lake Superior in order to connect with its line into Fort William. At the northern end of Long Lake the two railways were only about 30 miles apart.

When the two railways were consolidated it was realized that by constructing this 30-mile connecting link at Long Lake it would be possible to reduce the distance between Toronto or Montreal, and Winnipeg by 102 miles and the distance between Quebec and Port Arthur by 99 miles. The greater advantage of the cutoff is, however, in the saving in all rail freight movement between Winnipeg and Toronto or Montreal both in distance and in vertical rise and fall formerly required on the C.N.R. route in going down to lake level at Fort William.

Work was started in January, 1923, and the new train schedule over the cutoff went into effect in January, 1924. The total cost was about $2,000,000 and the annual saving is estimated at about $400,000.

An article describing the Longlac–Nakina Cutoff, from *Engineering News Record,* 1923 (left).

Longlac station, *c.*1930 (above).

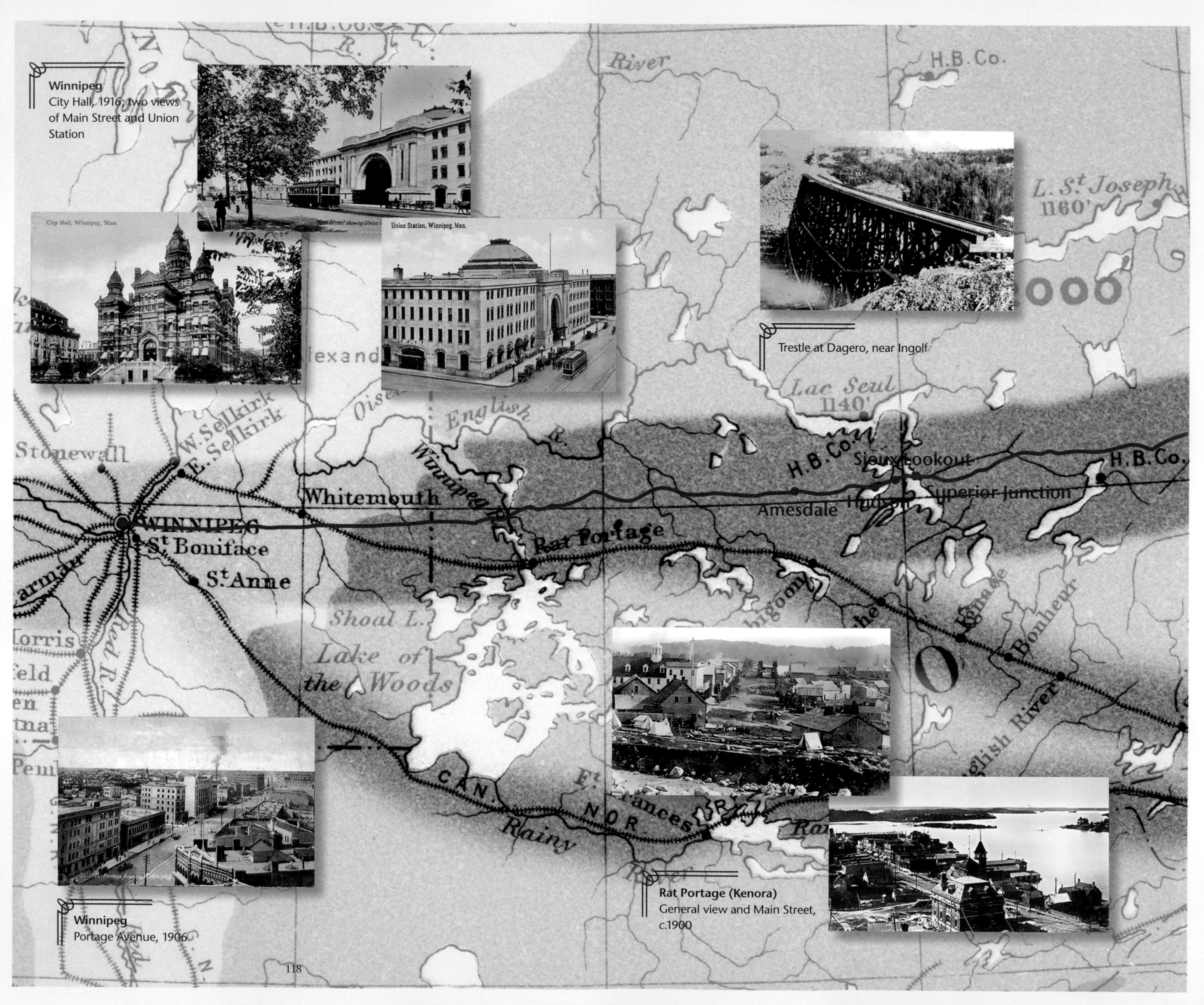

Winnipeg
City Hall, 1916; two views of Main Street and Union Station

Trestle at Dagero, near Ingolf

Winnipeg
Portage Avenue, 1906

Rat Portage (Kenora)
General view and Main Street, *c.*1900

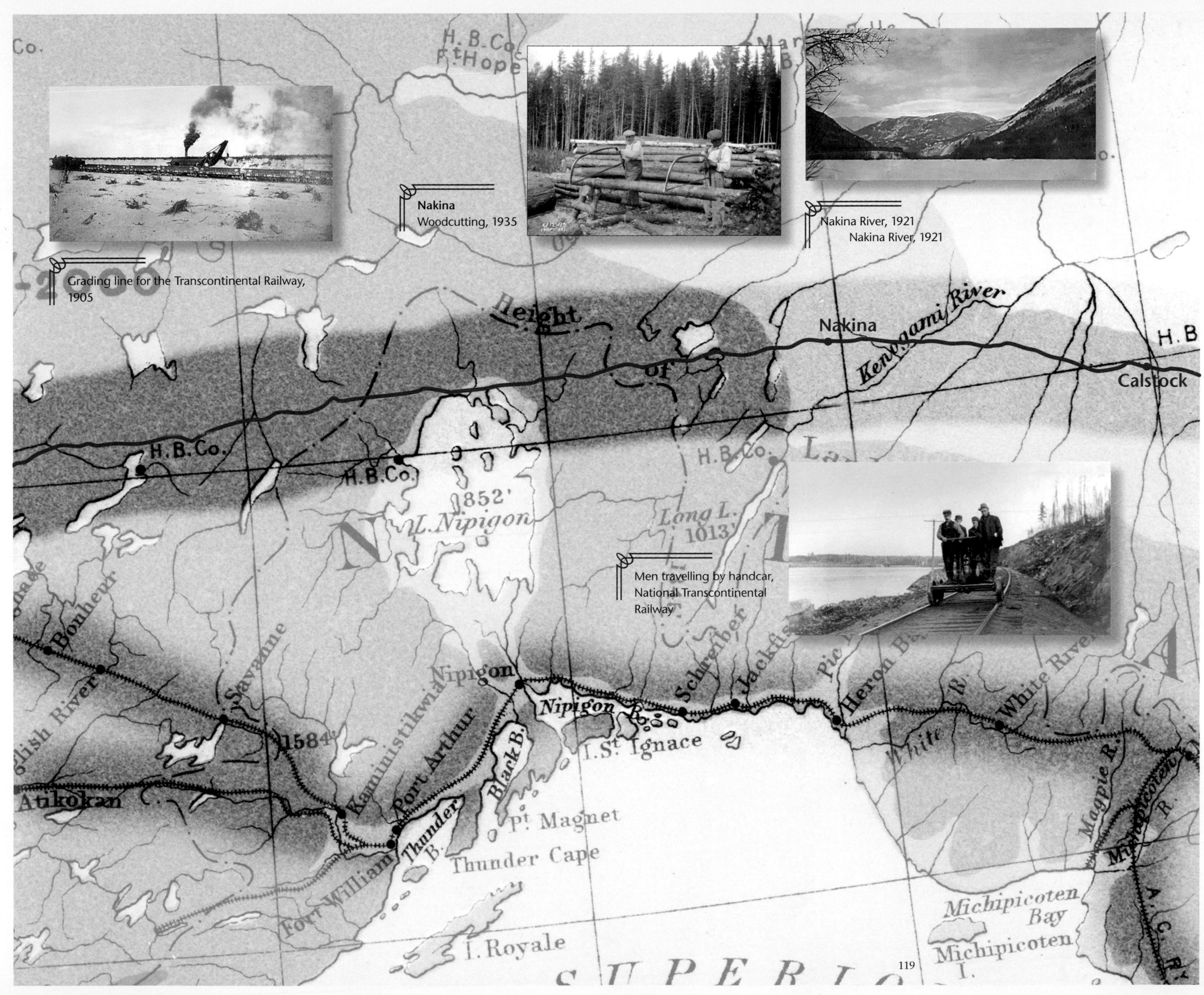

Grading line for the Transcontinental Railway, 1905

Nakina
Woodcutting, 1935

Nakina River, 1921

Nakina River, 1921

Men travelling by handcar, National Transcontinental Railway

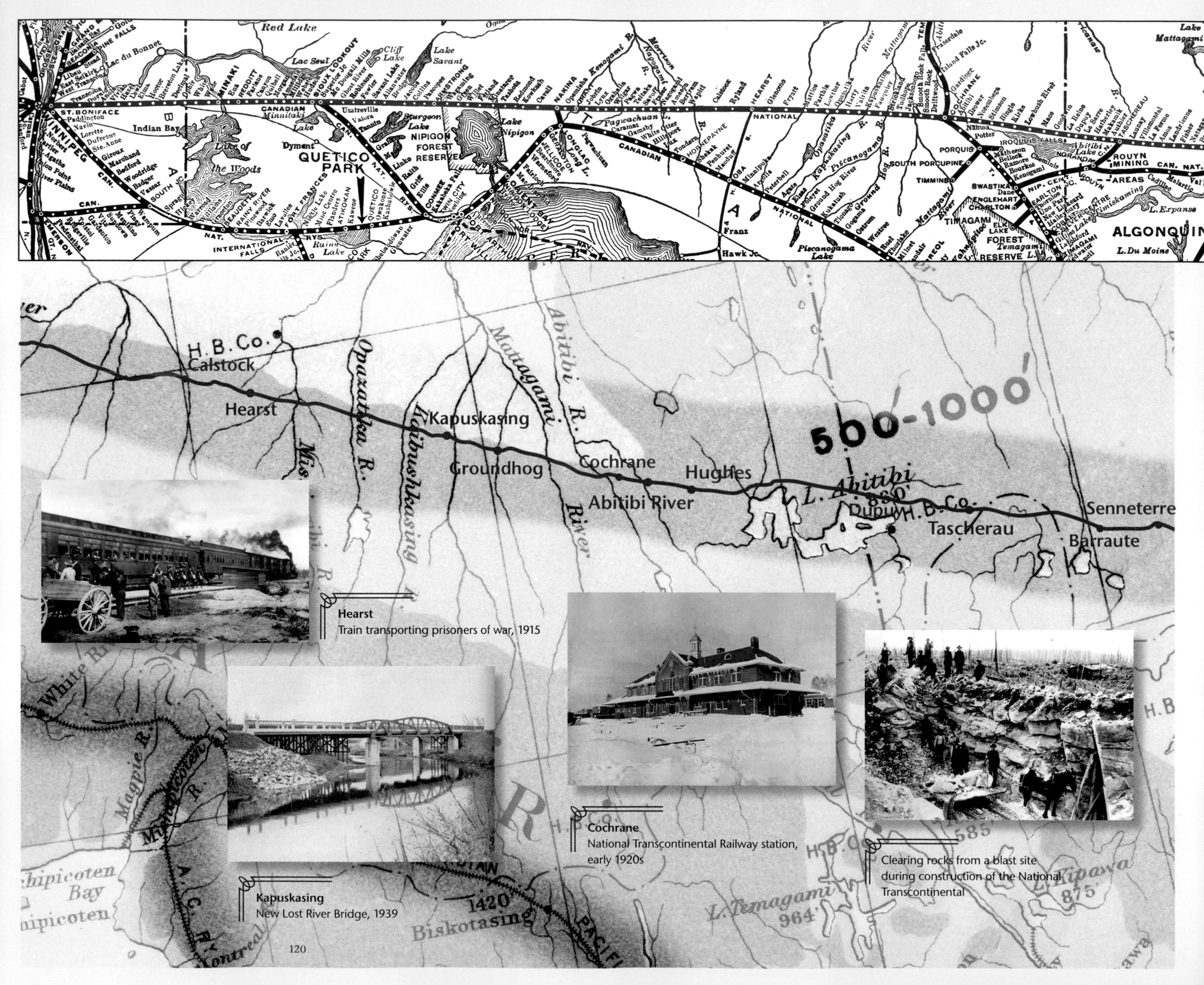

Hearst
Train transporting prisoners of war, 1915

Kapuskasing
New Lost River Bridge, 1939

Cochrane
National Transcontinental Railway station, early 1920s

Clearing rocks from a blast site during construction of the National Transcontinental

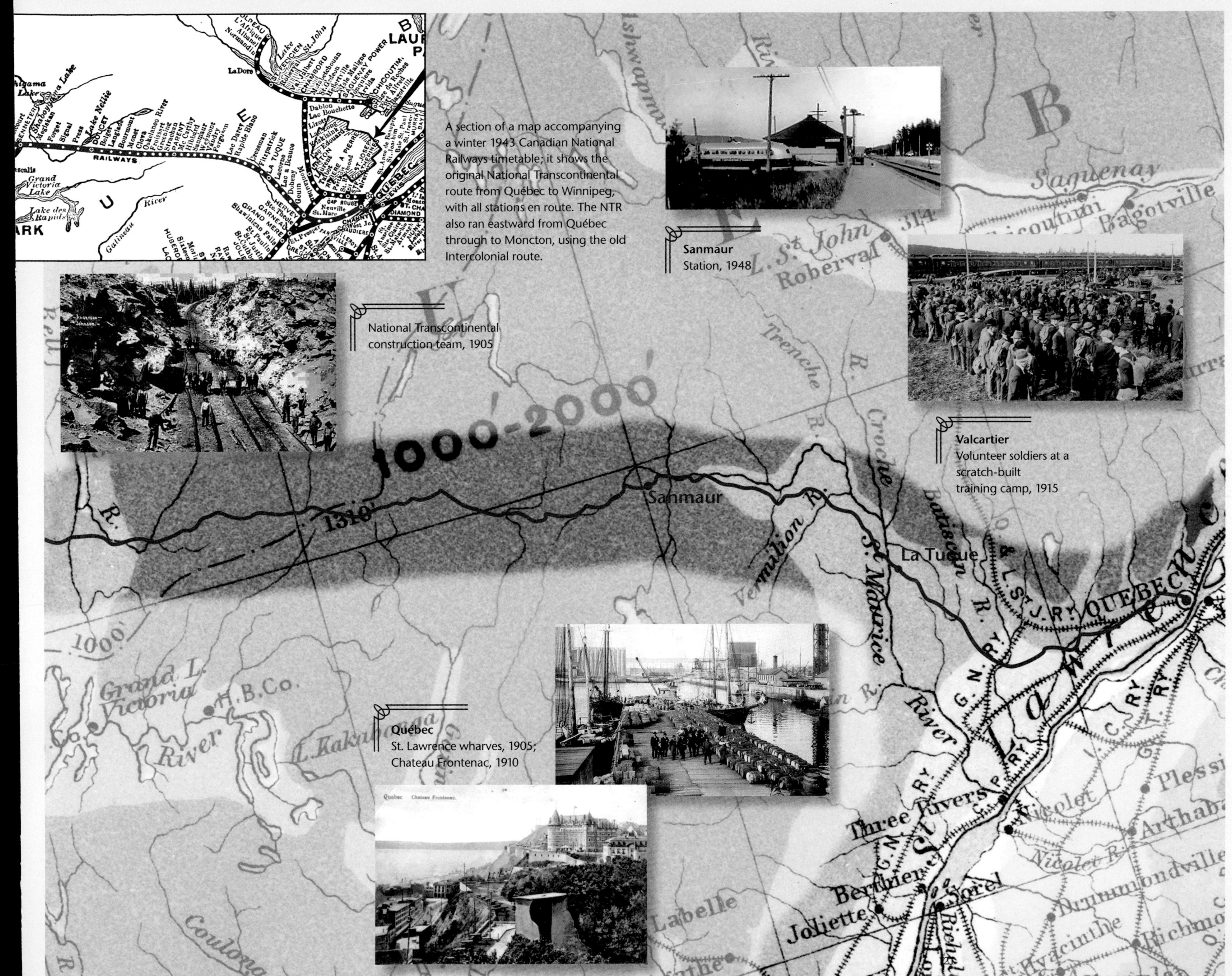

A section of a map accompanying a winter 1943 Canadian National Railways timetable; it shows the original National Transcontinental route from Québec to Winnipeg, with all stations en route. The NTR also ran eastward from Québec through to Moncton, using the old Intercolonial route.

Sanmaur
Station, 1948

National Transcontinental construction team, 1905

Valcartier
Volunteer soldiers at a scratch-built training camp, 1915

Québec
St. Lawrence wharves, 1905;
Chateau Frontenac, 1910

THE GRAND TRUNK PACIFIC

FROM WINNIPEG TO PRINCE RUPERT

On this continent wide, where our loved ones reside,
We have railways, both "great" and "small";
But of first-water brand, ours alone is styled "Grand",
So the Grand Trunk leads them all!
... And we all declare, that no chief can compare,
With the chief of our road—Mr. Hays!
The great legal lights, in the fierce railroad fights,
Seem anxious to make a figure;
Let them swagger and frown in their biggest gown,
Still the Grand Trunk has a "Biggar"!

"For the Reunion of Official Family
of the Grand Trunk Railway System,"
W.H. Rosevear, May 16, 1907

The road of a thousand wonders
The trail of a hundred hell's [sic]
The story of a thousand blunders
Is the tale the death roll tells.

In a tale of a future grandeur
And the dream of a judgment day,
I stand by the sorrow and wonder
Who is great—God or Laurier.

"The Grand Trunk Pacific,"
by J.A. McKechnie (John Houston)
Prince Rupert Evening Bulletin, March 30, 1909

Public opinion of the Grand Trunk Pacific Railway (GTPR) varied widely in Canada, as illustrated by these two poems. A subsidiary of the Grand Trunk Railway, the GTPR was formally established in 1903. After years of planning and construction, it formed a 2,983-mile (4,800 km) system of track that served to provide the eastern GTR with access to the West and helped it remain competitive with the Canadian Pacific Railway and the Canadian Northern Railway. Funded by loans from the Canadian government, the GTPR had a mandate to build track between Winnipeg, Manitoba, and the Pacific coast at Prince Rupert, British Columbia. The original plan was for the Grand Trunk Railway to run both the GTPR and the National Transcontinental Railway (NTR) as a unit, therefore creating a transnational line all the way from Moncton, New Brunswick, to Prince Rupert, but a lack of funds prevented this from taking place.

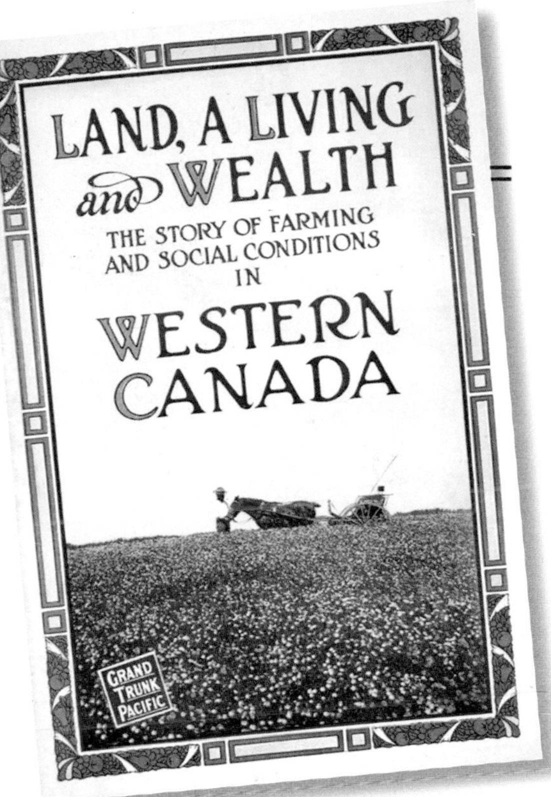

A Grand Trunk Pacific publication of 1913, encouraging European immigration to the northern prairies.

Originally, the GTPR outlined a transcontinental rail route that in the West was even closer to Asia than the Canadian Pacific terminus of Vancouver. The proposed route followed the recommendations of surveyor Sandford Fleming by ending at Port Simpson, on the boundary between Alaska and British Columbia, but plans went "off the rails" when tensions over the Alaska boundary decision of 1903 led to US President Theodore Roosevelt threatening to send an occupation force to the area. Prime Minister Wilfred Laurier consequently chose to relocate the terminus to a less contentious but still CPR-competitive spot at Prince Rupert, British Columbia.

Construction of the GTPR began on September 11, 1905 when Wilfred Laurier turned the sod at Fort William, Ontario in an opening ceremony. Subsequently the Grand Trunk Pacific Construction Company connected the Fort William

Setting the steel of the Battle River Viaduct of the Grand Trunk Pacific (opposite).

The first passenger train crossed the newly-opened High Level Bridge at Edmonton on June 2, 1913 (postcard above and GTPR stamp above right).

terminus to the NTR line, 190 miles (306 km) away. That same year, construction began across the Prairies, with the railway crews reaching Saskatoon, Saskatchewan in 1907 and Edmonton, Alberta two years after that. From Edmonton, the tracks ran through Jasper and up to the Continental Divide at Yellowhead Pass throughout 1910 and 1911. Construction of the line was finally completed on April 7, 1914 at Prince Rupert's newly constructed seaport. By the time of its completion, the GTPR had more than 1,118 miles (1,800 km) of track in Saskatchewan alone, with 97 depots, 138 loading platforms, 23 warehouses, and 50 stockyards.

The main branch of the GTPR passed through southern Saskatchewan on a northwesterly route, with Melville and Biggar as the two main divisional points. The railway entered Saskatchewan from Manitoba just southeast of Spy Hill, and then progressed through Melville, Watrous, and Biggar, and on to Edmonton. At Melville, branch lines went north to Canora, southwest to Regina, and all the way south through Weyburn to the Saskatchewan/United States border. An additional line continued west from Regina through Moosejaw. Branch lines also broke away from the main line at Young, heading north to Prince Albert, and at Biggar, where branches split south to Calgary and north to Battleford.

DISAPPOINTMENT AND DEMISE

The completed line did not fulfill expectations as quickly as hoped. The new competition for the CPR lacked the marketing expertise, government financial support, and service population of the older line. Furthermore, plans to draw immigrants to towns along the route were put on the shelf by World War I. The war was also accompanied by a worldwide economic slowdown that crippled the GTPR's ability to turn a profit. In 1916, steel was torn from the GTPR lines in the Rockies to assist the war effort in France. Coupled with high construction costs, these factors led to the ultimate demise of both the GTPR and its parent company, the Grand Trunk Railway, since the Grand Trunk had guaranteed Grand Trunk Pacific securities. The GTR tried and failed to escape these obligations, and was dragged down into financial default and nationalization along with the GTPR. In 1916 and 1919 the Canadian Northern Railway and GTPR became components of the newly formed Canadian National Railways. Over the next few years several lines of the original two railways were consolidated, with the GTP lines generally surviving because they were built to a higher standard than those of the Canadian Northern Railway.

Although the GTPR itself did not survive, it made a lasting impact on the culture and physical structure of western development. One of the major legacies that the railway left to Canada is the names given to the communities along its routes. First, many of the communities in Saskatchewan along the GTPR line are named after railway executives: Biggar is named after general counsel William H. Biggar; Melville for President Charles Melville Hays; and Watrous for vice-president and general manager Frank Watrous Morse. Second, in between Winnipeg, Manitoba and Prince Rupert, British Columbia, the GTPR established a large number of railway stations which later became towns. With so many similar-looking places for conductors to keep track of, the planners thought it best to use some kind of logical and easy-to-remember system; sensibly enough, they chose the alphabet.

Track layers working on the Grand Trunk Pacific line at Lazare Bridge, April 1908 (right).

ALPHABETICAL TOWNS

The GTPR named its stations in alphabetical order from Portage la Prairie westwards, which helped both in thinking of new names and in knowing how one's train was progressing.

Beginning in Manitoba, they were

Alpha
Bloom
Cave
Deer
Exira
Firdale
Gregg
Harte
Ingelow
Justice
Knox
Levine

Myra
Norman
Oakner
Pope
Quadra
Rea
Uno
Treat
(they backtracked, adding Uno later)
and Victor

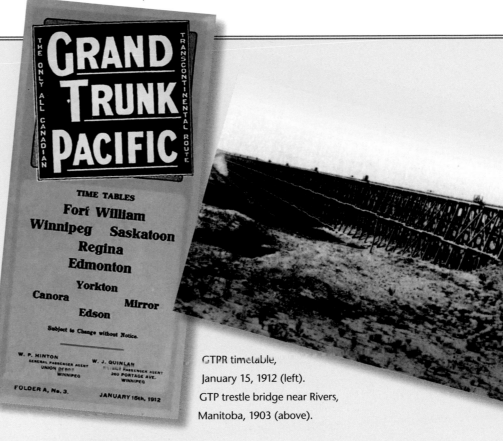

GTPR timetable, January 15, 1912 (left). GTP trestle bridge near Rivers, Manitoba, 1903 (above).

Crossing the border into Saskatchewan, they continued with

Welby
Yarbo
Zeneta
Atwater
Bangor
Cana
Elroy
Fenwood
Goodeve
Hubbard
Ituna
Jasmin
Kelliher
Leross
Lestock
Mosten
Punnichy
Quinton

Raymore
Semans
Tate
Undora
Venn
Watrous
Xena
Young
Zelma
Allan
Bradwell
Clavet
Duro
Earl
Farley
Grandora
Hawoods
Ivana

Juniata
Kinley
Leney
Mead
Neola
Oban
Palo
Reford
Scott
Tako
Unity
Vera
Winter
Yonker
Zumbro
and
Artland

Then, crossing the border into Alberta, they continued again with

Butze
Chauvin
Dunn
Edgerton
Greenshields
(Wainwright)
Fabyan
Hawkins
Irma
Jarrow
Kinsella
Meighen
Nestor
Poe
Ryley

Shonts
Tofield
Uncas
Ardrossan
Bremner
Clover
(Bar)
Edmonton
Fallis
Gainford
Hargwen
Imrie
Junkins
Keston
Leaman

Mackay
Niton
Otley
Peers
Rosevear
Thornton
Wolf Creek
Yates
Ansell
Bickerdike
Dalehurst
Entrance
Fitzhugh (later changed to Jasper)

JASPER

A Forest Park

Magnificently positioned in the Canadian Rockies, the Jasper area was a rough and wild fur-trading centre for decades before civilization came to call. Located on the west bank of a widening of the Athabasca River called Brule Lake, the trading centre known as Jasper House was first established in 1813 as a North West Company outpost. It later fell under the auspices of the Hudson's Bay Company on the trade route to Fort Vancouver. It was named after well-known North West Company clerk Jasper Hawes. The area attracted Stoney, Beaver, and Shuswap people, as well as Iroquois and Métis free traders.

With the decline of the fur trade, Jasper House was abandoned in 1884. The Dominion government subsequently used it as a marker for establishing Jasper Forest Park, an area of roughly 5,000 square miles (13,000 sq km), in 1907. In 1910, a coal mine named Pocahontas opened nearby with a settlement of seventy houses, and since the men who were building the railway were also camped in the area, the population was large enough to justify a cable ferry crossing the Athabasca—a boon to tourism. The small town of Fitzhugh (named as part of the Grand Trunk Pacific alphabet line) grew up around the new railway station, and in 1913 it changed its name to Jasper to match the park. All the amenities of community life (hospital, school, post office, churches) soon followed as the town of Jasper came into its own. For several decades, one of the most notable features at Jasper's railway station was a Haida Native Canadian totem pole that stood facing the station. Carved in the late nineteenth century in Masset on the Queen Charlotte Islands in British Columbia, the cedar pole was acquired by the GTPR in 1915 and shipped to Jasper by train.

Even before the advent of the twentieth century, the Jasper area was popular with tourists. Tourism was the successor to the fur trade in the uneasy preservation/exploitation plan of the national park service, and tourism and the railway went hand in hand in the creation of profit. "It would appear to be the duty of the Department [of the Interior]," wrote James Bernard Harkin, the first commissioner of Dominion Parks, to William Wallace Cory, deputy minister of the Interior in 1912, "to provide the Parks [with] the machinery at once for opening up the beauty spots and thus helping to promote the tourist traffic which is one of the best paying businesses that any district can have."

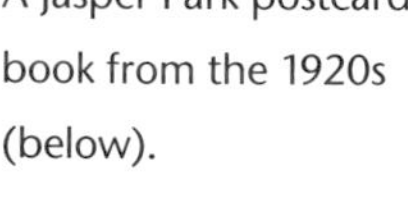

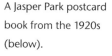

A Jasper Park postcard book from the 1920s (below).

Jasper Forest Park was granted national park status in 1930, with the passing of the National Parks Act in Ottawa. Jasper National Park is now the largest national park in the Canadian Rockies, covering an area of 4,200 square miles (10,878 sq km). In addition to the breathtaking mountains, the major tourist attractions of the area include the glaciers of the Columbia Icefield, the Miette Hotsprings, limestone caves, lakes, and waterfalls. Wildlife in the area includes elk, caribou, moose, bighorn sheep, wolves, wolverines, mountain lions, and both grizzly and black bears. The major river systems in the park provide excellent fishing and recreation opportunities. They include the North Saskatchewan River (which is part of the Hudson Bay basin) and the Athabasca and Smoky Rivers (both part of the Arctic Ocean basin).

Jasper House, in a photograph of *c.*1872 (left).
A Canadian National Railway passenger train steams through Jasper National Park, 1947 (above).

YELLOWHEAD PASS

A Low and Mild Crossing

Yellowhead Pass, at 3,642 feet (1,110 m) above sea level, is a remarkably low pass for the North American Continental Divide. It lies on the border of British Columbia and Alberta, within the boundaries of Jasper National Park. The pass was named after Iroquois–Métis trapper Pierre Bostonais, who went by the nickname "Tête Jaune" (Yellow Head). Working for the Hudson's Bay Company, Bostonais had led expeditions to the interior of British Columbia beginning as early as 1820.

Early in western railway history, much attention was paid to Yellowhead Pass as a potential crossing point over the Continental Divide. Surveyor Dr John Rae took a trip through Yellowhead Pass in 1865, sponsored by the Hudson's Bay Company and the Canadian government. He explored the possibilities of passing rail tracks, a wagon road, and a telegraph line through the region. In 1871, Walter Moberly headed up a survey party on behalf of Sir Sandford Fleming, the new engineer in charge of the Canadian Pacific Railway. As he worked through the upper reaches of the Columbia River, Moberly dispatched Roderick McLennan to survey the vicinity of the North Thompson across Albreda Pass to Tête Jaune Cache and up the Yellowhead. A.R.C. Selwyn of the Geological Survey of Canada travelled with McLennan to make detailed observations and maps. Inspired by the possibilities found there, in 1872 Sandford Fleming directed Moberly to focus his survey efforts on Yellowhead Pass. Moberly organized an expedition and set out to follow the proposed railway route all the way from Halifax to Victoria.

"The Railway Pathfinders" by E.P. Kinsella. In searching for a route through rugged country, the surveyor often had to be slung on a log platform over a raging torrent (right).

The events of the expedition were recorded by the Reverend George M. Grant, who kept a detailed diary: "At the summit, Moberly welcomed us into British Columbia, for we were at length out of 'No-man's-land' and had entered the western province of our Dominion. Round the rivulet running west the party gathered, and drank from its waters to the Queen and the Dominion. The work that the surveyors are engaged on requires a patience and forethought that few who ride in Pullman cars on the road in after years will ever appreciate."

The railway survey continued along the north side of Yellowhead Pass, where the bluffs were not quite as steep as they were on the south.

Ultimately the CPR passed over Yellowhead Pass in favour of a more southerly route over the difficult Kicking Horse Pass, which was more competitive with American railways. When this happened, the preparatory activities that had been taking place in the Yellowhead area slowed to a trickle. In 1898 geologist James McEvoy reported that fire had devastated the valley. By 1900 when the GTPR began discussing the possibility

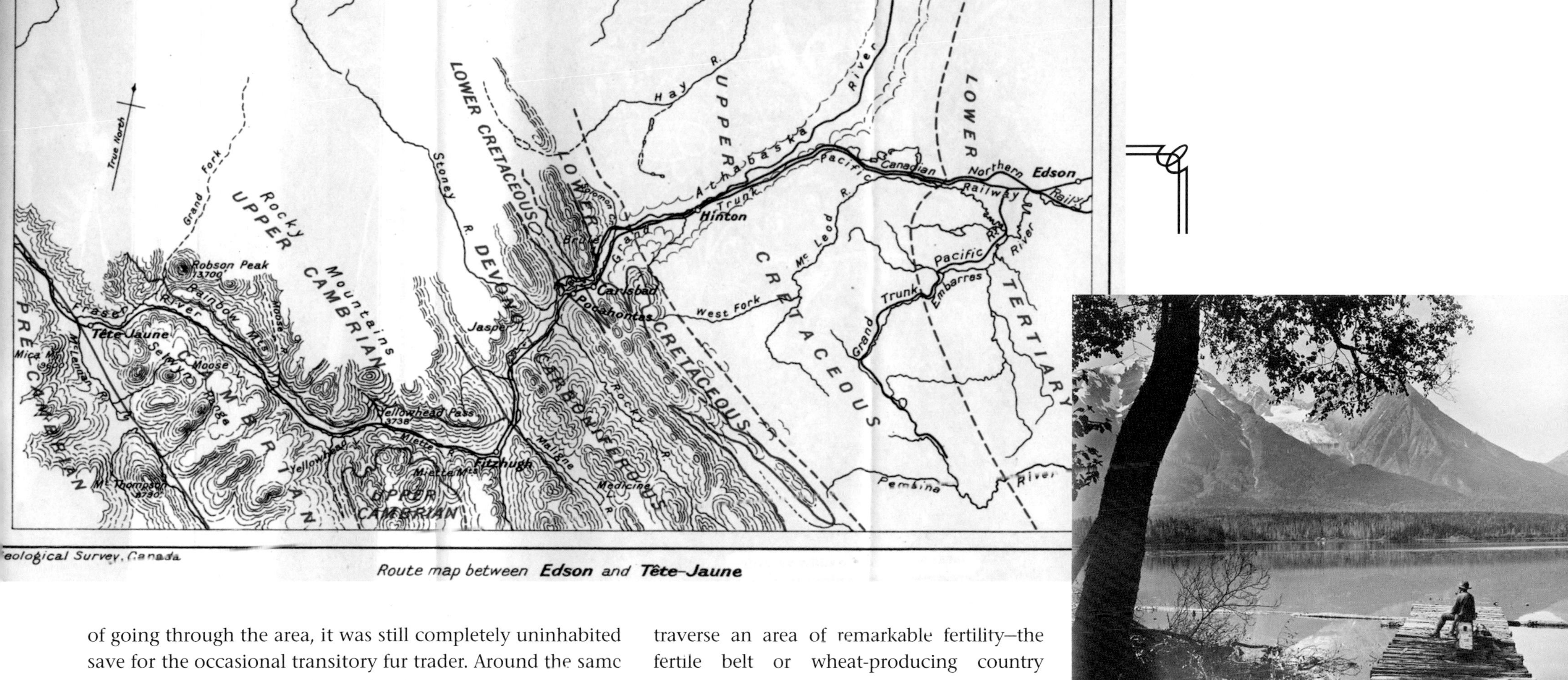

of going through the area, it was still completely uninhabited save for the occasional transitory fur trader. Around the same time, the Canadian Northern also began sending surveyors and pack trains through the pass to investigate its possibilities as a transport route.

The GTPR's charter specified that the company would lay track "by way of either the Peace River Pass, or the Pine River Pass, or such other Pass in the Rocky Mountains as is found most convenient and practicable." The Pine River Pass route cut a swath through a belt of fertile agricultural land, extending 300 miles (483 km) further west than the Yellowhead Pass before reaching the Rockies, and correspondingly cut the distance needing to be crossed in that beautiful but uninhabitable mountain range. A survey report from March 1904 estimated that the Pine River route traversed 560,000 acres of arable land on the east side of the Rockies—while the Yellowhead route only traversed 20,000 acres. Prime Minister Laurier spoke publicly for Pine River Pass and against Yellowhead Pass, saying, "In place of a bleak sterile country, the line by the Pine River route would traverse an area of remarkable fertility—the fertile belt or wheat-producing country extends nearly 300 miles further to the west before the Rocky Mountains are reached than by the route over the Yellowhead Pass."

When B.B. Keliher was appointed GTP chief engineer in July 1905, however, he reviewed the Canadian Pacific profiles of the Yellowhead route created in the 1870s and came to a different conclusion. He estimated that a 0.4 per cent gradient could be achieved on both sides of the pass, and that the advantage of a mild gradient outweighed the benefits of traversing fertile land. During the following year, GTP engineers located a practicable route that achieved that gradient with the exception of 20 miles (32 km) of eastbound track at Tête Jaune Cache. In 1906, Tate filed a route map for Yellowhead Pass. At the same time, however, the Canadian Northern filed a route map that conflicted with GTPR's plans, and eventually both railways ended up building over their respective passes in the period from 1910 to 1913.

"Pondering the Yellowhead Pass," a photograph taken *c.*1872 (above).

Route map between Edson and Tête Jaune, from *Guide Book No. 9, Transcontinental Excursion C2, Toronto to Victoria and Return*, produced by the Canada Department of Mines in 1913 (above left).

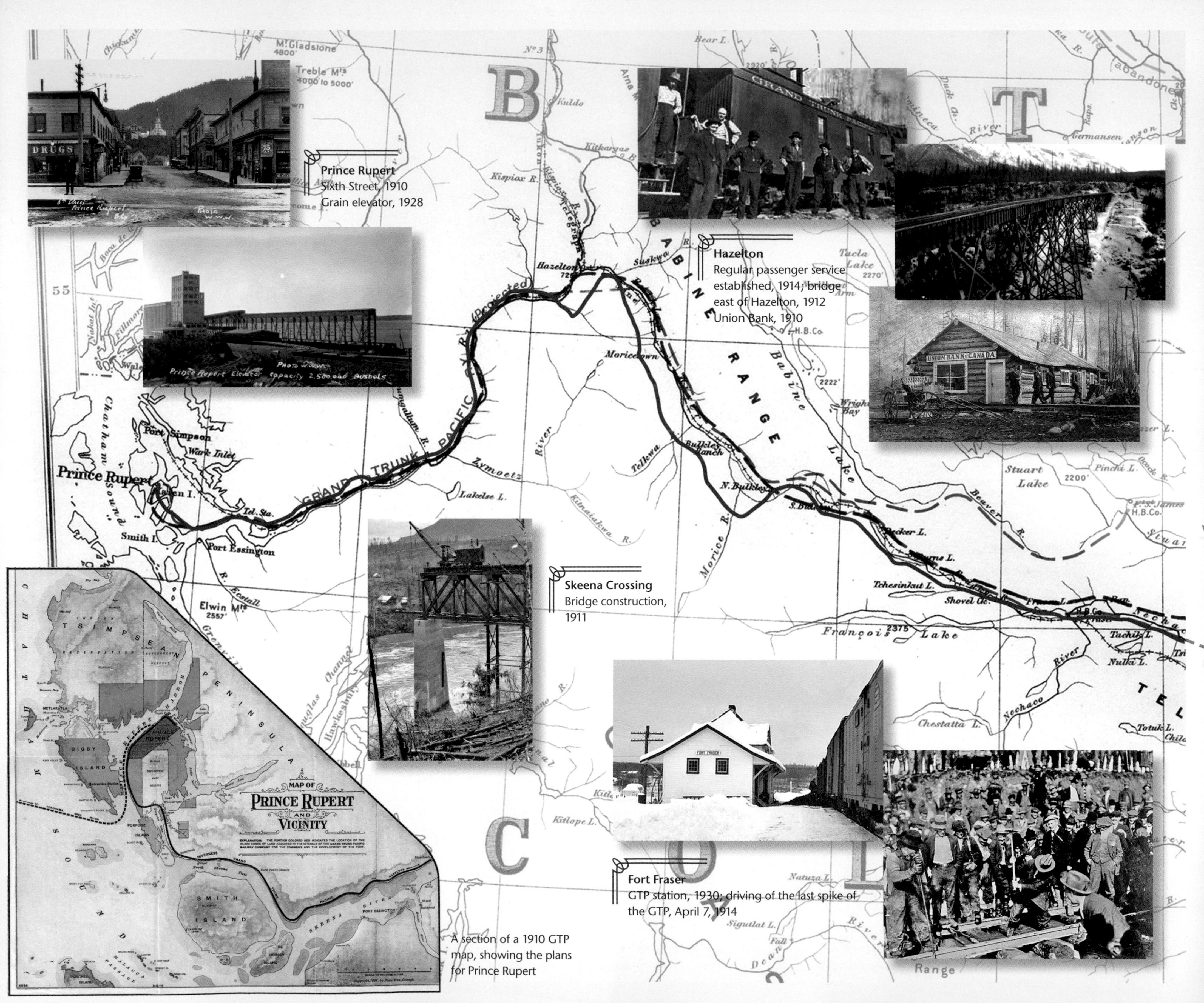

Prince Rupert
Sixth Street, 1910
Grain elevator, 1928

Hazelton
Regular passenger service established, 1914; bridge east of Hazelton, 1912
Union Bank, 1910

Skeena Crossing
Bridge construction, 1911

Fort Fraser
GTP station, 1930; driving of the last spike of the GTP, April 7, 1914

A section of a 1910 GTP map, showing the plans for Prince Rupert

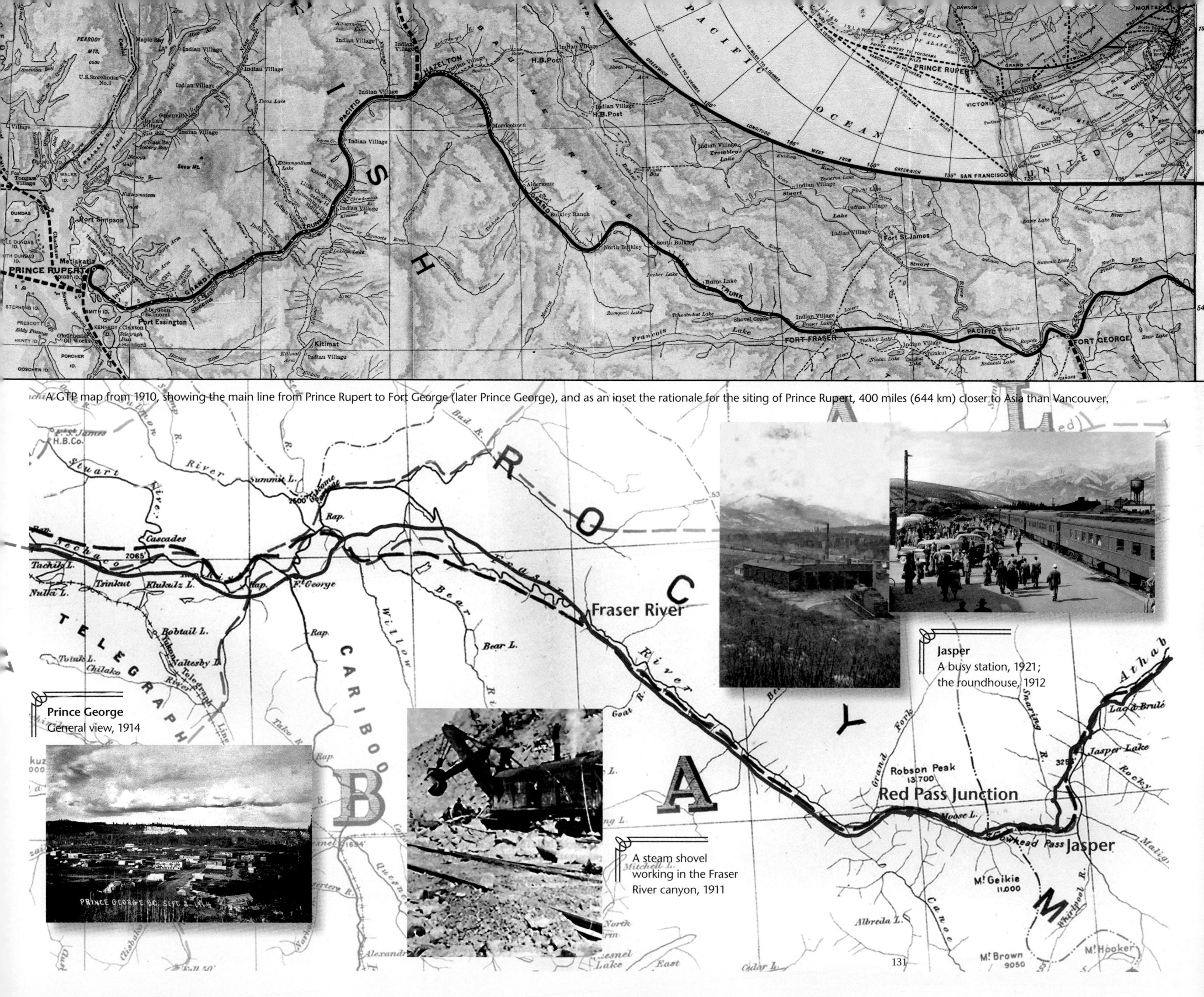

A GTP map from 1910, showing the main line from Prince Rupert to Fort George (later Prince George), and as an inset the rationale for the siting of Prince Rupert, 400 miles (644 km) closer to Asia than Vancouver.

Prince George
General view, 1914

A steam shovel working in the Fraser River canyon, 1911

Jasper
A busy station, 1921; the roundhouse, 1912

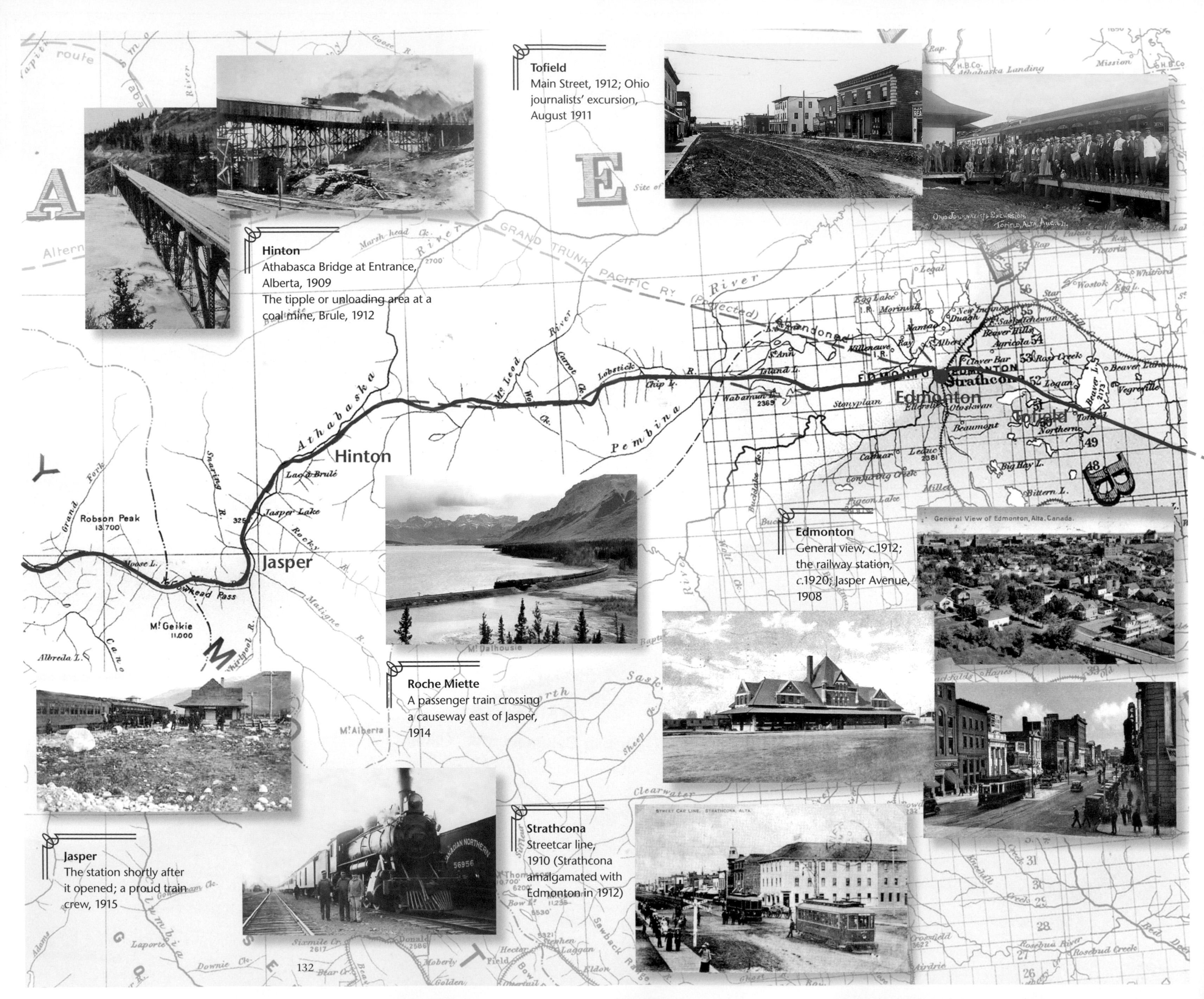

Tofield
Main Street, 1912; Ohio journalists' excursion, August 1911

Hinton
Athabasca Bridge at Entrance, Alberta, 1909
The tipple or unloading area at a coal mine, Brule, 1912

Edmonton
General view, *c.*1912; the railway station, *c.*1920; Jasper Avenue, 1908

Roche Miette
A passenger train crossing a causeway east of Jasper, 1914

Strathcona
Streetcar line, 1910 (Strathcona amalgamated with Edmonton in 1912)

Jasper
The station shortly after it opened; a proud train crew, 1915

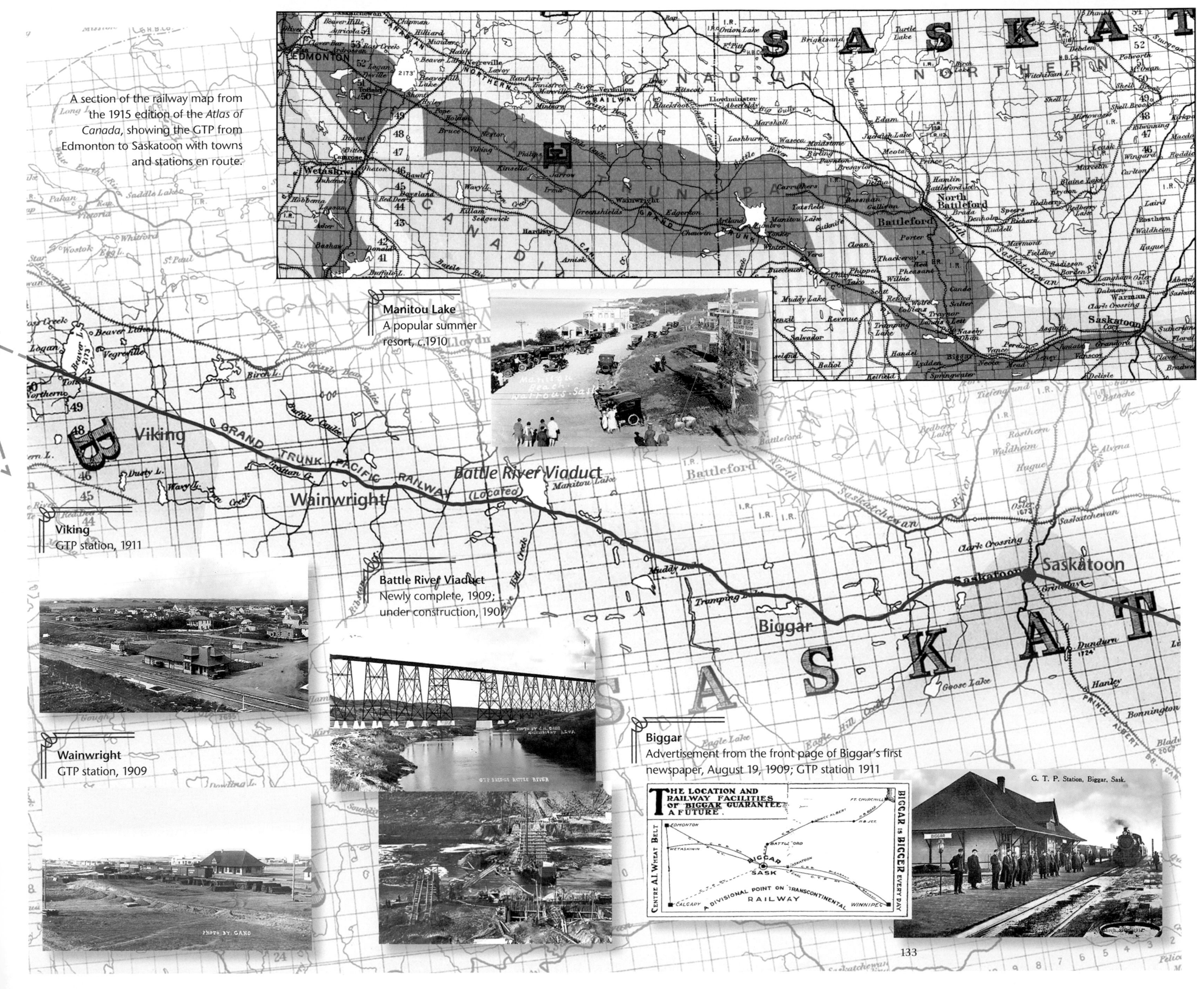

A section of the railway map from the 1915 edition of the *Atlas of Canada*, showing the GTP from Edmonton to Saskatoon with towns and stations en route.

Manitou Lake
A popular summer resort, c.1910

Viking
GTP station, 1911

Battle River Viaduct
Newly complete, 1909; under construction, 1907

Wainwright
GTP station, 1909

Biggar
Advertisement from the front page of Biggar's first newspaper, August 19, 1909; GTP station 1911

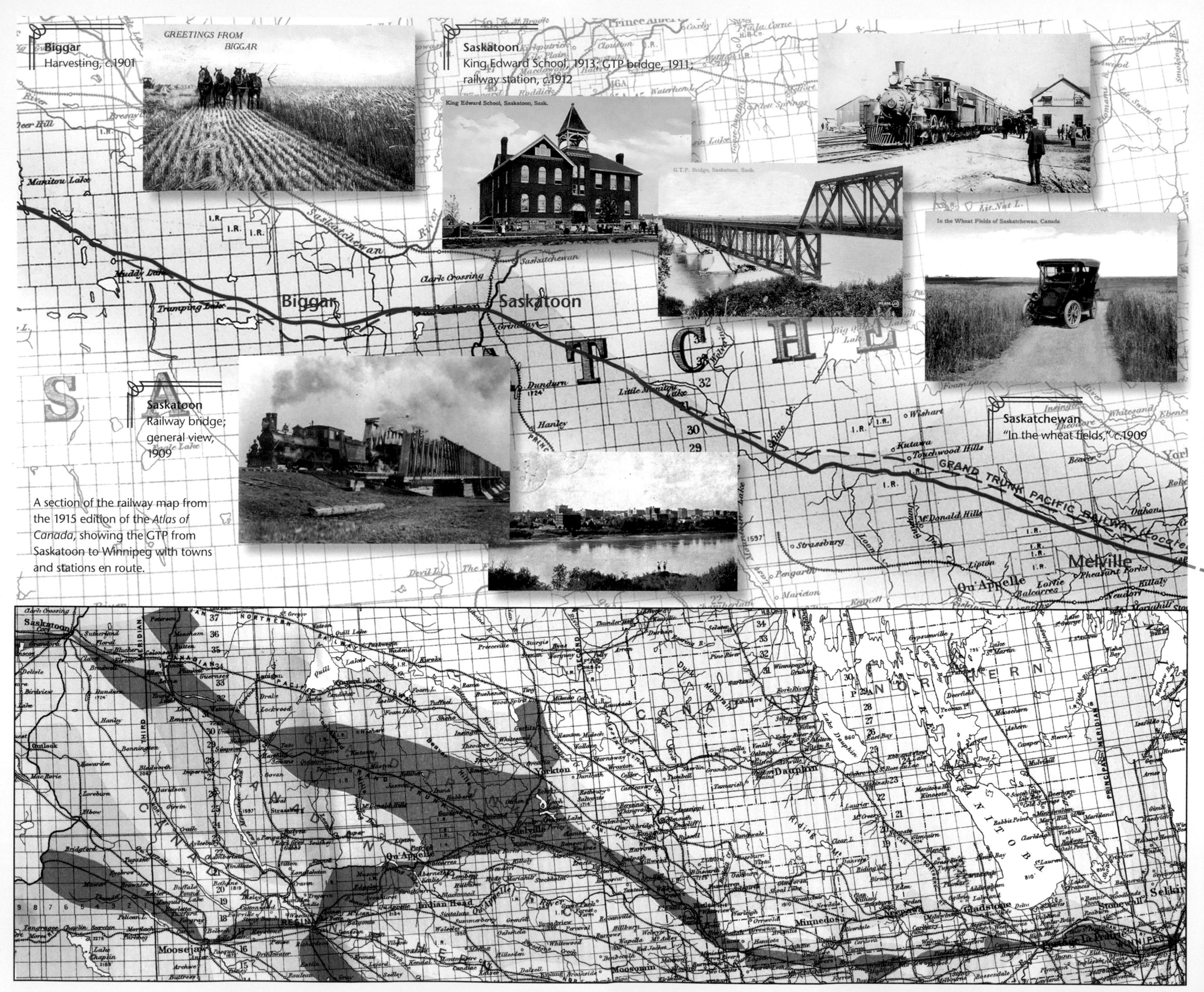

Biggar
Harvesting, c.1901

Saskatoon
King Edward School, 1913; GTP bridge, 1911; railway station, c.1912

Saskatoon
Railway bridge; general view, 1909

Saskatchewan
"In the wheat fields," c.1909

A section of the railway map from the 1915 edition of the *Atlas of Canada*, showing the GTP from Saskatoon to Winnipeg with towns and stations en route.

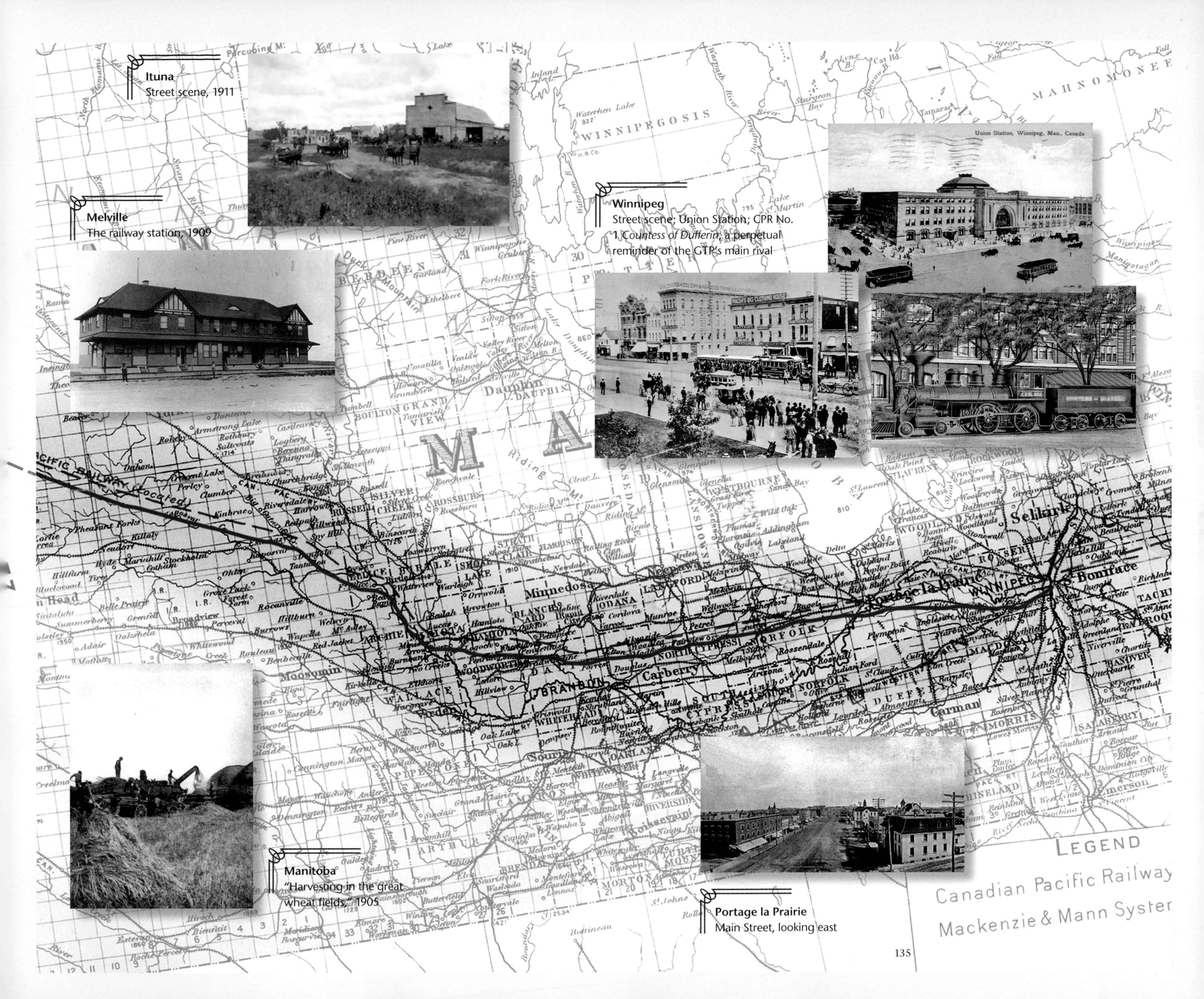

Ituna
Street scene, 1911

Melville
The railway station, 1909

Winnipeg
Street scene; Union Station; CPR No. 1 *Countess of Dufferin*, a perpetual reminder of the GTP's main rival

Manitoba
"Harvesting in the great wheat fields," 1905

Portage la Prairie
Main Street, looking east

CANADIAN NORTHERN
RAILWAY.
1642
CANADIAN NORTHERN
2602
C.N.R
2602

THE CANADIAN NORTHERN

CONNECTING THE PRAIRIES TO THE LAKEHEAD AND MONTREAL

When he learned of the outbreak of war in September 1914, Sir William Mackenzie's face turned ashen. "I'm finished," he mumbled. Sir William (1849–1923) knew that the war would consume enormous amounts of global capital, which had once been enamoured of the millions of dollars of government- and railway-guaranteed construction bonds issued by the Canadian Northern Railway (CNoR) and its subsidiaries.

In truth, even before World War I had been declared, the CNoR was barely generating enough profit to pay the interest on those bonds. By 1915 however, with government assistance, Mackenzie and his business partner, Sir Donald Mann (1853–1934), had completed the CNoR from Québec City to Port Mann near Vancouver.

In October 1915, the two men hosted a grand opening of their railway on a stage stretching almost across Canada: a special excursion train from Québec City to Vancouver, and on by ferry to Victoria. On board were members of parliaments and legislatures, businessmen, financiers, journalists, and a medical doctor, as well as a Nordheimer piano. With some exceptions, such as Calgary's satiric *Eye Opener*, the Canadian press was impressed. "Sir Donald Mann et Sir William Mackenzie veulent que l'inauguration de leur nouveau chemin de fer," reported Montréal's *la Presse* on October 12, 1915, "soit fait d'une manière digne de l'importance de cet évenement." Most people on board the train to Vancouver were equally impressed.

The official opening was the culmination of twenty-one years of dreaming and scheming on the part of Mackenzie and Mann, who, in 1911, had been knighted by King George V for their contributions to the development not only of Canada, but also of Brazil, Mexico and the Caribbean. The two entrepreneurs had been born in pre-Confederation Canada, Mackenzie in the hamlet of Kirkfield, northeast of Toronto, and Mann in the hamlet of Acton, northwest of Toronto. They had met during the early 1880s while building bridges and snow sheds for the Canadian Pacific Railway in the mountains of eastern British Columbia. Later in the 1880s they had worked as contractors on three CPR-controlled railways, one in Maine, and two others in what would become the provinces of Alberta and Saskatchewan. By 1896 contracting had made Mackenzie and Mann experienced and wealthy businessmen.

That year they moved into promoting and operating railways when they acquired control of a charter of the Lake Manitoba Railway and Canal Company (LMRCC), a modest company designed to serve the fertile farmland northwest of Winnipeg, with an option of building towards Hudson Bay. On Christmas Day of 1896, the LMRCC made its inaugural run from Dauphin south to Gladstone, and, with running rights on the Manitoba and Northwest Railway, it reached Portage la Prairie in Manitoba where passengers and freight could transfer to the transcontinental CPR. On board were twenty-one passengers, some of them, no doubt, newcomers to Dauphin, which had been founded only a few weeks earlier when the LMRCC had chosen the site for its station.

Until 1896, Canadian railways had been financed almost entirely by government land grants and subsidies, which had helped companies sell construction bonds on national and international markets. Now, importantly, the LMRCC introduced Mackenzie and Mann to a new method of financing railway construction: government-guaranteed bonds. In 1896, the government of Manitoba provided to the LMRRC a government-backed guarantee on construction bonds of up to $8,000 per mile for the first 125 miles (201 km) of railway. In return, Mackenzie and Mann agreed to keep freight rates attractive to farmers, who suspected that the CPR had been charging too much for shipping

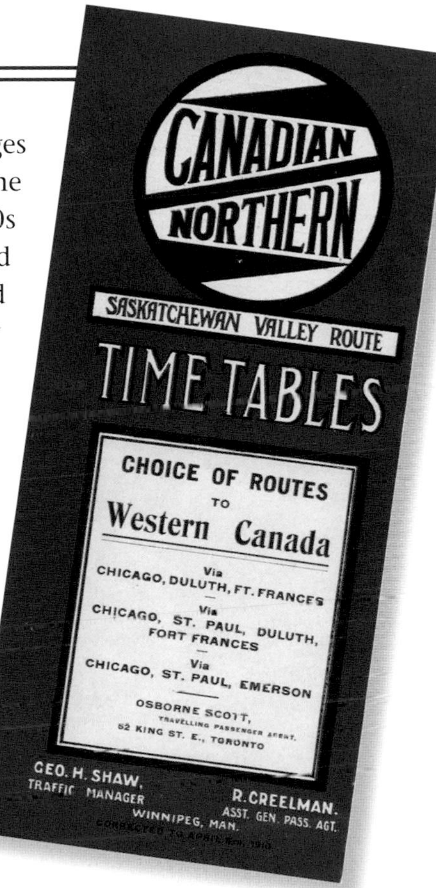

Canadian Northern timetable for the Saskatchewan Valley route, April 1910 (above).

A Canadian Northern train at a grain elevator in northern Manitoba, 1910 (opposite).

Canadian Northern locomotive No. 702 (above).

The arrival of the first Canadian Northern train at Ottawa on December 5, 1909 (below).

their grain. At the same time, the Dominion government supported the new railway by offering it land grants of 6,400 acres for every mile built as well as an annual grant of $40,000 for transportation of federal goods such as the mail.

In 1897 the LMRCC extended its line a few miles north to Sifton Junction, named for Clifford Sifton, a local supporter of Mackenzie and Mann's new railway, and, in July 1896, the first minister of the interior in the Liberal government of Sir Wilfrid Laurier. In order to fulfill the terms of the LMRRC charter, Mackenzie and Mann built a short line from Dauphin to Lake Winnipegosis, which gave them the option of a water and rail link northward to Hudson Bay. However they realized that a more profitable and logical option would be to build westward through the fertile farmland between Dauphin and the town of Prince Albert on the North Saskatchewan River.

In 1897 and 1898, the two contractor-promoters began to assemble other local charters, one for a railway south and east from Winnipeg towards Lake of the Woods, and another for a line farther west, in northwestern Ontario. When the two men formed the Canadian Northern Railway company in December 1898, they were in charge of what was no more than several small regional rail lines. By 1901 when the CNoR had grown to 512 miles (824 km) of completed grade with seven hundred more under construction, it still remained essentially a Prairie railway designed to serve the fertile agricultural lands between the Red River and the Saskatchewan.

However, in 1902, with the prospect of transcontinental competition from the Grand Trunk Railway, the CNoR made clear its own transcontinental ambitions. That year and the next the company acquired control of several Québec and Nova Scotia railways as well as an entry point into east-end Montréal, and in 1905 it became the first transcontinental railway to reach Edmonton. In 1905–6 the Canadian Northern Ontario Railway connected Toronto with the CNoR's east–west main line near Sudbury, Ontario, and between 1910 and 1915 the railway pierced the craggy mountain ranges of British Columbia to reach Port Mann, near Vancouver. By 1913 it had punctured Mount Royal with a tunnel designed to provide an entry into the centre of Canada's metropolis. From a mere 101 miles (163 km) in 1896, the Canadian Northern had grown to just over 9,433 miles (15,180 km) of railway by 1915, linking the heights of Québec to the valley of the Fraser. During that same time period, the number of employees had risen from fourteen to more than 23,000—a remarkable achievement indeed.

Nevertheless, when the CNoR was officially opened in October 1915, it was effectively broke. The recession of 1912–13 had made investors wary, and earnings fell as the war drove up costs of labour and *matériel*. Had the CNoR declared bankruptcy then, however, it would have seriously damaged the Canadian Bank of Commerce, its chief Canadian financier, and also the reputation of Canadian enterprise in international financial markets.

With the help of emergency government loans given in exchange for more and more company stock, the railway managed to soldier on for another two years until, in November 1917, Prime Minister Sir Robert Borden had no option but to tell a shattered Mackenzie that his dream of co-owning a profitable transcontinental must end. In September the following year, Mackenzie and Mann resigned as officers and directors of the company, which by then was completely government-owned. Thus the CNoR became the first major component of the new Crown corporation, the Canadian National Railways.

With the demise of their railway, Mackenzie and Mann became two of the favourite whipping boys of Canadian historiography, at least until 1976 when historian T.D. Regehr's revisionist history of the Canadian Northern was published, showing the line to be a true pioneer.

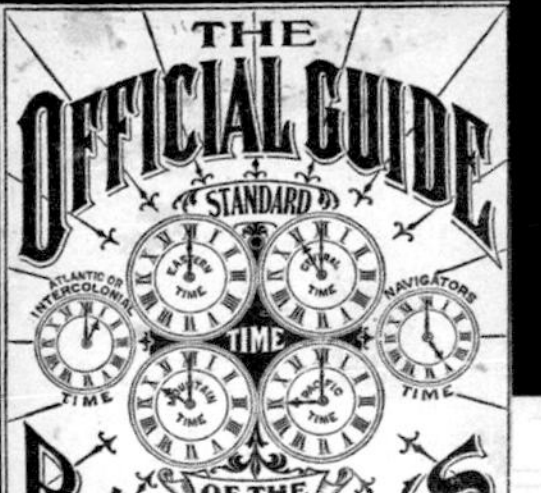

CANADIAN NORTHERN TIMETABLE, 1906

MAP OF THE CANADIAN NORTHERN RAILWAY AND CONNECTIONS

The Short Line Through Winnipeg to Edmonton and the Great Saskatchewan Valley

CANADIAN NORTHERN RAILWAY.

EXECUTIVE.

WM. MACKENZIE, President, Toronto, Ont.
D. D. MANN, Vice-President, "
D. B. HANNA, Third Vice-President, "
Z. A. LASH, Chief Solicitor, "
W. H. MOORE, Secretary, "
HUGH SUTHERLAND, Executive Agent, Winnipeg, Man.

TRAFFIC.

GEO. H. SHAW, Traffic Manager, Winnipeg, Man.

FINANCIAL AND ACCOUNTING.

A. W. MACKENZIE, Treasurer, Toronto, Ont.
C. E. FRIEND, Auditor, Winnipeg, Man.

LAND, IMMIGRATION AND INDUSTRIAL.

A. D. DAVIDSON, General Agent, Toronto, Ont.
A. R. DAVIDSON, General Agent, Winnipeg, Man.
A. D. McRAE, General Agent, "

EXPRESS AND TELEGRAPHS.

SCOTT GRIFFIN, Superintendent, Winnipeg, Man.

OPERATING.

E. A. JAMES, Manager, Winnipeg, Man.
A. SHIELDS, Master Mechanic, "
W. A. BROWN, General Superintendent, "
A. WILCOX, Superintendent, "
J. W. DAWSEY, Superintendent, Dauphin, Man.
J. R. CAMERON, Superintendent, Port Arthur, Ont.
W. J. PACE, Assistant Superintendent, Edmonton, Alta.
W. PRATT, Jr., Supt. Sleeping & Dining Cars & News Dept., Winnipeg, Man.
J. P. DRISCOLL, Superintendent Car Service, "

PRINCIPAL AGENTS.

WM. PHILLIPS, Gen. Eastern Agt., 52 King St. E., Toronto, Ont.
R. H. BELL, Trav. Fht. & Pas. Agt., 231-232 Board of Trade Bldg, Montreal, P.Q.
HENRY J. COWIE, Fht. Agt. Canadian Northern Ry., 5 Chapel St., Liverpool.

PURCHASING.

E LANGHAM, Pur. Agt. & Gen. Storekeeper, Winnipeg, Man.

CONDENSED TIME-TABLE—ST. PAUL AND WINNIPEG, VIA GT. NORTHERN RY.

Trains Nos. 9 and 10, Daily, are Solid, with Sleeping and Dining Cars.

No. 10	June 3, 1906.	No. 9
*5 15 P M	lve. St. Paul.....(G. N. Ry.) arr.	*7 30 A M
5 07 A M	lve. Emerson.....(C. N. Ry.) arr.	7 23 P M
6 06 A M	arr. Morris.......... " arr.	6 30 P M
*7 15 A M	arr. Winnipeg....... " lve.	*5 20 P M

CONDENSED TIME-TABLE—ST. PAUL AND WINNIPEG, VIA NO. PACIFIC RY.

Trains Nos. 7 and 8, Daily, are Solid, with Sleeping and Dining Cars.

No. 8	June 3, 1906.	No. 7
10 15 P M	lve. St. Paul.....(N. P. Ry.) arr.	*7 25 A M
11 22 A M	arr. Pembina.....(C. N. Ry.) arr.	3 57 P M
12 00 Noon	arr. Morris.......... " arr.	3 00 P M
*2 00 P M	arr. Winnipeg....... " lve.	*1 40 P M

MAIN LINE WEST.

43	3	1	Mls	June 3, 1906.	2	4	44
....	b8 05	*12 30	0	lve....+ Winnipeg[3] δ ..arr.	11 20	15 25	....
....	8 15	12 39	3	....Portage Junction...	11 10	15 15	....
....	8 34	12 57	12	........St. Charles........	10 52	14 57	....
....	8 56	13 15	21	........White Plains........	10 32	14 40	....
....	9 21	13 34	32	..........Eli..........δ	10 11	[illegible]	....
....	9 46	13 54	42	+ ....Oakville.........δ	9 46	13 54	....
....	10 03	14 06	49	..........Curtis..........	9 32	13 37	....
g8 00	10 23	14 20	56	+..Portage la Prairie.δ	– –	13 20	10 00
– –	10 28	– –	57	arr. Arizona Junction.lve.	– –	12 48	– –
....	10 28	....	57	lve. Arizona Junction arr.	....	12 48	....
....	11 24	....	79	........Lavenham........	....	12 01	....
....	12 41	....	109	.....Brandon Junction.....	....	10 53	....
....	13 22	....	113	........Carberry.......δ	....	10 45	....
....	14 12	....	131	arr...Carberry Junc...lve.	....	9 57	....
8 18	....	14 33	61	..........Walldon..........	9 03	....	18 40
8 57	....	15 06	75	..........Beaver.........δ	8 34	....	17 50
9 40	....	15 28	84	...Neepawa Junction...	8 13	....	17 20
9 40	....	....	84	...Neepawa Junction...	....	....	17 20
10 00	....	....	90	..........Mayfeld..........	....	....	17 00
11 22	14 12	....	107	...Carberry Junction...	....	9 57	15 37
11 35	14 23	....	111	..........Hallboro..........	....	9 47	15 24
11 55	14 40	....	117	+ ......Neepawa.......δ	....	9 30	g15 00
....	16 05	....	158	..McCreary Junction..	....	8 03	....
....	....	15 38	88	......Golden Stream......	8 02	....	....
....	....	15 50	93	+ .....‖Gladstone.......δ	– –	....	....
....	....	16 21	107	..........Plumas.........δ	7 16	....	....
....	....	17 13	128	........Glencairn........	6 23	....	....
....	16 05	17 38	139	..McCreary Junction..	5 50	8 03	....
....	16 07	17 40	140	........McCreary........	5 56	8 00	....
....	16 47	18 17	157	........Makinak.........δ	5 19	6 50	....
....	17 03	18 33	164	.......Ochre River.......δ	5 03	6 30	....
....	17 30	19 00	178	arr. ..‖+ Dauphin δ....lve.	4 35	a6 00	....
....	....	19 20	178	lve.......Dauphin......arr.	4 15	....	....
....	....	19 27	181	Gilbert Plains Junction	4 05	....	....
....	....	20 09	198	+ .....Gilbert Plains.....δ	3 27	....	....
....	....	20 34	208	+ ......Grandview.......δ	3 00	....	....
....	....	21 47	241	..........Roblin.........δ	1 41	....	....
....	....	23 20	279	ar. + Kamsack (Cent. time) δ lv.	23 45	....	....
....	....	22 35	279	lv...Kamsack (Mount. time).ar.	22 35	....	....
....	....	23 42	303	..........Canora.........δ	21 26	....	....
....	....	1 30	336	........Invermay........δ	19 37	....	....
....	....	2 52	366	..........Wadena.........δ	18 03	....	....
....	....	4 36	399	..........Watson.........δ	16 19	....	....
....	....	5 55	425	arr.......Humbolt δ ...lve.	15 01	....	....
....	....	6 05	425	lve.......Humbolt.....arr.	14 51	....	....
....	....	6 51	443	..........Bruno..........	13 50	....	....
....	....	7 59	469	..........Vonda.........δ	12 58	....	....
....	....	8 39	485	........Clarkboro........	12 15	....	....
....	....	9 35	507	........Langham........δ	11 24	....	....
....	....	10 10	521	..........Borden..........	10 49	....	....
....	....	10 30	529	........Radisson........δ	10 30	....	....
....	....	11 08	544	........Maymont........	9 53	....	....
....	....	11 29	553	..........Ruddell..........	9 33	....	....
....	....	11 47	560	........Denholm........	9 17	....	....
....	....	12 02	566	..........Brada..........	9 03	....	....
....	....	12 40	572	....North Battleford..δ	8 45	....	....
....	....	12 53	578	....Battleford Junction....	8 15	....	....
....	....	14 10	605	..........Paynton..........	7 00	....	....
....	....	14 35	615	..........Birling..........	6 31	....	....
....	....	15 55	644	..........Marshall..........	5 10	....	....
....	....	16 27	665	......Lloydminster.....δ	4 35	....	....
....	49	16 50	663	........Blackfoot........	4 10	50	....
....	†7 30	18 45	696	........Vermilion.......δ	2 25	18 30	....
....	8 00	19 10	704	........Claysmore........	1 45	18 00	....
....	9 10	19 55	719	..........Minburn..........	1 00	16 50	....
....	10 25	20 45	735	..........Ranfurly..........	24 10	15 45	....
....	11 05	21 20	744	..........Lavoy..........	23 45	15 05	....
....	12 30	21 40	753	........Vegreville.......δ	23 15	14 30	....
....	14 00	22 50	773	..........Hilliard..........	22 09	13 00	....
....	16 40	24 35	808	....Ft. Saskatchewan...δ	20 20	0 30	....
....	18 20	1 45	825	arr.....Edmonton δ ..lve.	*19 15	†8 00	....

STANDARD { Central time east of Kamsack and Swan River. Mountain time west of Kamsack and Swan River.

Connections.—[1] With Northern Pacific Ry. [2] and [3] With Canadian Pacific Ry. [4] With Great Northern Ry.

WINNIPEGOSIS BRANCH.

47	Ms	June 3, 1906.	48
o19 45	0	lve.......Dauphin δ ...arr.	4 30
20 00	3	Gilbert Plains Junction	4 15
21 17	13	....Sifton Junction....	3 08
21 47	27	.......Fork River.......	2 33
22 13	37	.........Gruber.........	2 08
22 20	39	arr...Winnipegosis δ lve.	f2 00

DELTA BRANCH.

Ms.	Freight only.
0	lv. P. la Prairie δ ar.
16	arr......Delta δ ..lve.

RIDGEVILLE BRANCH.

Ms	June 3, 1906.
0	lve....Emerson...arr.
12	arr...Ridgeville...lve.

*Daily; †daily, except Sunday; *a* Tuesday, Thursday and Saturday; *b* Monday, Wednesday and Friday; *f* Tuesday and Friday; *g* Tuesday only; *o* Monday and Thursday. ‖ Meals.

+ Coupon stations.

δ Telegraph stations.

MAIN LINE EAST.

2	Mls	June 3, 1906.	1
*16 00	0	lv. + Winnipeg[3] δ ar.	11 30
16 05	2	....St. Boniface....	11 25
16 34	15	......Lorette....δ	10 52
16 57	29	......Ste. Anne...δ	10 28
17 15	35	......Giroux....δ	10 10
17 45	48	....Marchand...δ	9 38
18 00	55	......Bedford......	9 22
18 26	66	....Woodridge..δ	8 56
19 11	86	......Vassar......	8 11
19 46	97	+....Sprague....δ	7 42
20 29	117	+...Warroad...δ	6 56
20 54	130	.....Roosevelt...δ	6 28
21 45	152	+. Beaudette..δ	5 39
21 57	153	+.‖Rainy River..δ	5 33
22 22	165	.....Pinewood.....	4 55
23 13	187	+.....Emo.....δ	4 05
24 02	208	ar. + Fort Frances lv.	3 18
24 02	208	lv..Fort Frances δ ar.	3 18
1 43	239	+. Mine Centre.δ	1 43
2 04	258	.....Glenorchy....	1 19
2 49	279	......Banning...δ	24 33
3 30	296	+..‖Atikokan....δ	23 57
5 32	357	....Kashaboiwe..δ	21 48
6 51	394	.....Mattawin...δ	20 28
7 46	420	.Stanley Junction δ	19 31
8 19	436	+ Fort William δ	18 59
8 30	439	ar. PortArthur[2] δ lv.	*18 50

PEMBINA, BRANDON AND MIAMI SECTIONS.

7	27	9	Mls.	June 3, 1906.	28	8	10
†13 40	....	*17 20	0	lve. + Winnipeg[3] δ .arr.	....	14 00	7 15
13 50	....	17 30	3	. Portage Junction .	....	13 50	7 05
14 13	....	– –	16	........Cartier........	....	13 24	– –
14 30	....	– –	24	......St. Agathe....δ	....	13 09	– –
14 36	....	– –	28	......Union Point......	....	13 02	– –
15 00	....	18 30	41	arr....+ Morris δ ..lve.	....	12 37	6 06
15 12	....	18 44	47	...St. Jean Baptiste. δ	....	12 23	5 54
15 30	....	19 02	57	........Letellier.....δ	....	12 05	5 36
15 47	....	19 23	66	+.....Emerson[4].....δ	....	11 45	*5 07
15 57	....	....	69	arr....Pembina[1] δ lve.	....	*11 22	....
....	†18 40	....	41	lve.....Morris δ ..arr.	12 00	....	....
....	19 55	....	62	.........Myrtle.........	10 45	....	....
....	20 30	....	67	+......Roland......δ	10 20	....	....
....	21 50	....	81	+.......Miami......δ	9 15	....	....
....	23 45	....	103	+......Somerset......δ	7 10	....	....
....	1 35	....	127	arr. + Greenway δ lve.	†5 00	....	....

CARMAN SECTION.

37	27	11	Mls.	June 3, 1906.	12	38	28
....	....	†9 00	0	lve... Winnipeg δ arr.	15 50	....	....
....	....	9 23	9	...Carman Junction. δ	15 28	....	....
....	....	9 58	22	.......Sanford.......δ	14 58	....	....
....	....	10 40	39	.......Sperling.....δ	14 20	....	....
....	....	11 00	46	......Homewood....δ	14 04	....	....
....	....	11 20	53	........Carman.......δ	13 45	....	....
....	....	12 10	72	..........Leary's..........	12 55	....	....
....	....	12 35	80	........Cardinal........	12 35	....	....
....	†23 45	13 15	87	......Somerset.....δ	12 15	....	7 10
....	24 15	13 30	93	......Swan Lake....δ	11 42	....	6 30
....	1 35	14 15	110	.....Greenway.....δ	11 03	....	†5 00
....	....	14 55	126	.......Belmont.....δ	10 30	....	....
....	....	16 40	144	......Wawanesa....δ	8 55	....	....
....	....	17 02	164	...Methven Junction. δ	8 10	....	....
....	....	18 10	184	arr....Brandon...lve.	†7 05	....	....
a14 15	....	†15 05	126	lve.....Belmont...arr.	10 25	11 45	....
15 15	....	15 38	139	.........Ninette.........	9 52	10 45	....
15 50	....	15 50	143	.........Dunrea.........	9 40	9 40	....
17 15	....	16 25	157	..........Minto..........	9 13	8 40	....
18 20	....	16 53	168	..........Elgin..........	8 48	7 30	....
19 30	....	17 20	180	.........Hartney.........	8 20	b6 00	....
....	....	18 15	204	.........Agnew.........	7 25	....	....
....	....	18 37	214	.........Maples.........	7 03	....	....
....	....	18 45	217	arr.....Virden...lve.	†6 55	....	....

MOUNT ROYAL TUNNEL

Grande Entrée to Montréal

In 1910 the Canadian Northern Railway (CNoR) had a presence in the downtowns of most Canadian cities, but not in Montréal, the country's largest city, which at the time was also Canada's financial capital. Because the westerly part of the city was already occupied by industry, housing, and by the rights-of-way of the Canadian Pacific Railway and the Grand Trunk Railway, the CNoR was effectively barred from entering downtown Montréal.

Mount Royal—winter's night. The illuminated cross was 130 feet (39m) tall and visible from 30 miles (48km) away (below).

However in 1910, Henry K. Wicksteed, chief engineer of surveys for the CNoR, had an idea: why not enter the city by way of Mount Royal, in northern Montréal? But not over the top of the 769-foot-high mountain on which rested McGill University, wealthy neighbourhoods, two cemeteries, the city's water reservoir, and a grand park. Instead, Wicksteed wondered, why not bore a tunnel three miles long through the mountain? To that end, William Mackenzie and Donald Mann created a company that would eventually be called the Mount Royal Tunnel and Terminal Company Limited (MRTTC).

In utmost secrecy the MRTTC began to buy land on both sides of the mountain—almost 5,000 acres of apple orchards on the northwest side, and several city blocks downtown that are the site of today's iconic Place Ville-Marie as well as Central Station, the Queen Elizabeth Hotel, and the headquarters of Canadian National Railways. In place of apple trees, landscape architect Frederick Todd laid out what became known as the Town of Mount Royal (TMR) on the model of central Washington, D.C.

In 1911 and 1912 the mountain was surveyed, and in July and August 1912, some 1,600 men began to use dynamite, air-powered jackhammers, and powerful boring machines to break through the rock and earth, using electrified wagons on rails to remove the debris. Three air shafts were drilled, one at Maplewood Avenue in Outremont on the northern side of the mountain, and two on the downtown side at Sherbrooke and at Dorchester, with the latter shaft being used for removing earth upward to a vacant lot. By early April 1913, men from the TMR end had bored through rock and earth into the Maplewood air shaft.

During the early morning hours of December 10, 1913, dynamite blasted open a hole large enough for workers from each end to squeeze through. Amazingly the two parts of the tunnel almost exactly aligned. When the newspaper *la Presse* hit the streets a few hours later, *les Montréalais* read about "l'un des plus beaux exploits du génie civil au Canada."

At 2.30 that afternoon, a long line of work wagons, suitably cleaned and each carrying four "dignitaries"—officials of the three transcontinental railways, McGill professors, mayors, businessmen, journalists, and photographers—set off warily into the tunnel. At 4.30, when they reached the point of the blast a few hours earlier, they broke into "O Canada," at that time a patriotic song sung in either French or English. Half an hour later, passengers glimpsed the glow of downtown Montréal.

Not all *Montréalais* backed the tunnel concept, however, as several houses built on clay had settled somewhat during construction while other homeowners complained that the dynamite blasts were shaking their houses. One evening over dinner, a visiting tunnel official assured his nervous host that the work directly underneath had been completed, just as a sudden huge blast broke all the front windows of the building.

In June 1914, Sir William Mackenzie toured the tunnel and construction site of an interim station on de la Gauchetière, just south of the site of a proposed, but never built, grand station. By 1916 the tunnel was reinforced with concrete, steel and iron, and in 1918 it was double tracked and electrified. Today, Montréal commuters are the beneficiaries of one of the most daring and imaginative construction projects in Canadian history.

Mount Royal Tunnel portal from Dorchester Boulevard (left).

Driving the tunnel through Mount Royal to give the Canadian Northern access to Montréal (below).

HELL'S GATE CANYON

Terror and Awe

The Vancouver branch of the Canadian Northern from Jasper, showing its relationship with the CPR and Pacific Great Eastern routes. This extract is from a Canadian National Railways timetable of 1943. Hell's Gate is just north of Yale station.

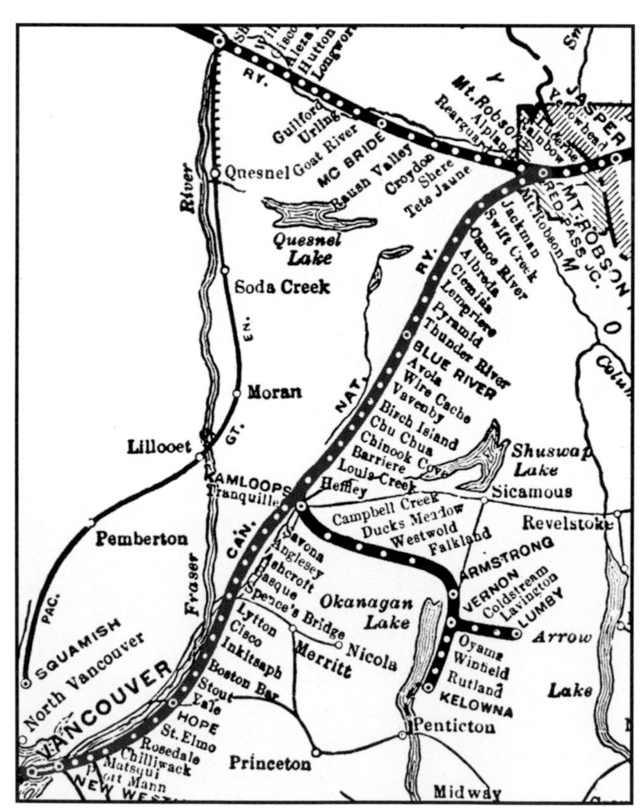

Simon Fraser's advice was sound. No human being, the explorer and fur trader wrote in his journal in June 1808, should venture near the rapids and rocks "cut perpendicular on both sides of the River." That year Fraser was searching for a navigable canoe route to the Pacific, and his warning referred to the boiling rapids and precipitous rock cliffs of Hell's Gate Canyon, located in southwestern British Columbia on the river that is named after Fraser.

Few people have heeded Fraser's advice. During the 1850s, impatient gold seekers travelling to the Cariboo gold fields were transported by horse and covered wagon over the Cariboo Trail which had been cut into the cliffs high above Hell's Gate.

During the early 1880s, the Canadian Pacific Railway was forced to confront the terrors of Hell's Gate as the craggy terrain of British Columbia gave railways running from Calgary or Edmonton to Vancouver little choice but to do so. As historian Pierre Berton once noted, contractors and labourers, many of them Chinese, some of them Irish, risked life and limb to blast into the rock cliffs over the canyon in order to create a flat bed on which to lay tracks. Construction companies tried, although not always successfully, to avoid despoiling the river below with tree splinters, mud, and chunks of rock.

Once the last spike of the CPR was driven at Cragellachie, British Columbia, on November 7, 1885, travellers such as Prime Minister Sir John A. Macdonald and his wife, Agnes, as well as Lord and Lady Aberdeen five years later in 1890, viewed Hell's Gate from the comfort of a CPR private coach. In her book *Through Canada With A Kodak*, first published in 1893, Lady Aberdeen wrote about "perpendicular cliffs" and the "rushing waters" that sound much like the cliffs and rapids of Hell's Gate which had left her transfixed. The train, she wrote, found its way along "ledges of rock, twisting and turning in every direction on the brink of the precipices below."

When the Canadian Northern Pacific Railway, the provincial branch of the Canadian Northern Railway, was building its line to Vancouver during the years 1910 to 1915, its contractors had no choice but to carve out a new route high above Hell's Gate. Once again, the blasting caused rock and mud slides so massive that the federal Department of Marine and Fisheries grew alarmed about harm to the river and salmon that swam down it to the canneries of Vancouver. Officials from Marine and Fisheries ordered the railway company to remove the rock barriers. When the company refused, Marine and Fisheries hired a dredging company which cleaned up the river at a cost of $90,000, although not before the salmon run was damaged.

In October 1915, the Canadian Northern was officially inaugurated with a run from Québec City to Vancouver, and on by ferry to Victoria. Early on the morning of 18 October, the train reached the most dramatic part of the journey, its route along the Fraser River. As amazed senators, members of parliament, and journalists peered straight down from the heights above Hell's Gate and observed other scenic wonders, they could barely believe that a railway could be constructed through such difficult terrain.

Today, Hell's Gate continues to amaze travellers, and although most visitors now arrive by automobile, it is still possible to experience the "horrible beauty" of the canyon in exactly the same way as Sir John A. Macdonald, Lady Aberdeen, and countless others—from the comfort of a passenger train.

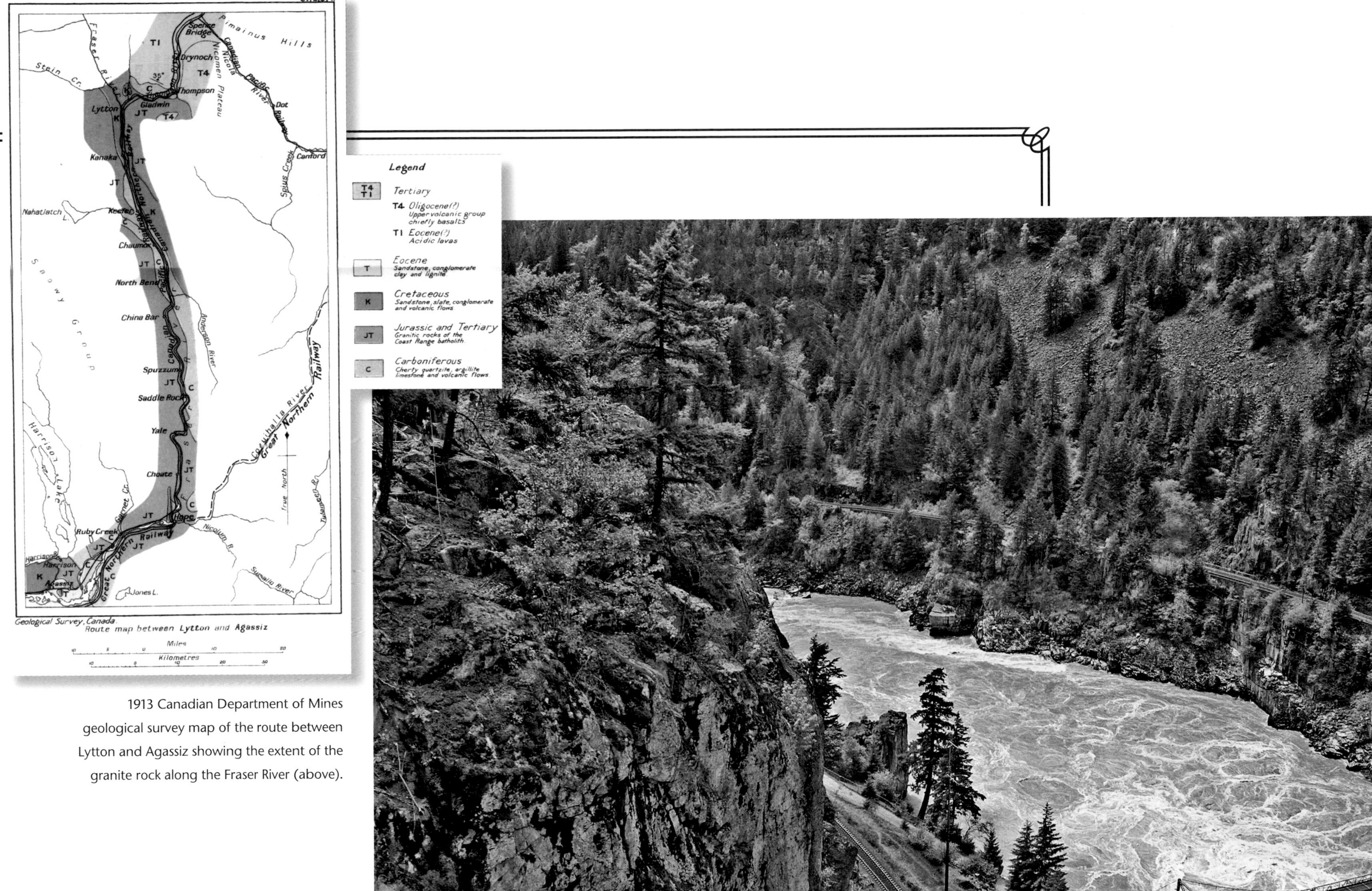

1913 Canadian Department of Mines geological survey map of the route between Lytton and Agassiz showing the extent of the granite rock along the Fraser River (above).

Hell's Gate Canyon showing the CPR line on the right—the east bank—and the Canadian Northern line to the left—the west bank— of the Fraser River (right).

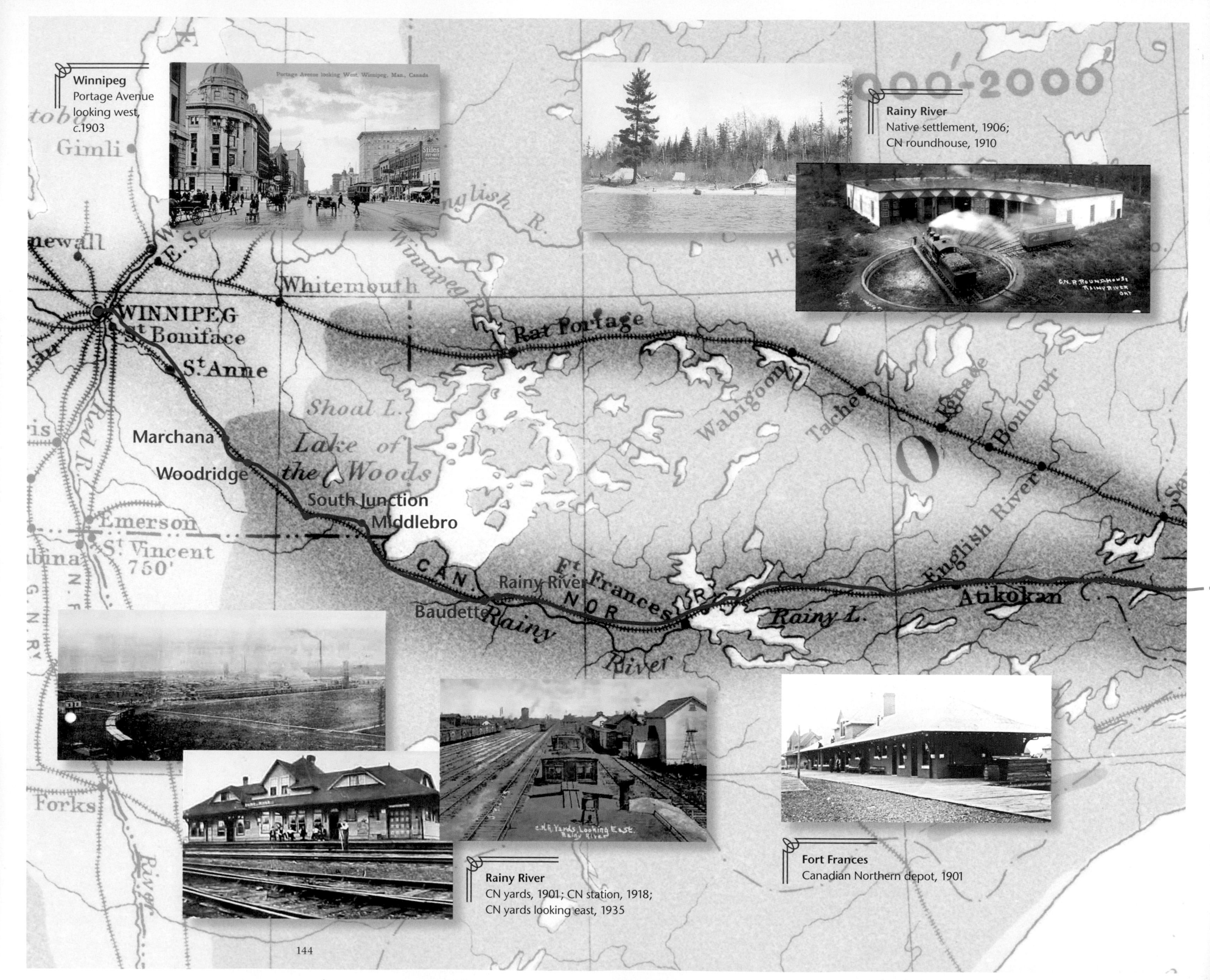

Winnipeg
Portage Avenue looking west, c.1903

Rainy River
Native settlement, 1906;
CN roundhouse, 1910

Rainy River
CN yards, 1901; CN station, 1918;
CN yards looking east, 1935

Fort Frances
Canadian Northern depot, 1901

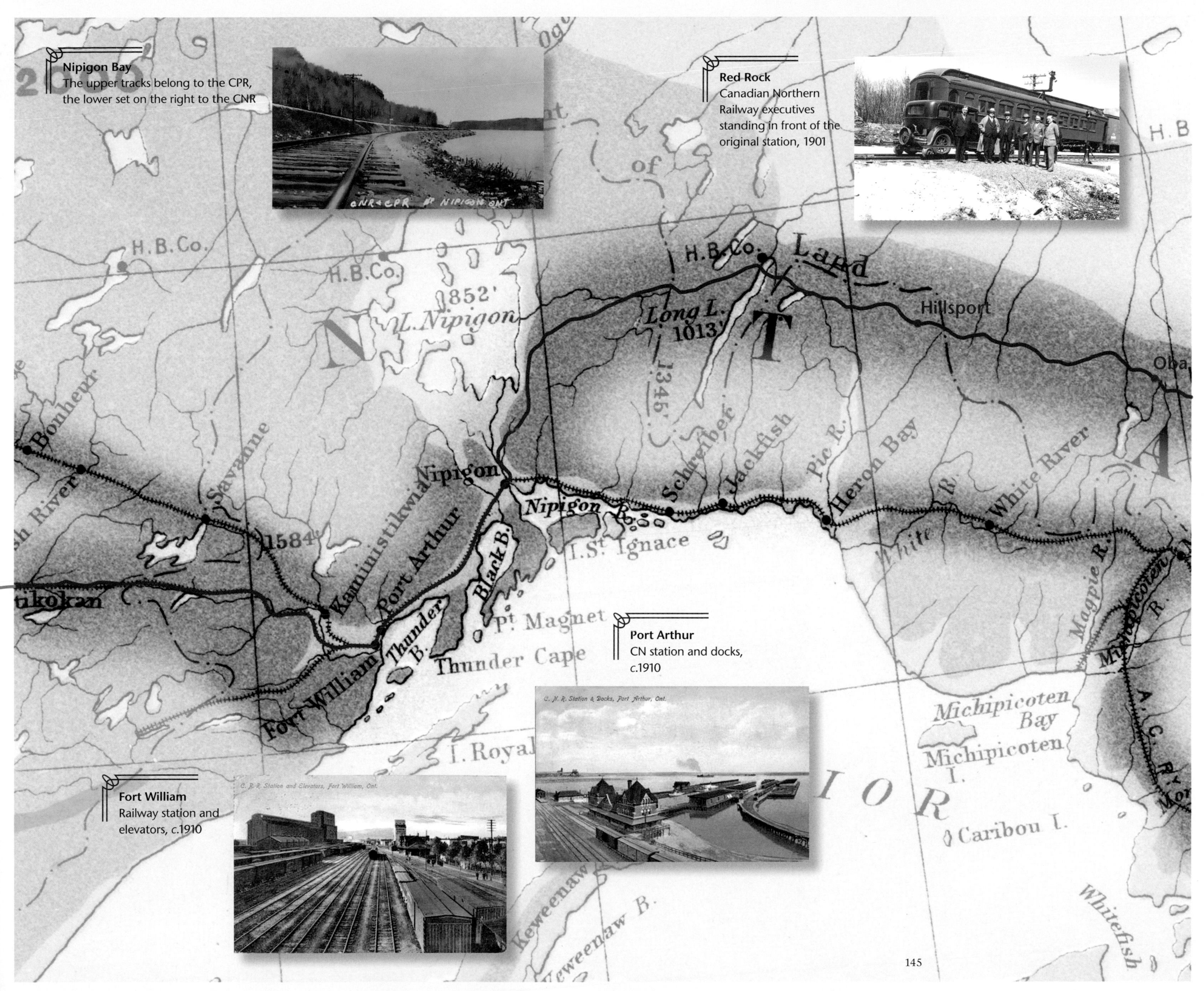

Nipigon Bay
The upper tracks belong to the CPR, the lower set on the right to the CNR

Red Rock
Canadian Northern Railway executives standing in front of the original station, 1901

Port Arthur
CN station and docks, *c.*1910

Fort William
Railway station and elevators, *c.*1910

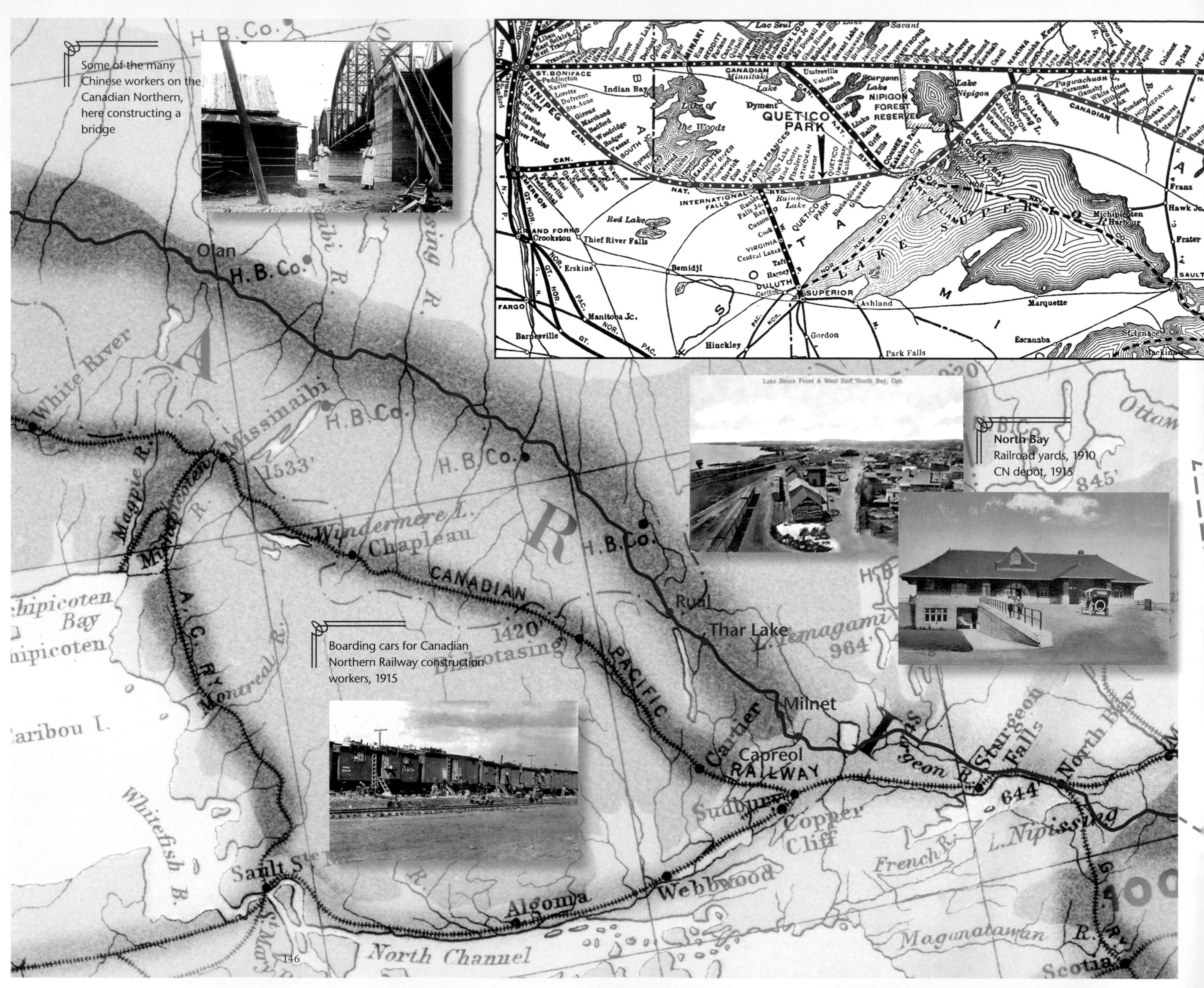

Some of the many Chinese workers on the Canadian Northern, here constructing a bridge

North Bay
Railroad yards, 1910
CN depot, 1915

Boarding cars for Canadian Northern Railway construction workers, 1915

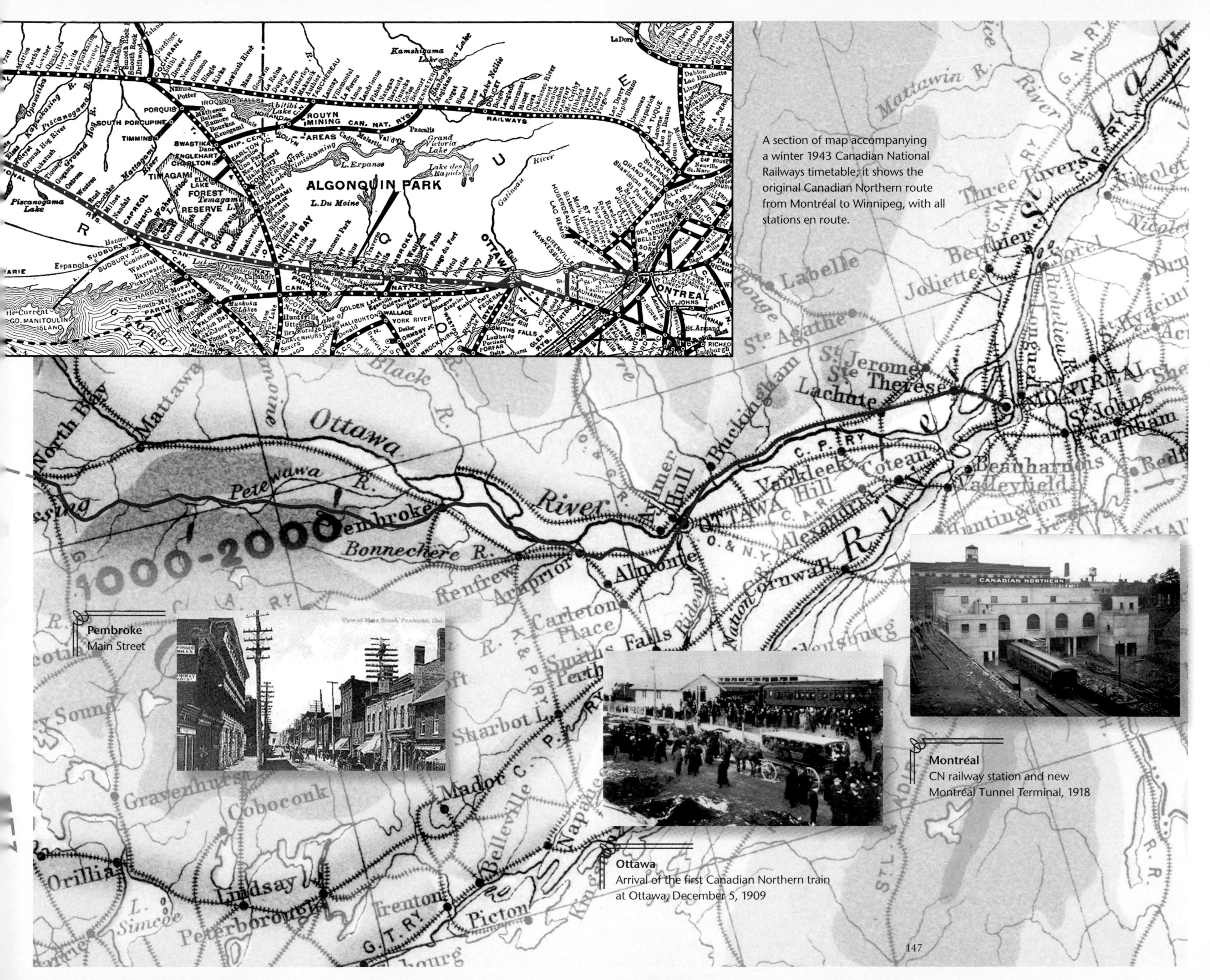

A section of map accompanying a winter 1943 Canadian National Railways timetable; it shows the original Canadian Northern route from Montréal to Winnipeg, with all stations en route.

Pembroke
Main Street

Ottawa
Arrival of the first Canadian Northern train at Ottawa, December 5, 1909

Montréal
CN railway station and new Montréal Tunnel Terminal, 1918

THE PACIFIC GREAT EASTERN

THROUGH THE MOUNTAINOUS HEART OF BRITISH COLUMBIA

British Columbia's Pacific Great Eastern Railway was known not only for its rural charm and beautiful scenery, but also for a complicated, often politically charged history. For many years the vast interior of British Columbia had depended on stage coaches and wagons traversing gravel mountain roads or on river steamers for transportation, but in the years before World War I railway expansion into the vast south central interior of the province was becoming a reality.

In 1907 the Howe Sound, Pemberton Valley and Northern Railway was incorporated to start at a remote settlement called Newport, later named Squamish, about 40 miles (64 km) north of Vancouver at the head of Howe Sound, and to build inland from there. The railway had only extended a few miles into the Squamish Valley when it was restructured and renamed the Howe Sound and Northern; however, little or no further construction was undertaken. Then in 1912 the Pacific Great Eastern Railway was incorporated to take over the earlier railway and build trackage from Vancouver through the mountains to the Cariboo District and eventually to a junction with the Grand Trunk Pacific Railway at Fort George, later called Prince George. Although the intention was to complete the section south to Vancouver at a later date, the British Columbia government guaranteed bonds for the company in order to encourage early investment and construction.

Construction progressed at a steady rate into the rugged Cheakamus Canyon where much bridging was required as the line crested the coastal mountains at Alta Lake some 30 miles (48 km) north of Squamish. From there work progressed by 1914 into the Pemberton Valley to Anderson and Seton lakes and into Lillooet, where the railway crossed the Fraser River and followed its course northwards. The line climbed over 2,000 feet (610 m) as it reached the mining and ranching country of the Cariboo Plateau. However, by 1916, when about 170 miles (274 km) had been built, the backers for the railway, as well as the contractors Foley Stewart & Welch, ran out of finances. This situation led to the province taking over the railway in 1918, and funding its construction and operation. With this change in the role of the province, the railway became forever immersed in politics as an instrument of government regional development policy.

Passengers on the inaugural run to Lillooet, February 20, 1915 (opposite).

The original bridge at Lillooet, which was demolished in 1931 (below).

PGE crew working along Cayoosh Flats, *c.*1915.

Passenger services were extended as the line was built, but terminated at the small town of Clinton 167 mountainous miles (269 km) from Squamish. In 1918, with provincial government funding, more construction work continued north and the PGE reached the ranching centre of Williams Lake and then Quesnel in 1921, 348 miles (560 km) from Squamish. Grading and some rails were laid south from Prince George but there was one major obstacle, the deep Cottonwood Canyon just north of Quesnel, and as a result the government decided to terminate the line at Quesnel until a feasible crossing could be found. Little did they know then that it would be forty years before the line would be built to its intended destination of Prince George.

In the south, meanwhile, the rugged section along Howe Sound was far too costly to build, aside from 13 miles (21 km) of line that was extended west from North Vancouver to Whytecliff. Although opened in 1914, this short section of track was closed just fourteen years later in 1928, and it was not until 1956 that the railway was completed between North Vancouver and Squamish. For many years the PGE could well have been described as a railway that ran from nowhere to nowhere, with no direct connections with other railways or even major urban centres, but it was graced with spectacular scenery. Passengers from Vancouver connected with the train at Squamish by steamship operated by the Union Steamship Company, which itself was a delight to travel on. A tug and barge service provided freight connections.

The first divisional point north of Squamish was East Lillooet, 122.1 miles (196.5 km) to the north and across the Fraser River from the town of Lillooet. Shops were erected and a freight yard built, much to the chagrin of the residents of Lillooet, who felt the railway should have been on the west side of the river. But the PGE had utilized a lower crossing of the Fraser River by means of a long wooden-decked Howe Truss span. East Lillooet was mainly a settlement for railway employees, and a suspension bridge across the canyon connected the two communities. However, in 1929 the railway did decide to move to the west side, crossing the Fraser River on a high steel bridge north of town, and this diversion was completed in 1932.

The PGE became one of the best-loved railways in Canada, with its unique rolling stock and a charming off-the-beaten-track personality. Passenger cars included former electric interurban cars and freight equipment that was varied and unusual, while the company's steam motive power was smart and well looked after. Travel on the PGE would take you back in time. Its passengers came from many backgrounds: First Nations people, missionaries, fishermen, tourists, farmers, and residents from the remote communities it served. Its train crews were the most cordial anywhere, and the meals in the diner were a delight. But above it all was the scenery, the roaring waters through Cheakamus Canyon north of Squamish to the beautiful setting of Alta Lake, with its pristine waters and the vast expanse of the Caribou region. Today across from Alta Lake is Whistler, the world famed ski resort and venue for the 2010 Olympic Winter Games.

For travellers a trip on the PGE in its early years held many thrills. All along the line were many high bridges that in the early days were of wooden construction, but were later rebuilt with steel. The high steel bridge over the mighty Fraser River at Lillooet was a highlight, and the spectacular climb into the interior dry country was breathtaking. In the Fraser Canyon a passenger could look down hundreds of feet to the river below. After cresting the mountains the train reached Williams Lake, a cattle town where huge stock pens held the thousands of cattle being shipped to market. Williams Lake was also another divisional point, 277 miles (445 km) from Squamish. From there it was just another 70-odd miles (115 km) to Quesnel, another cattle, mining, and

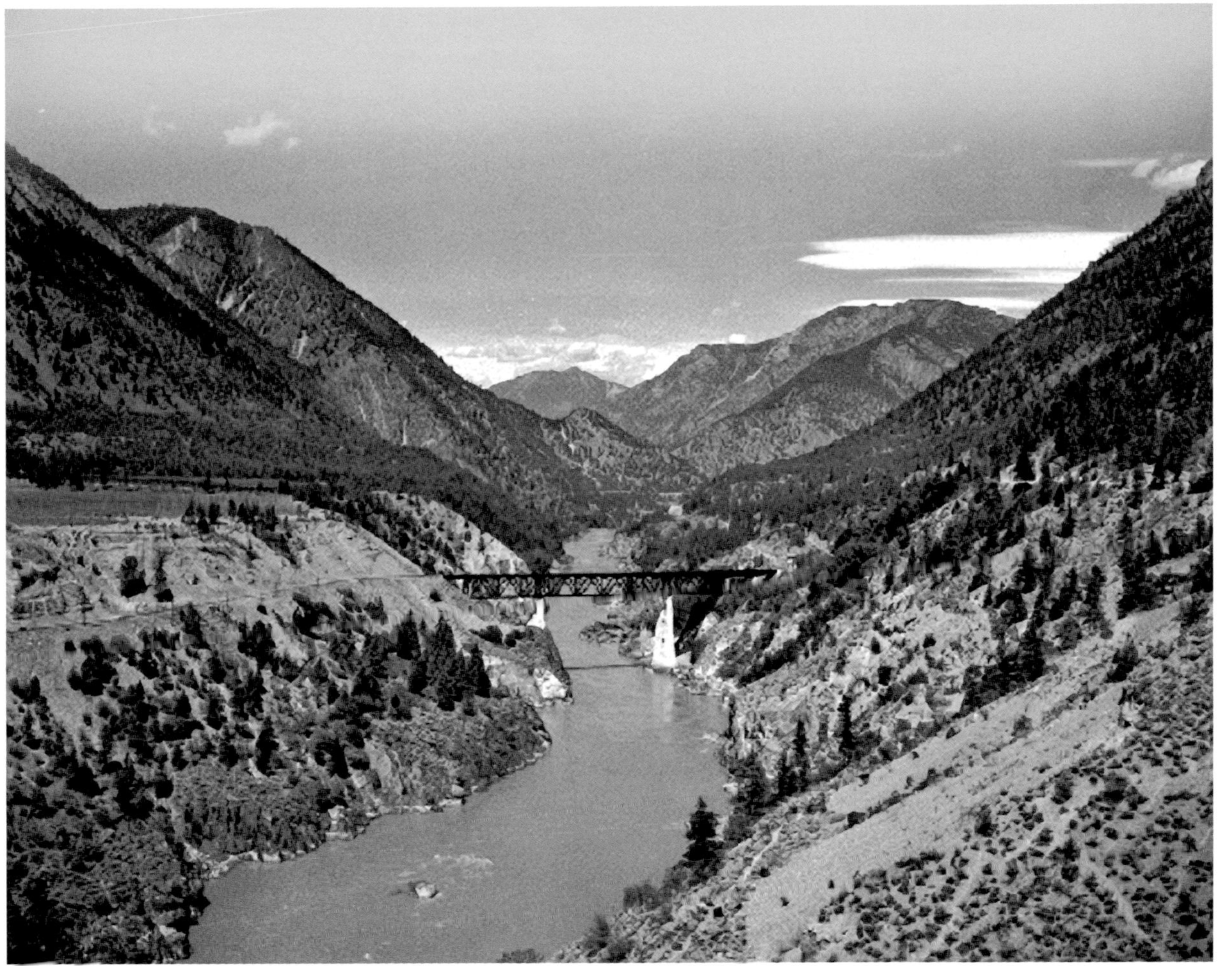

lumber town. To proceed north from there, a determined traveller took a bus to Prince George over poor gravel roads.

One of the features on the old PGE was an open observation car called a "Rubber Neck Car" because passengers were afforded so many opportunities to look at the scenery in all directions. To sit out in this open car, viewing the magnificent landscapes and drinking the best coffee made was a highlight of the trip, although it did have one downside: the PGE often picked up cattle cars and coupled them behind the engine, even on their passenger trains, because they made faster time than the freight trains. It was not uncommon to have ten cattle cars on a train, but with cattle there is the obvious odour problem, and on a summer day this would be quite pronounced in the open car, and even more so if a car were loaded with pigs. Trains were often not on time. One often-

The new Lillooet Bridge, completed in 1932 (above).

Original station at Cayoosh Flats on the west bank of the Fraser River near Lillooet in 1919 (top left).

The PGE's Lilloet Station built in 1932 and shown in the 1960s (bottom left).

A typical mixed PGE train at D'Arcy station, which also served as a meal stop before dining cars were used, 1913.

repeated story is of an old lady who was waiting for the train. When it arrived she congratulated the conductor for being on time, to which he replied, "No, madam, this is yesterday's train. We are twenty-four hours late." The pace of trains was leisurely, and the passenger trains might stop for an hour or two while express or mail was unloaded at some small settlement, or pause at a section house where the section man's wife had baked a pie for the crew and where newspapers or groceries were dropped off. Many of the freight train crews were known to go fishing along the way, as there was no real set time to be anywhere.

Deep Creek Bridge on Pacific Great Eastern railway, view from the north bank, October 1921.

Many a lonely settler along the line would stop a train and ask a crewmember to pick up some item of goods or just some tobacco, and it would be dropped off on the crew's next run north or south. Fishermen would take the Union steamer and then the train from the city to fish the beautiful lakes along the PGE, and for a time the railway operated a "Fisherman's Special" on weekends.

Fortunately the railway experienced few accidents to passenger trains, and in the history of the PGE there was only one fatal accident to a traveller, when a rock crashed through the roof of a train along Anderson Lake, killing the unfortunate man in his seat. One accident involving a passenger train was along Anderson Lake in 1944 when engine No. 56 crashed through a bridge that had been weakened by floodwaters. The locomotive went into the lake but no passenger cars were derailed, although the crew perished. In 1950 engine No. 53 went into Seton Lake and the crew died, but again no passenger cars derailed. With freight trains it was a different story, however, as there were many accidents, mostly involving snow slides in winter, washed out bridges, or avalanches along the lakes.

In the summer months a man on a small gasoline speeder would follow trains to see that no fires were started either by the locomotive or brake shoes. This fire patrol work was lonely but necessary to ensure the woods were protected from forest fires, which could devastate the woodlands.

Progress caught up with the PGE in the 1950s when it became one of the first railways in North America to fully dieselize its operations by 1956. It also went through a massive expansion and modernization phase as it was completed to Prince George and North Vancouver and extended into the Peace River District far to the north as well as to other regions needing modern and efficient transportation. The Province saw the PGE as an effective tool for natural resources development and economic expansion.

In 1972 the railway was to change again, at least in name, when it became the British Columbia Railway. Two years later the road initiated a popular summer steam-powered passenger service between North Vancouver and Squamish using restored former Canadian Pacific Royal Hudson No. 2860 and vintage passenger coaches. More expansion came with the opening in 1983 of the electrified Tumbler Ridge line, which was built to service coal mines in northeastern British Columbia. Then in 1984 the railway's name was simplified again to BC Rail.

Changes came rapidly in the early 2000s. Electric service on the Tumbler Ridge line ended and diesels took over following a reduction in coal production. The steam summer service was cancelled at the end of the 2001 season and regular passenger services ceased in 2002, then in 2003 the government leased the railway to the Canadian National Railway. As its flag fell, the saga that began in the early 1900s and is remembered as the "Please Go Easy" or "Past God's Endurance" was gone forever. Fortunately, seasonal luxury tour trains operated by the Rocky Mountaineer now run between North Vancouver and Whistler and also to the heart of the Cariboo, giving people a wonderful opportunity to relive the early days of the PGE.

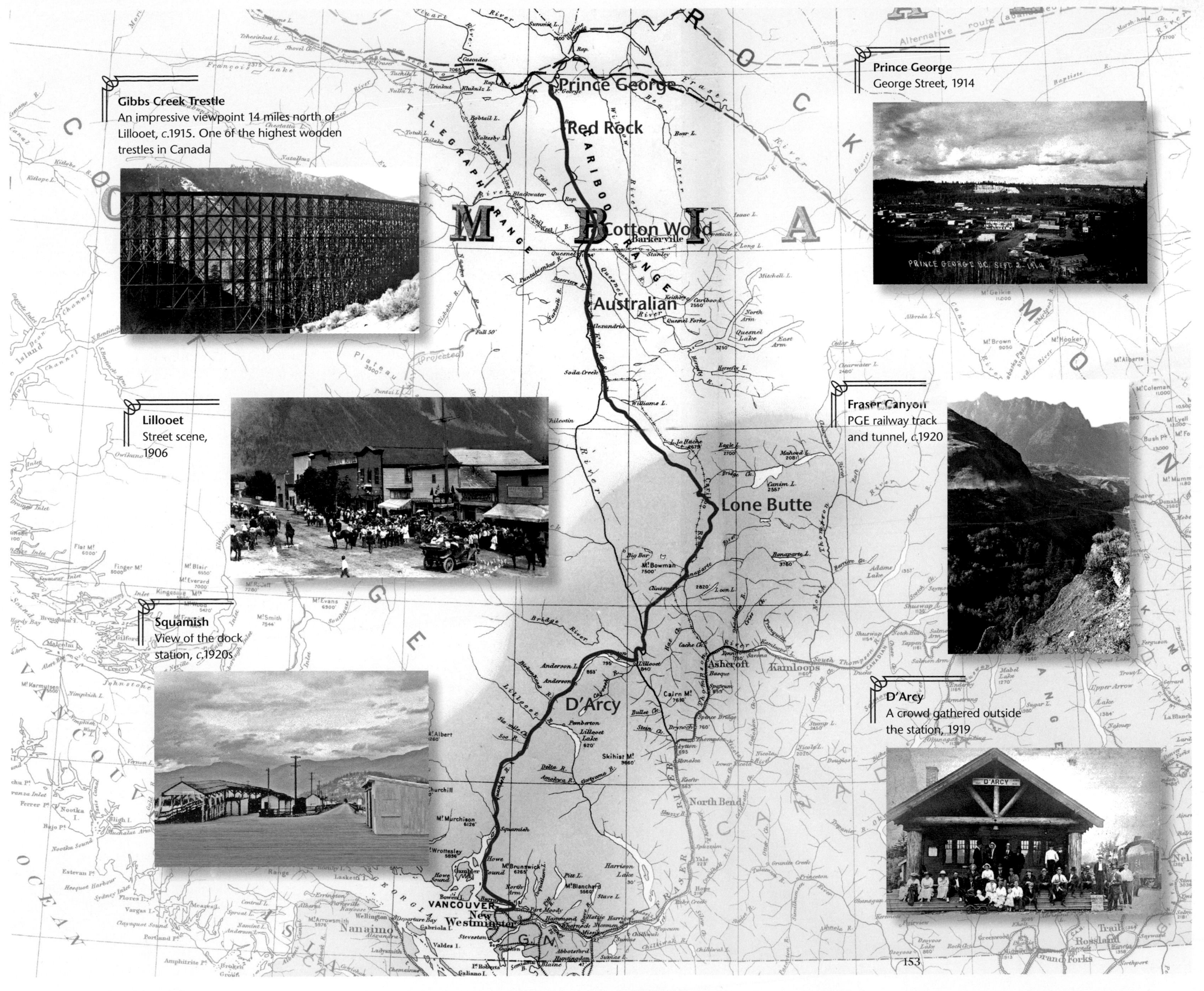

Gibbs Creek Trestle
An impressive viewpoint 14 miles north of Lillooet, *c.*1915. One of the highest wooden trestles in Canada

Prince George
George Street, 1914

Lillooet
Street scene, 1906

Fraser Canyon
PGE railway track and tunnel, *c.*1920

Squamish
View of the dock station, *c.*1920s

D'Arcy
A crowd gathered outside the station, 1919

CANADIAN PACIFIC
CANADIAN PACIFIC
KETTLE VALLEY
4

THE KETTLE VALLEY RAILWAY

McCULLOCH'S WONDER

After the completion of the Canadian Pacific Railway to the west coast of Canada in 1885, the CPR soon turned its attention to the growing mining district in southern British Columbia. William Cornelius Van Horne (1843–1915) of the CPR was worried by potential competition from the American Great Northern Railway, which was extending branch lines into the same mining areas. To counter the threat posed by the GNR to garner the rich trade of ores, the CPR built a railway route through the Crowsnest Pass in the southern Rocky Mountains to Midway on the southern border of British Columbia using a combination of railway and lake steamers. However, the CPR still required a route to the coast.

A brilliant engineer named Andrew McCulloch was hired to build a railway from Midway to a connection with the CPR main line near Hope at the head of the Fraser Valley east of Vancouver, and he immediately got to work laying out a route that would pass south of Kelowna but through Penticton and Princeton, climbing and twisting through the mountains. He was to meet many obstacles on the route, including Myra Canyon where many bridges had to be built. The railway then dropped down to Penticton where the newly established Kettle Valley Railway established its headquarters.

From Penticton the line climbed past Chute Lake and then dropped down to Princeton where McCulloch met the rival Great Northern of James J. Hill, built under the name of the Vancouver, Victoria and Eastern. Both Hill and McCulloch wanted to reach the west coast but conditions were difficult and construction extremely costly. Finally they reached an agreement to share trackage from Princeton through the mountains and across the formidable Coquihalla Canyon east of Hope. Both had surveyed the canyon but it was the KVR that actually built the line through the Coquihalla Canyon, cutting the famed Quintette Tunnels and connecting with the CPR main line at a point just west of Hope. In the end the Great Northern used only part of the line and never operated a through service, and the Coquihalla route became exclusively the domain of the KVR. The company was later to be given to the CPR on a 999-year lease.

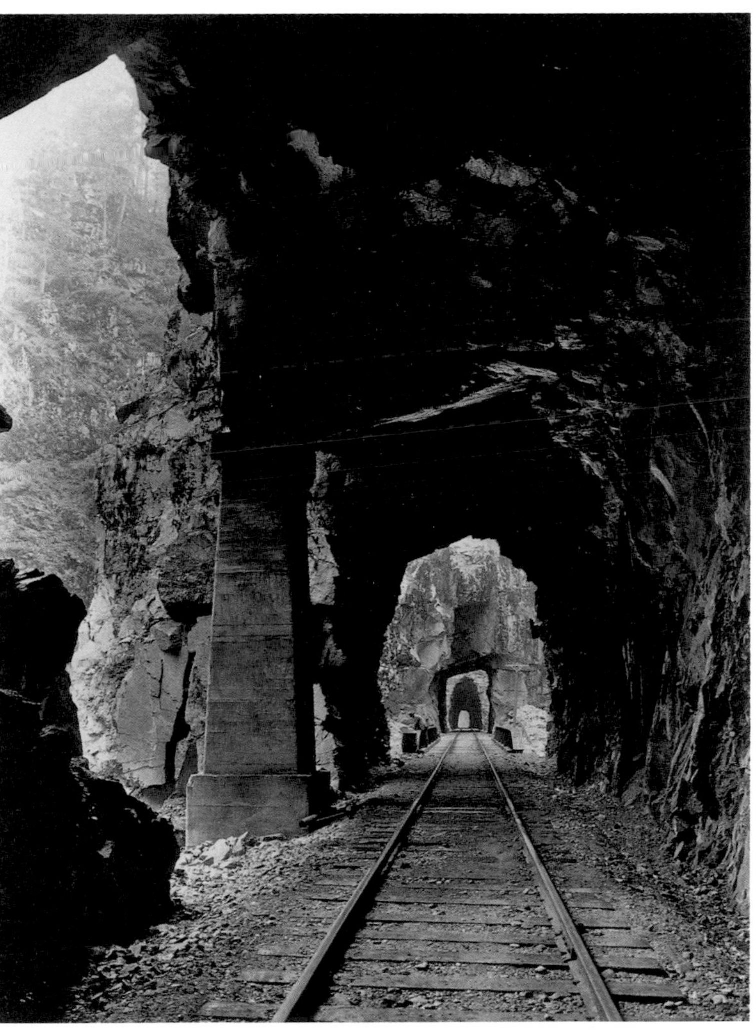

The first train into Penticton's lakeshore station, May 31, 1915, hauled by locomotive No. 4 (opposite).

The Quintette Tunnels in 1929 (left).

Operation on the KVR was never easy. Very harsh winters often deposited 30 feet (9 m) of snow at the summit of the Coquihalla Pass, and when winter snows melted, the run-off could take out bridges and embankments. But throughout all these operational difficulties the KVR proved invaluable to the CPR. In addition to freight, the KVR was a lifeline to the settlements of the Okanagan region, and daily passenger trains were operated. With the magnificent scenery it was a delight for the many who rode the trains. In addition, the railway proved especially useful during the 1939–45 war years when it carried millions of tons of war materials. In fact, after the war the CPR considered it their second main line and the company began to improve the line in many ways, including placing concrete lining in tunnels and installing heavier bridges.

However, with the heavy expense of keeping the line open in winter the CPR considered abandoning the line in the 1950s. Nature decided it for them, as huge washouts in the Coquihalla Canyon in November 1959 closed the line, and it was abandoned by 1961. Although part of the KVR laboured on, bypassing the Coquihalla Canyon and reaching the main line at Spences Bridge to the north, the end finally came for the whole line in May 1989.

One can still find many portions of the former grade, however, and some sections are now hiking and cycling trails. The dramatic Quintette Tunnels near Hope have become a park, while the famed trestles of Myra Canyon are now a National Historic Site of Canada, and have also been preserved. Many sections of the old right-of-way are now parts of the Canadian Trail System. A fine, steam-powered heritage railway operates on a section of the former KVR from West Summerland through the orchards and along the mountain slopes high above Okanagan Lake.

Surveyors at the site of Quintette Tunnels, 1914 (below).

Myra Canyon trestles (below right).

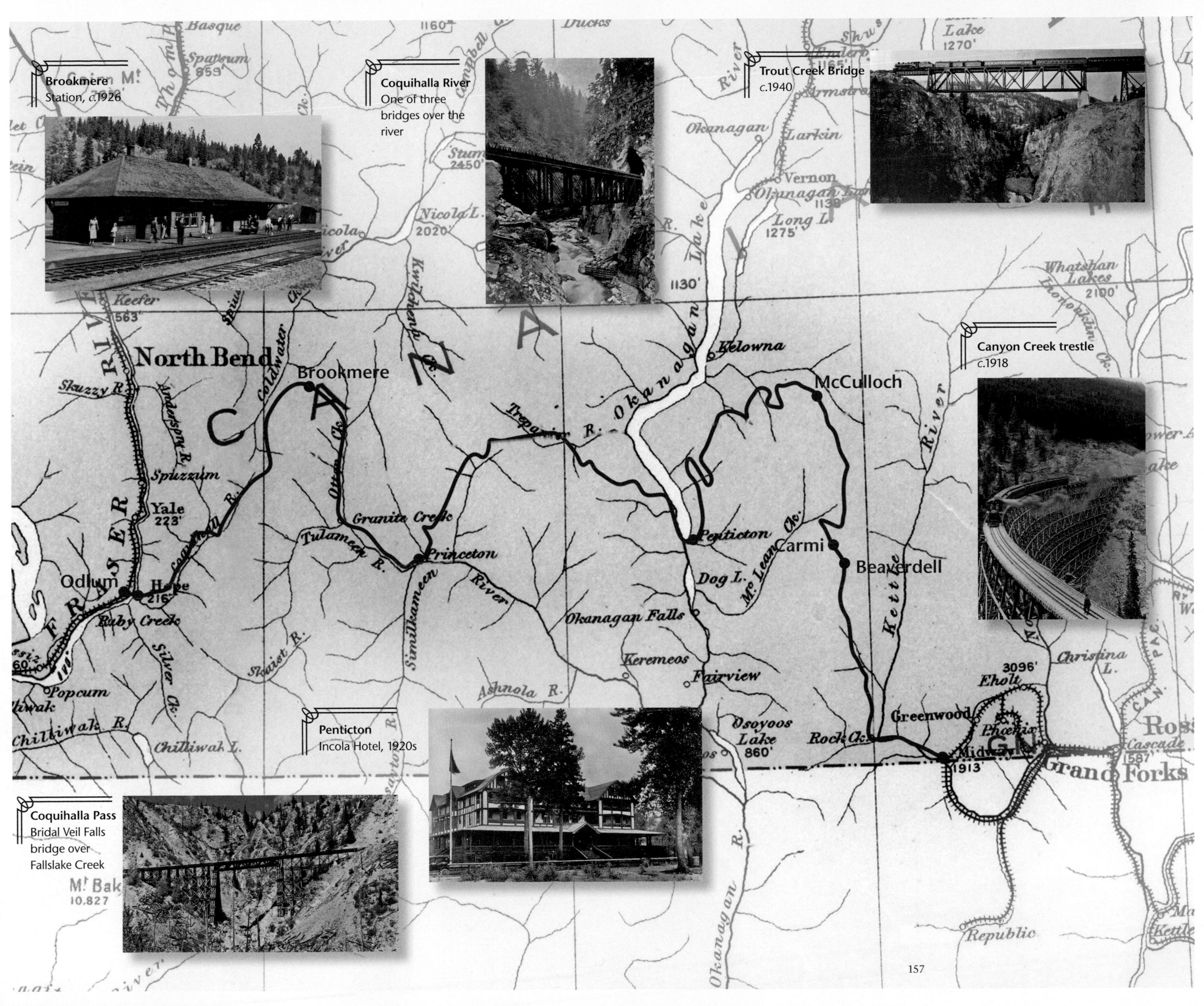

Brookmere
Station, *c.*1926

Coquihalla River
One of three bridges over the river

Trout Creek Bridge
*c.*1940

Canyon Creek trestle
*c.*1918

Penticton
Incola Hotel, 1920s

Coquihalla Pass
Bridal Veil Falls bridge over Fallslake Creek

THE ESQUIMALT AND NANAIMO RAILWAY

THE VANCOUVER ISLAND ROUTE

The Esquimalt and Nanaimo Railway (E&N) was incorporated in 1884 by Robert Dunsmuir (1825–89), who owned major coal mines on Vancouver Island, and his partners American businessmen and railroad magnates Richard Crocker, Collis P. Huntington, and Leland Stanford. The railway was originally planned as part of a trans-Canada line to go into operation when British Columbia joined Canada, but in the end the line was built as a separate entity, called the Esquimalt and Nanaimo because the line was actually built between these two points on the island. However, it was soon extended north to the coal-mining centre of Wellington and south to Victoria, the provincial capital. With the railway came a huge, timber-rich land grant that extended from southern Vancouver Island to Campbell River almost half way up the island.

In 1905 the Canadian Pacific Railway acquired the E&N along with its vast land grant. The CPR soon extended the line to Parksville in 1910, and from there to Port Alberni in 1911 and to Courtenay in 1914. A further line was built to Lake Cowichan in 1913, primarily to garner the tremendous timber resources that lay in the Cowichan Valley. The line was the catalyst for the settlement of large areas of Vancouver Island, providing access to the forest and mineral resources of the island, and thereby encouraging the growth of the population, towns, and settlements on the island.

The line passed through some of the most beautiful landscapes in British Columbia, and over the years it prospered and became one of the CPR's most profitable acquisitions. However, traffic declined in the 1940s and 1950s because of the advent of improved highways, and the railway was to see its freight revenues drop sharply. This trend continued

Esquimalt and Nanaimo Railway timetable, 1909 (above).

Esquimalt and Nanaimo passenger train near Shawnigan Lake, *c.*1886 (Robert Turner Collection, opposite).

Trestle over Niagara Canyon, *c.*1900 (left).

Truss bridge over the Cowichan River, 1912 (far left).

through the next decades and, by the early 2000s, there were few outbound freight shipments remaining. Passenger service, which had been modernized in the 1950s with the use of Budd Rail Diesel Cars, continued but passenger volumes declined slowly as most people travelled by road. However in 1979 VIA Rail assumed this service and continues to operate it today. But the CPR divested itself of the railway in 1999 through a sale and lease agreement to RailAmerica, which tried to continue the remaining freight services until it accepted that the operations were unprofitable. Eventually the railway was acquired by the Island Corridor Foundation, a local organization, which brought in the Southern Railway of British Columbia to operate the line. It continues a limited service but the future of freight and the VIA passenger services are tenuous, needing major investments in the right of way and new equipment.

Laying track on the Esquimalt and Nanaimo line to Alberni, 1911 (above).

E&N locomotive No. 3 leaving Victoria, *c.*1900 (right).

Nanaimo
General view, *c.*1900
Northfield Mine, *c.*1900

Dunsmuir
Dunsmuir Mine, *c.*1880

Victoria
E&N locomotive No. 62, late 1920s

Esquimalt
Harbour, 1890

THE WHITE PASS AND YUKON ROUTE

CANADA'S MOST NORTHERLY PASSENGER RAILWAY

North America's most northerly passenger railway owes its existence to the 1897 Yukon or Klondike Gold Rush, when thousands of people scrambled over the brutal Chilkoot Pass or White Pass from Alaska into Canadian territory, heading for Dawson City, Yukon, "the San Francisco of the North." The steep passes were so treacherous that each traveller had to make several journeys over the summit to take all his or her supplies.

The challenge of transporting all these would-be miners was irresistible to Railway Age entrepreneurs, so British investors bankrolled a railway to take gold-diggers the entire 110-mile (177-km) overland section of the gold rush route—Skagway in Alaska to Whitehorse, Yukon. From Whitehorse, travellers could board steam-driven paddle-wheelers for the 600-mile (966-km) journey down the Yukon River to the gold fields.

Construction began in May 1898. A three-foot narrow gauge was chosen because a narrower railbed made for big cost savings when that roadbed had to be carved out of the mountain rock. The narrow gauge also meant that the tracks could more easily follow the abrupt curves of the craggy landscape, rather than having to be blasted through it. Altogether, 35,000 men worked on the track, and 450 tons of explosives were used to blast aside 120-foot (36-m) cliffs and reach the White Pass summit, 2,885 feet (879 m) above sea level. The mountain sides were so steep that workers were suspended by ropes to prevent them falling off while cutting the grade, but even so thirty-five men died during construction.

On February 18, 1899, the tracks reached the summit, and many of Dawson's leading citizens (including Belinda Mulrooney, "the richest woman in the Klondike") boarded a ceremonial passenger train for the historic first round trip. The train stopped several times en route for photographs of the dignitaries, swathed in furs and wearing thick leather boots. In July 1900, the line was completed. A journey that had taken several weeks in the early days of the Gold Rush now took seven hours.

But by then the Yukon Gold Rush was over. Nevertheless, the WP&YR struggled along, carrying passengers and freight. During World War II, American servicemen posted in Alaska knew it as the "Wait Patiently and You'll Ride."

The railroad was dieselized in the mid to late 1950s, one of the few North American narrow gauge railroads to do so, and was an early pioneer of intermodal or containerized freight traffic. In 1969 the Faro lead-zinc mine in Yukon opened, and the railway was upgraded with seven new locomotives. In the fall of 1969, a new tunnel and bridge bypassing Dead Horse Gulch were built to replace the tall steel cantilever bridge that could not carry the heavier trains. Passenger traffic on the WP&YR was also increasing

The first passenger train en route to the summit, winter 1898 (opposite).

The "border post" at White Pass station, early 1900s (below).

Driving the last spike at Whitehorse, June 8, 1900 (right).

WP&YR's first full summer timetable, June 1901 (below).

Challenging conditions during the final winter of building (bottom right).

as cruise ships started to visit Alaska's Inside Passage. There was no road from Skagway to Whitehorse until 1978. In 1982, however, metal prices plunged, striking with devastating effect on the mines that were the White Pass and Yukon Route's main customers. The railway closed on October 7, 1982.

The shutdown, however, was not for long. Many cruise ships stopped at Skagway, and the dramatic scenery of the White Pass route was a great tourist draw. Cruise operators, remembering the attraction of the little trains, pushed for the line to be opened again. The White Pass Route was reopened between Skagway and White Pass in 1988 for tourist passenger traffic, and is now a key part of the local economy.

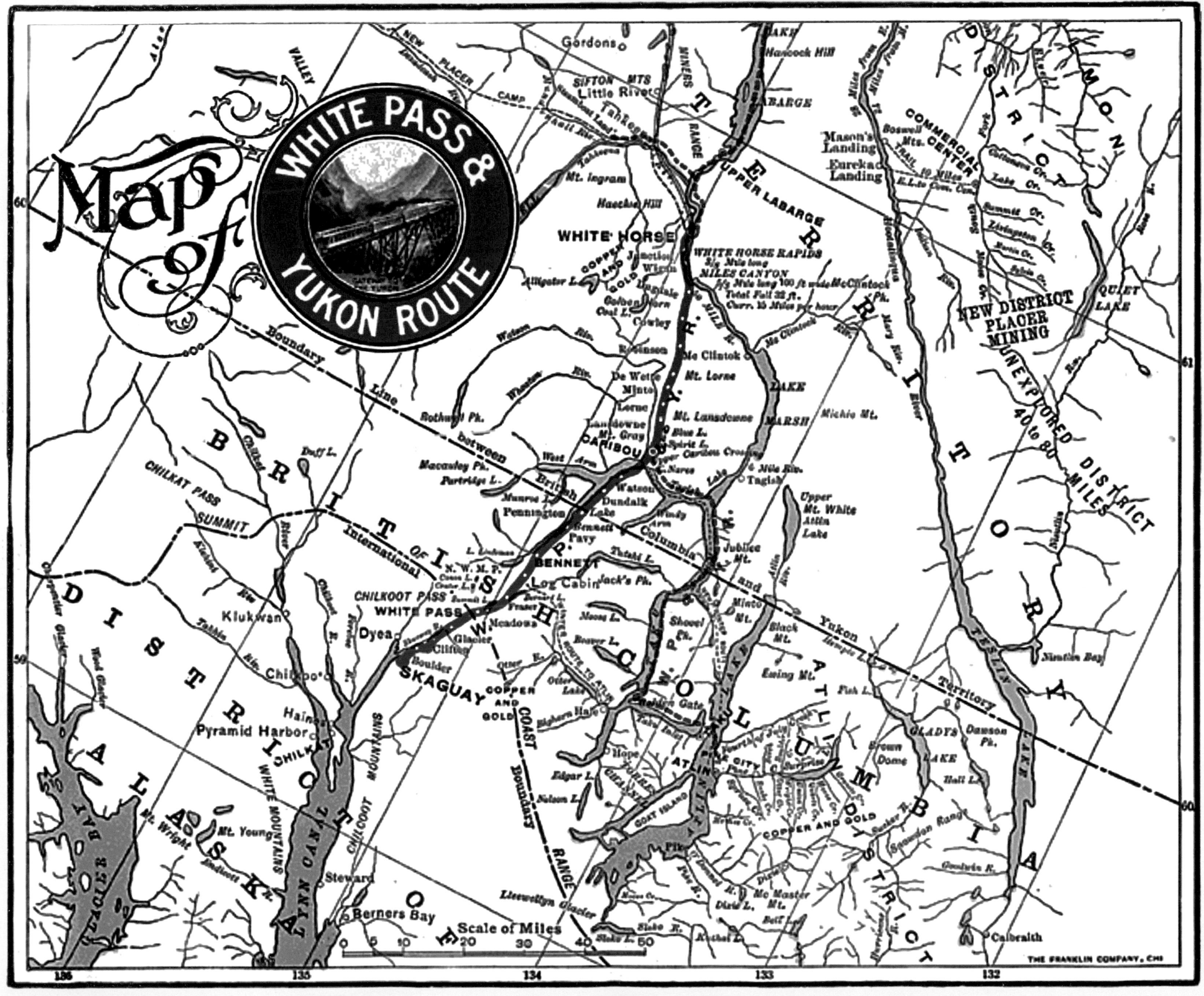

Map of
WHITE PASS & YUKON ROUTE
WHITE HORSE
UPPER LABARGE
WHITE HORSE RAPIDS
MILES CANYON
CARIBOU
BENNETT
Log Cabin
CHILKOOT PASS
WHITE PASS
Dyea
SKAGUAY
Klukwan
Haines
Pyramid Harbor
Steward
Berners Bay
LYNN CANAL
GLACIER BAY
CHILKAT PASS
SUMMIT
BRITISH COLUMBIA
DISTRICT OF ALASKA
YUKON TERRITORY
NEW DISTRICT PLACER MINING
COMMERCIAL CENTER
Mason's Landing
Eureka Landing
ATLIN
Boundary Line between British Columbia and Yukon Territory
COAST Boundary RANGE
COPPER AND GOLD
Scale of Miles
0 5 10 20 30 40 50
THE FRANKLIN COMPANY, CHI
136
135
134
133
132
60
61
59

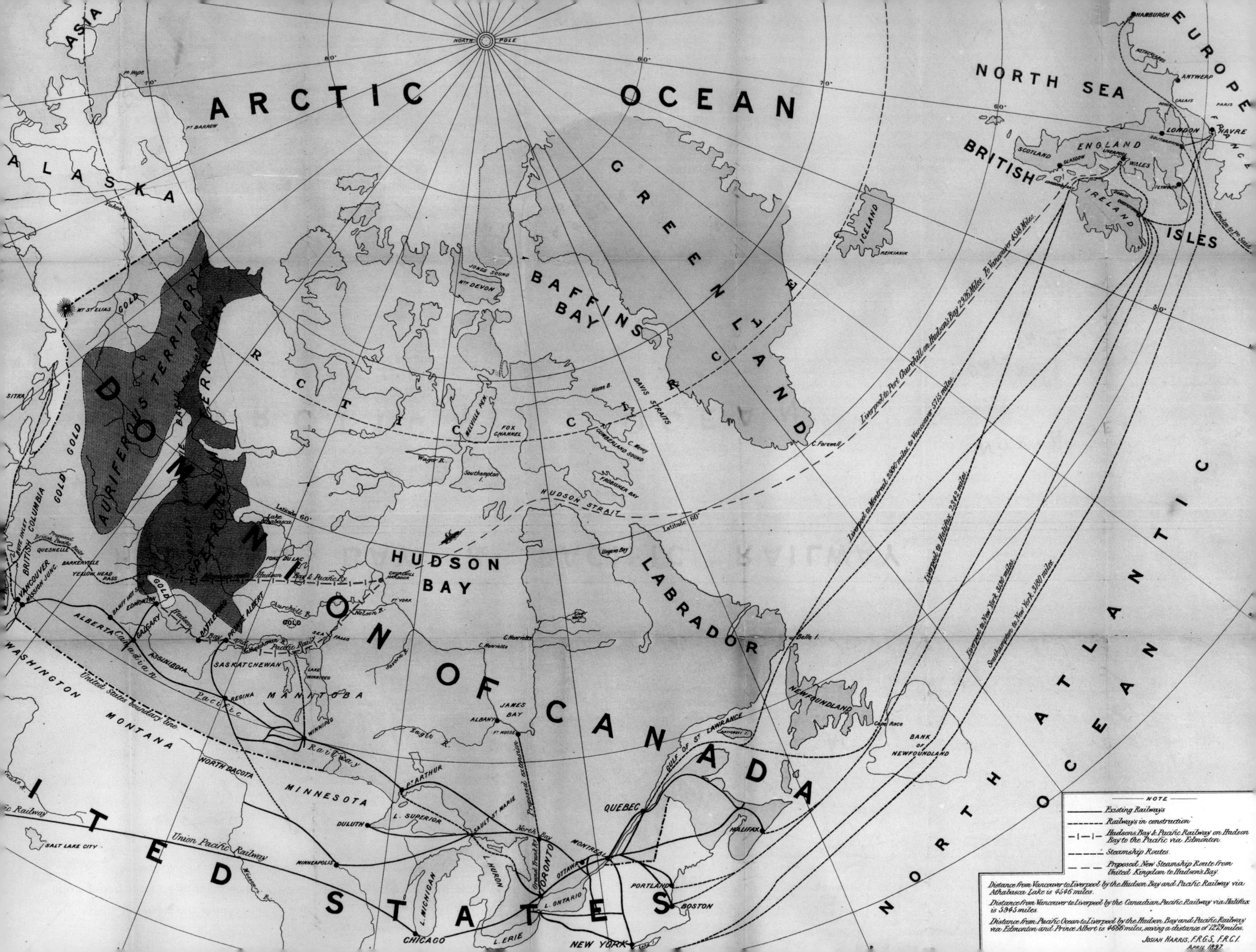
ARCTIC OCEAN
NORTH POLE
ASIA
EUROPE
NORTH SEA
ALASKA
BRITISH ISLES
SCOTLAND
ENGLAND
WALES
IRELAND
FRANCE
HAMBURGH
ANTWERP
CALAIS
PARIS
LONDON
HAVRE
GLASGOW
ICELAND
REIKIAVIK
GREENLAND
BAFFINS BAY
JONES SOUND
DAVIS STRAITS
FOX CHANNEL
HUDSON STRAIT
CUMBERLAND SOUND
FROBISHER BAY
C. Farewell
ARCTIC CIRCLE
Latitude 60°
HUDSON BAY
JAMES BAY
LABRADOR
NEWFOUNDLAND
Cape Race
BANK OF NEWFOUNDLAND
GULF OF ST LAWRENCE
Belle I.
Ungava Bay
DOMINION OF CANADA
AURIFEROUS TERRITORY
PETROLEUM TERRITORY
BRITISH COLUMBIA
ALBERTA
ASSINIBOIA
SASKATCHEWAN
MANITOBA
MT ST ELIAS
GOLD
SITKA
PT BARROW
Lake Athabasca
FORT DU LAC
CHURCHILL HARBOUR
FT YORK
Nelson R.
Churchill R.
VANCOUVER
MISSION JUNC.
QUESNELLE
BARKERVILLE
YELLOW HEAD PASS
EDMONTON
CALGARY
BANFF HOT SPRINGS
BATTLEFORD
PRINCE ALBERT
REGINA
WINNIPEG
ALBANY
FT MOOSE
PT ARTHUR
DULUTH
SAULT ST MARIE
North Bay
OTTAWA
TORONTO
MONTREAL
QUEBEC
HALIFAX
PORTLAND
BOSTON
NEW YORK
CHICAGO
MINNEAPOLIS
SALT LAKE CITY
L. SUPERIOR
L. MICHIGAN
L. HURON
L. ONTARIO
L. ERIE
WASHINGTON
MONTANA
NORTH DACOTA
MINNESOTA
UNITED STATES
United States boundary line
Canadian Pacific Railway
Hudson Bay & Pacific Railway
Union Pacific Railway
Proposed extension
Grand Trunk R.
Proposed British Pacific Railway
NORTH ATLANTIC OCEAN
Liverpool to Port Churchill on Hudsons Bay 2926 Miles. To Vancouver 4518 Miles.
Liverpool to Montreal, 2990 miles; to Vancouver 5715 miles.
Liverpool to Halifax 2342 miles.
Liverpool to New York 3180 miles.
Southampton to New York 3100 miles.
London to Pt. Said
NOTE
Existing Railways
Railways in construction
Hudsons Bay & Pacific Railway on Hudson Bay to the Pacific via Edmonton
Steamship Routes.
Proposed New Steamship Route from United Kingdom to Hudson's Bay.
Distance from Vancouver to Liverpool by the Hudson Bay and Pacific Railway via Athabasca Lake is 4546 miles.
Distance from Vancouver to Liverpool by the Canadian Pacific Railway via Halifax is 5945 miles.
Distance from Pacific Ocean to Liverpool by the Hudson Bay and Pacific Railway via Edmonton and Prince Albert is 4666 miles, saving a distance of 1279 miles.
JOSIAH HARRIS, F.R.G.S., F.R.C.I.
APRIL 1897

THE HUDSON BAY RAILWAY

THE NORTHERN VISION

With prairie settlement booming at the end of the nineteenth century, western farmers sought cheap methods of exporting their grain to Europe. The standard route was by rail on the Canadian Pacific Railway (CPR) east to Fort William (now Thunder Bay) on Lake Superior, then by inland shipping to Montréal and from there by ocean shipping to Europe. A salt-water port on Hudson Bay seemed to offer an alternative route that bypassed the traffic monopoly of the CPR and was 1,000 miles (1,600 km) closer to Europe than the route via Montréal.

In 1880 the Winnipeg Great Northern Railway was incorporated to build from southern Manitoba to the mouth of the Nelson River on Hudson Bay. Nothing happened until railway promoters William Mackenzie and Donald Mann (later of Canadian Northern fame) acquired this company in 1886 in order to obtain its large land grant. Since these entrepreneurs were not actually interested in building to Hudson Bay, track construction ended at The Pas in northern Manitoba in 1910.

Although the Canadian Northern and Grand Trunk Pacific began to build alternative transcontinental lines to break the CPR's monopoly, the Hudson Bay route remained politically popular in the West. The Dominion government agreed, therefore, to continue the line to Port Nelson on Hudson Bay as the Hudson Bay Railway. Work began in 1913 but ceased in 1916 due to wartime shortages. Following World War I, new surveys showed that Port Nelson was totally inadequate as a harbour. So in 1927 the government decided to relocate the terminal further north to the

Churchill station, Hudson Bay Railway, late 1930s (above).

Railway promoters Donald Mann and William Mackenzie (left).

A 1913 map showing how Churchill is on the shortest route from Europe to central and western Canada (opposite).

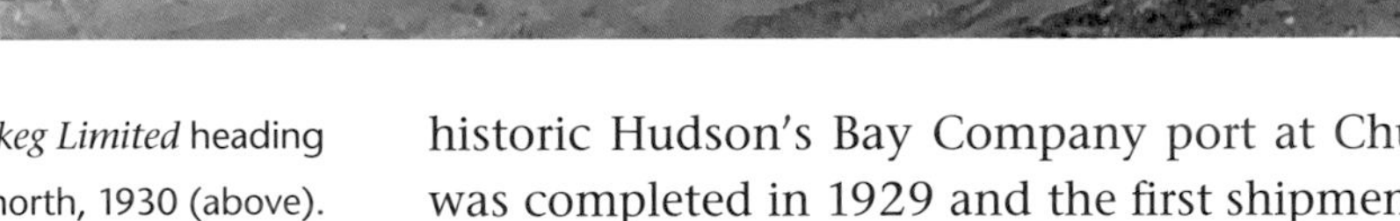

The Muskeg Limited heading north, 1930 (above).

Churchill station shortly after it was opened (top right).

Hudson Bay Railway bridge over Saskatchewan River, The Pas, 1919 (bottom).

historic Hudson's Bay Company port at Churchill. The line was completed in 1929 and the first shipment of grain left in September 1931.

The Hudson Bay line was never a commercial success. Perhaps the most obvious problem was a short shipping season; the build-up of ice at the entrance into Hudson Bay limited ocean shipping to early August to mid-October. Since few ships could use the port, freight and marine insurance rates remained high. The permafrost conditions (permanently frozen ground) made the rail line expensive to maintain. And, in any case, the well-established rail-water systems of southern Canada remained a cost-effective means of exporting western grain.

While the Hudson Bay Railway did not develop much export traffic, the line did, however, help to open northern Manitoba to mineral development. Branches were built into the nickel, copper, zinc, and gold mining areas around Flin Flon (1929), Lynne Lake (1953), and Stall Lake (1960–3), and its modern incarnation is still a vital freight transportation link in the region.

The Pas
The bridge over the Saskatchewan River shortly after it was opened in 1913

The Pas
Freighting, 1916
Hotel de Pas, 1918

Kettle Rapids
Bridge in morning fog

Regina
HB station staff, 1896
View of the HB station, 1897

Qu'Appelle Valley
1905

25
25
ALGOMA 25 CENTRAL

THE ALGOMA CENTRAL RAILWAY

THE HEARTBEAT OF THE WILDERNESS

The Algoma Central defied the primordial east–west logic of Canadian railway building. In a nation that consolidated its unity with railways that stretched laterally from coast to coast, the Algoma Central ran north–south, stubbornly pushing up from the rocky shores of Lake Superior into the uninviting Canadian Shield, and dedicating itself to opening up the resources of "New Ontario." Chartered in 1899, the Algoma Central reflected the optimism of the Laurier Boom—that surge of immigration, resource exploitation, and industrialization that floated Canada off the shoals of late-nineteenth-century economic despair.

Situated at the confluence of Lakes Huron and Superior, the town of Sault Ste. Marie sat at a crossroad of Canada's development. During the fur trade, *voyageurs*, or mobile trappers, used the town as a way station en route to the West, portaging around the mighty rapids that tumbled from Lake Superior into the Huron. When fur trading faded, the town languished. The Canadian Pacific Railway, intent on reaching the western prairies post haste, passed to its north, as would the later government-sponsored transcontinental railways in the new century. Prevailing wisdom saw the Sault's northland as barren of economic potential—a tortuous terrain of hard rock and boreal forest. However, in the late nineteenth century discoveries of nickel, copper, and silver began to hint at untapped wealth in the north.

It took an American entrepreneur—the eloquent and flamboyant Francis Hector Clergue (1856–1939) of Maine—to connect the Sault to burgeoning resource exploitation and industrialization as "Canada's century" dawned. The Sault's hinterland, Clergue told the Toronto Board of Trade in 1900, had hitherto been "unknown and inaccessible except to the woodsman inured to Indian hardships." Boasting well-heeled backers in Philadelphia and New York, Clergue painted a picture of the Sault as the might-be industrial Pittsburgh of the Canadian Shield. The surging St. Mary's rapids would provide the motive force for a cluster of industries that he would bring to the sleepy town. Iron and steel, pulp and paper, nickel smelting, street railways, and hydroelectricity generation would thrive on shared economies of scale and nearby resources—the great forests of the Canadian Shield and iron ore discovered north of the Sault at Wawa. "From the days of the first baboon down to the times of Carnegie," Clergue cockily assured investors, "there has never been an industrial failure where the raw material existed to the best advantage, combined with the force necessary for its transformation into practical use." The press dubbed Clergue "The Wizard of the North" and a "Napoleon of Promoters." Politicians in both Ottawa and Toronto welcomed him as the agent of progress, lavishing subsidies and tariff protection on his projects. And so the Lake Superior Corporation was born; by 1903 it would boast 7,000 employees.

To sew his industrial empire together Clergue needed a transportation network—of steamships to fetch coal from Pennsylvania for steel smelting and railways to draw ore and timber from the Sault's hinterland. So, in 1899, he obtained a federal charter for the Algoma Central Railway along with a land grant of 7,400 acres per mile endowed by Ontario's government. Clergue praised such "judicious" largesse, saying that his railway would create "an agency for immigration more efficacious than a legion of lectures and a million maps" in populating "New Ontario." He extravagantly promised to attract an influx of a thousand new Canadians annually over the next

Algoma Central and Hudson Bay Railway timetable for May 1909 (above).

Algoma Central locomotive No. 25, built by Brooks Locomotive Works in 1900 (opposite).

decade. But the Algoma Central was primarily to be a resource railway. The first objective was to connect the Sault's steel mill with iron ore from the Helen Mine near Wawa, 160 miles (257 km) to the north. A spur line would be pushed to the shore of Lake Superior at Michipicoten Harbour, where coal could be transshipped and iron ore delivered to ships in the ice-free summer. Elsewhere the line would collect timber for pulping at the Sault and deliver woodsmen to their forest camps. Eventually, the line would intersect the Canadian Pacific to the north and thereby tap into its lucrative east–west traffic. Ever the visionary, Clergue in 1901 added the phrase "and Hudson Bay" to the railway's name, prophesying that the line would reach the shores of James Bay on the southern end of Hudson Bay, and thus be in a position to deliver fresh northern fish to fishmongers in Chicago. "Hudson Bay" was eventually dropped from the railway's name in June 1965.

In 1900, construction began on the main line north out of the Sault and inland from Michipicoten, although from the outset it became apparent that Clergue was a better wordsmith than a railway surveyor. For all his talk of being a "backwoodsman from the wilds of Algoma," he had grossly underestimated the challenge of building a railway across some of the rockiest, steepest, forest-choked terrain in Ontario. From its lakeside terminal at the Sault, the railway's route rose a

An inspection team onboard an Algoma Central train, March 1910.

harrowing 1,040 feet (317 m) over its first 97 miles (156 km). At times, the gradient on the line reached a daunting one foot in 55. The route was not only steep, it was tortuous. Deep ravines, flashing rivers, and formidable rock walls had to be crossed, circumvented, and blasted. Construction costs soared. Furthermore, since the line was penetrating virgin territory, every construction need—ballast, structural steel, ties, rails, dynamite—had to be brought up the line to the end of the road. Locals took to jokingly referring to the Algoma Central and Hudson Bay as the "All Curves and High Bridges."

By 1903, track laying had inched 56 miles (90 km) out of the Sault, although progress on the Michipicoten branch line was quicker. Then, on September 28, 1903 the whole Clergue enterprise metaphorically came off the tracks. For all its bold talk of industrial synergy, the Lake Superior Corporation rested on a shaky and unscrupulous foundation. Its stock was "watered"—grossly misrepresenting actual asset value—and there was a chronic failure to make the various industries dovetail together. Costs outstripped earnings, and when the payroll failed to be met that September day, Clergue's workers rioted and the whole enterprise ground to a halt. The militia restored order, Clergue made himself scarce (he would loiter on the edge of Canadian business, listened to but not trusted until his death in 1939), and the Ontario government shored up the corporation's wobbly finances. The railway was clearly hobbled.

Construction proceeded fitfully, and it was not until 1914 that the line was completed to Hearst (a town named after a Sault lawyer turned provincial premier), 296 miles (476 km) north of the Sault. There it intersected with the new National Transcontinental, having already crossed the Canadian Northern at Oba (mile 244) and the Canadian Pacific (mile 194). Any talk of pushing on to Hudson Bay faded, however, as there was no commercial fishery accessible from Hearst—its hinterland was frozen solid half the year and muskeg swamp for the rest. Bowed by construction costs, the railway struggled to survive. Finally, in 1916, long-suffering bondholders in London, England, asserted their control, and understandably began a conservative regime. Pulpwood, coal, and iron ore gave the line a modicum of traffic, and two world wars provided a fillip for the railway as demand for primary materials soared. A modest passenger traffic also developed, but only a handful of immigrants found their way to the arable clay belt around Hearst at the north end of the line. In the regional and national economic sense, the Algoma Central never lived up to Clergue's roseate billing, and Algoma Central shareholders would not see a dividend until 1959.

The locks on the Sault Ste. Marie Canal, a postcard of 1911.

The glory of the Algoma Central—tourism—was completely unintended. Even the construction crews who toiled through the Sault's arduous hinterland saw the virginal beauty of the place. Moreover, these were years in which North Americans reacted to the grimy pressures of city and industry by seeking the solace of nature. "The time has come," an Algoma Central brochure touted in 1909, "when tired humanity seeks surcease from heat, smoke, toil, and trouble, and the exodus begins, to the waters, where blow cool breezes, and to the woods, where there is rest and shade." By 1920, the railway boasted that its rails led to "A Primeval Paradise for the Sportsman." In 1924, travel writer T. Morris Longstreth told his readers that to gaze upon the Montréal River Falls from the 1,550-foot (472-m) long Algoma Central trestle (mile 92) was to sense "the heartbeat of the wilderness."

J.E.H. MacDonald, a founding member of the Group of Seven artists, was inspired by his excursions into Algoma territory; pictured here are two of his best-known paintings, "Algoma Waterfall" (1920, above) and "Autumn, Algoma" (1918, top right).

Agawa Canyon is a favourite attraction on today's Algoma Central tourist railway (right).

Because of its gnarled route the Algoma Central moved slowly—the average speed of the ride from the Sault to Hearst was 19 miles (30.5 km) per hour—so there was ample opportunity to observe river and forest. Just 19 miles (30.5 km) out of the terminal, the Bellevue Trestle—1,510 feet (460 m) long and 160 feet (49 m) high—offered an example of engineering that stretched the imagination. Having attained its lofty summit at mile 97, the line then dropped precipitously into the stunning Agawa Canyon, where one could see the shift from the luxuriant Great Lakes forest of the south to the more stunted boreal forest of the north. Cascading water, autumnal colours and blanketing snow gives every season its distinctive character along the Algoma Central.

Few ever forgot what they saw on the Algoma Central. In 1918, a group of southern Ontario artists began an annual ritual on the railway. They rented a boxcar, fitted it out with bunks and a stove, hoisted their canoes aboard and headed north. The railway obligingly left them on a siding—the Agawa Canyon became a favourite spot—from where they painted the rugged landscape of the Shield. Eager to jettison foreign notions of how art should portray Canada, they embraced the rugged Algoma District as the embodiment of what it meant to be Canadian. Today, we remember these artists—Arthur Lismer, A.Y. Jackson, J.E.H. MacDonald, Lawren Harris, and others—as The Group of Seven. Their boxcar canvases have indelibly etched themselves onto the Canadian psyche. It is as if the Algoma Central has served as a route from which Canadians might gaze on the essence of their land.

A year later, in 1919, the Prince of Wales, later King Edward VIII, toured the Dominion, and the Algoma Central provided special locomotives to pull the Royal Train up the steep gradients north of the Sault. When the train reached the curving high trestle over the Montréal River Falls, the Prince was so smitten by the view that he yanked the train's emergency stop cord and brought the train to a jolting halt. While the Prince drank in the splendours of nature and shot some clay pigeons, railway officials fretted about the imminent arrival of the unalerted journalists' train coming up the line and worried about a collision.

In the 1950s, the railway began to systematically capitalize on its natural endowment with a dedicated winter Snow Train and a summer Canyon Tour supplementing the regular passenger run to Hearst. The line has a unique monopoly: in a land unpenetrated by highways, it offers the sole path to observe the area's natural wonders. Today, riding the Algoma Central into the Agawa Canyon has become a rite of nationhood for many Canadians, like a visit to Niagara Falls. The All Curves and High Bridges Railway has finally paid a dividend.

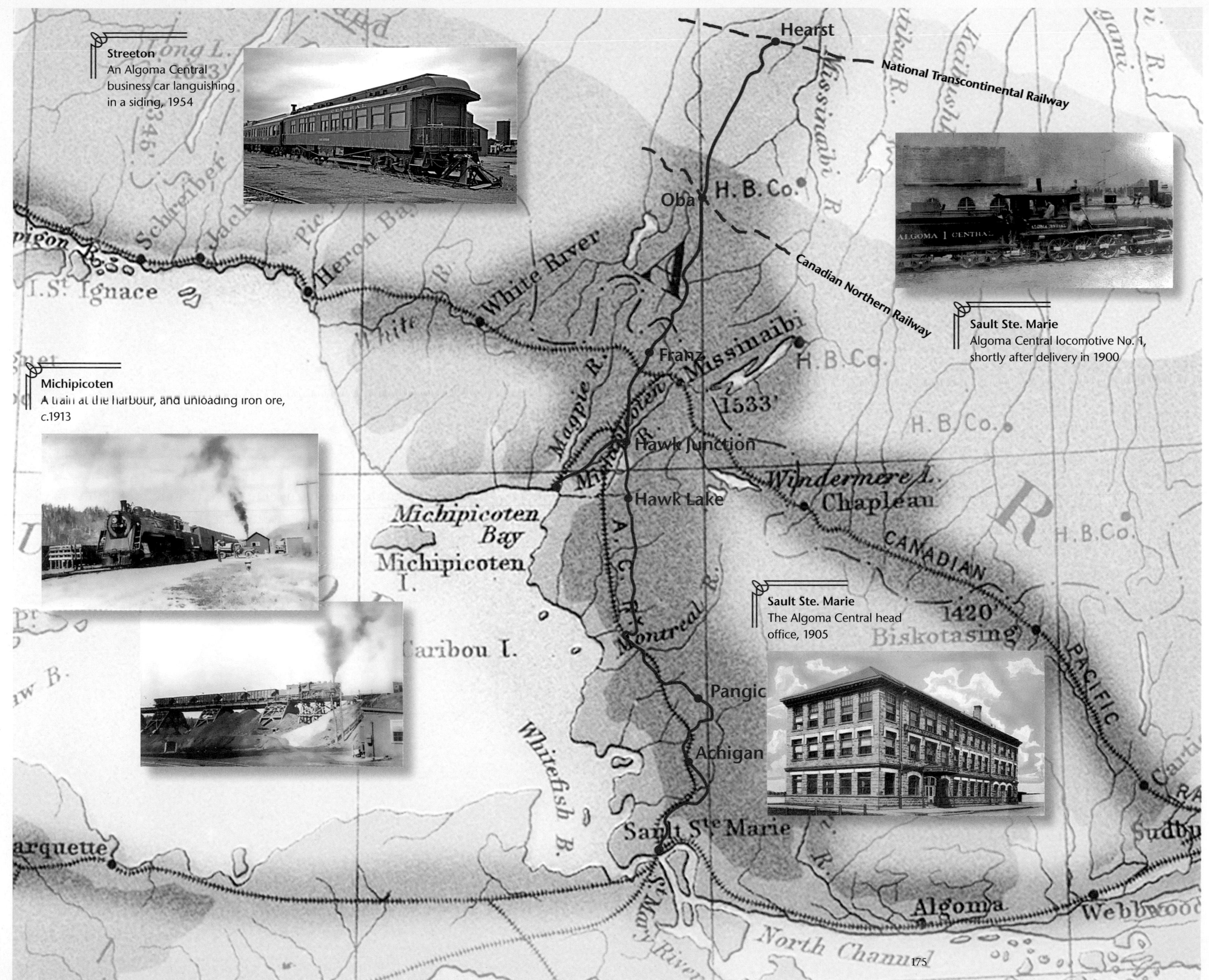

Streeton
An Algoma Central business car languishing in a siding, 1954

Sault Ste. Marie
Algoma Central locomotive No. 1, shortly after delivery in 1900

Michipicoten
A train at the harbour, and unloading iron ore, c.1913

Sault Ste. Marie
The Algoma Central head office, 1905

137
137
137

THE ONTARIO NORTHLAND RAILWAY

LIVING HISTORY

When the Ontario government created the Temiskaming and Northern Ontario Railway (TNO) in 1902 as a colonization railway, it never dreamed that the line would become the focus of the world's mining industry and the centre of Canada's richest silver strike. The provincial government was only interested in opening up the timber stands and clay belt of northeastern Ontario for logging and farming, but then, in 1903, a pair of railway timber scouts stumbled upon a fabulously rich silver find.

Soon, miners, businessmen, and con men were crowding onto the railway's wooden coaches bound for a rocky shack town known as Cobalt, at the centre of the strike. By 1910, the hardscrabble little community in northeastern Ontario had boomed to a boisterous town of more than 10,000 as 250 mines clanged into the ancient rocks. The station here was one of Ontario's finest.

By 1909, an extension had been completed between the Canadian Pacific Railway at North Bay and the National

Temiskaming station (left).

Cobalt station (above).

1913 Canadian Northern 2–8–0 locomotive 2164, from a 1950s postcard (opposite).

Ontario Northland Offices, North Bay, 1950 (left).

The Hon. E.C. Drury, George S. Henry and Mr. Latchford at the laying of the last spike of the railway to Moosonee, 1932 (below).

Transcontinental Railway at Cochrane. Shortly afterwards, the railway played a key role in evacuating hundreds of residents in Cochrane and Matheson from the ravages of fierce forest fires which destroyed entire communities and claimed hundreds of lives in 1911 and again in 1916.

One of the highlights of the route was situated where the tracks skirted the picturesque waters of Lake Temaskaming. There the company built a stunning stone station where tourists boarded steamers for the resorts along the lake.

Parlour area and furnishings, Temiskaming and Northern Ontario Railway parlour-café car, 1911 (above), and the same car from the outside (right).

In 1932 the TNO opened a further extension to Arctic tidewater at Moosonee, hoping for an ocean terminus. Although the shifting sand bars at the mouth of the Moose River dashed those hopes, the community became the hub for the scattered Cree communities on the remote James Bay coast.

In 1946, the TNO renamed itself the Ontario Northland Railway. Although the railway's glory days have faded, they have not disappeared entirely. The station at Temagami has been restored to its former grandeur while the near ghost town of Cobalt has been named "Ontario's Most Historic Town," complete with its fine brick station.

The line's Polar Bear Express still provides a vital lifeline for Moosonee while bringing summer tourists to this authentic frontier town. And six days a week, the legendary Northlander passenger train rolls into the North Bay station from Toronto to follow its century-old run northward to Cochrane on the historic tracks of the Ontario Northland Railway.

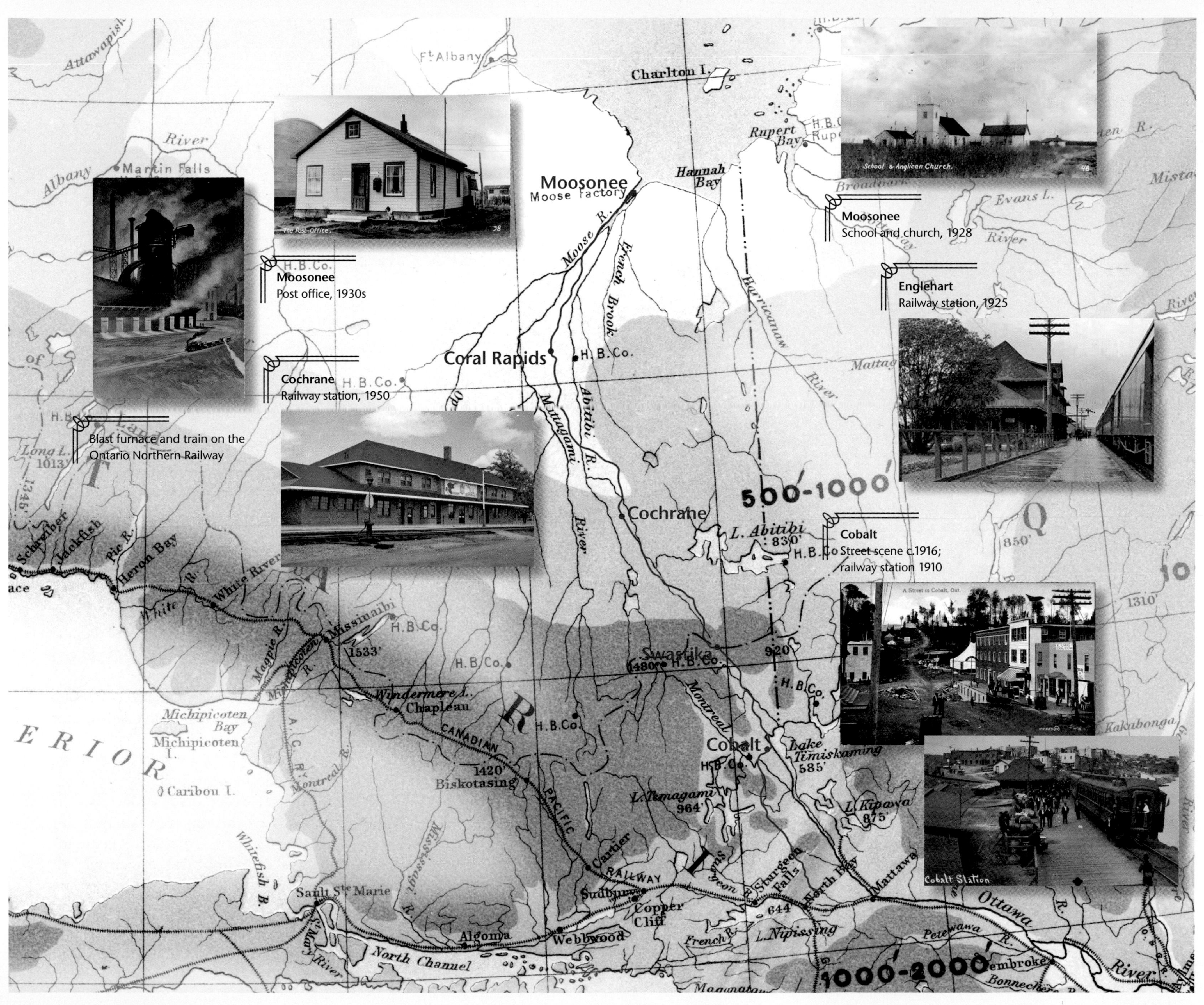

Moosonee
Post office, 1930s

Moosonee
School and church, 1928

Englehart
Railway station, 1925

Cochrane
Railway station, 1950

Blast furnace and train on the Ontario Northern Railway

Cobalt
Street scene c.1916; railway station 1910

CANADIAN STEAM LOGOMOTIVES

Slinging a 100-ton 2–6–0 locomotive at the Transcona Shops of the Grand Trunk Pacific Railway in Winnipeg, 1910.

Pioneering British engineers invented fundamental railway and locomotive technology. Shortly after the railway was established as a form of common carrier transport in England, American engineers and entrepreneurs travelled to Britain to transfer railway technology, including the reciprocating steam locomotive, to North America. While formative American railway technology was largely derived from British practices, American innovation quickly produced a divergent approach toward railway building and locomotive construction. Greater distances, less developed and less populated land, as well as less available capital, led engineers to adopt a flexible track structure in America, instead of the heavily and rigidly constructed track used in Britain. As a result locomotives with greater flexibility and requiring better suspension were developed.

Canadian railway development trailed both Britain and America by a decade. Canada, as a North American British colony, initially blended British and American locomotive practice. But since Canadian operations had more in common with those in the United States, however, by the mid nineteenth century Canadian locomotives largely emulated American design, although Canadian railways were more conservative in regard to overall design and styling. Locomotives were neater and tidier than on many railroads south of the border as Canadian locomotive design never reached the extremes found in the United States.

While Canadian lines were less inclined toward experimental designs and focused on the most common established types, the Canadian Pacific Railway in particular was noted for its progressive refinement of locomotive design and innovation in the application of modern appliances such as superheating to improve efficiency and performance.

THE EARLY YEARS

Canada's first locomotive produced great excitement when it arrived in Montréal in 1837. This imported British machine, named *Dorchester*, was built in 1836 by Robert Stephenson & Company for the Champlain and St. Lawrence Railway. This line was just 14.5 miles (23 km) long, running between St. John, Québec, and the Lachine Rapids (just a few miles from Montréal on the St. Lawrence River), and initially operated with horse-drawn trains. *Dorchester* was a primitive-looking machine using a twin pair of 40-inch drive wheels. Like its British contemporaries, it was not equipped with the trappings that typified North American locomotives of the Golden Era, having neither a bell nor a whistle, and not even a protective cab for the crew.

The second locomotive in Canada was rather different in appearance, however. *Samson* was built in 1838 by noted British locomotive manufacturer Timothy Hackworth. Designed for freight work in Nova Scotia, it featured three pairs of coupled wheels in the arrangement later known as an 0–6–0. (The Whyte classification system uses numerals by position separated by dashes to indicate the number of leading wheels, driving wheels, and trailing wheels, so an 0–6–0 has no leading wheels, six coupled drivers, and no trailing wheels. The common 4–4–0 has four leading wheels and four drivers, but no trailing wheels.) *Samson*'s boiler was protected by long lateral strips of wooden lagging and used vertically oriented cylinders.

GRAND TRUNK'S BROAD GAUGE LOGOMOTIVES

The most significant early railway in Canada was the Grand Trunk, established in 1853 and intended as a main line to compete for through traffic. The Grand Trunk had the misfortune of adopting the broad (or "Portland") gauge track that was the standard of its component company St. Lawrence and Atlantic—a line constructed to connect Portland, Maine, and Montréal. While the standard track gauge in Britain and on many railways in the United States was 4′ 8½″ (1.435 m) measured inside between rail heads, builders of the St. Lawrence and Atlantic came to the misguided conclusion that a broad gauge line of 5′ 6″ (1.676 m) had economic advantages. The theory was that a broader gauge would allow for larger locomotive boiler and firebox configurations and thus more powerful engines, while giving freight cars and passenger cars much greater carrying capacity without dramatically increasing their tare weight. The St. Lawrence and Atlantic's assumption was that all freight would require trans-loading at Montréal, therefore there was little advantage in allowing for easy interchange of freight cars. Here the builder's logic proved to be terminally flawed, however; the perceived advantages of broad gauge proved illusory while easy interchange of cars became standard. The poor decision to adopt a broad gauge was by no means unique to the St. Lawrence and Atlantic, however.

The Grand Trunk Railway also operated with the 5′ 6″ gauge for the better part of two decades, which resulted in some relatively unusual locomotives. Among these were the so-called Birkenheads of the 1850s—an order for fifty locomotives from British builder Peto, Brassey, Betts and Jackson who assembled them at their appropriately named Canada Works in Birkenhead, England. Their essential design was patterned after that used on the London and North Western, which employed the use of outside-inclined cylinders. The Birkenheads were largely 2–4–0s, but Sinclair wrote that some were designed as passenger locomotives with a single set of very large driving wheels—6 feet (2 m) in diameter. Most were ultimately rebuilt with leading four-wheel trucks to make them better suited to North American track.

In America, the 4–4–0 wheel arrangement successfully combined a powerful engine with a three-point suspension made possible by Joseph Harrison's equalization lever (first applied in 1837), and became the dominant universal American type in the nineteenth century. In 1853, James Good built a 4–4–0 in Canada named *Toronto*, which featured inclined cylinders, a spherical sand dome, a balloon stack, and a flared wooden "cow-catcher" pilot much in the spirit of the 4–4–0s built south of the border. In 1859, Grand Trunk's locomotive superintendent, F. H. Trevithick, designed and constructed a 4–4–0 named *Trevithick*, patterned largely along the lines of those built in the United States. It was the first locomotive Grand Trunk built in its own shops. Incidentally, F. H. was the nephew of locomotive pioneer Richard Trevithick of Cornwall, England who in 1804 had demonstrated the first practical steam locomotive.

By the 1860s, the 4–4–0 had become the most common new type of locomotive used in Canada. The Grand Trunk went on to buy numerous 4–4–0s from commercial builders, many of which were constructed in the United States by established locomotive manufacturers including Baldwin and Schenectady. Others were imported from the British Isles, such as the twenty-five so-called "Champagne Cup" engines built by Neilson & Company in Scotland during 1868, famous for the unusual shape of their smoke stacks.

LOCOMOTIVES IN THE GOLDEN AGE

In 1873, the Grand Trunk made the difficult yet necessary conversion from broad to standard gauge that required the re-gauging of all its tracks, as well as the expensive job of re-gauging or replacing all of its locomotives and rolling stock. This was accomplished in phases during 1873 and 1874. The railway also placed substantial orders for new locomotives, many from the United States, in addition to locomotives built or rebuilt for standard gauge operation by the Canadian Locomotive and Engine Company in London, Ontario. At this time, the Grand Trunk introduced the 2–6–0 Mogul type to its operations, a locomotive that had proven increasingly popular as a heavy freight locomotive in the United States.

Another type of locomotive that became popular in Canada was the 4–6–0 "Ten-Wheeler." This arrangement combined the benefits of a four-wheel leading truck and excellent suspension while offering greater pulling power and the ability for fast running. In the early twentieth century, the 4–6–0 arrangement would become one of Canada's most common locomotive types, although these later mass-produced 4–6–0s were significantly heavier machines than the earlier engines. The size of locomotives grew rapidly during the late nineteenth century, so a big engine of 1880 seemed relatively small by 1905. Also, while the earliest 4–6–0s were custom-built as specialized heavy main line engines—either with tall driving wheels for express passenger service or with low drivers for heavy main line freight—as the railroad evolved, later 4–6–0s were built for general service and routinely hauled both freight and passenger trains on main lines and branches. In later years, 4–6–0s largely worked branches and secondary services, with some engines surviving in branch service until the end of steam.

CANADIAN PACIFIC

Despite its enormous territory reaching from coast to coast, the CPR adopted a fairly standard fleet of locomotives with relatively few unusual designs in its early years. However, some of its earliest engines were anomalies as the railroad required engines for construction of the line. These were acquired from its contractors and consisted of a collection of secondhand locomotives built for US lines. CPR No. 1, named *Yale*, was a 2–6–0 built in 1869 by the Union Iron Works in San Francisco for Nevada's Virginia and Truckee (V&T). It was among locomotives bought by contractor Andrew Onderdonk and used for construction in British Columbia. He also acquired several other V&T 2–6–0s, including V&T No. 8 which became CPR No. 3 *New Westminster*; *Carson*, which became CPR's No. 4 *Savona*; and another which became CPR's *Lytton*.

The Canadian Pacific Railway focused new purchases on 4–4–0s as versatile machines that could work freight and passenger assignments across the system. Many locomotives were manufactured commercially, but in 1883 the CPR began to build engines itself at its Delorimier Avenue

Shops in Montréal. First was no. 285, a well-proportioned standard 4–4–0, featuring a classic "diamond" stack (containing screens to filter sparks that might escape the firebox), a "cow-catcher" style pilot, a large boxy headlight, and adorned with polished brass fittings. Yet the reign of the 4–4–0s as CPR's preferred standard type was short lived. By 1888, traffic demands resulted in the railroad requiring larger types. Briefly the CPR embraced the 2–6–0, but by 1889 it preferred 4–6–0s for most new locomotives. Over the next two-and-a-half decades the CPR bought or built nearly one thousand 4–6–0s, and the type would remain the most common power on the railroad well into the twentieth century.

BIGGER LOCOMOTIVES

Growth of the Canadian railway industry and infrastructure mirrored that in the United States, and as traffic grew, railway companies sought ways to handle their business with greater efficiency and speed. Heavier and faster trains were made possible by key technological innovations such as the introduction of the Westinghouse air brake and Janey knuckle couplers in the late nineteenth century, which promoted greater safety while enabling the operation of much heavier freight trains and much faster passenger trains. Although it took decades before these innovations were fully implemented, the need to run heavier and faster trains spurred significant growth in the size and power of locomotives in both the United States and Canada. This was achieved through the introduction of new technology, improved wheel arrangements, and a substantial increase in the size and weight of main line locomotives. Even more powerful engines were necessary in the twentieth century as railroads first embraced steel-framed rolling stock, and later all-steel rolling stock, which significantly increased the tare weight of trains.

Bigger locomotive types could not be universally adopted, however, as they first required substantial upgrades to bridges and other infrastructure. As a result, the newest and heaviest motive power was normally assigned to main line trains, while some branch lines remained unmodified and so continued to employ antique locomotives and cars well into the twentieth century. In the late nineteenth century, the 2–8–0 had become a standard for heavy freight service as the CPR had bought a fleet of 2–8–0s in the 1880s for service on its steepest grades in the Canadian Rockies, while the Grand Trunk also bought a substantial fleet of them.

Among the significant innovations that allowed for a substantial increase in locomotive output was the introduction of the radial trailing truck in the 1890s. In the United States this resulted in the wide-scale development of 4–4–2 Atlantic types and 2–6–2 Prairie types. Neither of these locomotives were particularly popular in Canada (although the CPR operated a few Atlantics in express passenger service), but the early-twentieth-century development of the 4–6–2 Pacific as a main line passenger locomotive and the 2–8–2 Mikado as a main line freight engine (the 2–8–2 was first built for North American service as a narrow gauge engine) resulted in widespread adoption by Canadian railroads. For passenger trains, the Pacific offered excellent stability and tracking characteristics, with ample boiler capacity allowing for movement of long heavy passenger trains at relatively high speeds. The Canadian Pacific Railway bought its first Pacific in 1906, and continued to order them as late as 1948.

As traffic continued to grow, heavier trains required ever bigger engines and a number of new types entered service after World War I. Coincident with rapid traffic growth was the consolidation of several Canadian railways under government ownership between 1918 and 1923 that ultimately resulted in the creation of the Canadian National Railways. In the final decades of steam locomotive operation, Canada's two primary railways (CNR and CPR) adopted distinctly different strategies toward locomotive development and purchase.

The CPR relied largely upon heavy 2–8–2s and 4–6–2s, respectively, for main line freight and passenger services, while assigning 4–6–0s and other older types to branch lines. For heavy freight service it built some 2–10–0s and 2–10–2s. (The CPR's first 2–10–0s were rebuilt from articulated Mallet compounds—the only examples of their type in Canada.) Noteworthy for their size were the CPR's 2–10–4 Selkirks which were built from about 1929 for freight service in the mountains. About the same time, CPR adopted the 4–6–4 Hudson for its heavy long-distance trains. The Hudson was essentially an expansion of the 4–6–2 with even greater boiler capacity made possible by a four-wheel trailing truck. Ultimately the CPR proved one of the greatest proponents of the Hudson for long-distance passenger services and bought more than sixty of the type. These outstanding locomotives were noted both for exceptional performance and their good looks, and the CPR routinely operated its 4–6–4s on 800-mile-long runs. Best known were its semi-streamlined Royal Hudsons—so named because in 1939 two of this class hauled the special trains that brought King George VI and Queen Elizabeth across Canada—which were specially decorated with an embossed crown. Unusual among North American locomotives were the CPR's 4–4–4 Jubilees built in the mid-1930s for light and relatively fast work on branch passenger trains.

CPR 4–6–2 express locomotive No. 2300, *Railway Magazine*, October 1919.

By contrast, the Canadian National's locomotive philosophy favoured eight-coupled types. Where its predecessors had embraced the 2–8–0 and later the 2–8–2 for general freight work, and 4–6–0s and later 4–6–2s for passenger work, in the early 1920s the CNR ordered 4–8–2s for general main line service. Significantly the CNR was among the first railways in the world to adopt the 4–8–4 type which was known as the Northern in the USA, while the CNR patriotically referred to its 4–8–4's as Confederations in honour of the federal union of the Dominion of Canada. The CNR, along with its US subsidiary the Grand Trunk Western, ultimately operated the largest fleet of 4–8–4s in North America, consisting of more than two hundred locomotives. Like the 4–8–2, the CNR's 4–8–4 design was also a universal main line locomotive for both freight and passenger service. While the CNR's 4–8–4s were big locomotives, they had comparatively light axle-weight compared to similar engines on US lines, but as a result they were capable of service on many secondary lines. For lighter passenger trains, the CNR maintained its sizeable fleet of inherited 4–6–2 Pacifics, yet only bought five 4–6–4 Hudsons which it assigned to Montréal–Toronto express trains.

At the end of World War II, and before Canadian railways embarked on large-scale dieselization, there were an estimated 4,100 steam locomotives serving Canada's two principal railroads. Of these, most were products of two domestic commercial locomotive manufacturers: the Canadian Locomotive Company founded in the 1850s, and the Montréal Locomotive Works established in the first decade of the twentieth century which functioned as the Canadian subsidiary of the American Locomotive Company (Alco).

LOCOMOTIVES BIBLIOGRAPHY

Abdill, George B. *Pacific Slope Railroads.* Seattle: Superior Publishing Co., 1959.

Alexander, Edwin P. *American Locomotives.* New York: Norton, 1950.

Bruce, Alfred W. *The Steam Locomotive in America.* New York: Bonanza Books, 1952.

Chappell, Gordon. *Steam Over Scranton: The Locomotives of Steamtown.* United States Department of the Interior National Park Service, 1991.

Dorsey, Edward Bates. *English and American Railroads Compared.* New York: John Wiley & Sons, 1887.

Drury, George H. *Guide to North American Steam Locomotives.* Waukesha: Kalmbach Publishing, 1993.

Dubin, Arthur D. *Some Classic Trains.* Milwaukee: Kalmbach Publishing, 1964.

— *More Classic Trains.* Milwaukee: Kalmbach Publishing, 1974.

Forney, M.N. *Catechism of the Locomotive.* New York: Railroad Gazette, 1876.

Hilton, George W. *American Narrow Gauge Railroads.* Stanford: Stanford University Press, 1990.

Holland, Rupert Sargent. *Historic Railroads.* Philadelphia: MacRae Smith Company, 1927.

Lamb, W. Kaye. *History of the Canadian Pacific Railway.* New York: Macmillan, 1977.

Middleton, William D. with George M. Smerk, and Roberta L. Diehl. *Encyclopedia of North American Railroads.* Bloomington: Indiana University Press, 2007.

Morgan, David P. *Steam's Finest Hour.* Milwaukee: Kalmbach Publishing, 1959.

— *Canadian Steam!* Milwaukee: Kalmbach Publishing, 1961.

Ransome-Wallis, P. *World Railway Locomotives.* New York: Hawthorn Books, 1959.

Reagan, H.C., Jr. *Locomotive Mechanism and Engineering.* New York: John Wiley & Sons, 1894.

Sinclair, Angus. *Development of the Locomotive Engine.* New York: Angus Sinclair, 1907.

Solomon, Brian. *The American Steam Locomotive.* Osceola: Motorbooks International, 1998.

— *Super Steam Locomotives.* Osceola: Motorbooks International, 2000.

— *Locomotive.* Osceola: Motorbooks International, 2001.

— *Alco Locomotives.* Minneapolis: Voyageur Press Inc., 2009.

Swengel, Frank M. *The American Steam Locomotive: Volume 1, Evolution.* Davenport: MidWest Rail Publications, 1967.

White, John H., Jr. *A History of the American Locomotive.* Toronto: University of Toronto Press, 1968.

PERIODICALS

Locomotive and Railway Preservation. Waukesha, Wisconsin [no longer published].

RailNews. Waukesha, Wisconsin [no longer published].

Railroad History, formerly *Railway and Locomotive Historical Society Bulletin.* Boston, Mass.

Railway and Locomotive Engineering [no longer published].

Railway Mechanical Engineer 1925–1952.

Railway Age, Chicago and New York.

Railway Gazette, 1870–1908, New York.

RAILWAY EQUIPMENT AND ROLLING STOCK

CANADIAN ROLLING STOCK

Locomotives tend to draw the greatest attention from railway observers, but it is passenger cars that are most familiar to travellers. Confusing to the casual observer is the common term "train," which in railroading has specific meanings, but is too often used inappropriately to describe any piece or group of rolling stock. Together a locomotive and cars may be assigned to a "service," and it is this service we know as a "train." However, unless specified by schedule or railroad operating order, individually locomotives and cars are merely railway "hardware" and do not constitute a train as such. This is no different than modern airline travel where a specific aircraft may become "Flight AC102" when so assigned by the Air Canada schedule. This important distinction in railway parlance is often lost on both its travellers and historians, who fail to separate the individual equipment from the service it is used to provide. Furthermore, while specific cars might be designed, constructed, and decorated for a specific train service, in actual practice this equipment may be used for a variety of different runs. A car built for a premier service may be used elsewhere at a moment's notice, cascaded permanently to a lesser service, or sold to another railroad—even one beyond the nation's borders.

CANADIAN PASSENGER CARS

From the earliest days, Canadian passenger cars tended to emulate designs developed in the United States. The reasons for this are easy to understand. As Canadian long-distance passenger services developed in the 1850s, many trains crossed the border to reach their destinations in the United States. That being the case, passenger cars needed to be compatible with those used by American railroads. Furthermore, as services matured it became common to find trains running between cities in Canada and the United States operating with equipment built for service on both sides of the border. The Pullman Company, which built and operated sleeping cars for North American railways, had close ties with several Canadian lines, so many passenger cars built for Canadian railways were designed and constructed by that company as well as by other commercial American car builders. In general Canadian passenger cars shared common technology with their American counterparts, although in some instances distinctive car types were also developed for Canadian lines.

DESIGN EVOLUTION

Early North American passenger cars were crude, lacking most of the amenities associated with later railway travel, although they set in motion more than a hundred years of technical improvements. Unlike European and British cars that evolved from traditional stage coach practice and tended to favor compartmental designs, American coaches were built on hardwood frames riding on a pair of trucks with a continuous central corridor arrangement, seats on either side, and doors at the ends of cars. Early designs were box-like with flat roofs, panelled wooden exteriors, simple windows along the sides, minimal ornamentation, and had seats for approximately 20–24 passengers. By the early 1860s, the typical car had grown to 50–60 feet (15–18 m) in length, was equipped with a wood stove for heating, a simple toilet at one end, and basic lighting in the form of candles or oil lamps. Designs evolved rapidly in the later 1860s with the introduction of a clerestory roof raised over the centre aisle and small windows capable of being opened, which not only improved ventilation but also brightened the interior.

Car design continued to mature rapidly in the 1870s when larger, heavier, and more elaborate cars became the norm. Also, specialized designs such as sleeping and parlour cars augmented the basic passenger coach of earlier years. Most car exteriors were constructed from hardwood coated with layers of clear varnish for protection from the elements and, because of this treatment, passenger trains became known collectively to railroaders as the "Varnish." The finest cars of this era would often also be elegantly decorated using gold leaf or ornate embellishments. Among the notable technological improvements were the introduction of improved lighting and steam heating systems, and Janey knuckle couplers that eased the joining of cars, reduced the slack action between them, and minimized the possibility of train separation. Most importantly, however, was the adoption of the new Westinghouse air brakes which greatly advanced the ability to reliably and smoothly stop trains, thus vastly improving safety while allowing for faster and more accident-free operations.

Because wooden-bodied passenger cars tended to splinter and burn when wrecked, iron and steel framing was introduced in the 1890s, and after 1912 steel-bodied cars became standard, although for a few years "composite" designs with wooden sides and steel frames continued to be built for Canadian lines. The main advantages of composite construction were its superior appearance and better insulation—an important consideration in Canada where winter temperatures are notoriously cold.

The clerestory roof remained standard on most cars through the 1940s when new air-conditioned, lightweight and streamlined designs were adopted.

Further innovation came in the 1960s, when the Canadian National adopted the United Aircraft tilting TurboTrains for select corridor services, and then in the 1980s, when national passenger operator VIA Rail bought a fleet of LRC—"light, rapid, comfortable"—lightweight, tilting passenger cars, many of which survive to the present day. After 2000, imported cars from Britain began to replace 1950s-era streamlined cars on some services.

GRAND TRUNK AND GNR PREDECESSORS

In his book, *More Classic Trains*, Arthur Dubin notes that in 1867 the Great Western Railway's Hamilton, Ontario shops built the first "Hotel" car for George Pullman. This significant car, named *Western World*, helped establish a long-lasting relationship between the Great Western, and later the Grand Trunk (after melding of the two lines in 1882), regarding the operation of Pullman sleepers on Canadian lines. Great Western's early sleeping cars were noteworthy for their use of eight-wheel trucks using cast wheels—an anomaly in North American practice where four- and six-wheel trucks were standard. Pullman emerged as not only the foremost North American sleeping car operator, but also one of the largest car builders in North America. This leads to an important distinction: not all cars Pullman built were sleepers, for the company also built chair cars as well, so while references to "Pullman cars" implies sleeping cars and services, a car or trainset built by the Pullman Company (later Pullman-Standard) is not necessarily a sleeper.

The relationship between Pullman and Grand Trunk (which provided services to American cities as well as to those in Canada) continued well into the twentieth century, and was carried on by Grand Trunk successor Canadian National Railways after

CPR rotary snowplow, Revelstoke, BC, 1928.

1923. Grand Trunk's Pullmans could be found as far off-line as Boston, New York, and Philadelphia as a result of through trains operated in conjunction with other carriers. The Grand Trunk's Pullman sleepers of the nineteenth century typically were heavy, wooden-bodied cars ornately decorated in the high Victorian fashion. A common variety rode upon six-wheel trucks and featured twelve sections (where seats would be converted into berths in the evening, and passengers provided a degree of privacy only by heavy drapes), and a single large drawing room. In later years, exteriors were painted in a solemn dark green with gilded lettering and trim, and had brass fittings. As was common, the Pullman name was written above window level, sub-lettered for the Grand Trunk Route at one end, with a selection of destination cities at the other.

Sleeping cars with their fancy and elaborate decorations, high degrees of comfort, and distinctive and memorable names tended to garner the greatest amount of attention, but they were only a small portion of the Grand Trunk's fleet. Far more common was the ordinary day coach riding on four-wheel trucks with its conventional corridor-style seating. These would have made up the bulk of equipment on the railroad's passenger trains and worked main line long-distance intercity services, as well as secondary and branch line trains. Another common car, although by no means glamorous, was the "headend" car used to carry passenger baggage and express shipments. These typically rode directly behind the locomotive, which allowed for easy access by train crews during station stops while also providing a degree of protection for passengers in the event of a head-on crash or derailment. Some passenger trains might operate with just a single baggage car, while others, especially the long-distance "limiteds," would often carry several. A hybrid variety was the "combination car" where half of the car was reserved as a baggage compartment with large sliding doors on each side, with the other half equipped as a passenger coach.

For extra-fare, first-class passengers, luxurious comfort was offered by elaborately decorated Parlour cars. Typically these featured rows of plush, spacious individual seats running the length of each side of the car. These could be turned to suit the passenger's liking and in later days might be arranged to swivel on a central axis. Large plate glass windows topped with arched, stained-glass

CPR observation car interior, *Railway Magazine*, October 1903.

subsidiary windows lined the length of the cars. After 1900, parlour-car design was augmented with an open-end observation deck and rear-facing windows, and sometimes parlour cars were combined with first-class compartment sleepers. Dining cars with on-board kitchens that served up customized menus were another feature of railway journeys in the golden age of travel. Dining cars, parlour cars, and first-class sleepers typically rode upon six-wheel trucks which offered a significantly smoother ride than ordinary cars.

THE INTERCOLONIAL RAILWAY

Famous for its Montréal–Halifax luxury express trains including *The Maritime Express* and *Ocean Limited*, the Intercolonial Railway provided service using state-of-the-art passenger equipment from the late nineteenth century until its amalgamation into Canadian National Railways after World War I. Dubin notes that many of its sleepers and diners were built domestically by Canadian Car & Foundry, or in the United States by Pullman. An example of the latter was a plush-looking, outside-braced, wooden-sided sleeper named *Tantramer* built in Chicago about 1905. With its six-wheel trucks, gilded trim around its decorated, arched windows, and similar fine trim lines top and bottom along the full length of the car, it had all the airs associated with Edwardian rail travel in North America. Few who boarded such a vehicle for the trip from Montréal for an up to 24-hour ride to the Maritime Provinces would have been disappointed.

THE CANADIAN PACIFIC RAILWAY

When the Canadian Pacific Railway inaugurated transcontinental passenger service to Port Moody, British Columbia, in 1886, its trains were more than mere transportation, they were a national treasure as well. Most prominent were the CPR's first-class accommodations, which spared little expense and represented the epitome of late-Victorian travel with all the ornate excesses and opulence that characterized the period. First-class dining cars were equipped with fine china, expensive silverware, and exquisite interior decoration while the menus onboard were designed to tempt the palate of the most distinguished traveller. Unlike the Grand Trunk, which worked with Pullman, the CPR preferred to operate its own sleeping cars although some of its trains also carried Pullmans in later years. Early CPR sleepers included products of car-builder Barney & Smith of Dayton, Ohio, which were named for principal cities along the line. According to Dubin, these were relatively short compared with cars of later generations (measuring just under 59 feet/18 m long), rode upon six-wheel trucks, and featured open-end platforms. Later Barney & Smith cars for the CPR were built with heavily varnished mahogany exterior finish while their interiors were finely decorated using expensive wood, brass, and mother-of-pearl in a Japanese-inspired design that reflected the Pacific trade. This trade was encouraged by the opening of the CPR to the West Coast.

First-class passengers were afforded deluxe amenities which included marble bath tubs located at one end of the sleeping car and close to the truck centre in order to minimize vibration and shocks from movement over the line. While the first-class sleepers are the best remembered, far more passengers were carried by the line's so-called "Tourist Sleepers" which were less elaborate in décor, yet provided comfortable accommodation for the more budget-minded traveller. At the bottom of the scale were Colonist sleepers which offered only the minimum of accommodation that today might be described as "hard class." While sleeping areas were kept clean, their interiors were minimal and spartan, and neither cushions nor linen were provided by the railroad. These cars were intended to carry new arrivals in Canada to their places of settlement in the western prairies. Untold Canadian immigrants travelled across country in these cars which were often carried on the same transcontinental limiteds as first-class sleepers.

In his *History of the Canadian Pacific Railway*, author W. Kaye Lamb reports that in 1912 the railroad had 2,290 cars for passenger services, including baggage cars and mail cars, that routinely operated as part of long-distance trains. Of these, 403 were first-class sleepers, parlour cars, and dining cars, and 690 were first-class coaches. The CPR was famous for its pioneering use of observation cars that were designed to offer passengers views of the stunning scenery of the Canadian Rockies. These came in several varieties, the most basic of which was simply an open car fitted with laterally facing seats that gave passengers unobstructed vistas but no protection from soot, cinders, or weather. Dating from about 1906, the railway produced a unique type of observation car which featured elevated cupolas at both ends—similar in concept to the cupola used on the common caboose in freight service—with large windows in the central section between the cupolas. By 1909, CPR had adopted the more conventional type of open-end observation lounge sleeping car, as previously described and made famous by American whistle-stop campaign tours.

For many years the CPR was the preferred mode of transcontinental travel even after other lines opened competing services to the coast. At the end of its peak in the early 1930s, the railroad was operating no fewer than five scheduled transcontinental trains daily in the summer season. From 1929, its *Mountaineer* was an exclusive, all-sleeper service operating in conjunction with CPR's American affiliate Soo Line between Chicago and Vancouver. This was patterned along the lines of similar all-sleeper services in the United States such as New York Central's *Twentieth Century Limited.*

Although the volume of passengers declined following the onset of the Great Depression, the CPR continued to improve its passenger services. In the 1930s, it introduced new steam-hauled lightweight trains on routes in eastern Canada. Then during 1954–5 it completely re-equipped its transcontinental service with the introduction of the new *Canadian* (Montréal–Toronto–Vancouver) using Budd-built stainless steel streamlined cars hauled by new General Motors diesels. Most famous were the elevated dome cars that gave passengers an excellent forward view of the train as it crossed the Canadian prairies and traversed the craggy passes of the Canadian Rockies. At the back of each train was one of the road's eighteen "Park Cars"—round-end dome observation cars decorated in art deco style, each named for one of Canada's National Parks. The *Canadian* was continued by VIA Rail after the CPR discontinued its own services. While the train still operates in 2010, since 1990 it has served the less scenic Canadian National transcontinental route, rather than the traditional CPR crossing.

ROLLING STOCK BIBLIOGRAPHY

Berton, Pierre. *The Last Spike: The Great Railway 1881–1885.* Toronto: McClelland and Stewart Limited, 1971.

Currie, A.W. *The Grand Trunk Railway of Canada.* Toronto: University of Toronto Press, 1957.

Dubin, Arthur D. *Some Classic Trains.* Milwaukee: Kalmbach Publishing, 1964.

— *More Classic Trains.* Milwaukee: Kalmbach Publishing, 1974.

Fitzsimons, Bernard. *150 Years of Canadian Railroads.* Toronto: Royce Publications, 1984.

Hilton, George W. *American Narrow Gauge Railroads.* Stanford: Stanford University Press, 1990.

Holland, Rupert Sargent. *Historic Railroads.* Philadelphia: MacRae Smith Company, 1927.

Lamb, W. Kaye. *History of the Canadian Pacific Railway.* New York: Macmillan, 1977.

Mika, Nick with Helma Mika. *Railways of Canada.* Toronto and Montreal: McGraw-Hill Ryerson Ltd, 1972.

Murray, Tom. *Canadian National Railway.* St. Paul: MBI Publishing, 2004.

Whitehouse, P.B. *Great Trains of North America.* London: Hamlyn, 1972.

PERIODICALS

Official Guide to the Railways. New York.

Railway Age. Chicago and New York.

Railway Gazette, 1870–1908. New York.

Trains. Waukesha, Wisconsin.

Vintage Rails. Waukesha, Wisconsin [no longer published].

"Probably the most perfectly-appointed train ever constructed," wrote *Railway Magazine* in November 1903 of the CPR train which carried the Duke and Duchess of York on their Royal Tour through Canada earlier that year. Shown here are the royal bedroom and dining room, and the rear observation platform.

MUSEUMS AND PLACES TO VISIT

Canada's vast landmass means that, although a sizeable railroad network still criss-crosses the country, museums and heritage centres are by necessity relatively few and far between. Indeed, perhaps the most obvious starting point for the modern traveller wishing to gain a glimpse into a bygone era of transcontinental journeys is via one of several scenic trains operated both by national operator VIA Rail and a number of private firms.

The first transcontinental railroad, the Canadian Pacific Railway, marked its completion with the famous driving of the Last Spike at Craigellachie in the heart of the Selkirk mountain range on November 7, 1885. Visitors can still take a train along the original alignment, although many cut-offs and diversionary tunnels have been built over the intervening years to ease the gradients for freight traffic. Rocky Mountaineer Vacations operates the Kicking Horse Route from Vancouver to Jasper and Banff at regular intervals from April to October each year, allowing travellers to visit the monument and a small museum alongside the railroad.

For those wishing to recreate the transcontinental journey of a century ago, national long-distance passenger operator VIA Rail runs "The Canadian," a three-times-a-week train from Toronto to Vancouver, taking four nights from end to end.

Those seeking to view the Last Spike itself, however, should head for the Canada Science and Technology Museum on the southeastern outskirts of the capital, Ottawa. The Canadian Pacific presented the spike to the museum to mark the event's centenary in 1985. (Unlike the gold or silver spikes used in similar ceremonies for many other major railroads, the CPR's Last Spike was a conventional iron one identical to those used throughout construction of the line.) The spike, which was bent while being driven into the tie at Craigellachie by Lord Strathcona, was subsequently removed, and pieces were chiseled off to make souvenirs for the wives of the CPR Board of Directors. In a sizeable rail-focused collection, the museum also has a number of examples of rolling stock from the late nineteenth and early twentieth centuries, including CPR 926, one of a class of very successful main line steam locomotives produced by the CPR's Angus Shops in Montréal in 1911.

The museum also stocks a large collection of railway engineering drawings, brochures, and manuals. Apart from standard operational publications such as timetables and rulebooks, in recent years an effort has been made to collect a small but representative number of brochures that illustrate and document the railway companies' efforts to encourage colonization in western Canada. These materials are supplemented by a substantial number of railway mechanical drawings from the Canadian Pacific Railway, the Canadian Locomotive Company and the Porter Locomotive Co. The 40,000 examples in the museum's collection provide detailed information on locomotive construction practices and standards from the 1880s into the 1940s.

The Canadian Pacific's Engine No. 374, the steam engine that pulled the first transcontinental train to arrive in Vancouver on May 23, 1887 can now be seen in a special pavilion in the city.

Toronto's historic Union Station—the eastern terminus of "The Canadian"—is worth visiting in itself. Although it is still an extremely busy transport hub at the heart of the GO Transit commuter rail network, the station retains its status as one of the country's most significant historic buildings. The Toronto Railway Historical Association and the City of Toronto have worked together to include Union Station as part of the Railway Heritage Centre project focused on the nearby John Street Roundhouse.

After eight years of campaigning, planning, and restoration, the Roundhouse re-opened as a fully-fledged railroad museum in May 2010. The development includes restoration of the workshop's turntable to operational condition, extra track to allow the display of historic railway equipment, and completely restored railway buildings such as a watchman's shanty and a tool shed.

While Toronto's attractions are still growing, Canada's largest railroad museum remains ExpoRail, located in Delson near Québec. Regarded as the national railway museum, ExpoRail includes the Angus pavilion—a 90,000-square-foot exhibition space that is home to a rotating roster highlighting forty-four of the museum's one hundred and sixty items of rolling stock, the largest single collection nationwide. A must-see among them is CNR 4100, a Santa Fe class 2–10–2 built by the Canadian Locomotive Company for the Canadian National Railway in 1924, and thought to be the most powerful steam locomotive in the British Empire at the time of delivery. Another noteworthy exhibit is *The Saskatchewan*, the personal saloon car of Sir William Cornelius Van Horne, general manager of the Canadian Pacific from 1883 and later its president, and a man regarded as one of the founding fathers of the transcontinental railway. In addition, ExpoRail holds a stock of around 10,000 items of memorabilia to contextualize the story of Canadian railroad development.

Moving to the other side of the Rockies, the West Coast Railway Association has amassed the largest collection of historic rolling stock in the country outside Québec. Located at Squamish, British Columbia, the organization has established its headquarters in a 12-acre park, permitting both indoor and outdoor exhibits. The association's collection consists of sixty-five pieces of heritage railway rolling stock plus a significant collection of railway-related artifacts. The oldest pieces are the business car *British Columbia* dating from 1890, and a Canadian Pacific Colonist sleeping car from 1905. The extensive WCRA archives are dedicated to preserving material that helps tell the story of railroading in British Columbia. The collection includes over 3,000 artifacts that can be accessed for displays, live demonstrations or documentary film production. A library also houses more than 600 books and 2,500 magazines.

A number of smaller rail-based attractions can be found across the country in towns and cities that owe their existence to the engineers and labourers who forged their way across the prairies and mountains in the second half of the nineteenth century, binding the new Canadian nation together as they went.

The Saskatchewan Railway Museum in Saskatoon is one such example. Although most of its modest collection of rolling stock dates from the second half of the twentieth century, the site includes a number of buildings that are significantly older. The museum's gift shop is housed in a six-person bunkhouse built by the Canadian Northern Railway in about 1919 that was originally in use in Maymont, Saskatchewan. There is also a portable freight and passenger shelter built at Debden in 1918. These buildings were used either as a permanent station in a very small village or as a temporary station in a larger town. They are small enough to fit on a standard flat car and can be easily moved from town to town. The main exhibition building and curators' office is a converted engineman's bunkhouse, equipped with ten bedrooms, kitchen, lounge, and washrooms, built by Canadian National for its Nantana yards south of Saskatoon.

The Northern Ontario Railroad Museum and Heritage Centre at Capreol is another museum firmly off the beaten track, the focal point of which is 6077, a Mountain-class steam locomotive dating from the early 1940s which was given the nickname *Bullet-Nosed Betty*. Canadian National caboose or brake van No. 77562 is also on show. Built of wood in 1899, it proudly carries the slogan "Serves All Canada." Also on display is a Canadian National Rules Instruction Car, built by Pullman Standard in 1912 for transcontinental passenger services and named *Stradacona*.

Lastly, the Alberta Railway Museum in Edmonton houses a collection of railway equipment and buildings with an emphasis on cars and locomotives from the Canadian National Railways, Northern Alberta Railways and industrial and short line railways from the province. Rides on heritage rail vehicles are also available on certain weekends during the summer.

ONLINE RESOURCES

ExpoRail – the Canadian National Railroad Museum
www.exporail.org

West Coast Railway Association
www.wcra.org

Canada Science & Technology Museum
www.sciencetech.technomuses.ca/english

Saskatchewan Railroad Museum
www.saskrailmuseum.org

Nova Scotia Museum of Industry
museum.gov.ns.ca/moi

Alberta Railway Museum
www.railwaymuseum.ab.ca

Northern Ontario Railroad Museum and Heritage Centre
www.northernontariorailroadmuseum.ca

The Rocky Mountaineer on Seat 61.com
www.seat61.com/RockyMountaineer.htm

Last Spike Museum, Craigellachie
www.railwaymuseum.com/last_spike.htm

Toronto Railway Heritage Centre
www.trha.ca/visionandmission.html

Locomotive production and technical data
www.steamlocomotive.com/santafe

An exhibit at ExpoRail, Delson, Québec.

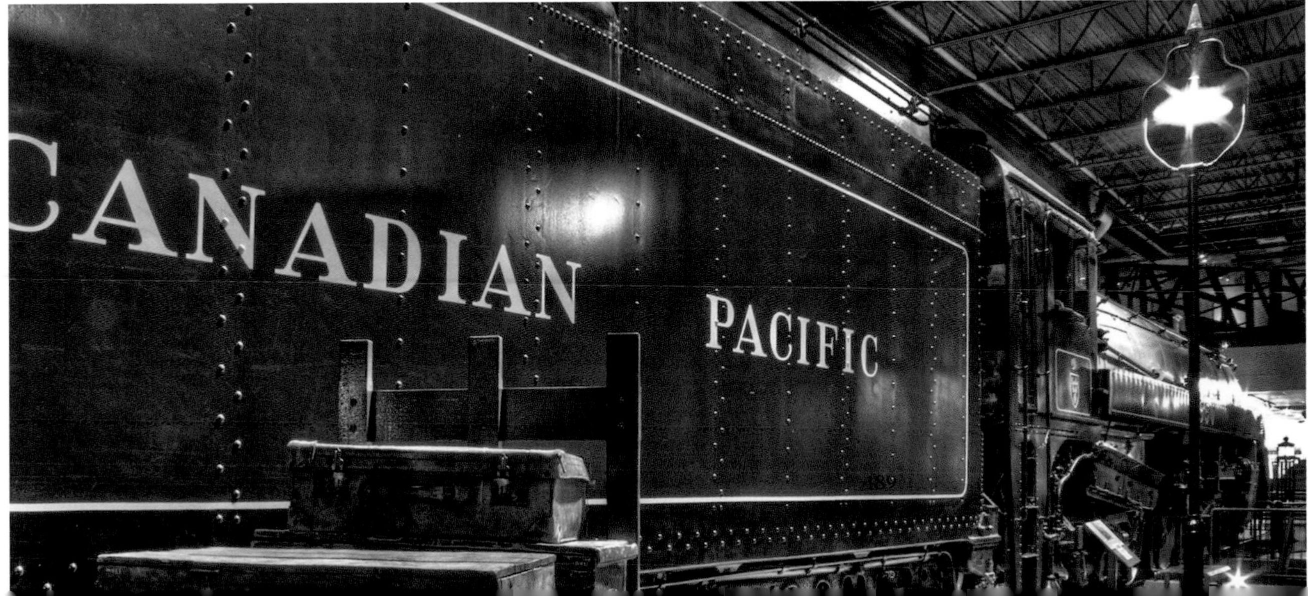

BIBLIOGRAPHY

Anderson, Allan and Betty Tomlinson. *Greetings from Canada: An Album of Unique Canadian Postcards from the Edwardian Era.* Toronto: Macmillan, 1978.

Andreae, Christopher. *Lines of Country; An Atlas of Railway and Waterway History in Canada.* Stoddart: Boston Mills Press, 1997.

— "Railways," in Ball, Norman R., ed. *Building Canada: A History of Public Works.* Toronto: University of Toronto Press, 1986.

Appleton, D. *Appleton's General Guide to the United States and Canada. Illustrated with Railway Maps, Plans of Cities, and Table of Railway and Steamboat Fares.* Part I: New England and Middle States and Canada. New York: D. Appleton and Company, 1898.

Artibise, Alan. *Winnipeg: An Illustrated History.* Toronto: James Lorimer & Company/National Museum of Man, 1977.

Bealby, J.T. *Canada.* London, Canada: The Mallagh Bookshop, 1909.

Berton, Pierre. *The National Dream: The Great Railway 1871–1881.* Toronto: McClelland and Stewart Limited, 1970.

— *The Last Spike: The Great Railway 1881–1885.* Toronto: McClelland and Stewart Limited, 1971.

— *The Great Railway Illustrated.* Toronto: McClelland and Stewart Limited, 1972.

Boulanger, L. *Autour du Monde: Aquarelles Souvenirs de Voyage*, Paris: *c.*1890.

Brennan, J. William. *Regina: An Illustrated History.* Toronto: James Lorimer & Company/Canadian Museum of Civilization, 1989.

Brown, Craig, ed. *The Illustrated History of Canada.* Toronto: Key Porter Books, 2002.

Brown, Ron. *The Train Doesn't Stop Here Anymore.* Toronto: The Dundurn Group, 2008.

Canadian Railway and Marine World, 1910–19, including February 1912, 69–70; October 1918, 430–2; and January 1919, 1–5.

Choka, Marc H. and David L. Jones. *Canadian Pacific Posters 1883–1963.* Ottawa: Meridian Press, 1995.

Clegg, Anthony. *The Mount Royal Tunnel.* Montréal: Trains and Trolley Book Club, 1963.

Collard, Andrew. "The Mount Royal Tunnel," *The Gazette* (Montréal), 16 January 1971.

Cook, Clayton D. *Tales of the Rails, Volume IV, The Newfoundland Railway 1881–1988.* St. John's, Newfoundland: Flanker Press, 2005.

Cowan, R.G. "A History of the Intercolonial and Prince Edward Island Railways of Canada." M.A. thesis, University of Toronto, 1918.

Creighton, Donald. *A History of Canada: Dominion of the North.* Boston: Houghton Mifflin, 1958.

Cruikshank, Ken. "The People's Railway: The Intercolonial Railway and the Canadian Public Enterprise Experience," *Acadiensis*, 16: 78–100, 1986.

— "The Intercolonial Railway, Freight Rates and the Maritime Economy", in Currie, Archibald W. *The Grand Trunk Railway of Canada.* Toronto: University of Toronto Press, 1957.

— *Canadian Transportation Economics.* Toronto: University of Toronto Press, 1967.

Due, J.F. *The Intercity Electric Railway Industry in Canada.* Toronto: University of Toronto Press, 1966.

Fleming, Howard A. *Canada's Arctic Outlet: A History of the Hudson Bay Railway.* Berkeley: University of California Press, 1957.

Fleming, R.B. *The Railway King of Canada.* Vancouver: UBC Press, 1991.

Fleming, Sandford. *The Intercolonial.* Montreal: Dawson Brothers, 1876.

Folkins, Wentworth and Michael Bradley. *The Great Days of Canadian Steam.* Hounslow Press: Willowdale, Ontario, 1988.

Foran, Max and Edward Cavell. *Calgary: An Illustrated History.* Toronto: James Lorimer & Company/National Museum of Man, 1978.

Fraser, John Foster. *Canada As It Is.* New York: Cassell and Company Ltd, 1905.

Garden, J.F. *British Columbia Railway.* Revelstoke: Footprint, 1995.

Gibbon, John Murray. *The Romantic History of the Canadian Pacific; The Northwest Passage of Today.* Toronto: McClelland & Stewart, 1935.

— *Steel of Empire.* New York: The Bobbs-Merrill Company, 1935.

Gillmor, Don. Canada: *A People's History.* Toronto: Canadian Broadcasting Corporation, 2001.

Glazebrook, G.P. de T. *A History of Transportation in Canada.* Toronto: Ryerson, 1938. Reprinted Toronto: McClelland & Stewart, 1964.

Gordon, Ishbel, Marchioness of Aberdeen and Temair. *Through Canada with a Kodak.* Edinburgh: W.H. White & Co., 1893. Reprinted London, Buffalo, Toronto: University of Toronto Press, 1994.

Grant, George M. *Picturesque Canada: The Country As It Was and Is.* Toronto: Belden, *c.*1882.

Hanna, David B. *Trains of Recollection.* Toronto: Macmillan, 1924.

Hilton, George W. *The Great Lakes Car Ferries.* Berkeley: Howell-North, 1962.

Hind, Patrick O. *Pacific Great Eastern Steam Locomotives.* Victoria: British Columbia Railway Historical Association, 1984.

— *The Pacific Great Eastern Railway Company, A Short History of the North Shore Subdivision 1914–1928.* Vancouver: North Vancouver Museum and Archives Commission, 1999.

Hubbard, R.H. *Canadian Landscape Painting 1670–1930.* Madison: University of Wisconsin Press/The Elvehjem Art Center, 1973.

Innis, Harold A. *A History of the Canadian Pacific Railway.* Toronto: University of Toronto, 1923. Reprinted 1971.

Inwood, Kris, ed. *Farm, Factory and Fortune: New Studies in the Economic History of the Maritime Provinces.* Fredericton: Acadiensis Press, 1993.

Jackman, W.T. *Economic Principles of Transportation.* Toronto: University of Toronto Press, 1935.

Klassen, Henry C. *The Canadian West: Social Change and Economic Development.* Calgary: University of Calgary Press, 1977.

Kluckner, Michael. *Vancouver: The Way It Was.* North Vancouver, BC: Whitecap Books, 1984.

La Presse, Montréal, 1912–15.

Lamb, W. Kaye. *History of the Canadian Pacific Railway.* New York: Macmillan, 1977.

Lavallee, Omer. *Narrow Gauge Railways of Canada.* Montréal: Railfare Enterprises Limited, 1972.

— *Van Horne's Road.* Montreal: Railfare Enterprises Limited, 1977.

Legget, Robert F. *Railroads of Canada.* Vancouver: Douglas, David & Charles, 1973.

Leonard, Frank. *A Thousand Blunders: The Grand Trunk Pacific Railway and Northern British Columbia.* Vancouver: University of British Columbia Press, 1996.

MacEwan, Grant. *The Battle for the Bay.* Saskatoon: Western Producer, 1975.

MacKay, Donald. *The People's Railway, A History of Canadian National.* Vancouver: Douglas & McIntyre, 1992.

MacLachlan, Donald F. *The Esquimalt & Nanaimo Railway. The Dunsmuir Years: 1884–1905.* Victoria: British Columbia Railway Historical Association, 1986.

MacLaren, I.S. "Cultured Wilderness in Jasper National Park." *Journal of Canadian Studies,* Vol. 34, Issue 3, 1999.

McDowall, Duncan. *Steel at the Sault: Francis H. Clergue, Sir James Dunn, and the Algoma Steel Corporation 1901–1956.* Toronto: University of Toronto Press, 1984 (hb) and 1988 (pb).

McKee, Bill and Georgeen Klassen. *Trail of Iron; The CPR and the Birth of the West, 1880–1930.* Vancouver: Douglas & McIntyre, 1983.

Middleton, William. *The Bridge at Québec.* Bloomington: Indiana University Press, 2001.

Mika, Nick and Helma Mika. *Illustrated History of Canadian Railways.* Belleville, Ontario: Mika Publishing Company, 1986.

Minter, Roy. *The White Pass: Gateway to the Klondike.* Toronto: McClelland and Stewart, 1987.

Nock, O.S. *Railways of Canada.* London: Black, 1973.

— *Algoma Central Railway.* London & Sault Ste. Marie: Adam & Charles Beck/Algoma Central Railway, 1975.

Putnam, Donald F. *Canadian Regions: A Geography of Canada.* London: J.M. Dent & Sons, 1952.

Ramsey, Bruce. *PGE – Railway to the North.* Vancouver: Mitchell Press Ltd, 1962.

Regehr, T.D. *The Canadian Northern Railway, Pioneer Road of the Northern Prairies.* Toronto: Macmillan of Canada, 1976.

Robertson, R.W.W. *Stand Fast Craigellachie: The Building of the Transcontinental Railway (1867–1885).* Toronto: Burns & MacEachern Limited, 1970.

Rocky and Selkirk Mountains Canada: The Canadian Rockies on Line of the Canadian Pacific Railway (photo album) Brooklyn, New York: CPR News Service, n.d.

Salloum, Habeeb. "Canada's Railroads." *Contemporary Review,* Vol. 281, December 2002.

Sanford, Barrie. *Mcculloch's Wonder: The Story of the Kettle Valley Railway.* Vancouver: Whitecap, 1977.

Sifton, Clifford. *Canada.* Ottawa: n.d.

Stemes, Dave. "The Mount Royal Tunnel, 75 years young." In *Branchline, Canada's Rail News Magazine.* December 1993, 7–8.

Stephens, David E. Iron Roads, *Railways of Nova Scotia.* Windsor: Lancelot, 1972.

Stevens, G.R. *Canadian National Railways.* Toronto: Clarke, Irwin, 1960 and 1962 (2 vols).

— *History of the Canadian National Railways.* New York: Macmillan, 1973.

Sullivan, Alan. *The Rapids.* Toronto: University of Toronto Press, 1972.

Surtees, Robert J. *The Northern Connection: Ontario Northland since 1902.* North York: Captus Press, 1992.

Talbot, Frederick A. *The Making of a Great Canadian Railway.* Toronto: Musson, 1912.

— *Railway Wonders of the World.* London: Cassell and Company Ltd, n.d.

Trout, J.M., and E. Trout. *The Railways of Canada for 1870–1871.* Toronto: Monetary Times, 1871. Reprinted Toronto: Coles, 1970.

Tucker, Albert. *Steam into Wilderness: Ontario Northland Railway, 1902–1962.* Toronto: Fitzhenry & Whiteside, 1978.

Turner, Robert D. *West of the Great Divide: An Illustrated History of the Canadian Pacific Railway in British Columbia 1880–1986.* Winslaw: Sono Nis Press, 1987.

— *Vancouver Island Railroads.* Winslaw: Sono Nis Press, 1997 (second edition).

Walton, Mark. "The Mount Royal Tunnel Electrification." Paper given to the Bytown Railway Society, 6 June 2000, published as www.railways.incanada.net/candate/tunnel.htm.

White, James. *Atlas of Canada 1906.* Issued by direction of Hon. Frank Oliver, Minister of the Interior. Ottawa, Ontario, 1906.

Wilgus, William T. *The Railway Interrelations of the United States and Canada.* New York: 1937. Reprinted New York: Russell & Russell, 1970.

William Norman & Son (photographers). *Through Mountains and Canyons: The Canadian Rockies.* Montreal: William Norman & Son, n.d.

Williams, Clara and George Williams. *The Railway that Glue Built.* New York: Frederick A. Stokes Company, 1908.

Wilson, Keith. *Donald Smith and the Canadian Pacific Railway.* Agincourt: The Book Society of Canada Limited, 1978.

Woods, J. Lawlor, ed. *Canada from Ocean to Ocean.* Toronto: Dominion Pub. Co., *c.*1899.

Woods, Shirley E. *Cinders and Saltwater: The Story of Atlantic Canada's Railways.* Halifax: Nimbus, 1992.

INDEX

Italics refer to illustrations